# Seamus Heaney's Gifts

# Seamus Heaney's Gifts

HENRY HART

Louisiana State University Press

Baton Rouge

Published with the assistance of The Noland Fund

Publication of this book was made possible in part by the Arts and Sciences Faculty Grants Fund at the College of William and Mary.

Published by Louisiana State University Press
lsupress.org

Manufactured in the United States of America
First printing

DESIGNER: Michelle A. Neustrom
TYPEFACE: Freight Text Pro
PRINTER AND BINDER: Sheridan Books, Inc.

Jacket photograph copyright © The Jane Bown Literary Estate/
National Portrait Gallery, London.

CATALOGING-IN-PUBLICATION DATA ARE AVAILABLE AT THE LIBRARY OF CONGRESS.

ISBN 978-0-8071-8256-7 (cloth) | ISBN 978-0-8071-8343-4 (epub) |
ISBN 978-0-8071-8344-1 (pdf)

*for Robert Crawford and Stephen Enniss*

*with gratitude for your gifts*

# Contents

*Photographs follow page 150.*

# Preface

Seamus Heaney always surprised me. When I first met him with a group of Emory University summer-school students at University College, Oxford, in 1984, he sauntered into the classroom, laughing and chatting with his host, Professor Ron Schuchard. His thick gray hair was ungroomed, and he kept squinting as he smiled. His wife, Marie, laughed beside him. During my seven years of graduate and postgraduate work at Oxford, I'd gotten used to lecturers wearing black gowns and speaking or reading from prepared scripts with somber British accents. Heaney stood before us in casual dress, had no notes, and spoke in a jovial Irish brogue. "I've been on holiday with my family and haven't prepared a formal lecture," he said at the lectern. "I want to talk to you about a poem, though—Thomas Hardy's 'During Wind and Rain.'" He began reciting the elegiac poem, which had been inspired by the death of Hardy's wife, but before he got to the resonant end—"Ah, no; the years, the years; / Down their carved names the rain-drop ploughs"—he stumbled and asked if anyone remembered the rest. Someone gave him the lines he'd forgotten, and he finished his recitation. The lecture that followed was more spontaneous than those by other well-known poets who'd visited Oxford, such as William Empson, Ted Hughes, and Geoffrey Hill. Nevertheless, what Heaney said was moving and insightful. When he finished, my dissertation supervisor, Richard Ellmann, introduced us, and I spoke to him briefly about my thesis on Hill.

Heaney surprised me again when I went to see him at Harvard in 1985. I'd started research for a book about his poetry, and he'd invited me to his apartment in Adams House. We met at the bottom of a stairway near the front door. "Hello!" he said in his cheerful Irish voice. We made small talk for a few minutes before he said he'd like to take me to a restaurant near Harvard Square. As we walked through the campus, his curly hair bounced in the breeze, and he kept laughing and smiling. He had a stocky build, and he'd written about enjoying food and drink, so I was startled when he only ordered an appetizer—a small plate of mushrooms—for dinner. While I ate a substantial entrée, he picked at his mushrooms. Worried he might go hungry, I asked if he wanted dessert. He replied, "No, I'm trying to lose some weight."

Adams House, as I soon learned, was one of Harvard's "Gold Coast" residences. Students lived there, but it was more like a mansion than a dormitory. It boasted a swimming pool in the basement, a common room modeled on a Florentine palace, and a dining hall constructed to look like an eighteenth-century British spa. The building was named for John Quincy Adams, the sixth U.S. president and Harvard's first Boylston Professor of Rhetoric and Oratory. (When I met Heaney at Harvard, he'd just been dubbed the new Boylston Professor.) Adams House had been built to attract the sons of wealthy and powerful families. Franklin Delano Roosevelt, William Randolph Hearst, R. Buckminster Fuller, William Burroughs, and Henry Kissinger had all lived there as undergraduates.

I expected Heaney to have a luxurious apartment befitting his august professorship. Yet, when he opened his door, I saw a room that resembled a monk's cell or the stage of a Samuel Beckett play. The walls were undecorated; the floors had no rugs; there was no TV or radio or stereo. It was as if nobody lived there. The only obvious signs of habitation were a few pieces of institutional furniture, a cardboard box from Farrar, Straus & Giroux (it contained copies of his new book, *Station Island*), and a small, framed picture of his wife on the fireplace mantel.

Sitting in a chair facing Heaney, I worried about how he'd react to my questions. When I'd asked Geoffrey Hill if he'd agree to an interview for my doctoral dissertation, he wrote me a hostile letter that never acknowledged my request to meet him at the University of Leeds, where he taught. I was afraid Heaney might resist my queries, too. "So what would you like to know?" he said as he leaned back on his couch. Surprised by his openness, I asked about some of the people, places, and events he wrote about in his poems. I also asked about the influence of spiritual exercises and mysticism on his work. He never hesitated to answer my questions.

At one point, though, Heaney said he needed to take a break. I wasn't sure what he wanted to do, but I soon heard something clinking in the kitchen. He returned with a bottle of Irish whiskey and two jars. Not glasses, jars—the sort used for jam or pickled vegetables. He poured whiskey for both of us into the jars, and we began drinking. I asked more questions, and he gave more answers. When we discussed his new book, *Station Island*, he mentioned a flattering review that had just appeared in the *New York Times*. "I don't like fulsome reviews," he said, "and that was a fulsome review." He used the word "fulsome" several times with scorn in his voice.

After consuming a few jars of whiskey, Heaney gave me a gift—a signed copy of *Station Island*. I'd told him about my difficult teaching job at The Citadel, The Military College of South Carolina, where I was required to teach English in an army uniform and join the South Carolina Unorganized Militia as a captain. I explained that I'd grown up in New England and gone to Dartmouth College before doing graduate work at Oxford, and I'd felt disoriented at the southern military college that was proud of its cadets fighting for the Confederacy in the Civil War. Heaney said he understood what it was like to be uprooted and displaced, and signed his book, "For Henry at his station at the citadel, with admiration and good wishes. Seamus, 7th March 1985." Around nine thirty that night, while we walked together to my car, I mentioned that my sister was living nearby and struggling to begin her career as an artist. With characteristic generosity, he promised to call her and offer assistance.

I learned more about Heaney's generosity in the spring of 2002, when I hosted his three-day visit to the College of William and Mary, where I'd taught since 1986. While preparing for class in my office the day he was due to arrive, he surprised me once again. The phone rang, and I heard a friendly voice say, "This is Seamus. I'm in Princeton now. I was wondering what poems you'd like me to read at William and Mary." I told him I'd been teaching a selection of his poems in the *Norton Anthology of Contemporary Poetry* that included "Digging," "Death of a Naturalist," and "Punishment." He said, "Fine. I'll make sure to read those for your students." No other writer had ever called me to ask what they should read on campus.

Heaney had more surprises for me after I picked him up later that day at the airport in Richmond, Virginia. As we made our way down Route 64 to Williamsburg, I asked him how the Nobel Prize for Literature, which he'd won in 1995, had changed his life. He suddenly went silent. I looked over at him, and he seemed shocked or angry. "Henry," he said emphatically, "you're not allowed to use the N-word in my presence. In my house, we have a strict rule against using the N-word." I wasn't quite sure what he meant. Then he chuckled and said, "You know—the Nobel."

That night, Heaney gave a reading at a large movie theater in Colonial Williamsburg. As with most of his public performances, hundreds of people attended and went away enchanted by the way he read his poems. At parties after the reading, he continued to charm people, whether they were students, professors, college administrators, or townspeople. For three days, he was an exemplary guest. On the way back to Richmond, though, he became strangely quiet. "Sorry, I'm tired," he said after one long silence. "I'm on a busy tour and I agreed to do some extra work—two readings in New York to raise money for Irish hospitals." I thought he might like to talk about something nonliterary, so I asked him about farming. I'd read about his love for his boyhood farm in Northern Ireland, and I knew something about the joys of living simply in the countryside, since my parents had bought farmland in New England, where we grew and sold Christmas trees. Like his farmhouse, Mossbawn, ours at first had no electricity, phone, or plumbing. "Do you miss farming?" I asked. "Not really," he replied. There was another long silence. "What sorts of things did you enjoy doing on your farm?" I asked. "I was good at herding cattle," he said. It was obvious that the three days of socializing in Williamsburg had exhausted him, and he didn't want to talk, so we drove on in silence.

Shortly after flying to Kentucky to give his next reading, Heaney called me in my office again. He had another surprise. "Henry," he said in an energetic voice, "thanks for hosting me in Williamsburg. Could you do me a favor?" I said I'd be glad to, even though I had no idea what he wanted me to do. "I left some Irish coins at the hotel [the Williamsburg Hospitality House], and I'd like you to go get them," he told me. I wondered why he was so concerned about a few Irish coins; they were useless in the United

States. I was about to ask if he wanted me to mail them to his Dublin address when he added, "I'd like you to give the coins to your children as gifts." Amazed that he'd bother with such a trifle while preparing for another reading at another college, I thanked him and said I'd go to the hotel right away. As it turned out, I found the attractive gold-colored coins with Celtic harps stamped on them, and gave them to my young son and daughter, who were delighted.

A few weeks later, after Heaney had returned to Ireland, it was my turn to receive gifts. For my work on his behalf at William and Mary, a college named for a seventeenth-century English king who'd caused centuries of misery in Ireland for Irish Catholics like himself, he sent me a large envelope containing signed, special editions of poems and lectures. It was another surprise. I'd organized many readings for well-known poets, scholars, and novelists over the decades, but none, except Heaney, had ever sent me such valuable gifts.

Poets often write obsessively about a few preoccupations. Heaney alluded to this in his first book of literary criticism, *Preoccupations*. From the beginning to the end of his career, one of his central preoccupations was the artist's "gift." He repeatedly wrote about the inspired, trancelike state in which poets received gifts from a muse. He was preoccupied with the ethical obligation to "Remember the Giver," as he said at the end of his poem "A Drink of Water," and he believed that those who were blessed with gifts should pay tribute to the sources of their gifts. He also believed that the gifted should share their gifts for the betterment of others. Heaney's devotion to gift-giving and gift-exchange rituals could be sacrificial and enervating, as his poems, essays, and letters attest. But throughout his life, he remained committed to producing and distributing gifts.

# Acknowledgments

Like most books, *Seamus Heaney's Gifts* was a collaborative effort, and I'm grateful for my collaborators. My primary thanks go to Seamus Heaney. During the three decades I knew him, he took time out of his hectic schedule to discuss his poetry with me, and in 2008 he gave me permission to consult his papers at Emory University. I'm also indebted to his wife, Marie, who took me on a tour of their house in Dublin, pointed out gifts her husband had received from other writers, and encouraged me as I wrote about her husband's preoccupation with gifts. Stephen Enniss, who purchased a substantial collection of Heaney's papers for Emory's Robert W. Woodruff Library, was instrumental in making the papers available to me. A scholar of modern Irish poetry as well as one of the most distinguished special collections librarians in the United States, Steve offered helpful advice after reading an early draft of this book. The Scottish poet, biographer, and literary critic Robert Crawford read an early draft, too, and suggested numerous ways to improve it. I also owe a debt to Professor Richard Rankin Russell, a scholar of Irish and British literature who gave me helpful suggestions for revision. Another collaborator was Kathleen Shoemaker, the reference coordinator at Emory's Stuart A. Rose Manuscript, Archives, & Rare Book Library, where Heaney's papers are housed. I appreciated her generous assistance when I made research trips to the library and later when I contacted her about documents I needed for my book. The librarians at the National Library of Ireland, who are in charge of another substantial Heaney archive, provided similar assistance during the summer of 2008. Claire Pittman and several other William and Mary students tracked down hard-to-find journal articles by and about

Heaney. My literary agent, Jacques de Spoelberch, was enthusiastic about this project from the start and helped me find a publisher. James Long at Louisiana State University Press has been an ideal editor. Last but not least, my wife, Susannah Livingston, read a draft of the book and kindly suggested numerous ways to streamline the narrative.

# Seamus Heaney's Gifts

# Introduction

Little in Seamus Heaney's background suggested that by the beginning of the twenty-first century he would surpass Shakespeare as the most-studied writer in British universities. While growing up near the small village of Castledawson in Northern Ireland, he worked at farming rather than writing. He herded cows, fed horses, churned butter, mowed hay, shoveled manure, and gathered potatoes. His parents didn't have much time or inclination to read or direct their son toward a literary career. His father had left school at the age of fourteen to raise and sell cattle. His mother had ended her schooling as a young teenager, too, and soon took care of a large family—nine children in all—without the aid of electricity, modern plumbing, phone, or car. She taught Heaney Irish songs and a few popular poems, but was in no way bookish.

Heaney was as surprised as others in his family when he discovered he had a gift for poetry. "The fact of the matter," he said after winning the Nobel Prize for Literature in 1995, "is that the most unexpected and miraculous thing in my life was the arrival in it of poetry."[1] He explained to a *Sunday Times* reporter in 1999, "Poetry entered my life as gift, surprise, bonus, grace."[2] Throughout his career, Heaney conceived of poems as gifts from a sacred, mysterious source. In an interview with the writer and artist Michael Huey that was published in the *Christian Science Monitor*, he said, "I do believe that poetry is in the realm of the gift and in the realm of the sacred."[3] He informed the American poet June Beisch, "I still cling to my first position that a poem is a gift and that it stirs unexpectedly and can't be summoned by the will."[4] During his later years, he often worried that his busy social life had led him away from the source of his gifts. He confessed to English professor John Breslin, "There's always panic, and you think, 'Am I doing the wrong thing? Am I neglecting a gift?'"[5]

At Queen's University, Belfast, in the late 1950s and early 1960s, Heaney experienced what he called a "magical transition" when he began publishing his poems. "I don't think anything ever equals the sense of change and gift that comes from young poetry," he told a writer for the *Guardian* newspaper.[6] Uncertain about the quality of his first poems, he adopted the pen name "Incertus," which in Latin means "uncertain." As his knowledge of poetic tradition expanded and he became more certain of his skill as a poet, he viewed relationships with precursors in terms of gift exchange. The great works of the past were gifts that young poets should respond to with countergifts, and teachers should be like priests passing on the gifts of tradition to students and encouraging them to believe they can also be gift-makers and gift-givers. Thinking of his own teachers, Heaney said, "The biggest gift a teacher can give to the gifted student is a transmission of some kind of confidence. What you gain from contact with another writer whom you respect is unnamable."[7] Heaney agreed with the Russian poet Osip Mandelstam, who believed "a kind of apostolic succession operated in the realm of poetry, that the young poet is never fully empowered until he has somehow been confirmed by an older poet."[8] Masterful poets "confirmed" their successors the way Jesus "confirmed" His apostles and the way priests "confirmed" members of the Church.

Heaney's literary criticism often explored the way poets discovered, articulated, and sustained—or failed to sustain—their individual gifts. In his essay about Sylvia Plath, "The Indefatigable Hoof-taps," he could have been speaking for himself when he said Plath thought of "the poem as a gift arising or descending beyond the poet's control, where direct contact is established with the image-cellar, the dream-bank, the word-hoard, the truth-cave—whatever place a poem . . . emerges from."[9] Heaney called the Welsh poet Dylan Thomas, who had a profound influence on his early poetry, "an enormously gifted storyteller and fantasist" with an "immense gift for dispensing hilarity," but he faulted Thomas's assumption that he was "God's gift to the art" and lamented the way Thomas had squandered his gift.[10] Robert Lowell was another immensely gifted poet who'd failed to preserve his gift. In a review of Lowell's last book, *Day by Day*, Heaney sided with those critics who felt "disappointment . . . about the direction his gift took" at the end of his career.[11]

Heaney repeatedly drew attention to the gifts of poets he admired. In a newspaper article about Michael Longley's *Poems 1963–1983*, he wrote, "Legend and folklore sponsor his gift for swift transitions and transformations."[12] He commended his friend Derek Walcott for his "Wordsworthian gift for being in touch with the elemental powers of sea and sky."[13] Another friend, the Scottish poet Norman MacCaig, "had the poet's gift for 'flying crooked,' down the paths of irony and surprise."[14] The English poet Philip Larkin had been blessed with a "gift for winning the respect of two kinds of readers: those scrupulously concerned about literary standards and those other non-specialist listeners-in to what is generally available."[15] During numerous social and political crises in Poland, Nobel Prize laureate Czeslaw Milosz had demonstrated a similar "gift to be able to speak as if everybody's fate was implicit in his fate."[16] Another Nobel laureate, Joseph Brodsky, overcame political hostilities in the Soviet Union to direct "the unstinted gift of himself to his vocation."[17]

Heaney traced his own gift back to an actual gift he received when he left home for a private Catholic secondary school in Londonderry (or Derry, as Catholics called the city in Northern Ireland out of disdain for British rule). Before dropping him off at St. Columb's College on August 29, 1951, Heaney's parents took him to the nearby town of Buncrana in the Republic of Ireland, where they bought him a Conway Stewart fountain pen. This was the material gift he associated with his literary gift for the rest of his life. More than a half century later, he commemorated the pen in "The Conway Stewart," a poem in his last book, *Human Chain*. With its impressive English name, "14-carat nib," and "three gold bands in the clip-on screw-top," the luxurious pen was Heaney's reward for getting admitted to a prestigious school, but it was also a useful tool for a writer before the age of word processors and laser-jet printers. In his poem, Heaney said he used the pen almost as soon as his parents drove back to the family farm to write a "longhand / 'Dear' / To them." Many of Heaney's poems, early and late, would try to do what he did in his first pen-written letter: restore the severed bonds with home and his gift-giving parents.

After Heaney's death on August 30, 2013, the Irish writer Theo Dorgan extolled his friend's devotion to gifts and to the sources of gifts: "He understood that the poetry was a gift. And he respected the gift. He knew that the gift came from elsewhere. And he understood that his duty was to immerse himself in the craft so as to do justice to the gift."[18] Heaney also recognized the obligations and burdens that came with being gifted. Casting an older man's cold eye on "the years / Of every . . . obligation / Imposed and undertaken" in one his last poems, "On the Gift of a Fountain Pen," he wondered if his years of inveterate gift-giving had been a "mistake" or a "virtue." Heaney had become increasingly bound up (the Latin roots of "obligation," *ob-ligare,* mean "to bind") with the exhausting business of gift-giving. His many admirers wanted him to give readings, lecture at conferences, attend book launches, receive honorary degrees, speak at university commencements, help with fundraising events, and appear at literary parties. Not long after the publication of his first book, *Death of a Naturalist* (1966), he metamorphosed from a shy "Incertus" into a poet nicknamed "Famous Seamus." Like many celebrities, he was eager to please his fans, but it came at a cost.

In his pioneering study *The Gift,* which was first published in 1924 as *"Essai sur le don; Forme et raison de l'échange dans les sociétés archaiques,"* the French sociologist Marcel Mauss catalogued the sort of benefits and burdens in gift-exchange relationships that Heaney became increasingly aware of as his fame grew. Mauss concluded that "the obligation . . . to give presents," "to receive them," and "to reciprocate" formed a network of responsibilities that bound people together, especially in precapitalist societies. Productive communication and commerce depended on strict adherence to the rules of gift exchange, but if one failed to follow the rules, "the bond of alliance and commonality" could lead to conflict. Gift exchanges with dead ancestors and gods could also be problematic. "One of the first groups of beings with which men had to enter into contract, and who, by definition, were there to make a contract with them, were above all the spirits of both the dead and of the gods," Mauss asserted. "Indeed, it is they who are the true owners of the things and possessions of this world. With them it was most necessary to exchange, and with them it was most dangerous not to exchange."[19] To believers, the gods had created a world full of gifts, and they expected gifts of gratitude in return. But gift exchanges between humans and gods could go awry. The gods might receive gifts and not reciprocate, or they might not like the gifts and punish the gift-givers.

Heaney's commitment to gift-giving was encouraged during his early years by the priests at St. Mary's Catholic Church, where he worshipped as a boy, and later by the priests who instructed him at St. Columb's. The Eucharist at the heart of his Catholic faith was based on Christ's sacrificial gift-giving. The word "Eucharist," from the Greek *eu-kharistia,* can be translated as "good grace-giving," or "good thanks-giving," or "good gift-giving." During the ritual, a priest praises God's life-sustaining gifts on Earth and offers God's gift of salvation in Heaven. Those who participate in Communion consume Christ's gifts—His flesh and blood—in the form of consecrated bread and wine. Communicants give thanks to God and promise to serve Him by following his example of gift-giving. The purpose of the Eucharist ritual is to restore the bond between God and His worshippers. When Heaney became a poet, he tended to think of literary communication in terms of a communion in which artist-gods and artist-priests disseminated symbolic gifts for the welfare of others.

Shortly after graduating from Queen's University in 1961, Heaney received a gift from a friend—Patrick Kavanagh's poetry book A *Soul for Sale*—that would transform his career. The two Irish poets had much in common. Like Heaney, Kavanagh had grown up in a large Catholic family on a farm, and both writers had an abiding sense of being blessed with miraculous gifts. "When Patrick Kavanagh looked for an image to express his sense of the origins of [his] poetic gift," Heaney wrote in a *Listener* article in 1979, "he returned again and again to the image of mist and fog. It is an image of creation that lies perhaps at the bottom of all our minds. A picture conjured up perhaps out of the Book of Genesis where God the Father breathes and incubates the world out of the steam and swirl of chaos. But Kavanagh . . . knew himself to be the son of a place as well as the son of a woman. In his imagination, the nurturing fog hung forever above his birthplace."[20] Kavanagh was one of the first authors who inspired Heaney to trace his gift back to a maternal muse and genius loci on his family farm.

Heaney revealed in his book of interviews, *Stepping Stones,* that he always sympathized with "the fundamentally Catholic mysticism in Kavanagh." Both poets had been introduced at a young age to the "divine mysteries: the sacrifice of the Mass, the transubstantiation of bread and wine into the body and blood of Christ, the forgiveness of sin, the resurrection of the body and the life of the world to come, the whole disposition of the cosmos from celestial to infernal."[21] The "divine mysteries" of the Catholic Church influenced the way the two Irish writers regarded their gifts and the origins of their gifts. Heaney could have been referring to himself when he said, "Kavanagh escaped [a farming vocation] through his gift of imagination [and had] an uneasy relationship with his own place and his own people." Albeit conflicted, his relationship with his family farm remained strong, and, according to Heaney, he possessed a "gift for recreating that Eden time" in his poetry. Like Heaney, he also felt a profound sense of "gratitude for the simple gift of life" and "was entranced with his own creativity and grateful for it."[22]

Heaney's wife, Marie, once said about her husband, "All he's ever wanted to do is go back [to his family's first farm, Mossbawn] . . . his paradise . . . his Eden."[23] Returning to this Eden became more difficult after the death of Heaney's younger brother Christopher in a road accident. To get distance from the traumatic loss, his parents sold Mossbawn and moved the family to The Wood, a different farm, in 1954. The uprooting intensified Heaney's desire to recapture his lost paradise in memory and in poetry.

Heaney's devotion to the boggy land around Mossbawn eventually drew him to P. V. Glob's accounts of fertility rituals in *The Bog People*, a book Heaney bought as a Christmas present for himself in 1969. In his first poem inspired by the book, "The Tollund Man," he identified with the Iron Age man embalmed for two millennia in a Danish peat bog. He called the bog man "a kind of Christ figure: sacrificed so that life will be brought back [to the land]." For Heaney, he was an archetypal "symbol . . . of sacrifice to the goddess of territory" as well as a symbol of "the political upheavals of Ireland, especially in the 20th century."[24] Glob speculated that the Tollund Man's community had assumed that if they offered a sacrificial gift to the Earth goddess Nerthus, she would reciprocate with gifts of spring vegetation and abundant crops. Heaney equated this sacrifice to sacrifices of Christ-like Irish rebels who'd given the gift of life to Mother Ireland with the hope that she would reciprocate with the gift of a "green" nation—a united, independent Ireland.

Heaney got another opportunity to ponder the aesthetic, religious, political, and ethical aspects of gift exchanges when he was asked to translate *Beowulf* in the early 1980s. The ancient Anglo-Saxon war story attracted him because, like Glob's *Bog People*, it seemed relevant to the political violence and possibility of peace in his homeland. He pointed out that Beowulf's warriors "conceive of themselves as hooped within the great wheel of necessity, in thrall to a code of loyalty and bravery, bound to seek glory in the . . . warrior world." To Heaney, Beowulf was a model of a half-pagan, half-Christian leader who maintained bonds with God and community by giving gifts. Yet Beowulf was also a serial combatant who presided over a culture in which "bloodshed begets further bloodshed, the wheel turns, [and] the generations tread and tread and tread" like the benighted generations that Gerard Manley Hopkins lamented in "God's Grandeur."[25]

Heaney worked on his *Beowulf* translation during the 1980s and 1990s, when the centuries-old conflict between Ulster's Irish Catholics and British Protestants erupted yet again. During the period known as the Troubles, he scrutinized other heroes engaged in sacrificial gift exchanges, too. His book *Seeing Things* (1991) begins with a translation of a passage from the *Aeneid* where the Sibyl utters "clear truths and mysteries" at her shrine and tells Aeneas he must procure a magic gift—a "golden bough"—if he expects to descend to the underworld and reunite with his dead father, Anchises. This bough, the Sibyl says, is Proserpina's "own special gift," and it must be plucked from a tree in a grove sacred to Juno and given to the goddess of the underworld, Proserpina. For Heaney, the broken branch is typologically related to the gift of the broken bread in the Eucharist. Both branch and bread enable communions between the living and the dead.

Heaney's next book, *The Spirit Level* (1996), begins with "The Rain Stick," another poem featuring a literal and mythical gift. In this case, Heaney writes about a Native American instrument that his bibliographer Rand Brandes gave him during a conference in North Carolina in 1992. The rain stick works according to the principles of sympathetic magic; when it's upended, seeds or other small objects falling against cactus thorns that have been inserted into the stick's hollow core make a sound like rain, which is supposed to make actual rain fall that will irrigate the soil. In Heaney's hands, the potent rain stick, like his Conway Stewart fountain pen, represents the artist's miraculous gift that keeps giving.

*District and Circle*, which appeared in 2006, alludes to more gifts that enhance fertility and magically transport the imagination into what Heaney now calls the "precinct of vision." The new poems, while acknowledging the potency of gifts, stress the sociopolitical constraints imposed on their production and distribution. Distressed by the way ethnic and racial "precincts" confine people, Heaney returns to the idea that gift-giving can unify factions in polarized societies. He again assumes the role of Aeneas offering sacrificial gifts to the gods so he can travel to otherworlds for the sake of union and communion. In his sonnet sequence "The Tollund Man in Springtime," he resurrects his favorite Iron Age persona and imagines him trekking through a modern "virtual city" of deracinated citizens. Accustomed to a precapitalist gift-exchange economy, the revenant Tollund Man wants to pay for goods with what he values: not cash, but "a bunch of Tollund rushes—roots and all— / bagged in their own bog-damp." The reeds recall Aeneas's golden bough and the boggy vegetation around Mossbawn. They are prized symbols of Heaney's origins and original gifts.

Ever since his departure from Mossbawn in 1951 to attend St. Columb's College, Heaney had agonized over the proper way to address the "givens" of his home territory in Northern Ireland. One sonnet about the resurgent Tollund Man proclaims, "The soul exceeds its circumstances." This statement about going beyond boundaries comes from an obituary essay about Heaney's friend Czeslaw Milosz, who died in 2004. ("Circumstance" and "precinct" derive from Latin words for what stands around or confines.) According to the essay's author, Leon Wieseltier, Milosz "discharged his obligations to his age and his obligations to his soul" out of a belief that he'd been endowed with a gift to transcend his circumstances. A stubborn realist, Milosz was also a mystic who conceived of God as a sublime gift-maker and gift-giver. Wieseltier claimed that he and Milosz "shared an envy of mystics" who regarded "the things of this earth" as gifts produced by a "miraculous" and "incomprehensible . . . mystery."[26] Catholic mysticism had helped Milosz maintain his equanimity during the Nazi and Communist occupations of Poland, where he lived during the middle of the twentieth century. His poem "Thankfulness," which Wieseltier quoted at the end of his eulogy, describes the sort of gift-exchange relationship he had with the Creator: "You gave me gifts, God-Enchanter. / I give you thanks for good and ill."[27] Throughout his life, Heaney articulated a similar attitude toward the divine origin of gifts.

When asked by an Irish journalist about the epitaph he wanted on his gravestone, Heaney said he might like a line about gratitude in Sophocles's play *Oedipus at Colonus,* which he translated after Milosz died. At the end of the play, a messenger witnesses the king's mysterious descent into the underworld and declares, "Wherever that man went, he went gratefully."[28] In a eulogy for Milosz published by the *Guardian,* Heaney wrote, "I could easily have repeated to myself the remark he once made to an interviewer, commenting upon his epigram, 'He was thankful, so he couldn't not believe in God.' Ultimately, Milosz declared, 'one can believe in God out of gratitude for all the gifts.'"[29] If Heaney believed in a God after abandoning orthodox Catholicism in his twenties, that God resembled Milosz's mystical gift-maker and gift-giver.

In addition to writing a eulogy, Heaney attended Milosz's funeral in Kraków, Poland, and composed an elegy for his friend based on the funeral Mass and a Mass he'd attended years before in Lourdes, the famous pilgrimage site in southwestern France. From the vantage point of an older man, he regarded his journeys to Kraków in 2004 and Lourdes in 1958 the same way he regarded his pilgrimages to St. Patrick's Purgatory in northwest Ireland as a university student. The journeys followed the pattern of the "monomyth," as explained by the scholar Joseph Campbell in *The Hero with a Thousand Faces,* a book Heaney read with enthusiasm as a young poet. Taking his cue from James Joyce's *Finnegans Wake,* who coined the word "monomyth," and from the ethnographer Arnold Van Gennep's schema for rites of passage (separation, transition, incorporation), Campbell contends that all myths of heroes have three parts: a departure from home, an ordeal in an otherworld, and a return to society *"with the power to bestow boons on his fellow man."*[30]

The three-part narrative of departure, initiation, and return had a special resonance for Heaney because it corresponded to his own rites of passage and stages in his writing process, as he made clear in his essay "'Apt Admonishment': Wordsworth as an Example." Published shortly before he died, his essay uses Wordsworth's poem "Resolution and Independence" to illustrate the poet's journey through bewildering and depressing ordeals to a rediscovery of gifts. Wordsworth is exemplary for Heaney because he meets a muse figure, in this case an old, stoical leech-gatherer, who both uplifts and guides him: "The poet arrives on the scene either abstracted or disoriented, and is then brought more fully alive to his . . . obligations and capacities—is helped, in fact, to get back in touch with his . . . proper poetic gifts." Wordsworth leaves home, experiences psychological distress on a moor in England's Lake District, encounters a ghostly man "not all alive nor dead," and ultimately restores his "power to bestow boons." The poem suggests that a "peculiar grace, / A leading from above, a something given" has bestowed on Wordsworth a miraculous gift, which is the poem itself.

In his essay on Wordsworth, Heaney notes that the photos of lifelike corpses in P. V. Glob's *The Bog People* affected him the way the leech-gatherer affected Wordsworth: "It was as if the Tollund Man and I had come from far away to a predestined meeting: a meeting where there was something familiar between us yet something that was also estranging and luminous." Glob's grotesque photos shocked Heaney at first, but then he realized that the Tollund Man resembled a familiar relative (his great-uncle Hughie) as well as familiar Irish martyrs and their prototype—the crucified Christ. Heaney calls this discovery of the familiar in the unfamiliar corpses "uncanny," and he borrows the German word "unheimlich" from Freud's famous essay "The Uncanny" (1919) to elaborate on the way he responded to the bog people. For him, Glob's images were "bathed in an uncanny light" that made him feel "unhomed [and] . . . *unheimlich*." (The German word can be translated as "unhomelike.") The images triggered thoughts of mythical journeys to the underworld, cognitive descents into the unconscious realm of memory, and returns to the home of one's "proper poetic gifts." When Heaney writes, "In the age of Freud there was a far more fluid awareness of the sources of inspiration, a much greater readiness to locate the radiance of the gift in those very areas of the psyche that have been the most repressed," he gives clues about the "home" of his own gifts and his obsessive desire to return to it.[31]

As Lewis Hyde points out in his study *The Gift: Creativity and the Artist in the Modern World,* many twentieth-century poets gravitate toward fertility myths and mystery cults designed to return participants to the mysterious sources of gifts. Heaney's elegy for Milosz, "Out of This World," reveals his own interest in mystery cults, and suggests that the Christian devotion to Christ's "Mystic- // al Body, the Eleusis of its age" is similar to the pagan's devotion to the gift-giving Persephone in the famous mystery cult at Eleusis, Greece. Persephone's gift was the vegetation in spring, but it was only made after a painful descent to the underworld and a sacrifice to the rapacious god Hades. Heaney's early Catholic training introduced him to the rituals and spiritual exercises that were intended to return the mind to sources of gifts, whether Christian or pagan or secular. As a poet, he came to believe that a silent meditative state—what Hyde called "the gifted state"—was essential for his ongoing fertility as a writer.[32]

Heaney considered his creative life to be a quest for the sort of "gifted states" he'd enjoyed at Mossbawn. In his Nobel Prize speech, he said his mind as a boy had been as "impressionable as the drinking water that stood in a bucket" in the family's scullery; "every time a passing train made the earth shake, the surface of that water used to ripple delicately, concentrically, and in utter silence."[33] The "motionless point" in the center of the bucket came to represent the silent, focused state of mind he needed for writing, and the water's circular ripples represented the lines of writing produced while in that state. Heaney valued this silent meditative state as much as mystics. (The word "mystic" derives from the Greek word *muein*, which means "to remain silent or mute" before mysteries.) In his *Paris Review* interview with the writer Henri Cole in 1994, he also compared these ripples to growth-rings in the self. "No matter how wide the circumference gets, no matter how far you have rippled out from the first point," he said, "that original pulse of your being is still traveling in you and through you."[34] Heaney's "original pulse" was the creative force inside him that he'd gotten inklings of as a boy. It originated in his "hearth culture," and he said it was "the ultimate *sine qua non* [the essential source] in the gift."[35] One of his principal goals as a poet was to pay homage to that "original pulse."

Discussing his formative early life, Heaney acknowledged to a London *Times* journalist that he'd been "a solitary child" who liked to gaze "timorously" at the world from quiet spots around Mossbawn. As a poet, he'd tried to recapture that "solitary gaze out on the world."[36] On a trip to

Pasadena City College in 1995, he told a reporter, "I write to make some verifying alignment between an intuited first place inside myself, the place of original being, and all that is vivid and contradictory and compelling in the life around me. Specifically, I have found that things remembered from my childhood in rural Ulster are like a kind of poetic fossil fuel that can be tapped and transformed."[37] That fossil fuel was the sine qua non powering his poetic gifts.

The Irish poet Padraic Fiacc was thinking of Heaney's early Words-worthian years at Mossbawn when he said, "To understand Heaney . . . you've got to accept him first and foremost as a child." Fiacc added, "[Heaney possesses] a strange loneliness for one so externally gregari-ous (the face always put on his vulnerability)."[38] Close friends often com-mented on the reserve behind his sociable mask, and how his need for silence and solitude made it hard for him to be a political spokesman, even though members of his Catholic community expected him to speak out on their behalf. If he reacted to crises in Northern Ireland with a quiet and judicious "faults-on-both-sides tact," as he wrote in his *Field Work* poem "An Afterwards," he also reacted with guilt. "I'm always thinking to myself—'when people are killing one another, what are *you* doing?'" he told an interviewer in 1979 during some of Northern Ireland's bloodiest sectarian clashes.[39]

Heaney repeatedly wrote about the reasons for his political reticence. In his long poem *An Open Letter*, he included an epigraph from the French writer Gaston Bachelard that betrayed the guilt his silences aroused in him: "What is the source of our first suffering? It lies in the fact that we hesitated to speak. . . . It was born in the moment when we accumulated silent things within us."[40] Heaney felt that accumulating "silent things," such as memories for poems, amounted to collusion with the enemy, since Ulster Protestants had systematically tried to silence Catholics for centuries. When pressed to articulate his political opinions, he normally said he favored constitutional nationalists like John Hume, who worked within a political framework to improve conditions for Ulster's Catho-lics and to secure the country's independence from Britain. He admitted he came from a "Papish house" that didn't support the Irish Republican Brotherhood, the Irish Republican Army, or Sinn Féin. He believed sectar-ian factions should share power. "The Protestants must be granted every cultural and personal and human right to define themselves," he told Henri Cole, although "they must not be granted the right to base the ethos of a new Northern Ireland upon their loyalism and loyalties alone."[41] Unlike Yeats, Frost, Pound, and Eliot, Heaney supported democratic ideals, such as those espoused by the United Irishmen, the revolutionary group of Protestants and Catholics who fought together against the British Empire at the end of the eighteenth century.

Heaney once told the *Arkansas Gazette* that poets "should always be the government-in-exile in any country, the alternative authority. . . . When I say they shouldn't get involved in politics, I mean they lose their mystery and authority if they become entangled in the machinery of politics."[42] Heaney sought to be an alternative political authority from the moment he began publishing poetry in the late 1950s. As a young poet, he said, he'd gone "delving straight away into the sectarian seam of Northern life." He wanted to bear witness to "the hurtful conditions" and the "battened-down spirit [of Catholics] that wanted to walk taller."[43] When those conditions led to the civil rights movement in the 1960s, the British occupation of Northern Ireland, and the battles between sectarian groups, Heaney continued to insist that poets should legislate for justice from a distance. Discussing poetry and politics with his old St. Columb's friend Seamus Deane in the mid-1970s, he said, "I think that poetry and politics are, in different ways, an articulation, an ordering, a giving of form to inchoate pieties, prejudices, world-views, or whatever. And I think that my own poetry is a kind of slow, obstinate, papish burn, emanating from the ground I was brought up on."[44] Heaney hoped his poetry would have a political effect, but he had no illusions about its power to change the status quo in the centers of power.

If Heaney became the most famous English-speaking poet of his generation, he also became one of the most conflicted about the poet's role in the world. He believed poetry should call for justice when governments abused human rights, but he treasured the hermetically sealed life of his Catholic childhood. His tug-of-war between introspective solitude and sociopolitical engagement never ended. "For better or worse," he confessed near the end of his life, "I was never a person who preserved myself for my writing. In fact, I do believe that your vocation puts you in line for a certain amount of community service."[45] His commitment to the well-being of his community, however, was always at odds with his commitment to the solitude and silence of his writing studio.

Heaney agreed with Lewis Hyde's assertion in *The Gift* that "The work of art is a copula: a bond, a band, a link by which the several are knit into one. Men and women who dedicate their lives to the realization of their gifts tend the office of that communion by which we are joined to one another, to our times, to our generation, and to the race. Just as the artist's imagination 'has a gift' that brings the work to life, so in the realized gifts of the gifted the spirit of the group 'has a gift.'"[46] Heaney also subscribed to Joseph Conrad's belief that the writer's job was to "appeal . . . to that in us which is a gift . . . , to our capacity for delight and wonder, to the sense of mystery surrounding our lives; to our sense of pity, and beauty, and pain; to the latent feeling of fellowship with all creation—to the subtle but invincible conviction of solidarity that knits together the loneliness of innumerable hearts, to the solidarity . . . which binds together all humanity—the dead to the living and the living to the unborn."[47] If Heaney's early poems about becoming a writer amounted to declarations of independence from his family and community, those poems also acknowledged his dependence on family and community. One reason for his great success as a writer was his ability to use his gift to establish a "feeling of fellowship" between himself, his origins, and a community of readers that became increasingly global as his career progressed.

# 1

# Ancestral Gifts

## A GENEALOGY OF GIFTS

Like his poet friend Robert Lowell, who once wrote: "Everything I do / is only (only) a mix of mother and father,"[1] Heaney came to believe that his gift arose from the creative contraries represented by his parents. He attributed his down-to-earth knowledge of rural life to his father, Patrick Heaney. "My father was a creature of the archaic world," he said in his *Paris Review* interview. "He would have been entirely at home in a Gaelic hillfort. His side of the family . . . belonged to a traditional rural Ireland."[2] Heaney's early exposure to this archaic way of life contributed to his interest in precapitalist gift-exchange economies, fertility rituals, mystery cults, and pastoral writers from Virgil and Theocritus to Frost and Kavanagh. Patrick also passed on his passion for fort-like houses to his son. The word "Mossbawn" originally referred to a fortified farmhouse on the "moss," or bog; *bawn* was the Anglicized version of a Gaelic word meaning "walled enclosure." For most of his life, Heaney would try, with varying degrees of success, to inhabit houses that reminded him of Mossbawn.

An ambitious, imaginative son, Heaney often found himself at odds with his father. Born on January 18, 1910, to James Heaney (spelled Heeney in some genealogies) and Sarah Scullion, Patrick was one of twelve children who grew up on a farm in Broagh, a small village between Castledawson and Mossbawn. Patrick's mother had left her father's farm, The Wood, which was about a mile north of the village of Bellaghy, to join her husband after they married. Both James and Sarah died when Patrick was a boy. Sarah's three brothers, who were bachelors working in the cattle trade, agreed to take care of the orphaned Patrick at The Wood.

The absence of maternal figures made him especially susceptible to the Scullions' "archaic" masculine values. "The house where he spent his formative years was a place where there were no women, a place where the style was undemonstrative and stoical," Heaney said about his father. "All that affected him and, of course, it came through to us in his presence and his personality."[3]

Heaney spent years trying to come to terms with his father's stoical silences. In 2000, he wrote a prose poem, "Brother Stalk," which suggests that Patrick's loss of his parents had stunted his emotional growth and prevented him from becoming an engaged paterfamilias. The poem compares Patrick to a stalk of cabbage or kale (and other vegetables, too) that struggles to survive "at the ends of fields in winter rain." Perhaps thinking of Sylvia Plath's portrait of an "undead" father figure in "Daddy," Heaney accuses his father of being "more undead than alive." Set in the Christmas season of gift-giving, "Brother Stalk" highlights Patrick's Scrooge-like ways. "If you don't behave," he says to his children, "you'll be getting a cabbage stalk this year from Santy." It's as if Patrick wants his family to experience the deprivations he suffered as a child. Unable or unwilling to emulate Father Christmas, he seems trapped in the role of "the gaunt boy" who was "fostered out, uncosseted among uncles" on the Broagh farm.

Heaney sent "Brother Stalk" to his friend, the poet and publisher Peter Fallon, with a letter saying, "My grandfather and grandmother Heaney died when he was quite young and the older I get the more I think something was put on emotional hold in him because of that shock to the system." Heaney respected his father's agricultural skills, as "Digging," "Follower," "Harvest Bow," and other poems attest, but "Brother Stalk" and the letter to Fallon reveal that he also resented his "father's deep fear of cossetting."[4] Heaney would try to redress his father's refusal to "cosset" by being generous to a fault.

Patrick's lack of a high school education—he left school shortly after graduating from New Row Elementary School in Castledawson—may explain some of his archaic ways. If he had cultural interests and political opinions, he rarely divulged them. He adopted the tight-lipped fatalism of the Scullions, who, according to Heaney, "had something of the stillness of the original hunters and gatherers about them."[5] In his book *Stone Age Economics,* the anthropologist Marshall Sahlins argues that in primitive hunter-gatherer communities often the rules of gift exchange "engender continuity in the relation[s] . . . [and] solidarity" between leaders and their followers. Sahlins draws on the principles of Mauss's *Essay on the Gift*: "All [gift] exchanges . . . bear in their material design some political burden of reconciliation. . . . The worse thing is not giving presents. If people do not like each other but one gives a gift and the other must accept, this brings a peace between them."[6] Heaney's criticism of his father and the Scullion clan was partly based on their refusal to give gifts, whether in the form of love, speech, or Christmas presents.

Heaney shared more traits with his father's "quietist, fatalistic tribe" of Scullion relatives than he wanted to admit.[7] Furthermore, the Scullions were not always taciturn and stingy. As Heaney conceded, they liked to discuss farming and family matters. They showed impatience with political discourse and small talk, but so did Heaney. In 1998, after his novelist friend Darcy O'Brien died, Heaney wrote O'Brien's widow that he felt especially close to her husband because Darcy had demonstrated "something of the fatalism I had grown up with in the rural Ulster of the 1940s, that pervasive, precautionary, almost utilitarian recognition that 'life, son, is a shaky venture.'"[8]

Despite Heaney's criticism of his father in letters and conversations, his poems usually give a balanced assessment of their relationship. "Digging," for example, extols Patrick's ability to dig up potatoes with a spade; "Follower" commends his skill with a horse-plow; "The Harvest Bow" acknowledges the way his father's hands "harked to their gift" as they plaited a "love-knot of straw." Following Robert Frost, Heaney associates plowing lines in a field with writing lines of verse on paper. (The Latin root of "verse"—*versus*—refers to the turn of a plow at the end of a furrow.) What distinguishes father from son in "Follower" is the father's silent expertise and the son's garrulous clumsiness. By the end of the poem, though, roles have reversed; now the father is the clumsy one who stumbles in the wake of the successful son. Heaney's point, though, is that father and son are linked by their different ways of versing.

Heaney was a classic Oedipal son whose gift destined him to surpass his father. Because of his filial struggles, his poems about his father are often tinged with disappointment, embarrassment, anger, confusion, or guilt. A poem written in 1965, "Boy Driving His Father to Confession," for example, belittles his father the way "Brother Stalk" would do thirty-five years later. In the earlier poem, Patrick appears old-fashioned, remote, and vulnerable: there are "chinks in the paternal mail."[9] Other poems written around the same time deplore his father's macho enthusiasm for blood sports. To the German translator, Wilhelm Brockhaus, Heaney wrote on June 3, 1996: "My father, like it or not, was involved with the (illicit) sport of cock-fighting. One of the deplorable aspects of that pastime is the lapping or binding of steel spurs onto the heels of the cocks themselves."[10] For Heaney, cockfighting was an example of Ireland's perverse attraction to violence. If the blood sport demonstrated "phallic consciousness," to borrow D. H. Lawrence's phrase, Heaney—like Ireland's legal system—was against it. In a poem written in the 1960s, "On Hogarth's Engraving 'Pit Ticket for the Royal Sport,'" which was later revised and included in "Triptych for the Easter Battlers," an epigraph states, "Cockfights, or 'battles,' are still held in parts of the country on Easter Monday, despite severe legislation to the contrary."[11] The expanded poem suggests that for Ulster's Catholics and Protestants, cockfighting as well as sectarian fighting are as irresistible as sex.

Heaney's 1973 BBC radio script *Today and Yesterday in Northern Ireland: Cuchulainn and Ferdiad* examines cockfighting again. Here Heaney retells the story of the Irish heroes as if they were combative roosters. According to the ancient epic, the *Táin Bó Cúailnge* (sometimes translated as *The Cattle Raid of Cooley*), Cuchulainn and Ferdiad were once best friends, foster brothers, and possibly lovers, but they ended up fighting each other. After each day's combat, they exchanged gifts of healing herbs and food. Heaney's script dwells on the efficacy of this gift-giving and points out that, on the night before the final battle, "There was no exchange of gifts." The two warriors stay awake "thinking of the *gae-bolga* . . . the magic weapon," which is a barbed spear that Cuchulainn received as a gift from a mythical female warrior. A satisfactory exchange of gifts could end the battle peacefully, but the powers that be are determined to have a winner and loser. Cuchulainn looks back nostalgically to the time when he and his foster brother "made one bed and slept one sleep / in the forest nights." The possibility of renewing that intimacy comes to an abrupt end when Cuchulainn uses his gift—the *gae-bolga*—to kill Ferdiad. Rather than take responsibility for his friend's death, though, he blames those who control his fate and the fate of his rival: "They groomed us and spurred us / like two fighting cocks: / they put iron and danger between the feathers of friendship / and we flew in the face of our love."[12] Heaney scored his Scullion relatives' fatalism, his father's passion for cockfighting, and his country's addiction to ethnic combat into the plot of his radio script.

Heaney's later poems about his father uphold the practice of gift exchange as a way to settle disputes and restore peaceful bonds. "The Harvest Bow," which was published in *Field Work* in 1979, revisits Patrick's cockfighting but contrasts it with his penchant for making artful bows out of straw, which are traditional Irish gifts and symbols of love. When Heaney remembers how his father's hands "harked to their gift and worked with fine intent" to make the bows, he again confirms their artistic bond as skillful craftsmen. As an older man, Heaney found it easier to sympathize with his father's silences, which were partly due to the exhausting farmwork he did to support a large family. For the first fifteen years of Heaney's life, his father labored without a car, truck, tractor, or machines that depended on electricity. He normally asked his farming partner Patsy McWilliams, who lived in the nearby village of Toomebridge, to give him rides to cattle fairs and farms where he bought and sold livestock. Later, another partner, Jim McKenna, who lived in Maghera, agreed to drive him. Despite this inconvenient arrangement, Patrick enjoyed going out on the road to do business. He had a knack for buying the best cattle at the best prices, and for selling the cattle to farmers or butchers after they grazed in the fields around Mossbawn.

Patrick's traditional business practices were disrupted in the early 1960s, when farmers began buying cattle at auctions. He tried to adapt by hiring himself out as a consultant, but the change was difficult for him and for his Scullion relatives. Heaney's elegiac "Ancestral Photograph" in *Death of a Naturalist* recalls how his father and relatives used to haggle with other farmers at cattle fairs and "clinch the bargain" with a gift: "a round of drinks." When the old, sociable way of negotiating was replaced by more impersonal transactions, Patrick was made redundant. Heaney expresses empathy for how his father, who was "sadden[ed] when the fairs were stopped" and "farmers shopped / Like housewives at an auction ring." The implication is that gift-giving and masculine bonding ended when the cattle were simply regarded as commodities to be bought by female shoppers.

## A MOTHER'S GIFTS

For much of his life, Heaney pined for the simplicities of his father's agrarian background but chose to live in urban environments (Belfast, Boston, Dublin) that he associated with his mother, who was a housewife and shopper. Born on September 4, 1911, Margaret Kathleen née McCann was the one who introduced Heaney to the commercial world beyond the fortified farmhouse. She usually took him to her hometown, Castledawson, about a mile west of Mossbawn, to meet her relatives who worked in the nearby linen factory. Heaney's comment in his Nobel Prize speech, "Crediting Poetry," about growing up "in suspension between the archaic and the modern" refers to his journeys back and forth between his parents' different homes and different cultures.[13] As he told one interviewer, his mother "was more a creature of modernity" than his father;[14] she appreciated the modern appliances her McCann family could afford, and she struggled to adapt to the archaic conditions at Mossbawn.

Established in the early 1700s, the linen factory built by the Clark family in the village of Upperlands, about eight miles north of Castledawson, was the oldest of its kind in Ireland and famous for making high-quality fabric with its "beetling" machines that beat the linen to a lustrous sheen. During wars, when governments bought large quantities of fabric for uniforms, tents, and other military supplies, the company prospered. Droughts, floods, fires, changes in fashion, and competition from other textile mills threatened its business. As Wallace Clark notes in *Linen on the Green,* the company was one of only two or three that survived into the twentieth century. In a letter written to the Castledawson historian Ivor Hawe on July 26, 1992, Heaney admitted that the factory seemed glamorous to him as a boy, partly because he'd never been inside it. He'd heard stories about the factory's owners from his mother and from an aunt who'd worked as a maid for the Clark family. Heaney's poem "The Old Team" in *The Haw Lantern* mentions that the Clarks sponsored a local football team. The original Clark, a Presbyterian who fled Scotland during the seventeenth century, was sensitive to religious persecution, and at least some of his descendants tried to please Catholics and Protestants by building a football pitch on company grounds that both could use. The poem, though, reveals little about the actual factory.

As a child with few contemporary amenities at home, Heaney was proud of his mother's connection to the wealthy Clarks. As an adult, he took a more ambivalent view. Several of his poems about the linen-making business give graphic accounts of the pollution it caused and allude to the political biases of the Clarks, who, despite their ecumenical gestures, generally backed pro-British rather than pro-Irish causes. Wallace Clark, who chronicled the history of the Clark factory in *Linen on the Green,* belonged to the Orange Lodge in Upperlands, became an officer in the Ulster Special Constabulary and attained the rank of major in the Ulster Defense Regiment (UDR), an offshoot of the British army that was implicated in sectarian killings.

Heaney refers to the pernicious aspects of the Clarks' linen-making business at the beginning of "Death of a Naturalist," where he declares: "All year the flax-dam festered in the heart / Of the townland." The lines refer to artificial ponds called "dams" built by the Clarks so that flax, the fundamental component of linen, could be soaked until it rotted. The rotting plants suggest the sociopolitical rot at the heart of the country. Another poem about the linen factory, "Lint Water," which appeared in the *Times Literary Supplement* (TLS) on August 5, 1965, documents the rotting flax and pollution it caused in more gruesome detail. Here workers harvest flax, soak it underwater, and dry it on land "like half-gone carcasses." To stress the ecological damage of the Clarks' factory—and, by implication, the cultural damage of powerful Protestant figures like the Clarks—Heaney describes the "unseen contamination" of the linen-making process and the "nauseating fall-out" of the water released from the flax-dams that "sickened fish to death."

Much of Heaney's poetry arose from the conflict between his parents' industrial and agrarian legacies. Searching for ways to reconcile them, he found one guide in his great-great- aunt Catherine Bradley, who had sewn into a piece of linen a poem about "Ireland as she ought to be" (free from the contaminating effects of modern Britain) and, right next to the poem, the patriotic British dictum "God Save the Queen."[15] The needlepoint made in 1843 conjured up the plantation system and linen industry that the British Empire had foisted on Ireland to the country's social and environmental detriment. But the artifact was also a testament to the rich cultural legacy Britain bestowed on its colonized people. His aunt had stitched her divided cultural affiliations into one of the by-products of British imperialism—the attractive linen. From the beginning to the end of his career, Heaney tried to do something similar in his poetry.

Heaney considered his maternal grandfather, who worked in the boiler room of the Clark factory, to be another guide through the British-Protestant and Irish-Catholic labyrinth of his homeland. Grandfather McCann appears in Heaney's sonnet sequence "Clearances" as a godlike figure who gives his grandson intimations of the comfortable life he might someday enjoy. "My grandfather McCann," Heaney said in *Stepping Stones,* "was like any central-casting grandfather of that era: shining bald head, shining wire-rimmed glasses, shining-backed dark waistcoat, collarless shirt sporting its front stud, reading the paper at the end of the table, gazing at you over the glasses."[16] In "Clearances," his house at 5 New Row, Castledawson, radiates conventional respectability and prosperity; everything—including McCann—seems to shine. As Heaney would explain in another poem, "Electric Light," the shine was partly due to the fact that, unlike Mossbawn, the McCann's house had electric lights.

Following the pattern of Oedipal relationships, Heaney as a youth was determined to surpass his paternal relatives out of love for his mother and her relatives. He relished intimate moments with Margaret, even when they involved menial chores such as peeling potatoes or folding sheets. "Clearances," which is dedicated to Margaret, catalogues the "highpoints" of his Freudian family romance. In their *"Sons and Lovers* phase," as he calls it in one sonnet, he plays the role of Paul Morel, who in D. H. Lawrence's novel *Sons and Lovers* (1913) reveres his mother, Gertrude, and rejects his hardworking coal-miner father, Walter. Gertrude gradually withdraws from her husband, whom she considers beneath her social status, and transfers her love to Paul. A similar dynamic was at work in the Heaney household. Often frustrated by her incommunicative, hardworking husband who disdained cosseting, Margaret cosseted her gifted son.

Heaney's Catholic training as a boy encouraged him to revere his mother as another Virgin Mary or maternal saint. "My sensibility was formed by the dolorous murmurings of the rosary, and the generally Mar-ian quality of devotion," he said. "The reality that was addressed was maternal, and the posture was one of supplication. The attitude to life that was inculcated into me—not by priests, but by the active, lived thing of prayers and so on, in my house, [was] *through my mother.*"[17] He told Dennis O'Driscoll: "Religion was a powerful compensation for her. There she was, doomed to biology, a regime without birth control, nothing but parturition and potato-peeling in *saecula saeculorum* [forever and ever], and the way she faced it and, in the end, outfaced it was by prayer and sublimation, toiling on in the faith that a reward was being laid up in heaven. . . . The whole theology of suffering, the centrality of sacrifice, of the cross, of losing your life to save it, all that fitted in with what I saw in her." Heaney also saw in his mother a noble example of the way one's "travails could earn grace for others" through "selfless endurance," and he hoped to emulate these attributes in his own life.[18]

Heaney's sympathy for his mother's ethos of sacrifice was so intense that in some of his early poems he assumed her identity as a persona. "Mother," collected in *Door into the Dark,* is an act of ventriloquy that laments her travails at Mossbawn. Having pumped water for cows in the barn, she says, "I am tired of walking about with this plunger / Inside me." Pregnant once again, she compares the fetus moving in her womb to a calf. As with the cows that surround her, her existence seems to be an endless routine of sex, pregnancy, labor, birth, and feeding. "The Wife's Tale" in *Door into the Dark* also speaks for a mother who is tired of her work providing for others on the farm. A wife resembling Margaret brings lunch to workers threshing grain in a field. A man like Patrick asks her to inspect the grain, even though he knows she has little interest or expertise in such things. She obliges but soon leaves so the men can eat the food she has laid out on a linen cloth. Despite feeling estranged from those she serves, she fulfills the responsibilities of a traditional housewife: she patiently keeps giving, even though the men are "saying nothing." If they're grateful for her gifts, they never tell her.

Near the end of his life, in a speech given at a party for the president of Magdalen College, Oxford, Heaney paid tribute to the sort of patient, gift-giving spirit his mother exemplified. He quoted an interview in which the retiring president, Anthony Smith, had criticized capitalism and endorsed the conception of "the world as a series of gifts." Heaney agreed with his friend, who said, "We need somehow to create a new image of the economy, one which somehow takes into account all the things that are done for nothing, from giving birth to mourning, from giving presents to paying attention to people in trouble. Most of the real value we create in the world is given without hope of recompense. Unfortunately, the economics we learn about totally represses the world of gifts."[19] Heaney remembered the gifts his mother gave to others and also the little gifts she gave to herself, such as a warm footbath after a long day of work. "The Swing" in *The Spirit Level* describes his mother "majestic as an empress / Steeping her swollen feet one at a time / In the enamel basin." For a fleeting moment, the bath delivers her to a world of comfort beyond the austerities of Mossbawn. Heaney ends this domestic idyll by contrasting the realities of her workaday life with the sort of luxuries she forfeited when she left her McCann relatives to marry his father. "There should have been / Fresh linen, ministrations by attendants, / Procession and amazement," he says, knowing full well that such things were only fantasies.

Heaney's father was aware of his son's close relationship with his mother and worried that she and his two sisters—Sarah (nicknamed Sally) and Mary—would spoil him to the point he would refuse to take up farming as a career. They tended to treat him differently from his siblings, partly because he was the oldest child. His Aunt Mary, for example, took him on holiday to Portstewart, a popular seaside resort near Londonderry/ Derry. In his *Field Work* poem, "In Memoriam Francis Ledwidge," he portrays Aunt Mary as another maternal gift-giver, and he features her in "Mossbawn: Two Poems in Dedication," which he placed at the beginning of *North* to highlight her prominent role during his formative years. He also acknowledges her in his introduction to *Beowulf* as a muse whose voice and vocabulary (especially her use of the archaic word "thole") motivated him to translate the poem. As for his Aunt Sally, who was a schoolteacher, her books by Thomas Hardy, Rudyard Kipling, and William Butler Yeats, which she'd inscribed with her name "*S. Heaney,*" instilled in him the hope that someday he'd write his name in his own books. Aunt Sally boosted his literary aspirations with material gifts, as well. She gave him a glass-doored bookcase for his twenty-first birthday and, after he married, a £500 gift for a down payment on a house.

During his childhood and adolescence, though, it was Margaret

Heaney who played the central role of muse and gift-giver. She introduced her son to nationalist songs about Irish rebels who sacrificed themselves for Irish independence, and she tried to impart her family's "gifts for contention" to him by discussing social issues.[20] Margaret's directive, "Whatever you say, say nothing," which parroted the sentiments of Protestants who wanted to silence Catholics, became one of the goads for Heaney as a writer. He used the statement as the title of a poem in *North,* a book in which he repeatedly criticized himself for not exhibiting his mother's "gifts for contention" forcefully enough. "My mother's attitude was not at all expressed by the phrase 'whatever you say, say nothing,'" Heaney said. "Her use of it and my use of it put it very much in inverted commas. The phrase was a knowing acknowledgement of the power structure. . . . It was ironical rather than instructional. It was fundamentally an expression of anger rather than of acquiescence."[21] Margaret encouraged her son to reject her husband's view that "argumentation, persuasion, speech itself" was "otiose and superfluous."[22] Perhaps because she realized her son had inherited his father's penchant for silence, she urged him to speak up.

One of the ways Margaret demonstrated her nationalist sympathies was by naming her son "Seamus." Heaney's paternal grandfather was James, but Margaret, who was attuned to her country's sectarian codes, chose the Irish form of James. She and her husband decided on Justin for a middle name to remind their son of his Catholic heritage; the feast of Justin Martyr occurred in the church on February 14, the day after his birthday. Another way Margaret passed on the family's Irish-Catholic heritage to her son was by singing ballads about Irish patriots. One of her favorites, "Boolavogue," eulogized the militant Father Murphy and his parishioners, who had died fighting the British during the Irish Rebellion of 1798. In the song, the priest cries, "Arm! Arm! . . . / For Ireland's freedom we'll fight or die!" Patrick Joseph McCall, who composed the song in 1898 for the centenary of the Irish Rebellion, imagined the rebels sweeping "o'er the land like a mighty wave" with "pikes . . . reeking / With the crimson blood" of their enemies. In the end, though, the British defeated the rebels at the Battle of Vinegar Hill on June 21, 1798. For McCall, Father Murphy was another doomed freedom fighter in a long line of Irish martyrs. McCall called on God to glorify Murphy and predicted, "The cause that called you may call tomorrow / In another fight for the

Green again." Heaney's "Requiem for the Croppies" in *Death of a Naturalist* recycles imagery from the song while commending the fighters' ecumenical principles.

Many of Heaney's other elegies about Irishmen sacrificing themselves for the nationalist cause can be traced back to his mother's singing. Another one of her favorite ballads, "Who Fears to Speak of '98," began as a poem, "The Memory of the Dead," that envisioned spirits of killed rebels rising up in the future: "The same land that gave them birth / Has caught them to her breast." After Mother Ireland nourishes them at "her breast," they can be reborn "to act as brave a part" as their militant predecessors. These lyrics about death and rebirth contributed to Heaney's later fascination with vegetation myths and fertility rituals in which men die, descend into the earth, and meet a goddess who resurrects them. The song also prompted Heaney to regard British-Irish conflicts in Oedipal terms—as battles between Irish sons and British fathers that culminate in productive (or reproductive) unions with an Earth Mother who, at least in theory, will engender an independent, "green" Ireland.

Another ballad Margaret sang at home, "Roddy McCorley," pays homage to a martyr who died during the Rebellion of 1798 near the Toome Bridge on the Bann River, not far from Mossbawn. (Heaney wrote about the site in "Toome," "Bann Clay," "At Toomebridge," "Perch," and "Bann Valley Eclogue.") The legendary McCorley was a Protestant leader of the Society of United Irishmen who began life as a Catholic. The song's composer, Anna Johnston, portrays McCorley as an idealistic fighter who "loved the Motherland" and goes "to meet the martyr's fate / With proud and joyous mien." His optimism arises from the prospect of a romantic union with the motherland: "Oh Ireland, Mother Ireland, / You love them still the best, / The fearless brave who fighting fall / Upon your hapless breast." Heaney's elegies about similar "heroes" explore the Oedipal impulses behind sacrifices in which men give the gift of life to Mother Ireland with the expectation that she will reciprocate with gifts of personal glory and national independence.

Margaret's devotion to political ballads intensified in the 1950s, when she heard songs on the radio about recent victims of sectarian violence such as Seán South and Feargal O'Hanlon, two members of the Irish Republican Army (IRA) who died in 1957 during a raid on the Royal Ulster

Constabulary barracks in Brookeborough, County Fermanagh. One song, "Seán South of Garryowen," which was sung to the same tune as "Roddy McCorley," refers to South as "another martyr for old Ireland." Both IRA fighters were in their twenties when they died. Another song Margaret liked, which distinguished itself from the others by refusing to romanticize martyrs, was "The Patriot Game." Its narrator declares, "Come all ye young rebels, and list while I sing, / For the love of one's country is a terrible thing." The song calls for a united Ireland, but, like many of Heaney's poems, it refuses to condone or recommend the self-destructive zealotry of nationalists in "the patriot game."

Other songs Margaret taught her son, such as "Loch Lomond" and Robert Burns's "Coming thro' the Rye," focus more on the ordeals of ordinary lovers than on martyrs who die for the love of country. Heaney would develop a lifelong interest in the liberal-minded farmer-poet Burns, who wrote musical poems in both a Scots dialect and traditional English. The poem his mother liked to sing about lovers in a field of rye would become famous after J. D. Salinger had his alter ego Holden Caulfield allude to it in *Catcher in the Rye*. Margaret introduced her son to another poet who would have a permanent influence on him: John Keats. She liked to recite Keats's lighthearted poem "Song about Myself" that tells the story of a "naughty boy" who, out of disappointment with England, runs away to Scotland in search of a better life, only to discover that Scotland is similar to England. It was Keats's musical diction and self-mocking criticism of those who do nothing but "scribble poetry" that caught Heaney's attention.

### GIFTS OF SAINTS AND FARMERS

Unlike Shakespeare's star-crossed lovers in *Romeo and Juliet* who want to forget their family names and the historical baggage they carry, Heaney obsessively examined names and the historical events that produced them. He once said about the area where he grew up: "In the names of its fields and townlands, in their mixture of Scots and Irish and English etymologies, this side of the country was redolent of the histories of its owners."[23] Heaney's family name was also "redolent" of the region's complex history. In his 1978 BBC talk "Omphalos," he mentioned that his paternal ancestors were Gaelic and belonged to an ancient ecclesiastical family whose most famous member was Saint Muredach O'Heney. This O'Heney had settled in Banagher, about twenty miles northwest of Bellaghy, and had built a church there during the twelfth century. According to family lore, if one of the saint's descendants dug up sand on the site and threw it behind a person going to court, that person would win the case. If a descendant threw sand at football players as they ran out on the field, they'd win the game. Heaney valued the land of his ancestors in a similar way—as a repository of potent gifts. His alter ego in the poem "Antaeus" thinks of sand as a gift from his mythical mother, the Earth goddess Gaea, who "wombed," "cradled," and "nurtured" her son in the Earth. A compulsive wrestler whose name in Greek means "opponent," he says, "In fights I arrange a fall on the ring / To rub myself with sand // That is operative / As an elixir." He doesn't want to be "weaned / Off the earth's long contour, her river-veins" because it's from Mother Earth that he derives his supernatural strength.

Like the "facts" of most early genealogies, those about Heaney's Banagher ancestors are hard to verify. One story claims that the twelfth-century patriarch, St. O'Heney, battled a Grendel-like monster called a *peiste* and dispatched it into a deep pool in Banagher Glen. According to another legend, O'Heney rode through the countryside on a deer, balancing a book on its antlers until the deer stopped on a hill where a voice commanded the saint to construct a church. While some believe the builder was St. Patrick, citing as evidence the date AD 474 chiseled into a nearby stone, other historians argue that O'Heney built the church around AD 1120, served as abbot of a Banagher monastery, and is entombed there in a mortuary house. The church's ruins, which can be visited today, are a testament to the fragmentary historical record. One thing is certain: the superstition about valuable sand in the ground near the church is based on fact; it has been profitably quarried for years.

When Heaney scrutinized the history of his home ground, he usually did so through both realistic and mythical lenses. Many of his poems give down-to-earth descriptions of the hard work done by his family and ancestors on their land, but the poems also represent that land as a mythical source of gifts. In his BBC talk about Mossbawn, he calls the family farm his "*omphalos,* meaning the navel, and hence . . . the centre of the world."[24] In Greek mythology, the *omphalos* was a stone with magic powers that Zeus placed at the center of the world. It supposedly belonged to Antaeus's mother, Gaea, and it rested in a temple at Delphi, where a prophetess communed with Apollo. The idea of divine gifts—of prophecy or poetry—originating from a geographical "navel" fascinated Heaney and informed much of his writing.

Heaney felt umbilically connected to the "navel" of Mossbawn, but also to a navel at Banagher. In a letter to Roger Haney, a real estate agent in Omaha, he traced his paternal lineage back to "erenachs of the monastic lands at Banagher" who were involved in "some kind of hereditary tutelage of the property—farm-management rather than soul-cultivation."[25] Heaney suspected that both he and Haney were related to St. O'Heney and the ancient erenachs, since their names had devolved from the Gaelic Ó'hÉighnighs, a group of eleventh- and twelfth-century kings who ruled Fermanagh, a region in the western part of what is now Northern Ireland. Among the numerous Anglicized forms of Ó'hÉighnigh were: O'Heney, O'Heaney, O'Henaghan, Heney, Hegney, Hanye, Hanney, Hannay, Hiney, Heeney, Haney, and Heaney. The original Banagher O'Heneys and Heneys who served as erenachs (spelled "airchinnech" in old Irish) were typically heads of clans. They collected parish revenues such as tithes and rents, constructed churches, and maintained church buildings. In addition to their ecclesiastical duties, they farmed.

Due to the hereditary nature of the erenach's job, St. O'Heney's descendants had an elevated status in medieval society that made Heaney proud. Their duties and fortunes deteriorated, though, after the Protestant Reformation and King Henry VIII's draconian "Dissolution of the Monasteries" edict in the middle of the sixteenth century. The O'Heneys' fortunes also declined as a result of British military campaigns against Ireland in the sixteenth and seventeenth centuries, the policy of allowing Protestants from England and Scotland to confiscate large tracts of land in Ireland for plantations, and the Penal Laws that disenfranchised Irish Catholics.

In its spelling and pronunciation, the name "Heaney" registered the incursions of Scottish and English settlers in Gaelic Ireland. When the British colonized the island, Irish surnames were usually Anglicized. Because some of the medieval Ó'hÉighnighs were illiterate, and because the English and Scottish colonists were bent on suppressing Gaelic names, British officials for many years spelled the name as they saw fit at christenings, marriages, deaths, and other significant events. For example, after the Hannays came to Ireland from Scotland and the Henneys came from England (their names derived from the Old English word "henn-ieg," which meant "dweller by the river frequented by birds"), record-keepers used the British names as models for the Gaelic name Ó'hÉighnigh. Angered by the way they were misrepresented and mistreated, some of the original Ó'hÉighnighs left the country. Nevertheless, a number of Heaney's forebears stayed close to St. O'Heney's original parish of Banagher.

Heaney must have found the relationship between his name and birds intriguing, and even prophetic. (*Ean* in Gaelic means "bird," and "Ó'hÉighnigh" has been translated as "descendent of the son of Bird.") As a famous poet jetting around the world to give readings or receive awards, Heaney often felt like a high-flying bird. He identified with James Joyce's alter ego, Stephen Dedalus, who was supposed to resemble the mythical Greek figure Daedalus, who fashioned giant bird wings to escape a tyrant's labyrinth. Heaney also identified with the ancient Irish bird-man Suibhne, and in the 1970s he began translating *Buile Suibhne,* the long Gaelic poem about the legendary creature's flights around Ireland. Heaney meant for his title, *Sweeney Astray,* to suggest "Heaney Astray," since both he and his persona had experienced numerous displacements and always seemed to be flying from place to place.

Heaney sent his potential relative in Nebraska, Roger Haney, the poem "At Banagher," which he later collected in *The Spirit Level.* Its narrative begins with a genealogical vision in which Heaney's great-grandfather appears as an itinerant, Daedalus-like artificer who makes clothes in a meditative trance. He sits "cross-legged" in a "self-absenting" state of mind as if emulating "Lord Buddha." As with so many of his family portraits, Heaney eulogizes his relative as a fellow poet or "maker." (*Poetes* in Greek means "maker"; *makar* in Scots means "poet.") Like Heaney's mother, who used to tear apart flour sacks and sew the pieces into bed sheets, the Banagher tailor is also an "unmaker" who deconstructs garments before reconstructing them. In this composite portrait of the artist, Heaney's great-grandfather unstitches and restitches text-like textiles into useful, attractive artifacts. And he pursues his craft with St. O'Heney's indomitable spirit.

# 2

# Mossbawn

There were so many births, of both humans and animals, at Mossbawn that it should come as no surprise that Heaney thought of his birth as part of a long succession. Having been in the house when the family doctor helped his mother give birth to siblings, he knew something about deliveries. On April 13, 1999, he wrote jokingly to his former student, the poet Paul Muldoon, "According to the original sources, I came in Dr. Kerlin's bag this day 60 years ago."[1] His poem "Out of the Bag" in *Electric Light* uses the Latin word *miraculum* (a "marvel" or "miracle") to describe Dr. Kerlin's work as a gift-giver at Mossbawn. From Heaney's boyhood perspective, everything about the birthing process was related to gifts. The special sheets put on his mother's bed to prepare for births were "wedding presents," and the babies Dr. Kerlin carried in his bag were presents, too.

Less tutored in the facts of life than in the doctrines of the Catholic Church as a boy, Heaney imagined Dr. Kerlin to be another St. O'Heney or Santa Claus. "And what do you think / Of the new wee baby the doctor brought for us all / When I was asleep?" Heaney's mother asks her children in the poem, playing along with the notion that the doctor is a Santa Claus–like magician who can pull gifts from his bag. "Out of the Bag" compares Mossbawn to "shrines like Lourdes" where the Virgin Mary appeared, to the rustic manger where the Magi brought gifts for the baby Jesus, to the "Sanctuaries of Asclepius" where the Greek god of medicine offered healing gifts, and to the Delphic oracle where Apollo dispensed his gifts of prophecy through the medium of a priestess. Dr. Kerlin, according to the poem, is a mythical figure. He has "Hyperborean, beyond-the-north-wind blue" eyes, like the Hyperboreans in Greek mythology who lived in a sunny paradise beyond Boreas, god of the north wind, and who were credited with establishing the Delphic oracle.

To Heaney's mythopoetic sensibility, Mossbawn was the site of an ongoing *miraculum*. If Dr. Kerlin appeared to be a gift-giving miracle worker to the young Heaney, so did the hand pump in the yard. In his radio broadcast "Mossbawn," he called the pump an "iron idol . . . marking the centre of another world."[2] It, too, was an *omphalos,* a navel providing nourishment to the Heaneys and to other families in the neighborhood. His prose poem "Sinking the Shaft" in *Stations* (1975) suggests that the pump draws life-giving water from "a big wound" in the ground the way Christ gave life-giving blood from his wounds on the cross. Heaney's later poem "A Drink of Water" in *Field Work* emphasizes the sacred nature of the pump's water, which is now in a neighbor's cup. The poem's directive—"be / faithful" to the "admonishment on her cup, / *Remember the Giver*"—echoes Jesus's words to his disciples at the Last Supper: "This cup is the new testament in my blood: this do ye, as oft as ye drink it, in remembrance of me" (1 Cor. 11:25). Paul's Epistle, which recalls the Last Supper, also praises the "spiritual gifts" and "diversities of gifts" (12:1, 4) that the Holy Spirit bestows. As a writer, Heaney associated these spiritual gifts with the literary and reproductive gifts from the *omphalos* of his first home.

At a British Library ceremony where Heaney received the David Cohen Prize in 2009, he told his audience that "A Drink of Water" was "about receiving a gift and being enjoined to [reciprocate]." The neighbor alluded to in the poem, Rosie Keenan, had received gifts of water from the Heaneys' pump, and, in return, she'd acted as a "muse offering the cup of poetry to the child Incertus."[3] She was one of the only neighbors devoted to the arts (she played the piano and violin and sang Irish ballads), and she shared her enthusiasm for music with Heaney. Although his parents couldn't afford to pay Keenan for music lessons, which he wanted, she taught him valuable lessons simply by pursuing her passion for art in a place that seemed unartistic. The poem "At the Wellhead" in *The Spirit Level* also honors Keenan, the "blind-from-birth, sweet-voiced, withdrawn musician" who was one of Heaney's first models for the gifted and gift-giving artist. At the awards ceremony in London, Heaney wanted his audience to know that he considered the David Cohen Prize to be a generous gift, just as Rosie Kennan had considered her cup of water to be a gift.

As a sensitive child whose imagination was shaped by Catholic doctrine, Heaney thought the region around Mossbawn was full of extraordinary people like the Christ-like Rosie Keenan and supernatural Dr. Kerlin. His family farm, in fact, was ordinary by the region's standards. There were about ten acres of adjacent fields near the house and about forty acres of outlying fields. The whitewashed, thatched, one-story farmhouse was set back from Hillhead Road and screened by beech trees, alder trees, a boxwood hedge, and a thorn hedge. Lorries, cars, buses, and horse-drawn carts occasionally passed on the road. The Heaneys did most of their chores by hand. In the scullery—a brick room near the kitchen—they washed dishes and prepared meals from homegrown vegetables. They cleaned themselves and their clothes in the scullery, too. The family's bucket of drinking water rested on a stool there. Near the bucket was a wooden churn used for beating fermented milk into butter, a process Heaney remembered as both laborious and magical in his early poem "Churning Day." The scullery also contained a small pantry stocked with milk and other provisions.

The kitchen was one of the main rooms of the house and served multiple purposes. Here Margaret Heaney and Aunt Mary used a coal-burning stove, with the unlikely brand name "The Modern Mistress," to cook gruel for calves, scones and cakes for the family, and potatoes that were mashed for chickens. The Heaney children ate porridge and buttered bread for breakfast before walking to school. They had "dinner" when they returned at three thirty or four o'clock, and sat down at seven o'clock in the evening for supper, often without their father, who might be at a cattle fair or outside tending the cows. On weekends, the family ate home-cured bacon, meat stew, and tinned salmon. Sometimes on Sundays they enjoyed a pot roast with lettuce, eggs, and scallions. For holidays, such as Christmas or Easter, they opened leaves of a table in a bedroom, laid out a tablecloth, took down fancy china that Margaret and Patrick had received as a wedding present, and feasted on goose and apple sauce. In the absence of electricity, candles lit the bedrooms and an oil lamp lit the kitchen.

The Heaneys listened intently to a battery-driven Cossor radio set up in the kitchen. Heaney especially liked the BBC's *Dick Barton* detective serial, which aired every evening from 1946 to 1951. The show featured Special Agent Barton and his two sidekicks, Jock Anderson and Snowy White, who solved crimes and saved Britain from disasters. Heaney also tuned in to the BBC's popular *Children's Hour* so he could follow the exploits of the dashing World War I pilot James Bigglesworth (nicknamed "Biggles"). While Heaney preferred British stories full of masculine daring, his parents listened to comedies and football commentaries on Radio Athlone, an Irish broadcasting company started in 1932. Ireland's Radio Éireann, as it would soon be called, appealed to conventional Catholic listeners like his parents, while the BBC catered to a more cosmopolitan audience.

Heaney knew the radio programs were designed for different ages and different cultures, and as a boy he felt torn between them. He also felt torn between the different versions of English transmitted by the radio. His family's guttural English was the primary language in the house. The British voices on the BBC and the American voices on the American Forces Network sounded foreign. The adventure stories he liked also seemed out of place in his Irish-Catholic hearth culture, signs of which (a Catholic calendar, a commemorative picture of the Eucharistic Congress in Dublin, a red lamp lit for the Sacred Heart, Saint Brigid's crosses, portraits of Ireland's patron saints) surrounded him. He grew up divided between the worldly narratives on the kitchen radio and the otherworldly narratives of a cosmos ruled by God and his representatives, which is one reason he said his childhood was a "mixture of the kitchen and cosmos."[4]

Heaney's poems suggest that life on the family farm was so ordinary at times that, in a dialectical way, it whetted his appetite for journeys to extra-ordinary realms in the cosmos. His poem "A Sofa in the Forties" in *The Spirit Level* recalls how he and his siblings transformed a mundane piece of kitchen furniture into a train that could transport them—at least in their imaginations—on "heavenbound" journeys beyond the walls of Mossbawn. Without running water or electricity for the large family, Mossbawn could feel cramped and uncomfortable. Heaney's younger sisters Sheena and Ann had to sleep with their Aunt Mary in a small bedroom. Heaney's parents slept in a room that often had an infant in a baby carriage beside their bed. Heaney and his six brothers (Hugh, Patrick, Charles, Colm, Christopher, Daniel) shared two large beds next to their parents. Most mornings, Heaney had to wake early to milk the cows with his Aunt Mary. At other times, he had to shovel dung from the barn, pile hay or unthreshed corn on the "haggard" (the enclosed hay-yard), tend the vegetable garden in the backyard, and herd cows from the Broagh farm to The Wood farm. In addition to their crops, the Heaneys raised and butchered pigs, chickens, geese, and turkeys. Plowing and mowing fields with horse-drawn equipment, hauling water from the outside pump that froze in winter, using an outhouse rather than a toilet, and doing all the other daily tasks without modern machines required a patient, pragmatic approach to life. No wonder Heaney admitted that Mossbawn was "a small, ordinary, nose-to-the-grindstone place."[5]

One of Heaney's most vivid childhood memories was of getting lost in Aunt Mary's pea garden between the backyard and the railway line. His prose poem "Cauled" at the beginning of *Stations* asserts, "A caul of shadows stretched and netted round his head." Though lost, young Heaney finds himself in an Eden or womb. (A "caul" refers to the amniotic membrane around a fetus.) In his 1978 BBC talk about Mossbawn, he also refers to the pea garden as a womb: "a green web, a caul of veined light . . . full of assuaging earth and leaf smell, a sunlit lair." Another "lair" is the notch in a beech tree where he imagines he is "at the heart of a different life, looking out on the familiar yard as if it were suddenly behind a pane of strangeness." His withdrawal to a dreamlike space resembles Robert Frost's sleepy withdrawal in "After Apple-Picking." Frost says he tries to "rub the strangeness" from his eyes that he gets from looking at his farm through a "pane of glass," which is actually a sheet of ice he takes from a drinking trough. Heaney's "secret nests," as he calls them in "Mosbawn," are boyhood prototypes of the "gifted states" he would cherish as a poet.[6]

Heaney's experiences of "a different life" from the vantage point of a beech tree or pea garden were rites of passage as he matured, and they had an uncanny way of recapitulating his initial passage from womb to world. One of the most memorable of these initiatory rites occurred when Heaney was about nine and went with a friend to a marshy stretch of ground near Lough Beg, a lake about three miles east of Mossbawn. The area was supposed to be haunted by bogeys and a recluse nicknamed Tom Tipping, so it took courage for Heaney to strip off his clothes and jump naked into a muddy bog hole. He emerged, he later said, "somehow initiated [and] . . . betrothed . . . [to] the watery ground."[7] During this vaguely sexual plunge, he seemed to marry an Earth goddess like Gaea or the one P. V. Glob's bog bodies unite with in their Iron Age fertility rituals. Once again, he intimates a maternal figure is the source of his gifts.

"Waterbabies" in *Stations* dramatizes a similar rite of passage, although this one involves plunging the gift of a kaleidoscope, rather than his body, into a muddy puddle near Mossbawn. "I once fouled a gift there and sank my new kaleidoscope," Heaney says in the prose poem. This incident appears again in section XI of "Station Island," where the gift-giving initiates a mystical "dark night of the soul" in which Heaney returns to both poetic and divine sources of creation. In the muddied "prisms of the kaleidoscope," the poet sees a monk speaking "again about the need and chance // to salvage everything, to re-envisage / the zenith and glimpsed jewels of any gift." The monk instructs Heaney to translate a poem by the famous sixteenth-century Spanish mystic St. John of the Cross, and Heaney chooses one about the "eternal fountain [that] hides and splashes / within this living bread that is life." In Heaney's version of the mystic's Eucharistic gift exchange, a communicant recapitulates his union with a fertile source—in this case, with the mysterious "fountain" of the Creator and the origin of all creative gifts.

### GIFTS OF PEACE AND WAR

Because of his parents' financial constraints during and after World War II, Heaney took very few actual journeys beyond what he could see from Mossbawn. "If Lough Beg marked one limit of the imagination's nesting ground," he said about his childhood, "Slieve Gallion marked another."[8] Slieve Gallion was a 1,732-foot, flat-topped mountain about ten miles to the west of his house. There the countryside was more populated than the region to the east around Lough Beg. Periodically, his mother would take him on a bus from the intersection of Broagh and Hillhead Roads to Castledawson, where she'd leave him with her parents so she could shop by herself. On special occasions, she let him accompany her to nearby Hillhead and Anahorish, where she bought supplies for the farm. This was about the extent of his childhood travels.

In the 1980s, Heaney waxed lyrical about these excursions in a long letter to the historian Ivor Hawe. One reason he remembered them so fondly was because he was given gifts (mainly free candy) at a shop owned by his father's cattle-dealing friend Jack McMillan. He was also dazzled by the abundance of goods in the shops. McMillan's shelves were stocked with hurricane lamps, bags of sugar, sides of bacon, containers of tea, whitewash brushes, and other useful commodities. Heaney liked to visit the family friend, Johnnie Brown, too; his shop was a "warmly protective . . . haven" full of colorful wool. The owner of a cobbler shop, Robert Hueston, and the owner of a butcher shop, Bobby Garvin, struck Heaney as "archetype figure(s)" who presided over similar havens. Another "great wonder," he said, was a pressurized water pump called "The Fountain" near his grandparents' house that could fill a bucket with astonishing speed. Castledawson's large Nestlé factory, which was built in 1943 to produce sweetened condensed milk, filled the youthful Heaney with awe, as well, especially when it was lit up at night. A poem in *The Haw Lantern*, "The Milk Factory," recalls the factory as "a bright-decked star-ship." A later poem, "Moyulla" in *District and Circle,* acknowledges his boyhood enchantment with the factory but also its pollution of the Moyola River. Heaney liked visiting the train station, too, and never forgot the time a train window fell on his fingers. "Some kind of pain and public embarrassment starts at the verge of my memory of that day," he said.[9] Compared to his family farm, Castledawson seemed to be part of a modern world that was both attractive and potentially traumatic.

From an early age, and partly because of his Catholic training, Heaney regarded the pastoral fields around his home as Edenic and the world beyond its walls as a seductive world where things—such as train windows—could suddenly fall and cause pain. His fall into knowledge, though, came in increments. News of World War II, which had commenced in Europe the year Heaney was born, certainly contributed to his growing awareness of a world that was fallen or falling. At first, he found it hard to understand why Germany attacked Northern Ireland and why some Catholics welcomed the Nazi bombing of Protestant sections of nearby cities. When German planes blew up "the bitter Orange parts" of Belfast, he wrote in his *Stations* poem "England's Difficulty," Catholics cheered. When a German pilot bailed out of his plane and visited Mossbawn, the soldier didn't strike Heaney as the demonic "enemy" depicted by British propaganda.

The killing of animals for food that Heaney witnessed on his farm and on nearby farms, though, began to merge with the military killing he heard about on the radio or from his parents and neighbors. "Testimony: Anahorish 1944," which was first published in a book by one of Heaney's relatives about the American Eighty-Second Airborne Division stationed in Ulster, combines scenes of local and foreign slaughters. The poem begins with a blunt statement by someone in the Gribbin family about slaughtering pigs when American soldiers arrived in the area to prepare for war. The Gribbins did this every Tuesday on their farm a short distance from Mossbawn, and Heaney could hear the squeals of fear and pain. In hindsight, he realized that the soldiers preparing to invade Normandy on D-Day would suffer a fate similar to the pigs.

The harsh realities of World War II impinged on Heaney's childhood Eden in unexpected ways. On one occasion at his grandparents' home, he and his siblings discovered gas masks that the government had issued to protect citizens from German bombs. Another sign that something was amiss was the routine of pulling down blinds over windows at night. His parents informed him that this had to be done so German pilots wouldn't target houses in Northern Ireland. There were also ration books to remind Heaney of the war's economic hardships. At first, bacon, ham, sugar, and butter were rationed. Later, milk, coffee, eggs, cheese, jam, and other foodstuffs were added to the list.

The Allied presence near Mossbawn became more visible when Heaney was four years old and saw fighter planes landing at the Toomebridge aerodrome as part of President Roosevelt's Operation Magnet. (The plan called for about one hundred thousand Allied soldiers to train in Northern Ireland.) Although some of the troops ended up in the Pacific, thousands of Americans went to northern France. Sergeant Len Lebenson, who was part of the contingent near Mossbawn, recalled, "When we got there, we discovered our camp to be bare-boned basic—corrugated iron [Nissen or Quonset] huts for accommodation, single coal burning stoves for heat, limited bathing facilities and a scant supply of hot water."[10] The soldiers struggled to keep warm in the primitive buildings. They washed in basins of cold water and used outdoor latrines, just as the Heaneys did on their farm. Eager to leave their Spartan camp on the Moyola Park Estate about a mile and a half west of Mossbawn, the soldiers frequented pubs and dance halls. There they could stay warm while meeting women and drinking with locals.

Heaney was sequestered in his favorite beech tree "nest" when he first saw two columns of American soldiers marching beside tanks and armored cars on the road beside Mossbawn. He viewed the soldiers, he said, "with much the same sense of wonder as the native Indians must have felt four and half centuries earlier as they witnessed the arrival of Columbus and his Spanish troops on the shores of America."[11] The soldiers were supposed to be liberators, but they resembled invaders. When British soldiers came to Northern Ireland during a resurgence of sectarian violence in the 1970s, Heaney regarded them with similar trepidation. The Allied soldiers, however, won Heaney over with gifts. As "Anahorish 1944" recounts, they gave him "gum and tubes of coloured sweets." Other residents thought of the foreign soldiers as gift-givers, too, because they pumped cash into the local economy. When they left for England on February 13, 1944, the economy sagged. The troops in France experienced a different kind of misfortune. Nearly half of the twelve thousand men in the Eighty-Second Airborne Division were killed, wounded, or lost during the D-Day invasion, which began on June 6, 1944.

During World War II, Heaney got some of his first lessons in the way gift-giving could create cordial bonds between potential antagonists. A story that was often told in his household involved a gift from Protestant neighbors to Heaney's father. Shortly after the Allies defeated the Axis forces in Europe, George and Alan Evans returned from Italy, where they'd fought in Britain's Eighth Army. One of the brothers joked about pilfering rosary beads from the pope's dresser while visiting the Vatican. Patrick Heaney asked lightheartedly, "Did they make a papish of you over there?" Heaney, who was only six years old at the time, never forgot Evans laughing at the joke and giving his father a gift of rosary beads. He wrote in the prose poem "Trial Runs" in *Stations* that his neighbor and father were like "two big nervous birds dipping and lifting, making trial runs over a territory." Heaney's father jingled silver coins in his pocket, as if he might betray his friend the way Judas had betrayed Jesus for thirty pieces of silver. But no money was exchanged, and there were no hard feelings. The beads were a free gift, and, as a result, these Protestant and Catholic neighbors made their "trial run" as allies rather than as enemies.

# 3

# Anahorish
# Primary School

The year the Allies stormed the beaches of Normandy coincided with Heaney's first year of primary school. Realizing how frightened he was about leaving home, his parents asked an older girl who lived across the street, Philomena McNicholl, to accompany him on the three-quarter-mile walk along Lagans Road to Anahorish School. As it turned out, even the attractive, ginger-haired girl with the saintly name couldn't assuage Heaney's fears about going to school. His father, who was shaving in the kitchen and eager to get to a cattle fair, got angry, or at least he pretended to get angry, as his son sobbed and whined. Finally, after much parental prodding, Heaney left the house.

In retrospect, Heaney's reluctant walk with Philomena had all the *Sturm und Drang* of an epic journey. He may have felt like a soldier going off to war in a foreign land, since the school was housed in two zinc-roofed Nissen huts that the Allies had left behind when they went to Normandy. In any case, Anahorish School came to represent a mythical otherworld in Heaney's imagination. Years later, he compared himself to a Native American in the Pacific Northwest who felt "lost and homesick" on his final trek to "the land of the dead."[1] Approaching the small huts, he was particularly concerned about his handmade, leather shoulder bag, which his Uncle Peter had used to carry money when he sold bread from a cart. He felt the bag looked shabby and lower-class and would be ridiculed by the other students.

Heaney commemorated his first morning at Anahorish School in "The Schoolbag," a poem collected in *Seeing Things*. (*The School Bag* was also the title of a poetry anthology he edited with Ted Hughes for Faber in the 1990s.) His poem treats his journey past the hedged meadows and bog holes on Lagans Road as if he were Dante descending with Virgil into the infernal "land of the dead." Heaney imagines being "in the middle of the road to school," echoing Dante's line at the beginning of the *Inferno* about being in the middle of his life's road: "Nel mezzo del cammin di nostra vita." Heaney refers to his secondhand schoolbag as "a handsel," a gift intended to bring good luck to someone at the beginning of a new endeavor. Although he showed little gratitude for the bag as a schoolboy, as an adult he considered it to be what anthropologists call a "threshold gift"—a gift that marked and helped facilitate his rite of passage as a child heading off to school for the first time.

The fact that the school accepted girls as well as Protestants may have been one reason for Heaney's initial anxiety. He would soon learn that in the Nissen huts the students were grouped according to age and sex. Miss Walls, who talks about the differences between "daddy" frogs and "mammy" frogs in "Death of a Naturalist," taught the youngest boys in one hut, and in the same hut the sixty-year-old Master Bernard Murphy taught the older boys. In an adjacent hut, Miss Gribbin instructed the younger girls in reading and writing, and Murphy's wife taught cooking and sewing to older girls. There was a blackboard, a teacher's desk, and an iron stove for heat at one end of each hut. Eight-foot planks and wood benches served as desks for six or seven students. Younger students sat at the front, older students at the back.

If the buildings seemed Spartan and militaristic, so did the discipline. Miss Walls and Master Murphy punished students by hitting them with rods, although Walls used her rod less frequently than Murphy. "The rod of correction" (or "the stick," as the boys called it) was about a half inch thick. "Master Murphy wasn't a slasher but he was stern and could 'slap' without compunction," Heaney said.[2] Most parents respected Murphy, despite—or perhaps because of—his punitive ways. He ingratiated himself with several adults by giving them advice about pension documents and farm-subsidy forms. Heaney's family was grateful to him for helping Aunt Sally prepare for her King's Scholarship exam. Murphy launched Heaney's career as a writer and scholar, which may explain why his poems tend to overlook the master's punishments and regard Anahorish School as the place where he began to discover his gifts. Alluding to its original Gaelic name, *anach fhíor uisce* in his *Wintering Out* poem "Anahorish," Heaney idealizes the school as his "'place of clear water,' / the first hill in the world / where springs washed into / the shiny grass." It's as if Anahorish were an Eden or Ararat coursing with life-giving streams. The fact that the teachers didn't slash or slap Heaney as often as they did the other students may have reinforced his sanguine memories of the school. As a boy, he abided by the rules and concentrated on his lessons, impressing his teachers with his diligence and intelligence.

One profound lesson Heaney learned at Anahorish was that writing could renew his bond with home. It was in Miss Walls's class that he began to detect relations between written letters and familiar objects at Mossbawn. For someone as homesick as Heaney, letters were like magic wands that could whisk him away to a happier place and make absent things present. According to the poem "Alphabets" in *The Haw Lantern*, if he sketched "Two rafters and a cross-tie" to make the letter A, he re-created his farmhouse roof. Writing, if done properly, could elicit a teacher's check mark that looked like the "little leaning hoe" he used in his family garden. Fetching water near the school to make ink for fountain pens (there was no running water in the Nissen huts) also reminded him of home. As soon as he left a hut, he said, he "felt a world away" from the other students because the countryside looked just like it did around Mossbawn. Decades later, he spoke about this uncanny feeling of being at home and not at home in the second person to emphasize its strangeness: "You . . . had a taste of yourself [outside] in all of your own solitude and singularity."[3] He was at school in buildings set up by foreigners, but he felt as if he'd been transported to one of his solitary nesting places on the family farm.

Heaney's phrase "a taste of yourself" comes from Gerard Manley Hopkins's commentary on *The Spiritual Exercises of St. Ignatius Loyola*. Hopkins declares, "I consider my selfbeing, my consciousness and feeling of myself, that taste of myself . . . [to be] more distinctive than the taste of ale or alum, more distinctive than the smell of walnutleaf or camphor." Like Catholic mystics before him, Hopkins believed that God's ability to create—His "selving" power—was incomprehensible and "incommunicable by any means to another man."[4] In a letter to his friend Robert Bridges written in 1882, the year he finished his commentary on the *Spiritual Exercises*, Hopkins cites a passage from Walt Whitman's "Song of Myself" in which "leaves of grass" are referred to as an example of the Creator's "selving." Whitman says the grass must be "the handkerchief of the Lord, / A scented gift . . . / Bearing the owner's name someway in the corners, that we may see and remark, and say *Whose?*" Among other things, the grass is a sign of the Lord's and also the poet's identity. "It must be the flag of my disposition," Whitman writes. As for answering the fundamental questions about why and how the gift of grass—or the gift of God or gift of self or gift of poetry—came to be, Whitman responds like other mystics: "I do not know."[5] In *Stepping Stones*, Heaney indicated that he sympathized with this mystical view of the world.

Heaney's sense of "solitude and singularity" was caused in part by his recognition that he was a Catholic in a predominantly Protestant community. As he walked to school, signs of his Catholic heritage were all around him. On clear days, from the top of a small hill on Lagans Road called Mulholland's Brae, he could see the 1,434-foot-high Slemish Mountain to the northeast where St. Patrick had reputedly herded sheep. To the east, a Catholic church steeple rose above an island in Lough Beg. According to local lore, the imprint that St. Patrick had made on a churchyard stone while praying still collected healing water. Heaney should have felt at home among all these reminders of his Catholic faith, but Catholic students at Anahorish were treated differently from Protestant students. Protestants enjoyed the privilege of going home for lunch, whereas Catholics had to stay at school to recite the catechism and pray. Protestants praised King William of Orange and mocked the pope. Decades after he graduated, Heaney could still recite sectarian verses aimed at Catholics, such as: "Up with King William and down with the Pope / Splitter splatter holy water / Scatter the Papishes every one." The ditty ended: "If that won't do / We'll cut them in two / And give them a touch of the red, white and blue." The colors referred to the British flag. Sometimes Catholic students responded: "Up the long ladder and down the short rope / To hell with King Billy and God bless the Pope." Or they shouted: "Red, white and blue / Should be torn up in two / And sent to the devil / At half-past two."[6] The humor had a sharp edge, especially for students aware of the country's history of religious persecution.

Many of the "official" poems and songs in the school's curriculum sought to bolster, in subtle or not-so-subtle ways, the same prejudices articulated by Protestants in their juvenile lyrics. British literature was promoted, Irish literature demoted. Teachers made students memorize Robert Browning's patriotic poem "Oh to Be in England," which portrays Protestant Britain as if it were a springtime Eden. The students also learned a song popular in the British military, "The Lincolnshire Poacher," which told the story of an obedient apprentice ("I served my master truly") who decides to take up poaching to make extra money. Perhaps because many in Britain sided with the Confederacy during the Civil War (their textile mills depended on cheap cotton picked by slaves), Stephen Foster's "Poor Old Joe" became part of the school repertoire. In this song, a former slave pines for the good old days in the cotton fields when "hearts [were] once so happy and free." Drawing on blackface minstrel shows and the Lost Cause myth, Foster glossed over the sufferings of enslaved laborers on southern plantations, just as patriotic Protestants glossed over Britain's harsh treatment of Catholic laborers on plantations in Ireland. For Heaney and his Catholic peers, these songs were bitter reminders of past and present injustices.

## THE MASTER'S ROD

Heaney became more conscious of the British Empire's effects on his culture after he graduated from Miss Walls's class. One of his most enduring memories of his new classroom was a wall map of partitioned Ireland. Trained to think of Ireland as a big saucer with a wet center and a mountainous rim, he was surprised to see that Ireland on the map was more like a dish that had broken in half. Only the upper half was displayed; the lower half, which should have contained the Republic of Ireland, was missing. This was due to the 1921 War of Independence that had separated north from south. The rod at the bottom of the map reminded Heaney of the "rod of correction" wielded by his new teacher, Master Murphy. Each day, Murphy stood imperiously behind his desk in a blue serge suit with a starched collar and tie. Heaney in old age still winced at the way

Murphy had beaten a boy who had mispronounced the word "geography." Although Heaney got along with his strict master, Murphy came to represent the cruelty of British imperialism.

Heaney sometimes claimed he ignored the religious affiliations of his Anahorish friends, but he was certainly conscious of them. His prose poem "Kernes" ("kern" is an archaic term for a Scottish or Irish foot soldier) describes a fight with a boy named Jacky Dixon as if it was part of a long series of British-Irish battles. The Protestant Dixon holds the pole of a British flag as he sits on his expensive Raleigh bicycle. The brand name evokes memories of the powerful English Protestant Sir Walter Raleigh, who in the sixteenth century led British soldiers against a rebellious group of Irish Catholics at Smerwick in southwestern Ireland and ended up beheading and throwing the mangled bodies of many rebels into the ocean. Raleigh was involved in other imperialistic ventures as well. Dixon seems to embody the belligerence of the man whose name is on his bike as he rides toward Heaney's Catholic friends and shouts, "I could beat every fucking papish in the school!" Heaney would soon realize that childhood war games in Northern Ireland had a way of morphing into actual battles.

The British educational system was in place at Anahorish to maintain the status quo. Even though Heaney forgot the title of the first book he read as a student, he remembered its old-fashioned British views of bringing the light of civilization to benighted savages in foreign lands. Heaney read the book at home under an oil lamp while a neighbor, Hugh Bates, exclaimed, "Boys but this Seamus fellow is a great scholar."[7] Heaney's reading as a boy was generally confined to Catholic magazines such as *Far East*, which was published by the Missionary Society of St. Columban, and the *Irish Messenger of the Sacred Heart*, another Catholic magazine. Later, he moved on to British magazines with comic strips about Dennis the Menace, Roger the Dodger, Keyhole Kate, and Julius Sneezer. Although his parents disapproved of his tastes, his mother let him subscribe to an upscale British magazine called *Champion*, which was full of adventure tales and sports stories about characters like "Kalgan, the Jungle Boxer" and "Johnny Fleetfoot, the Redskin Winger." As soon as he finished the latest issue of *Champion*, he'd trade it for less wholesome magazines such as *Rover*, *Hotspur*, or *Wizard*. His parents tried to convince him, often with little success, to read *Our Boys,* an Irish-Catholic magazine published by the Education Company of Ireland and the Christian Brothers.

Heaney experienced what he called his "first literary frisson" in an Anahorish class that focused on Irish heroes such as Brian Boru, who died fighting Viking mercenaries in AD 1014.[8] Another story that had a powerful effect on his imagination involved the supernatural Celtic warrior Dagda, whose club could kill nine people with one swing and whose magic harp could control soldiers and seasons. Heaney was haunted by the way Dagda destroyed Balor of the Evil Eye. His poem "Hercules and Antaeus" in *North* resurrects Balor along with the defeated Antaeus and transforms them into archetypal Irish victims. The mythical Cuchulainn, who was also a subject of discussion at Anahorish, would resurface in his BBC radio script *Cuchulainn and Ferdiad.*

Pulp fiction and Irish mythology taught Heaney from a young age to conceive of life as an archetypal ordeal in which heroes use their gifts to triumph over adversaries. Two young adult books by the Scottish writer Robert Louis Stevenson, *Treasure Island* and *Kidnapped,* reinforced this view of life. Heaney especially liked *Kidnapped,* which he received as a Christmas present as an adolescent. In the novel, the protagonist David Balfour discovers he's supposed to inherit a substantial financial gift after his parents die, but an unscrupulous uncle tries to prevent him from receiving it. After a series of mishaps (he's abducted, shipwrecked, and chased by English redcoats in Scotland), he joins the Catholic Jacobite Alan Breck Stewart to evade his pursuers. Heaney said the action-packed story that romanticized a supporter of the Catholic King James II in his fight against the English in the Scottish Highlands made him "a Jacobite for life."[9]

The Irish ballads that Heaney sang at family gatherings appealed to the same embattled, nationalist mindset he found in *Kidnapped.* A travelling company of actors contributed to his early nationalist education, too. Their plays were inspired by ballads such as *Noreen Bawn, or The Curse of Emigration,* and by historical pageants about Irish heroes such as Robert Emmet, a martyred leader of the Rebellion of 1798. As a teenager, Heaney acted in a play about the Rebellion. Staged annually in the Ancient Order of Hibernians Hall not far from Mossbawn, the play offered a compelling alternative to the canonical British literature that Master Murphy taught at Anahorish.

When Heaney's teachers recognized his academic potential, they told his parents he should enroll in a college preparatory curriculum in secondary school. First, though, he had to take the "Eleven Plus" exam (so named because it was given to students in Britain at the age of eleven or twelve). The exam had been created by the Education Act of 1947 to determine where students should be placed in the Tripartite System. College-bound students normally went to grammar schools; other students attended schools that taught industrial skills or skills such as cooking and woodworking. The Education Act, as it turned out, became a catalyst for social change in Northern Ireland by giving scholarships to underprivileged students—often Catholics—who couldn't afford preparatory schools and universities. Heaney credited the Education Act for creating a new "generation with some sense of possibility and advantage and renewal."[10] The act also created a new awareness of the history of injustices in Ireland and the tools to redress them.

Heaney took the Eleven Plus exam in 1950 and did well enough to earn a scholarship to St. Columb's College. Master Murphy was proud of Heaney, but advised him to spend another year studying at Anahorish to get ready for the academic rigor of St. Columb's. So from 1950 to 1951, he went to Master Murphy for early-morning tutorials in Latin, Gaelic, and algebra. "Station Island" revisits these chilly sessions when "*mensa, mensa, mensam* / sang in the air like a busy whetstone." The Latin *mensa* refers to the top of an altar where sacrifices are performed, and *mens* refers to the "mind" that Heaney was trying to sharpen on his master's academic whetstone.

"The Wanderer" in *Stations* commemorates a rite of passage at Anahorish School during which Heaney received a "threshold gift." Referring to Master Murphy again, he writes, "On a day when the sun was incubating milktops and warming the side of the jamjar where the bean had split its stitches, he called me forward and crossed my palm with silver." Murphy announces to the other students that the gift of a silver half crown (a British coin first issued by King Edward VI in 1551 and worth about four dollars today) is for winning a scholarship to attend St. Columb's. The vignette, which borrows its title from a well-known Anglo-Saxon poem, portrays Murphy as a Beowulf-like "ring-giver." His gift is supposed to honor Heaney, make his passage to the new school easier, and establish a lasting bond between teacher and student. But the imagery in the poem is ominous. The bean in the jar that splits its stitches foreshadows the way Heaney's wounds will open again when he leaves home for boarding school. The half crown signals that he is the beneficiary of a British Crown and British Empire that have traditionally oppressed Irish Catholics. And the silver coin is a reminder of the pieces of silver paid to Judas for betraying Christ to officials in the Roman Empire before His crucifixion. Heaney's "crossed" palm seems to be an omen of future crossings and potential crucifixions. He accepts Master Murphy's gift, but his poem expresses the anxiety he felt about another departure from home.

# 4

# St. Columb's College

## CROSSING THE SHADOW LINE

Heaney once said that he had "crossed some kind of psychic shadow line" when he left home for Londonderry/Derry on August 29, 1951.[1] He may have been alluding to Joseph Conrad's autobiographical novella *The Shadow Line: A Confession,* in which the author gives an account of a painful rite of passage when, for the first time, he takes on the responsibilities of a sea captain in an unfamiliar part of the Pacific Ocean. Heaney's journey from his family farm to an unfamiliar city was similarly daunting. At the private, all-male school, as he would soon find out, no solicitous Philomena would arrive at his door each morning to usher him to class, no consoling mother or aunt would pamper him when he returned home, and no siblings would lift his spirits with their games. For the first time in his life, he had to fend for himself.

Four decades after an older friend drove him and his parents from Mossbawn to St. Columb's (the family still had no car), Heaney referred to the trip as his "Trail of Tears." The trauma of his first weeks at St. Columb's never left him. "On my first day, the leather strap / Went epileptic in the Big Study, / Its echoes plashing over our bowed heads," he wrote in "The Ministry of Fear," a poem in *North.* A decade before he died, he again remembered his brutal initiation at St. Columb's: "Everybody was lined up. I'd never seen such execution, such executive strapping as happened that day. . . . You had come from a home and suddenly you were in an institution. I was homesick for weeks, and very vulnerable."[2] The school was situated on the same street as the old city prison, and students often joked that the prisoners had better meals and fewer punishments than they did at St. Columb's. No wonder Wordsworth's lines "Shades of the prison-house / Begin to close upon the growing Boy" from "Intimations of Immortality" had such a special resonance for Heaney.

The friction between teachers and pupils, who were all Catholics, resembled the friction between Catholics and Protestants in Londonderry/Derry. It had not always been this way. During the first half of the 1940s, when the city had flourished as a naval port for Allied ships, sectarian tensions eased. Then, when the city's prosperity declined after World War II, relations between its citizens worsened. Surrounded by hostile Protestant city-dwellers and hostile Catholic priests, Heaney was initially so upset that he could barely eat. "I had no appetite for anything except grief," he confessed.[3] In hindsight, Heaney came to think of Master Murphy's half crown as the sort of coin given to a Roman or Greek corpse to pay for Charon's ferryboat ride across a river in hell.

Heaney had originally hoped to attend a good Catholic secondary school closer to home, but such schools were scarce in Northern Ireland. Protestant governments in the past had thwarted plans to establish Catholic training schools for priests. Several attempts to open a seminary in Londonderry/Derry had failed. Finally, Bishop Francis Kelly managed to buy land from the wealthy Bishop Frederick Hervey, who'd built a summer residence on the site where the school would later stand. Hervey, who was rarely content with his lavish residences, nicknamed his latest one "The Temple of Cloacina," after the Roman goddess of sewers. On November 3, 1879, a small group of students began classes at Hervey's renovated home. According to one historian, the school "consisted of a three-storey, seven-bay building in coursed green schist with a Venetian Gothic porch and two tiers of gabled dormer windows—the block later known as Junior House."[4] Near the end of the nineteenth century, builders added a Senior House, museum, library, and recreation hall. To remind students of the Church's global reach, the museum exhibited artifacts that missionaries brought back from their travels. Ten years before Heaney matriculated, a new chapel, oratory, infirmary, isolation room, and several science labs were constructed. As a result of the large influx of students made possible by the 1947 Education Act (about 650 enrolled in

1953), temporary "hutments" were set up on the campus to provide more classroom space.

Named after Saint Columba (also known as St. Colum and St. Colum Cille), St. Columb's College was close to the site of a sixth-century monastery that the saint had built on an oak-covered hill. The acorns in the school's coat of arms derived from local oak forests and Celtic history. The Gaelic name *Doire* referred to Derry's "oak grove," which was sacred to the Celtic tribes that gathered there. One of the first things Heaney encountered at the school in 1951 was the college crest and its Latin motto urging everyone "to seek first of all the kingdom of God."[5] Heaney would become an ardent Catholic seeker, even though he despised the harsh punishments of some of the priests and chose a curriculum that led to a secular vocation.

*Columba* in Latin means "dove," and Colum Cille means "dove in the church," a phrase bestowed on him because of his long hours studying scripture in churches. Convinced by St. Finian that Ireland needed Catholic missionaries, Colum Cille had established churches and monasteries around the British Isles, including on the island of Iona off the western coast of Scotland (a fact that Heaney mentions in his early poem "Gravities" in *Death of a Naturalist*). The saint also wrote poems and hymns and trained the monks who produced the exquisitely illustrated Book of Kells. Heaney's late poem "Album" gives a nod to the saint and St. Columb's College in the Latin line from the gospel of St. Matthew, "*Quaerite Primum Regnum Dei*" (Seek ye first the Kingdom of God [6:33]), which the school adopted as its motto in 1928. In Heaney's poem, however, the word "God" is missing from the biblical directive. Another late poem, "Loughanure," invokes the school's godly mission again when the narrator asks: "And did I seek the Kingdom? Will the Kingdom / Come?" Heaney revered St. Colum Cille and as a young man sought the saint's Kingdom, but he remained skeptical about the school's draconian methods of achieving its goals.

According to "The Ministry of Fear," Heaney dreamed of running away from St. Columb's as soon as he got there. He was especially attracted to Brandywell Stadium's football field and the large dog track that surrounded it. He had opportunities to go into the city (usually he saw movies, shopped, or visited friends in the predominantly Catholic Bogside), but he always returned. Londonderry/Derry, after all, was no sanctuary.

In the Bogside, so named because of its location by an old channel that had run through a bog, families generally lived in dilapidated buildings and unemployment was rampant (close to 60 percent when Heaney was a student). Protestant politicians contributed to the area's socioeconomic malaise by making it hard for Catholics to obtain well-paying jobs and vote for candidates who stood up for their interests.

Heaney gained an intimate knowledge of the Bogside from day students such as Seamus Deane, who lived there. Deane, to whom Heaney dedicated "The Ministry of Fear," would become a distinguished scholar and professor. In a short memoir about his friendship with Heaney published in the *New Yorker,* Deane pointed out that even though the city was only a few miles from the Republic of Ireland, its politics remained partisan: "[Londonderry/Derry] has a historical resonance for Protestants, because they endured a famous siege there in 1689 by the Catholic armies of King James II, and also for Catholics, because between 1922 and 1972 the city was notorious for discriminating against the local Catholic majority. The Protestants remained in power by openly gerrymandering the elections."[6] The siege occurred when King James II's Catholic soldiers, who were contemptuous of London and the Protestant King William III, nearly destroyed the city by cutting off supplies for 105 days. Many of the twenty thousand people trapped behind the city's walls were forced to eat cats, dogs, and vermin to survive. About half the population died from famine, disease, cannonballs, and mortar bombs before the siege was lifted on August 1, 1689. Memories of the debacle festered for centuries.

A native of the city, Robert Greacen, who was later Heaney's colleague at Queen's University, wrote in his autobiography that Protestants, including those in his family, vigorously suppressed Catholic culture in the past and present: "History meant Protestant history. Suffering and heroism meant that undergone by Protestants. There was never a whisper of the sixth-century Derry that had become a great centre of missionary zeal, long before we Scots-Irish had settled there—along with some English— sword in one hand and bible in the other. Nobody told me of Colmcille."[7] Despite Protestant animosity toward Catholics, few residents predicted the Battle of the Bogside in 1969 and the sectarian violence that followed.

St. Columb's tried to remain aloof from politics, but sometimes it was impossible to do so. During the partition of Ireland at the beginning of the twentieth century, Unionists had shot at United Irish Volunteers occupying campus buildings. British Protestants took charge of Northern Ireland's six counties in December 1920, which prompted the Catholic Church to issue a defiant statement that "the only satisfactory system of education for Catholics is one wherein Catholic children are taught in Catholic schools by Catholic teachers under Catholic auspices."[8] Protestant leaders attempted to deny academic privileges to Catholics and flaunted their alliance with Britain every July 12 by celebrating the 1690 victory of King William over King James at the Battle of the Boyne. Greacen remembered how in Belfast "street would vie with street in putting up decorative arches tricked out with the symbols we knew and loved: the open bible, William crossing the Boyne on his white horse, a black servant kneeling at the feet of his sovereign lady, Queen Victoria. . . . On the eve of the Twelfth, bonfires. . . . —pronounced 'bone-fires'—were held in districts where arches and red, white and blue bunting had already been put up."[9] Many Catholics hid behind locked doors while Protestants caroused around bonfires and marched in the streets.

During Heaney's years at St. Columb's, religious factions periodically clashed outside the school's walls. In 1951, the Royal Ulster Constabulary broke up a St. Patrick's Day parade with batons after the well-known nationalist politician Eddie McAteer raised an Irish flag in the center of the city. Seamus Deane, who was at the parade, ran into the Palace cinema to escape policemen who were beating Catholics. In response to the episode, the IRA rearmed itself by raiding British military bases in England and Northern Ireland. IRA attacks on Protestants grew more frequent, and in 1956 anti-Unionist guerrilla units from the Republic of Ireland attacked a BBC relay transmitter in Londonderry/Derry, a British army barracks in Enniskillen, and a courthouse in Magherafelt. More than three hundred assaults on British targets occurred in 1957, the year Heaney finished his studies at St. Columb's. The IRA's campaign lost momentum only after Ulster's prime minister, Basil Brooke, invoked the Special Powers Act, which allowed police to arrest IRA suspects and incarcerate them without trial. Lacking effective leadership, the IRA officially terminated hostilities on February 26, 1962.

To insulate students from these sorts of crises, St. Columb's prohibited radios and newspapers. The news blackout motivated some students to construct crystal radio sets so they could listen to Radio Luxembourg and other stations under their bed sheets at night. Heaney heard about the IRA offensive from friends and family, and on one of his bus trips home he saw where a bomb planted by the eighteen-year-old Seamus Costello had blown a hole in the roof and scorched the walls of the Magherafelt Courthouse. The building was close to where Heaney got off the bus when he returned home from St. Columb's. This was the first time outside of newsreels or books or photographs, he said, that he'd witnessed "evidence of destructive intent."[10] He wrote in "The Border Campaign," a poem in *Electric Light*: "When I heard the word 'attack' / In St. Columb's College in nineteen fifty-six / It left me winded, left nothing between me / And the sky beyond my boarder's dormer." It was as if the bomb had blown off his dormitory roof as well as the courthouse roof. He felt vulnerable because he knew Catholics would now be more exposed to reprisals from Protestant citizens, paramilitary groups, and police officers. No wonder he always felt safest in a house with thick walls and a sturdy roof.

## SHADOWS OF THE PRISON HOUSE

In the summer of 1951, before he arrived at St. Columb's, Heaney knew little about the school built on what was once an island in the Foyle River. His parents had told him that clever boys went there "to get the learning [because] a pen is lighter than a spade."[11] They also assured him that he'd be well fed. It was while visiting the scenic town of Buncrana in the Irish Republic, about six miles to the west, that Patrick and Margaret bought him the gift he never forgot. His father was not known for being a spendthrift, so the gift of a fancy pen was a surprise. Heaney came to think of the Conway Stewart fountain pen, with its Irish and British provenance (its name came from a London vaudeville team), as another emblem of his bipolar culture. In an interview, he said the "twelve and sixpence fountain pen" marked his "initiation into the higher condition" of a private-school education.[12] It was another "threshold gift" marking another rite of passage, another incorporation in a new community after an agonizing departure and transition. This time, the transition from spadework around his agricultural home to pen-work in an academic setting was more permanent. During his years at Anahorish School, he was able to return to his family farm every day and spend weekends there. Now he had to spend months away from home in a school full of sadistic priests and a city dominated by Protestants.

Heaney's room in Junior House, which he shared with a boy from Castledawson named Liam Donnelly, was as small and austere as a prison cubicle. It had six-foot-high walls, two beds, two lockers, and a wash basin. Toilets were outside. When his parents said their final goodbyes and walked down the path to the front gate, the feeling of being abandoned nearly overwhelmed Heaney. During the days and weeks that followed, his mother tried to mollify him with CARE packages of cake, biscuits, and Creamola (a drink mix). He admitted in "The Ministry of Fear": "I was so homesick I couldn't even eat / The biscuits left to sweeten my exile." After his first trip home for Halloween in 1951, he could barely force himself onto the bus back to St. Columb's. A Mossbawn neighbor, Mrs. Mitchell, observed him sobbing at the bus station by the Magherafelt Courthouse and told his mother she was "an old bitch" for sending her "child away like that."[13] Margaret was mortified by her son's distress but still believed she was doing the right thing by sending him to a reputable school; she later sent two other sons, Pat and Dan, to the school, as well.

Heaney had good reason to fear the "ministry" at St. Columb's. Many of the priests resented lower-class boys like Heaney who had gained access to the school because of the 1947 Education Act. These snobbish priests preferred students from middle- and upper-class Catholic families and tended to punish working-class students more severely. Deane remembered priests using sliding blackboards like guillotines, forcing students to place their necks beneath the board, and then bringing the board down hard. One priest hit a student with such force that his eardrum broke. The future civil rights leader and journalist Eamonn McCann said a priest in an Irish-language class knocked him unconscious. Priests made students soak their hands in cold water to make the sting of strap-beatings more painful. They condoned forced "duckings," the routine of making first-year students stick their heads under an outdoor, cold-water spigot on the first Sunday night of each term. According to the singer-songwriter Paul Brady: "Technically speaking, you were supposed to just have your head held under the outside tap of the school and get your head wet. But actually it was a very brutal experience." Some students accused the priests of being "clinically insane" in the way they conducted their "regime of terror."[14]

Like the teaching priests at Clongowes Wood College in Joyce's *A Portrait of the Artist as a Young Man*, those at St. Columb's could be cruel, but they could also be effective teachers. Heaney gradually got over his homesickness and learned a great deal at the school. He earned excellent grades and became head prefect at the beginning of his senior year. Despite his rise up the ranks, he remained ambivalent toward the powers that be he served. According to Deane, Heaney "was always 'well in' with those in power" but also "conspiratorially against them, holding them at arms' length by his humor, his gift for parody. To many people, this seemed merely to be an exercise in cunning, and it was. But it was also Heaney's way of dealing with his own contradictory sense of himself: his authority and his uncertainty."[15] At St. Columb's, his uncertainty would wane and his authority wax, but he was never entirely certain of his own powers and the way he should feel about those who wielded power over him and his peers.

### GIFTS IN A BOOK OF HOURS

As a young man hoping to succeed in a parochial environment, Heaney remained a devout Catholic. He served as an altar boy, abstained from sexual intercourse, obeyed his confirmation pledge to renounce alcohol, and prayed for lifelong temperance. As a teenager, he even enrolled in his Aunt Sally's Pioneer Total Abstinence Association. Because the British government paid his tuition, he regarded both his scholarship and his education as gifts that should be repaid with gratitude and hard work. If he had reservations about his British sponsors and Catholic teachers, he generally kept quiet about them.

Heaney realized early on that his personal gifts were more literary than religious. As a result, he opted for courses that prepared him for a vocation outside the Church. Usually, if a student took courses in Greek, he would later go to St. Patrick's College near Maynooth to study for the priesthood. St. Columb's instructors felt obligated to advise the first-year boys to enroll in Greek classes. President Anthony McFeely, who'd been ordained in Rome after graduating from St. Columb's, liked to say, "This isn't a school, this is a junior seminary."[16] Nevertheless, Heaney took French, science, math, English, and Latin. He was especially fond of his charismatic Latin teacher, Michael McGlinchey, who taught classical literature and Roman history. Heaney read the *Aeneid* in McGlinchey's class, and at the age of fourteen he imitated Virgil's style in a poem composed of rhyming Latin couplets that he showed to his teacher. It was one of his first attempts to write poetry. He said in his posthumously published translation, *Aeneid Book VI*: "[I had] a lifelong desire to honour the memory of my Latin teacher at St. Columb's College."[17] His translation of Book VI and his earlier translation of part of it, "The Golden Bough," were his gifts to a teacher who had helped him realize his gifts as a poet and who had introduced him to an epic that was preoccupied with gift-giving. From the Trojan horse, which was supposedly a Greek gift offered to Athena, to Aeneas's sword given to Dido and the golden bough presented to Prosperina, the *Aeneid* featured both enabling and disabling gifts.

The canonical texts and religious pattern of daily life at St. Columb's laid the foundation for Heaney's career as a poet and scholar. Each day, he rose with his peers at 7:30 a.m., attended Mass, ate breakfast in the refectory, and then went to classes until noon. After a short break for lunch, he returned to classes until 4:00 p.m. He and his peers did homework from 5:00 to 5:55 p.m., had a ten-minute cigarette break (seniors over the age of fifteen could smoke in the "reefing room"), returned to study hall at 6:05 p.m., began dinner at 7:30 p.m., studied again from 8:30 to 10:00 p.m. (some students were allowed to read approved novels for a half hour during this period), said night prayers, and went to bed at 10:30 p.m. Saturday classes were mandatory. On Saturday nights, the young men took showers and went to Confession. Every three weeks, they were allowed to leave campus for a brief foray into the city.

In "Cloistered," a prose poem in *Stations*, Heaney indicated that if he wrote a memoir about his six years at St. Columb's, it would resemble "a book of hours." This sort of book in the Middle Ages included prayers and psalms offered up to God as gifts. The school's spiritual director, as Seamus Deane noted in his autobiographical novel *Reading in the Dark*, wanted the boys to regard life as a sacred gift and not to misuse the "most mysterious power, the power of originating life itself" since "nothing else compares with it except the love from which that life springs, which is in

God."[18] St. Columb's students learned more about the central tenets of Catholicism on retreats, which usually began on the second Friday of the fall semester at the school's chapel. On these occasions, students would sing the ninth-century hymn "Veni Creator Spiritus" (Come Holy Spirit, Creator Blest), chant Benediction hymns praising God's sacramental gifts in the Eucharist, meditate in silence for sixty-five hours, and read theology or hagiographic biographies of saints.

In the Ignatian retreat that Joyce immortalized in *A Portrait of the Artist,* the rector vows to teach his charges how "to lead before God and in the eyes of men a truly Christian life." He explains that during a retreat a person leaves behind "the cares of our life, the cares of this workaday world, in order to examine the state of our conscience, to reflect on the mysteries of holy religion and to understand better why we are here in this world." The rector recommends that the students practice St. Ignatius of Loyola's "composition of place" in order "to imagine with the senses of the mind . . . the material character of . . . the physical torments which all who are in hell endure."[19] The diabolical scenes the rector "composes" have a purgative effect on Stephen Dedalus. He weeps, vomits, and rushes to a church to confess his sins. Heaney's meditations, by contrast, were more even-tempered and tended to dwell on uplifting mysteries rather than gothic horrors.

At St. Columb's, Heaney learned a great deal about the Catholic worldview from Charles Hart's *The Student's Catholic Doctrine,* which was assigned as a textbook. One of the book's central messages is that God-the-Father, Christ-the-Son, and the Holy Ghost are redemptive gift-givers. According to Hart, the principal "supernatural gift" from God is the spirit of charity. A person "approaches nearest to God" when she or he gives gifts to those in need. Christ is the embodiment of the gift-giving spirit that all should emulate. "The seven gifts particularly attributed to the Holy Ghost," Hart says, "are *wisdom, understanding, counsel, fortitude, knowledge, piety,* and *the fear of the Lord.*"[20] As a student, Heaney tried to abide by the Catholic ethos of gift-giving, and as an adult he tried to remain loyal to that ethos by sharing his work as if it were a redemptive gift.

If Heaney's religious education expanded his knowledge of divine gifts, English classes and theatrical productions gave him access to literary gifts and catalysts for his own creative gifts. He especially enjoyed acting because it allowed him to pretend to be someone else and externalize feelings and ideas he ordinarily kept hidden. During his first year, he played a small part in *The Arcadians,* a musical comedy about London turning into an agrarian paradise where people live simple, virtuous lives like the shepherds in ancient pastoral literature. First performed in 1909, the play features a prevaricating London caterer, James Smith, whose plane crashes in the mythical Greek land of Arcadia. Horrified by the foreign city-man's manners, the Arcadians throw him down a fairy well, where he metamorphoses into a younger, more innocent man named Simplicitas. Eventually, he returns to London to convert its residents to his new Arcadian lifestyle. *The Arcadians* exposed Heaney to a modern version of the pastoral tradition that he would later develop in his poems.

Heaney was given a more substantial part in Ian Hay's *The Sport of Kings,* another play that addressed modern English culture. He was the butler of a hypocritical English magistrate who rails against the sins of his countrymen, but who resorts to betting on horses to pay his high taxes. A year later, Heaney acted the part of an Indian army colonel in *The Private Secretary,* a farce about a playboy who dupes a weak-willed clergyman into helping him get access to his uncle's fortune and seduce a young woman. One of Heaney's most memorable roles, in J. M. Barrie's *The Admirable Crichton,* required weeks of rehearsals, but the play had to be canceled. Those who saw the rehearsals were especially impressed by the way Heaney played the lowly butler who follows his master, Lord Loam, to a tropical island after a shipwreck. On the island, master-servant roles reverse; the butler discovers, at least temporarily, that he possesses gifts that his lord lacks. The British Lord Loam ultimately colonizes the remote island and returns to England with his butler. Like *The Arcadians,* *The Admirable Crichton* dramatizes class differences between sophisticated and primitive cultures that resonated for Heaney.

Heaney had a knack for butler roles, perhaps because he was used to people considering him lower class. Many day students at St. Columb's regarded all boarders who came from rural parts of Ulster as inferior. One reason Heaney enjoyed acting alongside urban day students was because he got a chance to disabuse them of their prejudices. At times, his theater work was as comical as it was socially instructive. Philip Coulter, who played Ariel in Shakespeare's *The Tempest,* complimented Heaney's abilities as a comic actor. (Heaney's poem "The Real Names" returns the compliment with a reference to Coulter's resonant voice.) St. Columb's directors tended to assign male roles to boarders like Heaney and female roles to day students. Heaney at times mocked these gender and class assumptions in plays such as *The Merchant of Venice*, which Jack "Rusty" Gallagher directed. In this case, the priest gave Heaney the role of the young Venetian man Lorenzo and Deane the role of Jessica, the daughter of the Jewish Shylock. (Gallagher assumed that Heaney's country roots made him more masculine than the city-bred Deane.) In one scene, while holding up a purple rose and leaning back on some cushions, Deane waited patiently for Heaney to give him a romantic embrace. Instead, Heaney rolled on the stage in uncontrollable laughter. Sweating with frustration, Gallagher expelled the two boys from the play.

Most of the school plays were either set in London or written by Londoners, just as most of the writers in Heaney's literature courses were English. There was an assumption at St. Columb's that Irish speech and culture were inferior to British speech and culture. Heaney explained in 2002:

> People from my part of Northern Ireland talked from the back of their throats, in low, quick, thick accents. I began to be aware of this when I went to boarding school at the age of twelve; indeed, I could hardly help being aware of it since the English teacher took great delight in mocking the accent of those of us from beyond the mountain and would [make] . . . us repeat over and over again the phrase: "The lips, the teeth, the tip of the tongue. The lips, the teeth, the tip of the tongue. The lips, the teeth, the tip of the tongue." That exercise was a quick reminder that I was now living in two linguistic worlds, the world of what we might call the *lingua franca* and the guttural world.[21]

Heaney gradually adapted to the "proper" British way of speaking, although in his poetry he affirmed his roots in Ireland's guttural hinterland.

During his fifth year, Heaney learned more about his Irish heritage when his Gaelic teacher assigned extracts from Daniel Corkery's *The Hidden Ireland*, a study of Gaelic culture in eighteenth-century Munster, a southwestern province of Ireland. Heaney's classes on the Gaelic language prepared him to translate poems such as *Sweeney Astray* and *The Midnight*

*Court.* His exposure to visionary poems called "aislings," such as "Úr-Chill an Chreagáin," which tells the story of a dispirited man who wakes up in a cemetery to find a goddess-like woman kissing him, also influenced Heaney's later work. He especially admired the Gaelic poets Eoghan Ruadh Ó Suilleabháin, Aodhagán Ó Rathaille, and Séamus Dall MacCuarta. Back home, he continued to support his Irish heritage as the *fear á tigh*—the dance announcer—at *ceilidhs*. He joined the Bellaghy Dramatic Society, performing as a blacksmith in a play about Betsy Gray, a peasant girl who fought and died with the United Irishmen during the Rebellion of 1798. Much of his subsequent work as a poet and scholar attempted to resurrect the "hidden Ireland" that British colonizers had tried to hide.

### LOSS OF A BROTHER

One of Heaney's most upsetting experiences at St. Columb's occurred on a morning in February 1953. Before serving Mass in the chapel, he was summoned to President McFeely's office and told that his brother Christopher had been killed in a road accident. Heaney then went to the school's infirmary, where for several hours he listened in stunned silence to "bells knelling classes to a close," as he wrote a decade later in "Mid-Term Break." Jim McKenna arrived that afternoon in his car and drove Heaney back to Mossbawn. At home, according to the elegy he collected in *Death of a Naturalist,* his normally stoical father cried, while his mother seemed more angry than sad. His father had instructed Heaney in the past to set a good example for his younger siblings by not crying. Heaney, on this occasion, managed to stifle his tears.

The accident happened at the bus stop on the Broagh Road not far from Mossbawn. Christopher and another brother, Hugh, had been walking to the bus to give a letter to the conductor so he could mail it in Belfast. Two other brothers, Pat and Dan, were on their way to a friend's house to get paraffin lamp-oil. While the bus was pulling out, the three-and-a-half-year-old Christopher ran behind it toward his brothers on the other side of the road. An approaching car was unable to brake in time to avoid Christopher. Half a century later, Heaney said he still could "hardly bear to think about" the accident and Christopher's death several hours later in the Mid-Ulster Hospital in Magherafelt.[22]

Heaney's parents were as upset by the death as their children. To distance themselves from it, they sold Mossbawn and moved six miles away to their relatives' farm The Wood. Although Patrick looked forward to living on the farm where he'd grown up (his aunts and uncles were still there), Margaret Heaney worried about being cooped up in a single-story farmhouse surrounded by her husband's kin. The double loss for Heaney—of a brother and a beloved home—haunted him for decades. An elegy published near the end of his life, "The Blackbird of Glanmore," portrays Christopher as a familiar ghost who guides the older poet back to Mossbawn in 1951, when they played happily together after Heaney's "homesick first term" at St. Columb's. For Heaney, Christopher's death marked the end of his "Eden time."

Heaney explained to the writer Monie Begley that his family's departure in 1954 for The Wood "was a move from one world to another."[23] It was as if the family had crossed another shadow line, even though their new home was almost as familiar as Mossbawn. Some of the changes that came with the displacement turned out to be beneficial, at least for Heaney's father. He got a tractor to plow his fields and transport his crops. He had electric lights installed in the milking barn. Oddly enough, Heaney resisted his father's newfangled improvements. Rather than use the mechanical hay rake behind a tractor when he returned home, for example, he continued to use a pitchfork to turn and stack hay after it was cut. His poems would soon express nostalgia for the unmechanized way of life he'd enjoyed at Mossbawn before Christopher's death.

Heaney could have graduated from St. Columb's and gone to university in 1956 after receiving the equivalent of A's on the English Language and Literature, Irish, French, Mathematics, and Latin sections of his Senior Certificate exam. (He'd done especially well in Latin, scoring 394 out of a possible 400 points.) Despite his stellar grades, he worried that he wasn't ready for university, just as he'd worried six years before that he wasn't ready for St. Columb's. So he petitioned the administration for the right to take more courses and graduate in 1957. His parents and teachers thought this was a good idea, even though he'd already been promised one of twelve state bursaries, worth £1,000, to attend Queen's University. On August 30, 1956, in a letter mistakenly addressed to

"Mr. Shames Heaney," St. Columb's granted his request to stay at the school for an additional year.

Heaney took advantage of this time to strengthen his resumé and secure more funding for Queen's. He passed an exam for a State Exhibition scholarship and garnered one of the highest honors bestowed by St. Columb's. At a September assembly in 1957, President McFeely announced that Heaney would be the head prefect for boarders during his final year. It was like becoming an assistant priest. He was expected to serve Mass when a bishop or some other dignitary visited, establish seniority at student gatherings, and hand out medals at the annual summer sports day. He was also responsible for punishing students who bullied, stole, plagiarized, vandalized, smoked, or broke other rules. The dutiful Heaney took his job as prefect seriously and executed his responsibilities with vigor. Eamon McCann witnessed this when he made the mistake of talking one night in study hall. "Before I could turn around," McCann recalled, "Seamus Heaney [was] hitting me." At a meeting decades later, McCann told Heaney he owed him "a thump in the kisser."[24] Embarrassed by the memory of their study-hall encounter, Heaney tried to laugh away McCann's threat.

One of Heaney's most transformational classes during his final year was taught by Sean B. O'Kelly, an intense, learned man considered to be the best English teacher at St. Columb's. After graduating from the school, O'Kelly had received a master's degree from University College, Dublin, for a thesis on Thomas Hardy, a writer whose pastoral narratives Heaney admired. O'Kelly maintained that literature had both an aesthetic and ethical purpose, and he urged students to question conventional opinions and prejudices. When one student argued in class that Shakespeare's *Macbeth* was intended to be spoken in a Scottish accent, O'Kelly let the student read Macbeth's famous "tomorrow and tomorrow" speech like a Scotsman. O'Kelly once said he regretted teaching his students to be critics rather than creative writers, but he inspired Heaney to experiment with different poetic forms. While studying under O'Kelly, he wrote a blank verse description of a wallstead (a ruined building) at Mossbawn and dashed off notes to friends in Latin hexameters.

O'Kelly gave Heaney and his peers in the special A-level English literature class—Michael Cassoni, Paddy Mullarkey, Seamus Deane—an extensive introduction to the Western canon. Heaney later said he especially benefited from his teacher's insistence on memorization. By the end of the class, he could recite most of *Hamlet,* much of Chaucer's "Prologue" to *The Canterbury Tales,* and long passages by Wordsworth, Keats, and Hardy. Memorizing poetry prepared his mind to create his own poetry. Also included on the syllabus were texts by Francis Beaumont, John Fletcher, Sir Thomas Browne, George Herbert, John Dryden, Charles Lamb, William Hazlitt, Percy Bysshe Shelley, Alfred Lord Tennyson, Matthew Arnold, and Hopkins. O'Kelly honed Heaney's skills as a literary critic and also gave his student an intimate knowledge of the way masterful poets constructed their poems.

Summarizing his academic evolution at St. Columb's, Heaney told an interviewer, "The movement was from sorry to certitude, to some kind of independence and individuation." He agreed with Phil Coulter's comment that the school convinced students that, "If you have a talent, you have an obligation to do something with that talent. . . . The continuing mantra [was]: don't squander your brain power."[25] Four decades after graduating, Heaney told alumni at a reunion that his early teachers had convinced him that writing was a sacred gift that should honor precursors like St. Colum Cille. Everything written by St. Columb's students, according to Heaney, perpetuated the saint's legacy: "Each character formed on each line of each exercise book by pupils in the past, each figure entered on the graph paper, represents the penwork of the great scribe who is our patron. The many lives lived and the many letters formed are part of the one great work."[26] Following T. S. Eliot's precepts in "Tradition and the Individual Talent," Heaney believed that writing was a form of communion that unified writers in a spiritual community. To express gratitude to St. Columb's College, he suggested that all his poems, from "Digging" to "On the Gift of a Fountain Pen," contributed to a monomythical "great work" that derived from and paid homage to the school's patron saint.

# 5

# Queen's University

Queen's University, like St. Columb's College, was only about forty miles from Heaney's home, but it might as well have been in a different country. When he left Bellaghy in 1957 to attend the university, he once again felt like an explorer struggling to find his way through unfamiliar territory. "My first time to Queen's," he wrote a friend, "was almost my first time to Belfast."[1] His parents provided little guidance since, as he admitted in *Stepping Stones*, they "had no familiarity with universities."[2]

As with many institutions in Ireland, Queen's was a product of British-Irish conflicts and negotiations. The English prime minister Sir Robert Peel had argued for the Colleges (Ireland) Act in 1845 so that Queen's campuses could be established in Cork, Galway, and Belfast. Peel tried to mollify Catholics by insisting that the branches of the university accept all denominations, but his ecumenical idealism was rebuked by both Catholic and Protestant clergymen. After the university finally opened its doors, the controversy discouraged many students from applying. Dismal economic conditions after the potato famine of 1845 made the university's survival uncertain. It did survive, though, and the British government granted the Belfast campus independence in 1909.

Heaney and about three thousand other students matriculated at a propitious moment in the university's history. During the 1950s, the liberal-minded, hardworking vice chancellor, Eric Ashby, secured funds to increase the faculty by 90 percent. In addition to recruiting superb professors, he constructed new buildings and renovated old ones. Belfast's fortunes, unfortunately, lagged behind those of the university. The capital city was larger than Londonderry/Derry, but it resembled its northwest neighbor in many ways. Built near the mouth of the Lagan River, it enjoyed the economic advantages and suffered the military vulnerabilities of a large port city. Irish rulers had bestowed the Gaelic name Béal Feirste ("mouth of the sandbars" or "mouth of the sandy ford") on the small settlement by the river before English and Scottish citizens migrated there and Anglicized the name in the seventeenth century. The colonists turned Belfast into a thriving hub for shipbuilding and textile industries. By the nineteenth century, the city had earned the nickname "Linenopolis" because of all the linen factories operating there. At the beginning of the twentieth century, the prestigious company Harland and Wolff built the RMS *Titanic* in Belfast. During World War II, its thriving shipbuilding industry made it a natural target for the German Luftwaffe, which bombed the port in April and May 1941, killing nearly one thousand residents, destroying more than three thousand houses, and damaging many factories. After the war, the local economy declined, creating the angst and anger that exacerbated sectarian enmities.

Heaney's departure for Belfast in October 1957 lacked some of the *Sturm und Drang* of his journeys to Anahorish and St. Columb's. He was more mature now, and the prospect of having friends like Seamus Deane at Queen's made the uprooting less daunting than earlier ones. Nevertheless, he admitted that he felt "a bit at sea" after moving into a room on Belfast's Park Road opposite Ormeau Park.[3] In the city of a half million people and at Queen's, too, the old sectarian rules and class stratifications applied. Usually, Protestants at Queen's held the administrative positions, while Catholics worked as porters, kitchen staff, and groundskeepers. Catholic and Protestant students mingled at the "Literific" debating society, the Drama Society, the Student Union's billiard room, and the Wednesday- and Saturday-night dances, but most of the time they went their separate ways. Protestants congregated at the Bible Union and Officers' Training Corps, Catholics at the Irish Society and Catholic Students' Society. Heaney's "points of security," he said, were the library, the Union dining hall, and the Catholic Chaplaincy on Fitzwilliam Street.[4] For entertainment, he went to a few "hops" at the Student Union and big-band concerts in the city.

Some officials at Queens, such as the chaplain, recommended that Catholic students get to know Protestant students by joining their organizations. Other officials tried to accentuate religious differences and reinforce the status quo. Seamus Deane, who roomed with Heaney and took an English course with him during their "fresher" year, remembered how professors drew attention to sectarian divisions. In tutorials, Deane said, one of the most distinguished professors, the South African writer Laurence Lerner, would ask students if they could distinguish between Protestants and Catholics: "Usually everybody said yes: Prods [Protestants] were better dressed (because they had jobs, because they were Prods), and had thin mouths, blue noses, pinched, disapproving faces with starched expressions; Teagues [Catholics] had dirty shoes, curly hair, and nervous eyes, and didn't wear suits."[5] Another student in these tutorials, George McWhirter, recalled that Heaney distanced himself from Lerner's provocative remarks and learned a great deal from him about Emily Dickinson, Walt Whitman, and Wallace Stevens. It was Lerner, McWhirter believed, who "gave Seamus the start for precision and breadth of vision."[6]

At Queen's, Heaney signed up for the curriculum called Course B, which included English classics, English philology, early English poetry, and American literature with a concentration on works by Frost and Hemingway. American culture was a popular topic at Queen's, even though there weren't many courses that focused on it. One of Heaney's acquaintances, the poet and playwright Stewart Parker, hoped to get a teaching job in the United States so he could find out more about American drama, American Beat writing, and African American music. Parker may have passed on some of his enthusiasm for the United States to Heaney. In a decade, Heaney would spend a year in one of the liveliest centers of American literature and politics—Berkeley, California. For the time being, though, he spent most of his time studying the British canon.

While friends gambled, drank, danced, listened to pop music, and attended sporting events, Heaney concentrated on his books. His seriousness was on display in some of his arguments. Once he got into such a heated dispute with a roommate—a former St. Columb's classmate who held a grudge from Heaney's year as head prefect—that a fight broke out. Deane, who was the third roommate at the time, said, "I opened the door to find the two of them rolling in a furious, wrestling embrace on the floor. It was comic, but it was also serious. It was an early instance of a peculiar kind of hostility that Heaney could provoke."[7] In his own recollections of Queen's, Heaney prided himself on the "strong trust in the connections and friendships" he made there.[8] His many later poems about weighing and balancing, and even the titles of his books such as *The Spirit Level*, show that he wanted to remain level-headed in contentious situations. Sometimes, though, his strong principles and competitive zeal won out over his affable nature.

Once asked about his political activities at Queen's, Heaney replied that he had no idea how to get politically involved. He expressed his political sympathies, though, by speaking Irish at Gaelic Society meetings and performing in one-act Irish plays. During his third year, he visited a Gaelic-speaking section of Donegal with a group of students from the Celtic Department. Led to believe (perhaps as a result of reading Yeats) that the Gaeltacht was populated with romantic visionaries and rustic prophets, Heaney was crestfallen by the actual people he met. In *Stations*, he wrote about one conversation he tried to have in Gaelic: "I blushed but only managed a few words. Neither did any gift of tongues descend in my days in that upper room when all around me seemed to prophesy." Out of shyness or linguistic incompetence, he found it difficult to speak to the locals and conceded he was homesick for his native English tongue.

Heaney at St. Columb's had already begun his quest for a literary "gift of tongues," which he compared to the *spiritus* (Latin for life-giving "breath" or "wind") that came from an in-spiriting God in a moment of grace. His reference in his prose poem "The stations of the west" to the "upper room" betrays his hope to receive vocal and vocational gifts the way the apostles had received gifts of Jesus's symbolic flesh and blood at the Last Supper. According to Christian tradition, Jesus's Eucharistic act of gift-giving occurred in the "upper room" of David's Tomb Compound in Jerusalem, and more gift-giving followed His crucifixion and resurrection when He visited the apostles in the form of Pentecostal tongues of flame. For Heaney, the Holy Spirit's fiery tongues were analogous to gifts from a muse that in-spirited a poet's imagination and voice. In his essay "The Poet as a Christian," he wrote, "The discovery of a poetic voice [is] . . . the most important step on the unfinished journey towards wholeness and honesty. . . . The poetic vocation involves a pursuit of . . . a religious commitment to the ever-evolving disciplines of the art which the poet has to credit as his form of sanctity."[9] As an Irish Catholic, Heaney had hoped to receive an Irish-inflected "gift of tongues" in the Gaeltacht, but he realized that his gift came from his British-Irish "hearth culture" and from the British canon.

Heaney made an effort to reaffirm his Irish-Catholic identity at Queen's by becoming an official in the Catholic Student Union and going to weekly sodality meetings where a priest conducted services with homilies and prayers. Rather than return to his room at night after studying in the library, he frequently drank tea at the chaplaincy where the Catholic Society met. He joined Catholic students on pilgrimages to St. Patrick's Purgatory in the northwest corner of the Irish Republic. He also traveled to Lourdes, the famous holy site in the foothills of the Pyrenees. In "Brancardier," a section of the poetic sequence "Out of This World," he writes about assisting disabled pilgrims, carrying a censer of incense at Mass, giving choral responses to the rosary, and hoping to receive spiritual gifts from "the Mystic- // al Body" of Christ. The gifts he received, however, were more mundane: a plastic canteen of Lourdes's waters, a small snow globe containing figures of the Virgin Mary and St. Bernadette, and a certificate for his hard work carrying the sick on stretchers.

Heaney may have been disappointed by his pilgrimages, but he continued to study meditational and mystical texts that called for a withdrawal from social activities, followed by an initiation into sacred mysteries and a return to society with redemptive gifts. He had grown accustomed to this circular pattern of the "monomyth" in the rituals and retreats at St. Columb's. "All of the great spiritual writers were constantly being applied, in digested, pre-packaged form, by preachers at retreats, and were generally in the Catholic air I breathed at boarding school," he once said in a letter. One of these spiritual writers was the fifteenth-century monk Thomas à Kempis, whose most popular devotional book was *The Imitation of Christ*. Meditative withdrawal and prayer, according to *The Imitation of Christ*, should lead to a realization that the "powers of soul and body we possess, outwardly or inwardly, natural or supernatural, are . . . the bounty of the loving and good God, from whom we receive all good gifts. And whether we receive more or less, all gifts are [God's]. . . . Thus, whoever has received abundant gifts may not on that account boast of his merits, nor exalt himself above his fellows, nor despise any who are less richly endowed; for the greater and better a man is, the less he attributes to himself. . . . He who holds himself in humble esteem, and judges himself most unworthy, is most fitted to receive God's greatest gifts."[10] At Queen's, Heaney read "a book by Evelyn Underhill on mysticism" and remembered studying, "in a pious spirit, *Seeds of Contemplation* by Thomas Merton." To expand his knowledge of contemplative literature, he also "dipped into the *Spiritual Exercises* [*of St. Ignatius*]" and got "a sense of John of the Cross and St. Teresa" from his readings and conversations.[11]

St. Ignatius's *Spiritual Exercises* draws on *The Imitation of Christ* to explain how Christians receive God's gifts. "The more the soul finds itself alone and away from men, the more apt it is to approach and be united with its Creator and Lord," St. Ignatius declares. "The closer the soul approaches Him, the more it is disposed to receive graces and gifts from His divine and sovereign goodness."[12] Underhill's encyclopedic study *Mysticism* suggests that the Christian's "intangible quest" for union with a gift-giving Creator corresponds to the mythical hero's quest for worldly gifts, just as the mystic's sacred love for God corresponds to a person's erotic love for a beloved. According to Underhill, the mystical hero, like the secular hero, travels from a familiar community to an otherworldly realm where an initiation into divine "Mysteries" occurs, and returns to society bearing inspirational gifts. For Underhill, Dante's *Divine Comedy* is the paradigm of the "catholic" (from the Greek *katholikos*, meaning "universal") pattern of the hero's journey along "the Mystic Way."[13] Heaney would take the same view of Dante's journey and contend that it exemplifies the "monomyth" explicated by Joseph Campbell in *The Hero with a Thousand Faces.*

For Campbell, epic plots conform to a "universal mythological formula of the adventure of the hero." There is a "standard path" in these adventures based on the three stages of rites of passage: "*A hero ventures forth from the world of common day into a region of supernatural wonder: fabulous forces are there encountered and a decisive victory is won: the hero comes back from this mysterious adventure with the power to bestow boons on his fellow man.*"[14] With this in mind, Heaney pointed out that the "big shape" of *The Divine Comedy* is "the archetypal one" with three parts: a "faring forth into the ordeal," a descent "to a nadir" in a hellish otherworld, and a "return . . . to a world that is renewed by the boon won in that other place."[15] Dante's gift to the world was his poem about a journey toward a transcendent gift-making and gift-giving Creator. Like mystics before and after him, Dante reaches a sublime state in which his "mind, bedazzled and amazed, / Stood fixed in wonder, motionless, intent" on what he calls in the *Paradiso* "the love that moves the sun and the other stars" and "the final source of bliss and light." While contemplating the Prime Mover's "boon . . . [of] grace abounding," the poet admits, "How weak are words, and how unfit to frame / My concept."[16] He has gone as far as he can toward the origin of all being.

As Heaney struggled to develop an effective voice as a poet during his university years, he also struggled to figure out how to express the inexpressible mysteries of his faith. One of the most helpful guides for this endeavor was the Trappist monk Thomas Merton. Like Underhill, Merton believed that the mystical journey follows the pattern of the "monomyth." *Seeds of Contemplation* maps out a departure from "the old world of our senses," a purgatorial "dark night of the soul" that is "strange, remote and unbelievable," a state of union during which "a pure gift of God" is received "with thanksgiving, happiness and joy," and a return to society with the "the gift of God's love."[17] Like the Platonic and Christian mystics who influenced Dante, Merton envisions the Creator as an "invisible, transcendent and infinitely abundant Source" that is "beyond reason" and "beyond discourse." Communion with this "Source" depends on the "gift of awareness . . . of infinite Being" that allows a person to behold "contingent reality . . . as a present from God, as a free gift of love."[18] These conceptions of gifts and gift-giving had an enduring effect on Heaney.

Merton acknowledges in his "Author's Note" at the beginning of *Seeds of Contemplation* that his book will "follow lines laid down by the Spanish Carmelite . . . St. John of the Cross."[19] Heaney would pay similar tribute to the sixteenth-century mystical poet in his mini-epic "Station Island," where he juxtaposes the mundane Christmas gift of a kaleidoscope with a similar gift he envies—a friend's toy battleship. Heaney once said at a reading that he intended the poem to be "a parable about the abuse of a gift." He explained that "the kaleidoscope stands for the gift of imagination [and of] . . . introspective wonder." The moral of his parable was simple: "You should use any gift for what it's meant for."[20] Before he translates St. John of the Cross's poem "Cantar del alma que se huelga do conoscer a Dios por fe" as "penance," he points out that his goal is "to re-envisage / the zenith and glimpsed jewels of any gift / mistakenly abased." The gist of St. John of the Cross's poem is that all of Creation can be and should be reenvisaged as an "eternal fountain [that] hides and splashes / within this living bread that is life to us / although it is the night." This vision of communion with the mysterious gift-making and gift-giving Creator, which appears in "Station Island: Section XI," is similar to Dante's mystical vision at the end of *The Divine Comedy*. It's the vision that Heaney aspired to throughout his life.

### GIFTS OF HEARTH CULTURE AND ACADEMIC CULTURE

As an undergraduate, Heaney found the clash between his home culture and academic culture cause for both amusement and consternation. As he remarked in his John Malone lecture, *Among Schoolchildren*:

> I was studying English, reading Shakespeare and Oscar Wilde and Chaucer and Dickens . . . , considering the tradition of courtly love, learning to find my way among the ironies and niceties of Jane Austen's vicarages, discussing Tennyson's loss of faith and Lawrence's phallic consciousness, learning of the rituals of club life in India by reading E. M. Forster and learning the rituals of the sherry party by attending receptions at the house of our Oxford professor. . . . [And yet] at the weekends and during the holidays, far from the sherry parties of Malone Road, the secretary of the local Pioneer Total Abstinence Association was enrolling me as a probationer in the society; far from the elegances of Oscar Wilde and the profundities of Shakespeare, I was acting with the Bellaghy Dramatic Society in plays about [the Irish Rebellion of ] 1798, now playing a United Irishman, a blacksmith forging pikes on a real anvil fetched from Devlin's forge

at Hillhead, now playing Robert Emmet in a one-act melodrama and having my performance hailed in the crowded columns of the *Mid-Ulster Mail*. Far from discussing the Victorian loss of faith, I was driving my mother to evening devotions in the "chapel" or looking for my name in a list of "adorers" at the exposition of the Blessed Sacrament. Far from the melodies of courtly love, I was acting as *fear a' tigh* at the G.A.A. [Gaelic Athletic Association] *ceilidh* . . . and trying to master a way of coaxing a training college student into the back of our Austin Sixteen. And far, far from Lawrence's phallic candour, finding myself subsequently confessing sins of immodest and immoderate embraces [at church].

These town-and-gown oscillations prompted Heaney to wonder if he was "two persons or one."[21]

Considering his devotion to church and home at the time, it's surprising that Heaney was so besotted with his Queen's classes on the nightmarish dramas of Shakespeare's contemporaries John Webster and Christopher Marlowe. Webster's plays *The White Devil* and *The Duchess of Malfi* are rife with torture, incest, suicide, infidelity, poisoning, and imprisonment. With a similar gothic flair, Marlowe wrote about an unrepentant Doctor Faustus dragged off to hell after being assailed by demons, a Jew in Malta who poisoned his daughter and killed her fellow nuns, Catholics who executed thousands of French Protestants in the infamous St. Bartholemew's Day Massacre, and a shepherd named Tamburlaine who, in his pursuit of imperial power, murdered a son and treated prisoners so badly they committed suicide. Heaney was especially enchanted by Professor Terence Spencer's lectures on Marlowe and admitted to being "carried away by the sheer rhetorical power" of Marlowe's verse when Spencer read *Tamburlaine the Great* to his students.[22]

If the social injustices in Renaissance revenge tragedies reminded Heaney of injustices in Ulster, the poetry of Gerard Manley Hopkins suggested ways for those injustices to be resolved or transcended. Since first coming across Hopkins at St. Columb's, Heaney had sympathized with the Jesuit's vision of the world as God's wondrous gift. In classes taught by John Braidwood, he learned more about the Anglo-Saxon alliterative tradition that influenced the syntax and sonority of Hopkins's poetry. He also learned more about the Catholic and chivalric traditions of gift-giving that inspired Hopkins.

One of the long poems in that tradition that he studied at Queen's, the late fourteenth-century chivalric romance *Sir Gawain and the Green Knight*, appealed to Heaney because, like Hopkins's poetry, it dramatized miracles and gift exchanges in a style that was resonant with echoing consonants and vowels. Heaney liked the sonic effects of alliteration. He may have been intrigued, too, by the way *Sir Gawain and the Green Knight* expresses anxieties about the transition from a medieval gift economy to a modern capitalist economy. The poem tracks the successes and failures of gift exchanges in three intertwined storylines: the "Beheading Game" (two knights agree to exchange "gifts" of axe blows), the "Temptation Story" (a seductive woman offers erotic gifts to a man who feels morally compelled to refuse them), and the "Exchange of Winnings" (two men give each other gifts they've won). The poem shows what happens to a knight when he abides by some, but not all, of the tacit rules of gift exchange.

The narrative begins at a feast in King Arthur's court during the gift-giving season of Christmastide: "Lords and ladies leaped forth, largess distributing, / Offered New Year gifts in high voices, handed them out, / Bustling and bantering about these offerings." The ceremony ends when the mysterious Green Knight gallops into the hall on a green horse and proposes a gift exchange that makes a mockery of the one that has just taken place: he demands a severed head for a severed head. King Arthur agrees to "bestow the boon you bid us give"—an axe blow to the Green Knight's neck.[23] Gawain insists that he do the honor and proceeds to cut off the Green Knight's head. Like the crucified Christ, the Green Knight miraculously revives. He then tells Gawain to come to the Green Chapel so he can reciprocate with a similar "gift" of an axe blow to the neck. Both men take the biblical principle of "an eye for an eye" (or a head for a head) to its literal extreme.

The most significant gift that Gawain gives the Green Knight is the opportunity to prove his chivalry. According to the chivalric code, a knight who receives a gift must reciprocate with a gift. In this case, the Green Knight must behead Gawain on the first day of the following year, a day of gift-giving in the Middle Ages. Gawain intends to fulfill his pledge. He travels toward the knight's Green Chapel but gets delayed when he meets Lord and Lady Bertilak, who offer him gifts that test his virtues. Lord Bertilak gives him three prize animals he has killed while hunting (a deer, a boar, a fox), and Gawain gives Bertilak kisses that he no doubt intends for his wife. Lady Bertilak, acting like an erotic huntress, comes to Gawain's bed three times and tries to seduce him. Gawain upholds courtly principles by refusing Lady Bertilak's advances. He wavers, though, when she promises him her magic girdle (a green and gold silk belt) that has the power to protect him from bodily harm. (He's thinking of the impending axe blow from the Green Knight.)

Lady Bertilak hopes Gawain will give her "something as a gift," but he knows if he gives her a glove, that would indicate they're involved in a sexual relationship. So he tells her, "It is not to your honour to have at this time / A mere glove as Gawain's gift to treasure." His conscience only allows him to exchange gifts with men such as Lord Bertilak, the Green Knight, or God: "He told her that he could touch no treasure at all, / Nor gold nor any gift [from her] till God gave him grace / To pursue to success the search [for the Green Knight] he was bound on." A disappointed Lady Bertilak replies, "Though gift you give me none / You must have something of mine." Gawain knows the magical properties of the lady's girdle could prove useful when the Green Knight swings his axe, so he takes "the lady's gift" and "lapped his loins with his love-token twice / . . . to save himself when of necessity he must / Stand an evil stroke." Wearing women's clothing, though, is a sign that he lacks courage and other conventional masculine traits. His femininity—or at least his prudence—is born out when he refuses to sacrifice the gift of his head to the Green Knight. Afterward, the only way he can redeem himself as a chivalric knight is by confessing his "covetousness and cowardice" like a good Christian, going on a penitential journey and wearing Lady Bertilak's girdle as his "mark of shame."[24] By humbling himself in this way, he ends up with a greater gift than any of those given to him at King Arthur's court, Bertilak's castle, or the Green Chapel. He receives God's gift of grace.

Heaney learned more about medieval attitudes toward gift exchange when he studied *Le Morte d'Arthur,* the famous sequence of Arthurian tales published by Thomas Malory in 1485, a century after *Sir Gawain and the Green Knight* was composed. The central motifs in the Arthurian narrative—the Round Table, the sword Excalibur, the Holy Grail—are all gifts with supernatural powers. King Arthur's father-in-law gave him the Round Table as a wedding present; the Lady of the Lake gave Arthur his magical sword, Excalibur; an apparition of Jesus allegedly gave Joseph of Arimathea the Holy Grail, which he eventually brought to Arthur's kingdom. Gift exchange is treated as a sacred duty in the Arthurian tales. One of the early scenes in *Le Morte d'Arthur* shows what happens when a person fails to fulfill this duty. When the Lady of the Lake rides into King Arthur's court and asks the king for "a gift that he promised her when she gave him the sword" (she wants Sir Balin's severed head as a return gift), Arthur balks. Sir Balin finds out about the Lady of the Lake's demand, and, in an act of self-defense and revenge, he cuts off her head in front of King Arthur. Aware he has failed to honor his pledge to reciprocate, Arthur later has one of his knights, Bedivere, return the Lady of the Lake's gift of Excalibur to the lake: "And there came an arm and an hand above the water . . . [that] vanished with the sword."[25] Arthur abides by the chivalric code, but his gift-giving is belated, and he soon dies.

### GIFTS OF INCERTUS

In some of the poems he published in university magazines, Heaney incorporated themes and sound effects he discovered in *Sir Gawain and the Green Knight*, *Le Morte d'Arthur,* and *Beowulf.* Hopkins, though, was the prime mover of his early verse. "The revel and relish that the poetry of G.M.H. created in me at school got me going as a poet," he said.[26] His poem "October Thought" is one of the best examples of the way he reworked the alliterative style and Christian symbolism he found in Hopkins and his medieval precursors. Heaney's poem, which the journal Q published in 1959, envisions the world as an Eden of gifts that is menaced by satanic creatures, such as the "mice mealing the grain, gnawing strong / The iron-bound, swollen and ripe-round corn-barrel." Heaney hails the comforting sounds and routines on the farm: "Minute movement millionfold whispers twilight / And through the knuckle-gnarl of branches, poking the night / Comes the trickling tinkle of bells, well in the fold."[27] Still unsure of his poetic abilities, he signed his poem "Incertus."

Heaney signed a similar poem, "Song of My Man-Alive" published in the university magazine *Gorgon* two years later, with the same pseudonym. In this paean to pastoral love, he chants like a latter-day Hopkins or Dylan Thomas: "We were a giddy eddying; it was all tune-tumbling / Hill happy and wine-wonderful, / The lithe liquid spurts / Of the dancing thrush girls and hawk-boys spat round us."[28] Although he only drank Communion wine at the time, he seemed intoxicated with the "wine-wonderful" diction of his bardic predecessors. In more sober, rational moods, he realized that he had to curb his lyrical excesses—his spirited "gift of tongues"—to become an effective modern poet.

Of the various English instructors at Queen's, Lerner was the most crucial in Heaney's development as a writer. Lerner had come to Belfast from apartheid South Africa, and he possessed a keen understanding of Ulster's social divisions and strong opinions about how writers should address them. Unlike the New Critics who dominated literary criticism at the time, he believed texts should be regarded as social as well as aesthetic documents, and he took pains to prove literature was relevant to the lives of his students. Seamus Deane applauded him for "[reminding us] that our lives, too, were embroiled with these books," and for bringing "the streets of Belfast and the poems and novels we read into contact with one another."[29] Lerner's comments in class affected Heaney's poetry. One discussion in particular, of Frost's elegy "'Out, Out—,'" gave him the confidence to address rural traumas such as the death of his brother Christopher. After reading Frost's *Selected Poems* edited by C. Day Lewis, Heaney said he was moved by "the sheer recognition factor—of the people, the situations, the practices" and by "the rightness of making your own sounds in your own way."[30] Heaney especially admired Frost's "capacity-to-surrender-to-the-gift poem."[31] With Frost as his guide, he gradually shed his Incertus persona and learned to trust his gift for writing candidly about agricultural and sociopolitical subjects. In the 1960s, he bought Frost's *Collected Poems*, Lawrence Thompson's authorized biography of Frost, and a volume of Frost's *Selected Letters* to learn more about the gifts of the New England bard.

In a lecture titled "The Government of the Tongue," which Heaney delivered about twenty-five years after graduating from Queen's, he reflected on the importance for a poet to reach that disciplined stage where "the tongue (representing both a poet's personal gift of utterance and the common resources of language itself) has been granted the right to govern."[32] A poem such as "Aran," published in *Gorgon* in 1960, reveals that he could govern his linguistic exuberance if he tried. The poem describes the hard lives of people on the Aran Islands off the western coast of Ireland in the sort of straightforward style favored by Frost and also by John Synge in his nonfiction book *Aran Islands:* "They feed and worship, lancing the wizened veins / Of scanty soil, trying to draw life from the stones." The diction transmits the down-to-earth sounds that the islanders hear in their daily work: "As he digs, the islander's spade spangs off rock / And stops." Heaney would soon compare his pen to a spade cutting into the soil in "Digging." As he honed his craft at Queen's, he tried to use his pen to dig closer to his buried gifts and lance away the decorative rhetoric that had dazzled him as Incertus.

"Aran" also reveals Heaney's sense that as an undergraduate poet he was working alone like one of Frost's solitary figures or one of Synge's island laborers. Referring to the writing scene at Queen's, he said in a *Gorgon* article, "A lot of people of a generally literary bent were islanded about the place but they in no way constituted an archipelago. . . . We stood or hung or sleepwalked between notions of writing that we had gleaned from English courses and the living reality of writers from our own place whom we did not know, in person or in print."[33] In the absence of creative-writing courses and poetry readings, student poets were "trying to draw life from the stones." Lerner was one of the few professors who read the student literary magazines and encouraged Heaney to keep writing. When Lerner came across "Aran," he complimented his student on the poem's vivid descriptions. In the same issue of *Gorgon*, Deane had published a poem that was, by his own admission, "long, shapeless . . . , full of vacuous profundities, [and] based on Allen Tate's 'Ode to the Confederate Dead.'" Lerner advised Deane to emulate Heaney's less grandiloquent style. Deane later concluded, "Heaney was serving an apprenticeship. I was just being an undergraduate. Lerner put it nicely. Heaney, he said, was trying to write poems, and I was trying to write poetry."[34] Heaney's poems would soon get the notice of many other readers beside Lerner, and Deane would soon realize he had more of a gift for writing literary criticism.

Heaney's prose poem "Incertus" in *Stations* gives clues as to why he felt so uncertain at Queen's about his poetic gift and how difficult it was for him to gain confidence as a poet. "Incertus" places his literary genesis in the context of Stephen Dedalus's evolution in *A Portrait of the Artist as a Young Man*. Just as Dedalus reflects on his time as an awkward infant who desperately wants to mature as a writer, Heaney admits, "Oh yes, I crept before I walked." He makes an "expert obeisance" to dead literary masters and tries to imitate their expert craftsmanship, but, like Dedalus again, he also rebels against the idea of bowing down to writers in the British canon. He feels a growing affinity for Irish writers. It was hard, though, to learn much about Irish literature at Queen's during the late 1950s and early 1960s. In a keynote address given at his alma mater in 1995, the year he won the Nobel Prize, Heaney said, "By the late nineteen fifties the curriculum had indeed expanded, but still, in the course of my four years of study for the Honours Degree in English Language and Literature, the only reference I can recollect being made to Irish writing as such was a short account of Yeats's early poetry given by Professor Peter Butter, and that consisted of a slightly negative lecture about the dreaminess of Yeats's early style."[35] Books by Irish-born writers who had migrated to England, such as George Bernard Shaw and Edmund Burke, were on the syllabus during his first year, but they were treated as British texts. Burke's *Reflections on the Revolution in France,* which predicted that the French rebels would come to a disastrous end, was one book Heaney especially liked. George McWhirter, who studied Burke in the same class as Heaney, said, "I equate Seamus H with Burke's balancing, the measured demolishment and establishment of ideas."[36]

At Queen's, Heaney hoped to balance the academic emphasis on British culture with his devotion to his Irish-Catholic hearth culture. While his classmates experimented with alcohol and premarital sex, he remained remarkably devoted to Catholic prohibitions against them. One of his only bad habits was smoking, which he'd started at a wake for a neighbor's drowned son during a summer holiday. He bought his first pack of cigarettes in the fall of 1957 and smoked consistently for the next three decades. Cigarettes kept him alert at night while studying, and the nicotine highs helped assuage the anxieties in his love life. As a student, he became especially distraught in a relationship with a young woman who didn't seem to requite his passionate feelings for her. He worked some of his frustrations into "Song of My Man-Alive" and a short story titled "There's Rosemary———." Both appeared in *Gorgon* in 1961, when he was twenty-one. His story offers a double vision of himself as a young man and an old man. His alter ego Sean works in a seminary and is prone to "inferiority complexes and basic shyness and bad poetry."[37] Much of the narrative consists of flashbacks to a vacation in Galway, where Sean accidently impregnates a woman named Grainne. Later, he's horrified to learn that Grainne has had an abortion. Heaney uses the image of a dead belly, just as he did in "Song of My Man-Alive," to lament the gift of life being destroyed. Guilt-stricken and depressed, Sean concludes (like Dylan Thomas in many of his poems) that womb and tomb are linked, and sex simply leads to death.

Heaney meditated on sex and death with similar cynicism in his short essay "The Seductive Muse," which appeared in the same 1961 issue of *Gorgon*. Rather than an aborted fetus or dead dog (Sean in "There's Rosemary———" associates "the swollen corpse of a mangy grey dog" in Galway Bay with the aborted fetus), Heaney now uses the image of human waste to lament the result of intercourse.[38] He wants to have a productive—or reproductive—relationship with his muse, but she only produces "chronic diarrhea of image and metre" and "unfailing constipation of idea and incident." At times, Heaney comments insightfully on the frustrations of a young poet: "The amateur's first furtive verse usually imitates or parodies an actual poem that he has studied and enjoyed, recapturing the original turns of phrase and runs of rhythm. Thus it is true to say that the first poems spring from a nascent feeling for language—language as sounds, as a vehicle for emotional expression." He knows that emotions must be balanced with ideas, but he fears that too much thinking can lead to "poetic inspiration . . . being sicklied o'er with the pale cast of thought." His quotation comes from Shakespeare's famous "To be or not to be" speech, when Hamlet realizes that his long-winded rumination about life and death has deadened his will to act. Heaney at the time had arrived at a similar impasse. He had concluded that his "seductive muse" was a femme fatale and that he had become a "despicable . . . ex-poet."[39]

Heaney's disappointments with his muse were only temporary. By the end of his final year at Queen's, his diligence—at least with his writing—bore fruit. A national periodical, the *Irish Digest,* published a short article he wrote about the current style of "jive" dancing inspired by swing music and rock 'n' roll. Heaney's argument was that jiving should be incorporated into traditional Irish dancing. Written during his Christmas holiday in 1960 after teaching himself how to type on a rented typewriter, the article follows the precepts laid out in Eliot's "Tradition and the Individual Talent" and recommends that past forms merge with new forms. In this case, he hopes that a fusion of old and new dance styles will lead to "a renaissance of Celtic choreography" and be embraced by "young people in great numbers from every class and creed."[40]

Although Heaney showed promise as a poet and scholar in 1961, not all his professors were convinced that he was the top student in his graduating class. Lerner, for one, considered Deane to be a more accomplished critic. Nevertheless, Heaney earned a First Class Honours degree in English Language and Literature and won the prestigious McMullen medal for academic excellence. He bought books by Wilde, Synge, and MacNeice with the gift certificate that accompanied the medal. Heaney's father made graduation day special by letting Heaney drive the family's recently purchased car—a Humber. Heaney was also flattered by those professors who recommended that he apply to graduate school. Professor Peter Butter, who chaired the English Department, thought he should consider Oxford University. Heaney and his parents, though, weren't sure about his next academic step. "I remember just being bewildered," Heaney said about the possibility of going to Oxford. "My father and mother . . . wouldn't have stopped me . . . , but I suppose there was just some lack of confidence."[41] Heaney was still Incertus, at least when it came to pursuing a postgraduate degree in a different country. Instead of going abroad for further study, he decided to get certified as a teacher in Belfast so he could live close to his family and pay off debts to his parents.

Heaney's lack of a doctorate made him more eager to succeed as a teacher and scholar for the rest of his life. Looking back on his academic career in 2002, he explained to his Dutch potter friend Sonja Landjweer:

[I] always felt I would prove myself by doing what the academics were supposed to do—lecture and write criticism—but in a way that was still my own. I didn't want the mystique of "the poet" to be a union ticket. I wanted, in a proud, puritanical sort of way, to "pay my way," not be beholden, to be as good or better at the job than my "non-creative" colleagues. . . . And much of what I did was truly helpful to me: a clearing of the head, a declaration of loyalties to certain masters, a paying of creative debts, a standing-up for the art, a teacherly duty, a service of sorts.

This combination of competitive zeal and noble principles typified Heaney's approach to academia. He would try to outperform his colleagues with PhDs but still honor his unique "creative debts" out of loyalty "to certain masters." Heaney, though, worried that his pursuit of academic prestige would stifle his poetic gift. In 2002, having achieved his goals as a professor, critic, and poet, he told Landjweer, "Now I fear . . . [literary criticism] may have become an alibi. I desperately need rehabilitation with the muse."[42] He was still afraid his poetic imagination might become "sicklied o'er with the pale cast of thought" if he spent too much time away from his "seductive muse."

# 6

# From Incertus
# to Master

Heaney began writing his first mature poems during a relatively peaceful time in Northern Ireland. The IRA was dormant in 1962, and within a year Catholics had reason to hope for an easing of sectarian tensions. Unionists disenchanted with Prime Minister Brookeborough's economic policies pressured him to resign. Catholics were pleased. Earlier in his career, Brookeborough had bragged about his anti-Catholic biases. He once told a group of Protestants in the fraternal group known as the Orange Order, "Many in this audience employ Catholics, but I have not one about the place. Catholics are out to destroy Ulster."[1] In the early 1960s, Catholics looked forward to a Northern Ireland without Brookeborough.

For most of Heaney's early life, Brookeborough had ruled the country with an iron fist. Captain Terence O'Neill, who replaced Brookeborough as prime minister in 1963, displayed a new willingness "to promote a gradual healing of the sectarian sores in the politics of Ulster." Most Catholics expected him to follow through with his promises. "One trusted him," Heaney remarked, "because his personality . . . [was] redolent of honesty and good will."[2] Although O'Neill was the sort of upper-class Englishman who scorned Irish Catholics (he grew up in a conservative military family in London and trained at the Royal Military Academy Sandhurst), he tried to be evenhanded. When he took office, he called on lawmakers to stop drawing electoral boundaries that favored Protestant politicians, opposed the practice of Protestant landlords and homeowners casting multiple votes in local elections, supported funds for Catholics to purchase council houses, and vowed to curb anti-Catholic biases in the predominantly Protestant police force, the Royal Ulster Constabulary.

O'Neill quickly learned how hard it was to please one faction without angering another. When he tried to show goodwill toward Catholics by visiting a convent and by meeting with the Catholic prime minister of the Republic of Ireland, old animosities flared. Protestants suspected O'Neill would undermine their monopoly on power, and demagogues like Ian Paisley, the founder of the Free Presbyterian Church and Protestant Unionist Party, lashed out at him. In his jeremiads against Catholic "superstition and papalism with all their attendant vices of murder, theft, immorality, lust and incest," Paisley implored his followers to resist O'Neill's reforms.[3]

In 1964, the year Heaney wrote "Digging" and "Death of a Naturalist," a dispute involving Paisley and a Sinn Féin candidate turned violent after the candidate displayed the Irish national flag in a public place. Riots broke out that were the worst Belfast had seen in thirty years. Paisley demanded O'Neill's resignation and told fellow Protestants to take up arms against anyone who favored appeasing Catholics. In 1966, the year Paisley founded the *Protestant Telegraph* newspaper to air his grievances, one of his allies organized a paramilitary group, the Ulster Volunteer Force (UVF). The UVF soon declared war on the IRA and targeted Catholic homes, shops, and schools with petrol bombs. O'Neill tried to dismantle the UVF but failed. Angered by the attacks on Catholics, the IRA soon launched a guerrilla war in Ireland and England. Many of Heaney's poems would lament the resurgence of hostilities.

At the end of 1961, though, Heaney was more concerned with his academic future than his country's political future. Having decided to get a teaching job, he enrolled at St. Joseph's College of Education in Belfast. For his teaching certificate, he wrote an essay about Ulster's journals, which he published as "In Our Own Dour Way" in a 1964 issue of a St. Joseph's magazine, *Trench*. His research gave him a better idea of where to submit his poems, and it taught him that nationalist and unionist biases affected whose poems were accepted by certain journals. "In Our Own Dour Way" also gave Heaney an opportunity to articulate the sort of poet he wanted to be. "The artist is the custodian of human values, of sanity and tolerance," he writes, "and these are the qualities most needed in the North today." In another telling statement, he quotes from the ballad "The Man from God-Knows Where," which tells the story of the United Irishman Thomas Russell who was hanged for opposing the British during the Rebellion of 1798. The ballad's narrator boasts, "We men of the North had a word to say / And we said it then in our own dour way." Always sympathetic to the United Irishmen, Heaney counsels "their descendants of the 1960's [to] follow their example—with the pen, which is so much mightier than the pike."[4] Heaney's poem "Digging," which he wrote several months after publishing the essay, reiterates this idea, although there he renounces a gun in favor of a pen. His *Trench* essay also calls for a new Ulster journal that encourages writers to be regional and write about their native cultures. "No writer, however talented, should uproot himself in spirit from his native place," he contends. "An Ulster literary tradition must spring out of the life and speech of the province."[5] In 1968, his poet friend James Simmons agreed that a new journal might be the catalyst for a new "Ulster literary tradition" and, with that in mind, started *The Honest Ulsterman*.

Heaney devoted much of his time in the early 1960s to his teacher-training courses and to fulfilling St. Joseph's practice-teaching requirement. In 1962, he took a temporary position at St. Thomas's Intermediate School in Ballymurphy, about five miles southwest of central Belfast. The high school had been set up for boys who'd done poorly on the Eleven Plus exam and, as a result, had to take mechanical arts courses such as woodwork and metalwork. Most of these boys came from Catholic, working-class families in a run-down neighborhood on Belfast's Whiterock Road. In the school's hierarchical system, only the top quarter of the students got the opportunity to take English literature classes from Heaney. He tried hard to prepare these students for the exams that would allow them to get back on the college-bound track, but soon learned that most of them didn't care about college, didn't care about poetry, and didn't care about their future careers. (A number of them would join the Provisional IRA.) To them, poetry was an obscure, bourgeois art that had little to do with their hardscrabble lives. Heaney's earnest attempts to "demystify things" and "make them feel safer within the realms of poetry" got a chilly reception.[6]

One of the few consolations of his teaching job was his friendship with the school's headmaster, the fiction writer Michael McLaverty, who introduced Heaney to a number of contemporary authors. McLaverty had a habit of bursting into Heaney's classroom with a well-known writer in tow. He also liked to give Heaney books by some of his favorite writers: Hopkins, Rilke, Eliot, Kavanagh, and Edwin Muir. The poem "Fosterage" in *North*, which is dedicated to McLaverty, and the introduction that Heaney wrote for McLaverty's *Collected Short Stories* acknowledge the headmaster to be another gifted and gift-giving mentor: "In the 60s, when I was a beginner in both the writing and teaching trades, I was showered with gifts of books from him, and was made conscious of how serious and how solitary he had been in the quest for his own intellectual and imaginative identity."[7] McLaverty, like Eliot in "Tradition and the Individual Talent," believed writers should develop their talents by engaging in a kind of gift exchange ritual with writers of the past. Heaney wrote at the end of "Fosterage," "[McLaverty] fostered me and sent me out, with words / Imposing on my tongue like obols." Obols in ancient Greece were coins placed in the mouths of the dead as gifts for Charon, the mythical figure who ferried corpses through the underworld. Heaney implied that McLaverty's gifts of books and encouraging words were like obols for his journey among the great dead writers of tradition.

Although McLaverty played the role of literary guide at St. Thomas's, Heaney often felt as if his journey had stalled in a wasteland. The future journalist, poet, and novelist Jack Holland, who was one of the more attentive students in Heaney's classes, admitted that he and his peers scoffed at Heaney because of his farming background: "Country men were, by the nature of things, not taken seriously in Belfast. All city kids assumed they knew more about everything than people from the countryside, and set out to prove it on every available occasion."[8] Holland nicknamed his teacher "Sleepy" because Heaney was reserved and frequently nodded off in the library. Holland and his friends also mocked Heaney's attitudes toward sexual matters, which seemed old-fashioned. Sometimes they tried to embarrass him with explicit questions about sex. It took a while for the cocky city boys to realize their teacher was no country bumpkin.

Heaney eventually won over Holland by teaching Louis MacNeice's poem "Carrickfergus," which was in their textbook *Rhyme and Reason,* and by taking Holland and others in the class on a field trip to the coastal town north of Belfast where MacNeice had grown up. While roaming around the castle and pier, the students saw signs of the fateful landings by the British General Schomberg during the summer of 1689, and by King William III a year later. The fortunes of Irish Catholics had been forever altered when King William concluded Schomberg's military campaign by marching south from Carrickfergus to defeat the Catholic King James at the Battle of the Boyne on July 1, 1690. Heaney's poem "National Trust," which he wrote after he got back to Belfast, delineates different ways Protestants (like MacNeice) and Catholics (like Holland) commemorated—or failed to commemorate—Ulster's bloody history. While signs of defeated Catholics and their native saints have been eradicated from the area, the signs of the conquerors—"a horse-shoe, LOL, a three runged ladder"—are clearly legible. The horseshoe replicates the imprint that General Schomberg's horse made on Ireland in 1689, "LOL" refers to the Protestants' Loyal Orange Lodge established after William of Orange's victory, and the ladder was a Masonic symbol sewn into the orange sashes of Protestant Loyalists. Heaney's poem is another bitter testament to the suffering that British Protestants inflicted on Catholic Ireland.

During the summer of 1962, Heaney traveled to the cultural and political center of Britain where so many of the policies that hurt Irish Catholics originated. He had accepted a six-week job in the British government's passport office. Once settled in London, he commuted every day on the Green Line subway between Earl's Court and St. James's Park so he could write addresses on envelopes and make sure the information on applications was transferred correctly to passports. His poem "The Real Names" remembers some of the good times he had in the city, such as drinking with friends and going to an outdoor performance of Shakespeare's *Twelfth Night* in Regent's Park. He also attended BBC-sponsored classical concerts at Royal Albert Hall called the Proms, so named because they were once held in London's gardens, where audiences promenaded. He enjoyed these outings, but, as "Electric Light" attests, he often felt like an alien in the capital. The rock-'n'-roll era had begun, and many aspects of British culture were undergoing a seismic shift. The Beatles had completed their first recording session at Abbey Road Studios on June 6,

1962; the Rolling Stones had played their first gig at London's Marquee Club on July 12. As Bob Dylan would say about this period, "The Times They Are a-Changin'." Heaney would find himself at odds with many of the aesthetic and ideological changes of the 1960s, even though he appreciated the liberal-minded attitudes of many people who embraced them.

Heaney was still a devout Catholic in the early 1960s, but his students at St. Thomas's Intermediate School noticed he was mellowing. Ulster students tended to think of their teachers as aloof and unapproachable, but Heaney began to invite students, including Holland, to his apartment for informal conversations. On one occasion, he read his poem "Turkeys Observed," which he'd written at the end of 1962 after seeing slaughtered turkeys in a butcher's shop. He had recently discovered Ted Hughes's book *Lupercal* in the Belfast Public Library, and he tried to imitate the English poet's gritty realism and harsh diction in his poem about turkeys. With his students, he at first didn't reveal who'd written the poem; he felt if they knew, they'd respond accordingly and he wanted an unprejudiced assessment. Holland recalled, "I told him I did not think much of it and found it rather too self-conscious. He revealed that it was his. I shook my head. Sorry, Seamus, stick to teaching, I thought. The rest is history."[9] Heaney may have shared some of Holland's reservations about his early poem. Its metaphorical profusion of dead birds, funeral corpses, drowned bodies, ruined kings, complaining Confucian lords, and downed fighter planes was overwhelming at times.

Heaney told the English scholar Michael Parker that he was "floundering" as a teacher in 1962 and 1963.[10] He'd grown tired of slogging through reams of poorly written essays and tired of teaching literature to boys who had no aptitude for it. He also disliked many of his colleagues. He felt even more discouraged if he partied late into the night and had to hustle to school the next morning with a hangover. He began thinking of the school, with its iron railings and steel-framed windows, as a prison, and wondered if he should have gone to Oxford for a postgraduate degree or to Queen's to write a thesis on Wordsworth's theories of education.

A number of the poems Heaney wrote in the early 1960s express his discontent as an unmarried teacher. "Young Bachelor" laments his tedious daily schedule and lonely nights in his flat. Another uncollected poem, "Writer and Teacher," complains about his failed effort to educate "bone- / Heads" in his classes.[11] Disappointments at St. Thomas's, however, were offset by successes in poetry. One remarkable achievement was "Mid-Term Break," which he wrote in a Wellington Park Avenue flat he shared with two postgraduate biochemistry students. After a laborious day of teaching, and while waiting for one of his flatmates to cook dinner, Heaney dashed off the poem. Like many of his other best poems, it arrived as a gift after a long gestation.

## GIFTS FROM FRIENDS AND LOVERS

During his hard times at St. Thomas's, several people besides McLaverty made Heaney's life more bearable. One of these was David Hammond, a talented Ulster musician and singer who met Heaney in 1963 at Belfast's Lyric Theatre, where he was singing ballads in the production *See the Gay Windows*. Heaney was so moved by Hammond's performance that he invited him to sing at St. Thomas's in 1963. Although Hammond was a Protestant, he wowed the Catholic students. "He was as much at home with the Clancy Brothers [a Catholic group known for its traditional Irish music] as with the [Protestant] brethren of an Orange Lodge in Cregagh," Heaney said. "And the fetch of that liberated thing was in his singing voice."[12] Heaney would work closely with Hammond on BBC productions after the singer took a permanent job at BBC Radio Belfast in 1965. The education officer there, Leslie Davidson, had already approached Heaney about working on various projects, but someone higher up argued that Heaney was not well-known enough to attract a big audience. With Hammond's help, Heaney was able to launch a series of radio talks called *Over to You* that proved to be highly popular despite the London BBC's objections to Irish accents and obscure Irish references. Heaney also worked with Hammond in the Field Day organization, and he paid homage to Hammond in his poems "The Singer's House" and "The Door Was Open and the House was Dark."

Another new friend Heaney made in the early 1960s was T. P. Flanagan, an accomplished artist and poet from Enniskillen in southwest Ulster. Flanagan taught art at St. Joseph's sister school in Belfast, St. Mary's Training College, and he was also a school inspector. On a visit to St. Thomas's, he was introduced to Heaney by McLaverty. The two men hit it off immediately. Ten years older than Heaney, Flanagan acted as another mentor. To show his gratitude to the older artist, Heaney in a few years dedicated the poem "Bogland" to him. Heaney also wrote the foreword to *T. P. Flanagan*, a book about the artist published by Four Courts Press in 1995.

Perhaps the most transformational event in Heaney's life occurred when he met one of Flanagan's former students, Marie Devlin, at a retirement party for the Queen's chaplain. Marie shared Heaney's passion for poetry. (She'd written and studied poetry at St. Mary's Training College.) While walking her home one October night in 1962, he stopped at his flat so he could give her a copy of A. Alvarez's anthology *The New Poetry*. He thought she'd like Alvarez's eclectic selection of poems and his introduction that criticized the Anglo-American "gentility principle." He also hoped she would think of the book as a gift that would create a bond between them.

Heaney's plan worked; two days later, Marie visited his flat with the book so they could resume their conversation. One of the poems that may have interested them was Norman MacCaig's "Gifts," which tells the story of two lovers who want to give each other gifts to solidify their relationship. The poem's disgruntled narrator, though, tells his lover he hopes she will consider *him* as a gift, even though he admits he isn't perfect. "[It] is all / I have to give," he says of himself, knowing she would prefer the sort of romantic gifts that an "old Irish poet" (probably Yeats) writes about in a book she's reading.

Following their talk, Heaney offered to take Marie to a party hosted by Robert Sean Armstrong, a Protestant friend from Queen's who had edited the satirical magazine *PTQ*. (The initials were from the first three words in Belfast's Latin motto, *Pro Tanto Quid Retribuamus*, which came from the Psalms in the Bible: "In return for so much, what shall we give back?") It was at this party, as Heaney recounted in his *Field Work* poem "A Postcard from North Antrim," that he put his arm around Marie for the first time, and Armstrong shouted a line from a rugby song, "Oh, Sir Jasper, do not touch me!" They must have laughed, since the song's refrain refers to a woman who "lay between the lily-white sheets with nothing on at all." Written fifteen years after the party, "A Postcard" tells how Armstrong left Belfast for Sausalito, a bohemian city near San Francisco, and returned to do social work. (He worked for Voluntary Services International.) His efforts to live up to the city's motto about gift-giving, as Heaney noted in his elegy, were cut short. In 1973, a week after Armstrong's wedding, an unknown assailant who objected to Armstrong's willingness to cross Belfast's sectarian boundaries fatally shot him in his apartment. Heaney's elegy casts Armstrong as another Christ-like gift-giver who comes to a tragic end.

During the weeks following Armstrong's party, Heaney spent more time with Marie. He learned about her childhood and teen years in Ardboe, a fishing and farming village in the townland of Muinterevlin (the name derives from Gaelic words meaning "the height of cows") on the western shore of Lough Neagh about fifteen miles south of Mossbawn. According to her sister Polly, who wrote about the Devlin family in *All of Us There*, Marie (she is "Eiram" in the memoir, which is "Marie" spelled backward) was "a true Celt with her thin skin and fine features, her shining hair high-lighted with red gleams and her frisky, athletic body."[13] Heaney was attracted to her energy, beauty, and intelligence, and they soon fell in love.

Heaney admired Marie's attitudes toward sectarian issues, too. She had adopted the ecumenical outlook of her paternal grandfather, who'd married a woman of Scottish Presbyterian descent. As Polly remarked in her memoir, "The atmosphere in our home was particularly free from the taint of bigotry and prejudice which so poisoned and continues to poison much of life in Northern Ireland. In fact there was a long tradition of tolerance in both our parents' families, stretching back 150 years." Confronted with the biases of the status quo, Marie displayed "brave defiance." Yet, as Polly observed, Marie's "wild courage [was] mixed with great timidity."[14] Heaney's temperament was similar. He could confront troublesome situations bravely, but at other times he withdrew from them in silence.

Both of Marie's parents had steady jobs. Her mother was a schoolteacher, even though women during Ireland's prefeminist era were expected to be homemakers. Mrs. Devlin, in fact, scandalized some members of her community by driving a car when women rarely drove. Marie's gregarious, athletic father was more traditional. He ran a pub, which made it possible for his children to live in relative comfort. Although few local girls went to secondary school after primary school, Marie and her sisters attended convent schools as boarders or day students. Marie's enterprising paternal grandfather was partly responsible for the family's middle-class circumstances. He had worked as a magistrate and built a two-story Edwardian house that was the largest in the townland. His property, with its pleasant gardens and orchards, was the envy of Ardboe residents. Marie may have had bouts of timidity, but her family helped her gain the confidence she needed to succeed. After she completed her teacher-training program at St. Mary's, she took a job at St. Colmcille's High School in Crossgar, a small town south of Belfast.

Heaney's metamorphosis from Incertus and "ex-poet" to a confident craftsman was accelerated by his relationship with Marie and his breakup with his former girlfriend. "There was definitely a new charge, a quicker flow," he said about this period. "Everything happened quickly and at the same time—the development of our relationship, the entry into poetry, the marriage itself. Inside three years. One excitement quickening the other."[15] Whether she wanted to or not, Marie became Heaney's muse. As he told Suzanne Lowry, who wrote a profile of him for the *Belfast Telegraph* in 1968, "Writing requires courage—it's a terribly arrogant act to set down your own secret convictions as relevant to public attention."[16] Marie helped provide that necessary courage.

Heaney's talent as a poet led some, including Marie, to suppose that he'd always been self-assured. Marie told Polly that she was surprised that he did not share the Devlins' insecurities and angst: "I couldn't believe it when, after I had grown up, I discovered my husband didn't have this sense of loss, this feeling of being left behind. He thinks if a place is empty then he's the first there. That magical ring of confidence, that confidence in yourself and your own senses eluded us, eluded all our family." Marie traced Heaney's confidence back to his family, which she said "was utterly together, like an egg contained within the shell, without any quality of otherness, without the sense of loss that this otherness brings. They had confidence in the way they lived, a lovely impeccable confidence in their own style."[17] Like all writers, though, Heaney frequently suffered from a sense of loss and self-doubt. Even after winning the Nobel Prize and countless other honors, he admitted, "There's a residual Incertus at work in every poem I write."[18]

If Marie propelled Heaney's transition from Incertus to Certus, Ted Hughes played a subsidiary role that was almost as important. On May 24, 1979, Heaney acknowledged in a letter to Hughes, "Since I opened *Lupercal* in the Belfast Public Library in November 1962, the lifeline to Hughesville has been in its emergent differing ways a confirmation."[19] For a Catholic like Heaney, "confirmation" had a special significance. Primarily, it referred to the sacred rite when a young person received the seven gifts of the Holy Spirit and became a new member of the Church. During the rite, a bishop implores the Holy Spirit to bestow "the spirit of wisdom and understanding, the spirit of right judgment and courage, the spirit of knowledge and reverence, [and] the spirit of wonder and awe." After making a cross with chrism (perfumed oil) on the forehead of the initiate, the bishop says, "Be sealed with the gift of the Holy Spirit." Finally, the bishop addresses the congregation: "God, our Father, complete the work you have begun and keep the gifts of your Holy Spirit active in the hearts of your people."[20] As a writer, Heaney interpreted the confirmation rite the way Joyce did in *A Portrait of the Artist as a Young Man*. There, Stephen Dedalus prays "that one of the seven gifts of the Holy Ghost might descend upon his soul."[21] For Heaney, Hughes as well as Joyce became confirming gift-givers.

About four decades after reading *Lupercal* in the Belfast Library, Heaney said he still relished the way Hughes had "plugged into the power-point of Hopkins and was giving out the live energy."[22] His view of Hughes as a ritualistic energizer was encouraged by the book's title poem "Lupercalia," which alluded to a ritual in ancient Rome designed to provide gifts of reproductive energy to local women. In February, young Roman priests known as *luperci* (brothers of the wolf) sacrificed dogs and goats to a fertility goddess, Februus, and ran naked or half-naked through the streets, hitting women with thongs called *februa* that had been cut from the skins of the sacrificed animals. The flagellation was supposed to pass on the goddess's gift of fertility to nubile women and make childbirth easier. Hughes ended "Lupercalia" with a priestly prayer: "Maker of the world, /. . . . Touch this frozen one." The mythic gift exchange at the heart of *Lupercal* as well as the evocative poems about animals and natural landscapes had an immediate appeal for Heaney.

One of Heaney's many testimonials for Hughes, "On His Work in the English Tongue" in *Electric Light,* portrays Hughes as a godlike maker and redeemer who helped Heaney unify his disparate selves. Like the bridge over two railway lines in Anahorish that the poem alludes to, Hughes was essentially a bridge that allowed Heaney to connect his Belfast self and Mossbawn self, British-Protestant culture and Irish-Catholic culture, Anglo-Saxon alliterative verse and post-Chaucerian metrical verse, rural Ulster dialect and official British English. "On His Work" claims that when Heaney left the Belfast Library after reading *Lupercal,* he "felt like one come out of an upper room / To fret no more and walk abroad confirmed." The "upper room" of the library reminded Heaney of the biblical site where Jesus gave the symbolic gifts of his body and blood to his disciples. Heaney felt he'd received similar spiritual gifts from Hughes.

In 1963, Heaney had every reason to believe his life was on the sort of "shining" track he describes beneath the railway bridge in his poem for Hughes. He was in love and he was publishing poetry in national journals. In November 1962, "Tractors" had appeared in the *Belfast Telegraph;* a month later the same newspaper printed "Turkeys Observed." Before long, he published "Mid-Term Break" in the *Kilkenny Magazine,* "An Advancement of Learning" in the *Irish Times,* and "Essences" as well as "Welfare State" in the Queen's magazine *Interest.* As his reputation grew, so did his job prospects. Inspector of Schools John Ferguson told the British poet and Queen's professor Philip Hobsbaum, "The news of this man's teaching went far and wide. I had to haul him out of the school and make him an extra at St Joseph's College to teach the other teachers how to teach."[23] Tired of putting up with unruly teenagers and grading their countless exercise books at St. Thomas's, Heaney appreciated the opportunity to teach Shakespeare and Romantic writers at St. Joseph's, and he was even happier in 1966 to be offered a position as a lecturer at Queen's.

## THE BELFAST GROUP

Another person who was instrumental in "confirming" Heaney in the early 1960s was Philip Hobsbaum. Having grown up in a Jewish family in Yorkshire and studied at Cambridge University with the combative defender of English culture F. R. Leavis, and later with the scholarly poet-critic William Empson at Sheffield University, Hobsbaum was an unlikely mentor. Firmly entrenched in the English poetry scene, he'd organized literary soirées as an undergraduate at Downing College, Cambridge, and a well-respected poetry workshop in London when he took a teaching job there in 1955. Over the next four years, as the leader of "The Group" workshop, he invited talented writers to discuss their work at weekly meetings. Peter Redgrove (a former member of the Cambridge group), Edward Lucie-Smith, Peter Porter, George MacBeth, and Alan Brownjohn were regulars. Ted Hughes made several memorable appearances. The writing in London produced under Hobsbaum's aegis drew attention from publishers such as Oxford University Press, which published poems from his workshop in *A Group Anthology* in 1963.

One of the first readers to look closely at this anthology was Heaney. He wrote one review, "In Print," for the May 1963 issue of *Interest,* and another review, "Poetry from a Co-operative Society," for the September 1963 issue of *Hibernia.* The first review expressed skepticism about the viability of a Group workshop in Belfast, but the second review was more sanguine, even though it criticized the poets Hobsbaum promoted in the anthology for being infatuated with "a world whose god is Godot, whose scriptures are *Private Eye* and *The Observer,* [and] whose weekly worship is convened to the notes of a jazz-band or a TV commercial." His reservations notwithstanding, Heaney now welcomed the possibility of a workshop on Irish soil: "If there was a Group in Belfast, Dublin, Cork and Galway, our young poets would find it easier to meet an audience; beginners would have the benefit of criticism from the established and above all, interest should increase."[24] Heaney's hope for an Irish Group would come to fruition two months after the publication of his review.

In an attempt to recruit new talent in the early 1960s, Queen's University had lured Hobsbaum from London to Belfast. Heaney heard from the editor of *Interest,* Alan Gabbey, that Hobsbaum had accepted a lectureship at Queen's in 1962, and decided to meet him. Hobsbaum, in fact, was already aware of Heaney; he'd read the Hopkinsesque "October Thought" in Q; the recent poems in the *Belfast Telegraph, Kilkenny Magazine, Interest,* and *Irish Times*; and the review of *A Group Anthology* in *Interest.* Convinced that Heaney had great literary potential, Hobsbaum invited him to his flat in the spring of 1963. On a sunny Saturday morning, Heaney and Marie made their first visit to 5 Fitzwilliam Street, about a mile southwest of Queen's. "He seemed incredibly pleased to be noticed," Hobsbaum said of Heaney. "He kept grinning, a trait I didn't quite understand at the time, but I think it was in pleasure at being recognized."[25] Heaney was, indeed, pleased to be "noticed" by such a well-connected writer as Hobsbaum.

Hobsbaum formed a Belfast Group partly because he missed the camaraderie of his London Group. He also felt that Belfast needed an infusion of literary energy. Hobsbaum first spoke about a possible Group to Edna Broderick, who taught English at Queen's. He conferred with Stewart Parker, a graduate student. Warned that Catholics and Protestants would probably refuse to work together, Hobsbaum set about proving the pessimists wrong by welcoming the Anglican Broderick, the Protestant Parker, and the Catholic Heaney to his first workshops. Because of his Jewish roots, Hobsbaum was sensitive to religious prejudice and had a cosmopolitan outlook. "I've got double vision," he once said. "I never lose a sense of myself as a foreigner, as an alien."[26] He quickly disabused those in Belfast who assumed he'd be a single-minded partisan for British culture.

The Belfast Group convened in the sitting room of Hobsbaum's flat on a Tuesday evening in October 1963. (The meeting time eventually changed to Mondays.) Writers in various genres came, but poets took precedence. Among the workshop participants were the poet-songwriter James Simmons, civil servant and poet Joan Watton, Catalan language scholar Arthur Terry, and Queen's English Department chair W. J. Harvey. The secretary of the English Department along with Hobsbaum's first wife, Hannah Kelly, who'd been a member of the London Group, generously typed the poems and stories, and circulated copies before the workshops so everyone could prepare comments.

Parker began the Group meetings, often struggling to stand on his prosthetic leg to read his work. (His left leg had been amputated because of bone cancer when he was twenty.) "Once the meeting started," Heaney recalled, "[Hobsbaum] hunched forward like a man on a Harley Davidson coming down the road at ninety."[27] He and the others "workshopped" manuscripts for an hour or an hour and a half, then took a break for coffee and biscuits. After the intermission, poets read their favorite poems, and more discussion followed. By midnight, the room was thick with cigarette smoke. Hobsbaum, still glaring behind his thick glasses, ended the meeting by selecting a writer's work to discuss the following week.

Heaney flourished in the contentious environment of the workshops. Although Queen's colleagues told Hobsbaum that Heaney "had been thought by the University staff to be a relatively slight figure in comparison with the other first-class students," Hobsbaum quickly realized this assessment was wrong.[28] In November 1964, he wrote Lucie-Smith: "Seamus Heaney has just given me a most stupendous collection of poems. . . . I think that this will be his *annus mirabilis*."[29] Others outside the Group also recognized Heaney's talent. The poet Norman Dugdale remembered one night in 1964 when Heaney read poems he would later collect in *Death of a Naturalist*: "There was hardly a spare inch of space left in the living room. . . . I insinuated myself into this throng as best I could. Then a tall, well-built, personable young man, neatly dressed in sports jacket and flannels, Clydella shirt and tie, with short, jet-black hair, a long upper lip, and twinkly, small, intelligent eyes read his poems." Dugdale concluded that the young man was not simply a "promising beginner but . . . a potential master."[30]

Over the four years Heaney participated in the Belfast Group, he proved to be the most prolific and most accomplished poet, contributing forty-nine poems that were printed on seven worksheets and discussed on seven different nights. Heaney worried, though, that he was less sophisticated than Michael Longley and Derek Mahon. "They had an elegance, they had a self-confidence, they had met Louis MacNeice and W. R. Rodgers, they read contemporary poetry, they had collected slim volumes," he remarked years later. "I didn't have any of that at all." Hobsbaum did his best to assuage Heaney's concerns and convince him to have faith in his poetic gift. "Philip Hobsbaum was really the one who gave me the trust in what I was doing and he urged me to send poems out," he said.[31]

One of the poems Heaney submitted to a Group meeting in April 1965, "Boy Driving His Father to Confession," suggested that he was moving away from his family's Catholicism as he developed faith in himself as a poet and in poetry as an alternative religion. The poem associates his biological father with a divine father he can no longer communicate with in a meaningful way. His question "Does the same hectic rage in our one blood?" implies that his difficulties with his father and his father's Catholic beliefs are akin to the conflicts between Hamlet and his stepfather, King Claudius. Claudius says of Hamlet, "For like the hectic in my blood he rages" (act 4, scene 3, line 68). The king thinks—and hopes—that this "hectic" will end if Hamlet dies, and he wants Hamlet to die soon. Heaney was no raging Hamlet, but in his confessional poem he appears to rebel against both his father and his father's traditional ways of worshipping a patriarchal God. Patrick Heaney confesses his sins to a priest in church, while Heaney stays in the car and eventually confesses his troubled feelings in a poem.

As Heaney distanced himself from his father and his father's faith, he came to think of Hobsbaum as a substitute father. "He was impatient, dogmatic, relentlessly literary," Heaney admitted. "[Yet] he was patient with those he trusted, unpredictably susceptible to a wide variety of poems and personalities and urgent that the social and political exacerbations of our place should disrupt the decorums of literature. If he drove some people mad with his absolutes and hurt others with his overbearing, he confirmed as many with his enthusiasms. . . . I remember his hospitality and encouragement with the special gratitude we reserve for those who have led us towards confidence in ourselves."[32] As with Hughes, Heaney used religious terms such as "confirmed" to praise his mentor. Hobsbaum's "enthusiasms" (from the Greek *en theos*, meaning "inner god" or "inner spirit") were meant to in-spirit those like Heaney with poetic gifts.

Part of Hobsbaum's mission was to get Group members to write about the problems of Ulster. According to Joan Newmann, he intended his workshop to be a model for the way the larger community could resolve sectarian disagreements. "There was no need for the sublimation of differences—educational, class, political, gender or religious," she claimed, because these differences were addressed at Group meetings.[33] The scholar Heather Clark agreed with this assessment in her book *The Ulster Renaissance*: "Hobsbaum's Group was one of the few places in Belfast—perhaps the only place—where these writers felt free to voice social grievances and to explore the complexities of cultural identity."[34] Under Hobsbaum's supervision, Heaney felt emboldened to articulate his personal and political views. In some of the poems he wrote for the workshop, such as "Orange Drums, Tyrone, 1966" and "Requiem for the

Irish Rebels (Wexford, 1798)" (later titled "Requiem for the Croppies"), he voiced his disdain for those who had brutalized Ireland's Catholic population over the centuries. When he later praised the Group for inaugurating "a new political condition,"[35] he was thinking of the workshop as a paradigm of enlightened activity that might replace Northern Ireland's stultifying bigotry.

In many ways, the Group lived up to Hobsbaum's ideals. The Protestant poet Michael Longley once said that he had no close Catholic friends before meeting Seamus Heaney and Marie Devlin at Hobsbaum's flat. Longley's sense of cultural isolation and confusion contributed to his sense of kinship with Heaney. "From an early age," Longley admitted, "I drifted between Englishness and Irishness, between town and country." His English parents had moved to Belfast in the 1920s and remained proud of their English heritage. Longley was especially drawn to his father's British military service, but as soon as he left his British home, he felt pressure to conform to the working-class street culture of his Belfast school friends. At Trinity College, Dublin, in the late 1950s and early 1960s, he and Derek Mahon experienced the British-Irish schism all over again when they met those he called "upper-class [British] twits."[36] Forty percent of Trinity's students were English, and the others were predominantly Irish Catholics. When Longley graduated with a B.A. in classics in 1963 and began teaching in Belfast schools, the rancor between British and Irish factions only worsened.

The friendship between Heaney and Longley, and the friendships between other members of the Group, were not always free of the tensions in the larger community. Derek Mahon spoke for a number of Heaney's rivals in a letter to Longley when he said he was jealous of Heaney's reputation, which had been bolstered by Hobsbaum's literary contacts. Longley resented Heaney's popularity, too, and sometimes insulted him to his face. During their first conversation, Longley told Heaney he was "just another stage Irishman."[37] Heaney tried to disarm his potential foe with compliments about his poetry. The two men, in the end, became friends. Heaney attended the Longleys' wedding at Dalkey Church on December 28, 1964, and he took weekend trips with Longley and his wife in a Volkswagen "bug" he'd bought for his work at St. Joseph's. Occasionally, Marie joined them, singing Cole Porter songs and Irish ballads in between discussions of history, literature, and politics. Sometimes these excursions worked their way into poems. After driving around the Ards Peninsula southeast of Belfast, Heaney wrote "The Peninsula," which treats the trip as another monomythical journey away from home into a dark night that concludes with a return with the "boon" of lessons learned about writing poetry that is both meditative and realistic.

Longley enjoyed Heaney's company, but continued to bristle at what he considered to be Hobsbaum's favoritism at Group meetings. He acknowledged that he and his teacher had different aesthetic tastes. Longley preferred poetry that was "polished, metrical, and rhymed; oblique rather than head-on; imagistic and symbolic rather than rawly factual; rhetorical rather than documentary."[38] Hobsbaum preferred poetry that was rougher and more confessional. Stung by Hobsbaum's constant criticism, Longley pretended to ignore it. "I can honestly say that I didn't alter one semi-colon as the result of Group discussion," he claimed.[39] In fact, he did revise some of his poems, as Group worksheets prove, but only grudgingly. And in the late 1960s, he welcomed Hobsbaum's efforts to convince Macmillan to publish his first book, *No Continuing City*.

Heaney's Group sheets paint a complex portrait of their author. If he was a hard-nosed Hemingwayesque pugilist in "Ex-Champ," he was an idealistic Catholic nature-lover in "Saint Francis and the Birds." In other poems, he portrayed himself as a Darwinian naturalist who believed humans and animals displayed as much pride, lust, anger, greed, and gluttony as allegorical figures in medieval morality plays. On the same April night in 1965 that he presented his poem about St. Francis, he read "On Hogarth's Engraving 'Pit Ticket for the Royal Sport,'" a poem based on a parody of Leonardo da Vinci's *The Last Supper*. The MacKenna figure in the poem demonstrates the same vulgar lust for violence as Hogarth's English cock-fighters. "Death of a Naturalist" addresses the twin subjects of masculine sex and violence, too. Workshopped by the Group in the fall of 1964 and first published in *Poetry Ireland* as "End of a Naturalist," the poem views human instincts for sex and survival through a Darwinian lens.

Heaney considered "Death of a Naturalist" to be one of the first poems in which he brought his narrative and lyrical gifts to fruition. The poem, in fact, had come to him as an unexpected gift while he was sunbathing with Marie by some garbage bins behind her Belfast flat. The smell of rotting garbage conjured up memories of rotting flax in ponds near Mossbawn as well as the sectarian rot that "festered in the heart / Of the townland." Ted Hughes, who often compared violence in nature to violence in society, was another catalyst for the poem. Robert Lowell was an influence, too. Heaney's review of Lowell's *For the Union Dead*, which he published the same year he wrote "Death of a Naturalist," comments on Lowell's attempts to contain "the painful, disorderly, and terrifying side" of human experience. Lowell's imagination works like "a pressure cylinder where the piston is relentlessly descending," Heaney points out, and Lowell's poems are like "valves" that release the pent-up pressure. Switching metaphors, Heaney also suggests that Lowell's mind resembles the sort of festering "flax-dam" in "Death of a Naturalist," but one in which "the dykes of detachment are burst" and both poet and reader are "in danger of being overwhelmed."[40] In his own poetry, Heaney was determined to keep the pressure cylinders and dykes intact.

The "death" Heaney alludes to in "Death of a Naturalist" resembles the death Lowell laments in his title poem "For the Union Dead." Lowell reminisces nostalgically about going to the Boston aquarium as a child and watching the fish with his nose pressed against the glass. To the older Lowell, the aquarium represents an Edenic ecosystem and a stable, productive mind that have broken down. According to Lowell's apocalyptic vision, "the dark downward and vegetating kingdom / of the fish and reptile," which was once contained by the aquarium's walls, has broken out and invaded Boston like a conquering army. Heaney's fable about frogs is similarly apocalyptic, although in his historical narrative the violent, obscene "slime kings" resemble British kings that have invaded a bucolic landscape in Northern Ireland.

Heaney's aquarium in "Death of a Naturalist" differs from Lowell's in being more humble and domestic: it consists of "jampotfulls of the jellied / Specks" of frog-spawn arranged on windowsills at home and at school. Nevertheless, Heaney's reptilian life undergoes the same disturbing evolution as Lowell's "vegetating kingdom / of the fish and reptile." Once Heaney's spawn leaves the jam pots, the eggs inevitably metamorphose into tadpoles and bullfrogs. "Cocked / On sods," Heaney's big frogs seem to weaponize their sexual organs; they look like "mud grenades" about to explode. ("Prospero in Agony" deploys a similar grenade metaphor when it compares Lowell's "highly charged and controlled" poetry to "a grenade before the pin is pulled.")[41] The "jampot" in "Death of a Naturalist" could be another metaphor for potentially explosive violence. During World War I, soldiers packed jam pots and jam tins with explosives and used them as makeshift grenades or mortar shells. Sometimes empty cans of Nestlé's condensed milk, which could have been produced in the factory near Mossbawn, were turned into grenades. Heaney's journey to and back from a flax pond in "Death of a Naturalist" once again follows the three-part pattern of the "monomyth." In this case, though, after the departure from home and initiation into an otherworld of sex and violence, the only boon the youthful questor brings home is a new understanding of his vulnerability in a dangerous world.

Hobsbaum's Group workshops could be antagonistic, but they spurred Heaney to overcome his youthful fears and uncertainties and showed him how he and his peers could transcend at least some of Ulster's ethnic divisions. Hobsbaum also initiated Heaney into the world of poetry readings and publications. He invited Heaney to read with Stewart Parker, Hugh Bredin, Joan Watton, and John Bond at the Irish PEN meeting in Belfast's International Hotel on May 7, 1964. He made it possible for Heaney to lecture on Corkery's *Hidden Ireland* at Belfast's Festival of the Arts in 1964. He recommended that the Belfast office of the BBC broadcast Heaney's poems. At the end of 1964, he tried to convince Oxford University Press and Macmillan to publish Heaney's first book. He selected Heaney's "Scaffolding" and "Soliloquy for an Old Resident" for P. L. Brent's anthology *Young Commonwealth Poets*, which Heinemann published in 1965. (The book was distributed in Australia, Canada, and other British Commonwealth nations.) In 1964, after Hobsbaum introduced his London friend Lucie-Smith to Heaney at a dinner party in his Fitzwilliam Street flat, Lucie-Smith gave a sheaf of Heaney's poems to Karl Miller, the Scottish-born poetry editor of the *New Statesman*. Heaney had repeatedly submitted poems to the well-known London journal and another leading English journal, the *Listener*, but they'd all been rejected. Prodded by Lucie-Smith, Miller wrote Heaney a letter on November 25, 1964, accepting "Digging," "Scaffolding," and "Storm on the Island." Miller phoned Heaney at St. Joseph's to congratulate him on his success, which would lead to many more publications in London journals. As Heaney knew, Hobsbaum was the main reason this success came when it did.

### GIFTS FROM FABER

Charles Monteith, who had grown up in Ulster and studied at Oxford before working as an editor at Faber and Faber under T. S. Eliot, was impressed by Heaney's poems in the December 4, 1964, issue of the *New Statesman*. Shortly afterward, he asked Heaney if he had a book manuscript that Faber could consider for publication. "I just couldn't believe it," Heaney said after getting the query from Faber. "It was like getting a letter from God the Father."[42] In the past, Faber had favored Ulster Protestant writers like MacNeice. Monteith was himself a Protestant with Unionist connections, although his tastes were eclectic. Thrilled by his letter, Heaney gathered his best poems and sent them to Monteith.

Faber's interest in his poetry, while flattering, put Heaney in an ethical bind. He had already submitted a collection of poems to the Dolmen Press in Dublin, which had an excellent reputation: it published prominent Irish poets such as Thomas Kinsella and Austin Clarke, and its books were distributed around the world by Oxford University Press. A less distinguished company, MacGibbon and Kee, had also asked to see Heaney's manuscript. Luckily, Dolmen rejected the manuscript he'd sent under the title *An Advancement of Learning,* and Monteith accepted it with the stipulation that Heaney expand it. (Heaney would add "Blackberry-Picking," "Follower," "Barn," "Churning Day," "At a Potato Digging," "Personal Helicon," and several other poems.) At the beginning of 1966, Oxford University Press in New York issued a contract for the American edition of the book that now had the title *Death of a Naturalist.* Heaney later said he felt "steeped in luck"[43] and blessed with a "sense of change and gift"[44] when his first book was accepted. Since Hobsbaum had nurtured his gift and brought it to the attention of publishers, Heaney brought him a half bottle of whiskey as a sign of gratitude. Hobsbaum complimented Heaney on his good judgment, noting that if he'd brought a full bottle, they both would have gotten roaring drunk.

During the summer of 1965, Heaney had other reasons to be thankful:

he'd been engaged to Marie since the previous Christmas, and on August 5, 1965, they got married. A boisterous wedding reception at Drumsill House, an attractive eighteenth-century mansion surrounded by a park near Lough Neagh, followed the ceremony. Heaney was deeply in love with Marie, but he worried about the effect his marriage would have on his family, especially his close relationship with his mother. In his early poem "Wedding Day," he portrays himself as an Oedipal son who wants his wife to act as a comforting mother after he leaves his real mother and the rest of his family and friends behind. The companion poem in *Wintering Out,* "Mother of the Groom," underscores the close bond between mother and son that marriage threatens to sever. The mother in the poem remembers her son as a naked boy in the bath and regrets she can no longer hold him in her lap. Rather than welcome her daughter-in-law into the family, she complains that her son has left for another woman. The mother tries to be polite at the wedding, but her mind dwells on past occasions when she took off her wedding ring—the symbol of her attachment to her husband—and enjoyed the intimacy of bathing her naked son.

Like the London-bound Philip Larkin in "The Whitsun Weddings," another poem expressing ambivalence toward marriage, Heaney traveled to the English capital after his wedding. As it turned out, on the first day of his honeymoon—August 6, 1965—he met Larkin in his editor's office at Faber. The two poets shook hands, and then Larkin had afternoon tea with Monteith. According to Heaney, Larkin told their mutual editor "that young poets were now getting things far too easy, being published by Faber and at the same time marrying good looking young women."[45] Larkin and Heaney would meet on several occasions over the next two decades, and Larkin's jealousy of the younger poet would grow to the point where he denigrated Heaney as an untalented "gombeen man."[46] As well as mischaracterizing him as a village hustler out to make a quick profit at other people's expense, Larkin mischaracterized Heaney's poetry as unmusical, superficial, and overly erudite. Heaney's reaction to his embittered opponent was typically judicious: he recognized Larkin's flaws while praising his "abundant poetic gifts."[47]

Heaney also tried to be judicious with Monteith, even when his editor flaunted the same sort of bias against Irish Catholics as Larkin. While much of Heaney's first meeting on August 6 focused on Faber's publishing plans for *Death of a Naturalist,* his conversation with Monteith took an unexpected turn when Monteith seemed to praise Belfast's recent "Orangemen's Day" celebrations. Heaney admitted that he'd been in Belfast on July 12, the day local Protestants showed their loyalty to Britain with parades, bonfires, and other activities designed to antagonize Catholics. "Fine old folk festival," Monteith commented. "To some people," Heaney shot back.[48]

Heaney's postwedding fears of being cut off from his family and homeland were compounded by his fear of flying. "Honeymoon Flight" in *Death of a Naturalist* records his emotional state during his first time in a plane: "The sure green world goes topsy-turvy / As we climb out of our familiar landscape" and "air-pockets jolt our fears." Heaney was crossing another shadow-line, and both he and Marie felt "lost." His poem ends, "Travellers, at this point, can only trust." As with his difficult boundary-crossings in the past, Heaney received gifts (in this case, wedding presents) during his rite of passage and knew he had to trust his own gift for turning difficult experiences into redemptive poems.

Anxieties about his new marital status must have abated when invitations to read or publish his poetry arrived after his wedding. On August 12, 1965, Jack Sweeney, the curator of Harvard's Poetry Room, asked Heaney to record some of his poems for the library. Two weeks later, Friar Denis Hickey invited him to teach an "Appreciation of Literature" course at the Servite Priory in County Tyrone. The BBC Schools Program and Belfast Festival of the Arts requested that he read and talk about his poetry in November 1965. A young Englishman, Michael Emmerson, who'd stayed in Belfast after graduating from Queen's, was eager to publish a poetry chapbook by Heaney and to work with him on expanding the arts festival into a two-week affair at the end of each November. Emmerson began publishing pamphlets by Heaney, Longley, Mahon, and other talented Ulster poets to draw attention to the festival. Heaney's first significant publication, *Eleven Poems,* coincided with the festival in 1965. The English scholar and critic John Carey, having read the pamphlet, gave Heaney's reputation a boost in the *New Statesman* when he called some of the poems "masterly."[49] An *Observer* article about the festival in 1966 proclaimed excitedly that the city was "on the verge of a cultural utopia," and announced that the "newest star" was Heaney.[50]

Emmerson had a knack for finding and promoting world-class artists. At the Belfast Festival in 1966, he organized a concert by folk legend Pete Seeger, a production of Edward Albee's *Who's Afraid of Virginia Woolf?,* a reading of *The Autobiography of Malcolm X* by Alex Haley, and a lecture by Heaney and the American poet Daniel Hoffman. Rae Rosenfield announced in the journal *Hibernia* that Heaney had taken a sudden "leap . . . to fame" after the publication of *Eleven Poems.*[51] In 1967, Heaney joined the festival's lineup again, this time with rock superstars Jimi Hendrix and Pink Floyd. Other notable musicians and actors, from Ravi Shankar to Laurence Olivier and Billy Connolly, also graced the stage at the festival over the years. Heaney's dream of a cultural renaissance in Northern Ireland had become a reality, and the consensus was that he was playing a central role in it.

# 7

# Marriage and First Books

When Faber mailed Heaney his author's copies of *Death of a Naturalist* in the spring of 1966, he was startled to see his name on the dust jacket with such illustrious names as Auden, Eliot, Hughes, Larkin, Lowell, Mac-Neice, and Spender. The critical reaction to his book and the repeated references to his early life on a farm made him acutely self-conscious, too. At times, he found it hard to believe he was a farmer's son who'd become a Faber author. "The autobiographical creature begins to be implicated in the textual masquerade; you begin to read and hear about this composite who has written the book . . . [and who] sounds very like yourself, although there's always going to be a certain stand-off between the pair of you," he quipped,[1] perhaps thinking of Rimbaud's comment "Je suis un autre" (I is an other).[2] Heaney felt he had two principal selves now— the pre-Faber self and the post-Faber self. He was still the hardworking Irish-Catholic youth preoccupied with gifts rooted in his family's hearth culture, but he was also the adult poet in the Faber pantheon who, as Auden wrote in his elegy for Yeats, was being "modified in the guts of the living [readers]" and, at least in some cases, "punished under a foreign code of conscience."

To the Irish poet Padraic Fiacc, who asked what it felt like to be published by Faber, Heaney replied, "I feel I'll have to pay."[3] It was as if he'd suddenly entered a new social class and realized that life would now be more expensive. "There was obviously great fortification in what had happened," he said.[4] Nevertheless, he worried that his new gains would be offset by future losses. A number of his marriage poems in *Death of a Naturalist* dramatize his anxieties about pursuing an ambitious literary career where he might "have to pay."

In "Poem," which he dedicated to Marie when she was pregnant with their first child, Heaney stated his commitment to the sort of traditional family life that he had enjoyed at Mossbawn and that, to a certain extent, was at odds with his new life as a Faber poet. The poem begins with a promise to try to unify these two lives: "Love, I shall perfect for you the child / Who diligently potters in my brain." He conceives of his poem as an embryonic child gestating in his womb-like imagination, and he vows to deliver it to his wife as a "perfected" gift. In exchange, he asks her to "perfect" the child growing in her womb. From Heaney's androgynous perspective, both husband and wife have gift-creating and gift-giving wombs. Heaney, though, asks for more than just the delivery of a child: "Within new limits now, arrange the world / Within our walls, within our golden ring." He wants his wife to be a muse who enables him to "perfect" (from the Latin *per-facere*, to "completely make") his poems, and he also wants her to create an orderly "world" for him and the rest of the family at home. In other words, he expects her to be a "home-maker," "poem-maker," and "child-maker." Marie, in fact, delivered a healthy boy, Michael, in July 1966, assisted Heaney with his poems, and provided a stable home for a family that would eventually include three children.

Heaney's other early marriage poems, such as "Scaffolding" and "Storm on the Island," are as preoccupied with creating different forms of art and life "within limits" as Robert Frost was in his famous poem "Mending Wall." Like Frost, Heaney debated whether limits and walls were necessary ("Good fences make good neighbors") or unnecessary ("Something there is that doesn't love a wall"), and wondered about what he was "walling in or walling out." At the end of "Scaffolding," Heaney tells his wife, "We may let the scaffolds fall / Confident that we have built our walls." One kind of wall—the scaffolding—comes down, but only because another wall has been erected. In this case, walls seem necessary. The next poem in *Death of a Naturalist*, "Storm on the Island," portrays a married couple that values walls. They are "bombarded" by wind and rain, so they need "walls in rock" to remain safe and productive. Without the protection of walls, they would be as vulnerable to the destructive elements as the island's "wizened earth." Throughout his life, Heaney was highly sensitive to forces that threatened womb-like fortifications like his original "bawn," partly because Mossbawn came to represent a space that was conducive to domestic and spiritual gift exchanges.

As a Catholic from rural Northern Ireland publishing a book in London, Heaney had good reasons to suspect he'd "have to pay" for his success and that he'd need a safe zone behind walls. Michael Longley had already attacked some of the best poems in the book, such as "Digging" and "Death of a Naturalist," because he thought they were too "basic."[5] Other critics echoed Longley's remarks. Barbara Gibbs in the English journal *Strand* contended that the poems in Heaney's book were unoriginal. Howard Sergeant in *English* complained they were uneven, and James Reed in *The Use of English* said they were prosaic. Denis Donoghue in *Encounter*, a London journal funded by the CIA, belittled *Death of a Naturalist* as apprentice work. One of the most unsympathetic notices came from Peter Marsh in the *Observer*, a newspaper headquartered in London. Marsh dismissed the book as "strangely featureless" and "deeply mannered."[6] In the influential English journal *The Review*, Giles Sadler went further, mocking Heaney's poems for their "failure to get off the ground," and comparing Heaney to Worzel Gummidge, the children's-book scarecrow who changed his heads (usually made from turnips) to fit different occasions. As if those insults weren't enough, Sadler likened Heaney to a clumsy diver who indulged in "tremendous posing and limbering on the high-board" before launching himself into the air and hitting the pool in "a bad belly-flop."[7]

Heaney was especially angered by Sadler's reference to his "mud-caked fingers in Russell Square," which was Faber's London address.[8] According to Sadler, Heaney was an ill-bred farmer whose poorly crafted poems besmirched Faber's reputation. The insult was typical of those aimed at rural Irish Catholics by urban British Protestants. Heaney would soon discover that Sadler and Marsh were pseudonyms used by Ian Hamilton, the well-known English poet, editor of a prestigious journal, *The Review*, and future biographer of Robert Lowell and J. D. Salinger. Hamilton liked to write nasty reviews of writers whose talent he envied. His first magazine was aptly called *The Scorpion*.

Fortunately, some reviewers recognized the artistry and humanity in *Death of a Naturalist*. Irish poets such as John Hewitt, Brendan Kennelly, and Austin Clarke hailed the book as a triumph. A few important English critics were similarly enthusiastic. C. B. Cox, a poet and cofounder of *Critical Quarterly,* wrote in the *Spectator,* "[*Death of a Naturalist* is] the best first book of poems I've read for some time."[9] The most astute review came from the scholar Christopher Ricks, who dismissed Heaney's detractors with suitable hauteur: "Literary gentlemen who remain unstirred by Seamus Heaney's poems will simply be announcing that they are unable to give up the habit of disillusionment with recent poetry. The power and precision of his best poems are a delight, and as a first collection *Death of a Naturalist* is outstanding."[10] With characteristic insight, Ricks praised Heaney's poems as fables that drew parallels between the craftsmanship of poets and the craftsmanship of rural workers. In the end, the applause from Heaney's admirers drowned out the boos. The book won the coveted £1,000 Eric Gregory Award from the London's Society of Authors in the spring of 1966. It also won the Cholmondeley Award, the Somerset Maugham Award, and the first Geoffrey Faber Memorial Award, which Lady Faber, the wife of the late chairman of the publishing firm, presented to Heaney in person.

Ricks was one of the first critics to stress Wordsworth's influence on Heaney's subject matter and poetics. "Wordsworth grew up 'fostered alike by beauty and by fear,' and Mr Heaney writes with vivid strength about both,"[11] Ricks observed, alluding to Wordsworth's autobiographical epic *The Prelude, or, Growth of a Poet's Mind.* (A decade later in *North,* Heaney would quote Wordsworth's line about being fostered by beauty and fear in an epigraph to "Singing School.") *The Prelude* charts Wordsworth's obsession with past moments of inspiration that return to him as gifts. At times, he describes the process of recollection in Eucharistic terms, as if he were a priest transubstantiating memories into words for their restorative effect. He declares: "I would give, / . . . A substance and a life to what I feel: / I would enshrine the spirit of the past / For future restoration." Heaney shared Wordsworth's attitude toward recollection and his belief in "poetry as divination, poetry as revelation of the self," and poetry as in-spiriting gift. "The Diviner" in *Death of a Naturalist* presents this kind of divination in terms of a rural man using a rod to reveal the "hiding places" of water in the soil. Like the Wordsworthian poet who taps sacred moments buried in memory, the diviner specializes in tapping "secret stations" for the benefit of self and community. "You can't learn the craft of dowsing or divining," Heaney remarked in a discussion of the poem. "It is a gift for being in touch with what is there, hidden and real, a gift for mediating between the latent resource and the community."[12] Divining gifts depended on having a gift.

Wordsworth in *The Prelude* envisions the poet to be a similar kind of gifted and gift-producing diviner. He notes at the beginning of his epic that Nature—especially its sublime phenomena (awe-inspiring cataracts, lofty mountains, looming storms)—gives the mind inklings of the "first great gift, the vital spirit." This spirit appears in imaginative children and contemplative adults, as well. "With gifts," he says, the child "bubbles o'er / As generous as a fountain." Children apprehend "Nature's primitive gifts," and, if they become poets, like Wordsworth, they discover the "gift which God had placed within . . . [their] power." Wordsworth compares this divine gift to the Holy Spirit's "gift of tongues" that spoke to Jesus's apostles after He was crucified.[13] Heaney conceived of the artist's gift in a similar way.

Christopher Ricks may have been thinking of the quest for a redemptive "gift of tongues" when he noted that Robert Graves's mythopoesis had influenced *Death of a Naturalist*. Heaney had read Graves admiringly in the early 1960s, and Michael Longley had often recited Graves's poetry when they socialized. Longley was particularly fond of Graves's poem "To Juan in the Winter Solstice," which begins, "There is one story and one story only, / that will prove worth your telling." If Heaney believed "one story and one story only" was worth telling, it was based on the three-stage journey of the mythical hero who, like Adam or Christ, departed from a familiar place and descended into an otherworld of trials before returning with redemptive gifts. This "monomythical" story was not immediately obvious in Heaney's early poems since they were so realistic, but the mythical structure was there like his wall in "Scaffolding."

"An Advancement of Learning," which provided the initial title for his book manuscript, is a case in point. Heaney borrowed his title from Francis Bacon's famous seventeenth-century book about empirical ways of understanding the world, and in the title poem he indicates that his "advancement" will occur when he learns how to observe rats and other natural phenomena with scientific detachment. *Death of a Naturalist* contains a bestiary of frogs, hawks, corncrakes, gulls, turkeys, and snipes that are realistically, but also symbolically, portrayed. As an innocent Catholic boy, he tended to view these animals as satanic threats. In the mythical psychodramas of his later poems, rats play a central role as avatars of evil. He sees them everywhere on the farm. Sacks of grain look like "great blind rats" in "The Barn." A "rat-gray fungus" destroys the fruit in "Blackberry-Picking." A group of "big rats" scares him in "The Early Purges." In the book's final poem, "Personal Helicon," a well is "scaresome" because a "rat slapped" across his reflection in the water. Heaney told O'Driscoll in *Stepping Stones* that he was especially scared of "Mr Rat" scratching the ceiling boards above his bed at night.[14] If his Catholic upbringing made him prone to envisioning signs of evil, it also gave him a way to transcend them. In his "Advancement of Learning," he follows the path of a Christian Everyman as well as a modern-day empiricist who advances beyond his fears and doubts.

### UNIVERSITY LECTURER AND GROUP LEADER

Publishing a book with Faber had an immediate effect on Heaney's opportunities for advancement in his academic career. After Hobsbaum accepted an offer to teach at the University of Glasgow in 1966, Heaney applied for his position at Queen's. It was unusual for someone without a master's degree or doctorate to be hired by a major university, but Heaney was a highly regarded writer in Belfast. The impression he'd made at Group workshops on Professor John Harvey, the English Department chairman, worked in his favor. Harvey told Heaney not to worry about lacking a doctorate, but advised him to bolster his résumé by publishing scholarly essays. Heaney later credited Harvey for pushing him toward literary criticism.

Queen's hired Heaney in 1966 to give the First Arts poetry lectures and teach honors students in modern literature seminars. As a lecturer in English, he covered a wide range of writers from the Elizabethans (Sir Walter Raleigh, Sir John Davies, Shakespeare) to the moderns (Hopkins, Hardy, Yeats, Frost, Edward Thomas, Wilfred Owen, MacNeice). Heaney expected to encounter an anti-Catholic backlash when he got the job without having the normal credentials, but, in general, colleagues and students accepted him. He was a diligent, conscientious, friendly teacher, often rising early in the morning to prepare for his classes. What most students failed to realize about their amiable professor was his nervousness about stepping into the classroom. The publication of *Death of a Naturalist* had dispelled some, but not all, of his Incertus anxieties.

One colleague who sympathized with Heaney's insecurities in academia was the Irishman John Cronin, who also lacked a Ph.D. Cronin, who would complete his doctorate at Queen's in 1971, had come to Belfast via the University of the Witwatersrand in Johannesburg, South Africa. "Belfast was then a dreary and dull place," he said,

> with a violent future around the corner which would alter all of our lives. I had begun to introduce, for the first time at Queen's, courses in Irish writing, necessarily masquerading under the more academically acceptable title of "Anglo-Irish," and it was obviously very helpful to have a real, recently published poet in the department. . . . At that stage, I knew . . . [Heaney] as a contributor to our newly begun M.A. in Anglo-Irish Literature and also as a near neighbor since our houses were not far apart. I used to bump into him in Mrs. Cummins's tiny sweet-shop on the Lisburn Road.[15]

During the 1960s, Cronin and Heaney would become close friends.

Students appreciated the fact that Heaney, like Cronin, taught Irish writers who for decades had been considered second-rate and off-limits by Queen's professors. Introducing Irish writers, though, wasn't easy. At a Queen's conference in 1995, Heaney said he had to petition the English Department to put Joyce's *A Portrait of the Artist as a Young Man* and works by other Irish writers on the syllabus. In retrospect, he felt that he and a few like-minded colleagues were "taboo-breaking" when they "deconstructed *avant la lettre*" the hierarchical, Anglo-centric curriculum at Queen's.[16]

The number of talented poets Heaney fostered in his classes was remarkable, and their devotion to him was a testament to his effectiveness as a teacher and mentor. Paul Muldoon, Medbh McGuckian, Ciaran Carson, and Frank Ormsby were just a few of his students who went on to distinguished careers. Muldoon, who met Heaney in April 1968 at an Armagh Museum reading, had grown up in a Catholic family on a farm near Ulster Protestants and took to Heaney immediately. Not long after they met in Armagh, he mailed Heaney some verse and asked for comments. On May 30, 1968, while serving as a guest editor of *Threshold* magazine, Heaney accepted three of Muldoon's poems for publication. "I like these poems very much," he wrote, "and I think you don't need anyone to tell you 'where you're going wrong.' I think you're a poet and will go where you decide."[17] Their friendly correspondence convinced Muldoon to enroll at Queen's in 1969. Before long, Heaney would urge Muldoon to submit his poems to Karl Miller at the *Listener*, and later to Charles Monteith so he could publish them at Faber.

Medbh McGuckian, who entered Queen's in 1968, also benefited from Heaney's mentoring. So did Ormsby, who became the editor of the *Honest Ulsterman* while studying at Queen's in the early 1970s, and Ciaran Carson, who took a practical criticism class from Heaney. Critics would soon dub these four students the leaders of a new generation of poets in Northern Ireland. This designation was partly the result of another Queen's student, Michael Foley, relegating Heaney, Mahon, and Longley to an older generation that was already past its prime. Miffed by Foley's comments—he called the three older poets the "Tight Assed Trio" in the *Honest Ulsterman*—Heaney sent the journal a verse letter at the end of 1971 that lambasted Foley as an "editorial dope" and threatened him "with a clip on the ear or rabbit punch."[18] Heaney was in his early thirties and at the beginning his career and didn't want to be considered obsolescent.

After Hobsbaum left Belfast, Heaney invited McGuckian, Muldoon, Carson, Ormsby, and several other young writers to attend a new series of workshops with Group regulars Stewart Parker, Jack Pakenham, Joan Newman, and Michael Longley. This revamped Group met in the Queen's English Department, the Club Bar, Heaney's Ashley Avenue house, or the Four in Hand pub. Sometimes during their sessions, a beer break replaced the old coffee break. This Belfast Group published no anthology like the London Group, but when Heaney and Longley edited the *Northern Review* from 1965 to 1969, they often featured the new Group poets. Harry Chambers also published poems by Heaney's Group in his journal *Phoe-*

*nix.* Group poets and critical discussions of them appeared in the *Honest Ulsterman,* too. Around 1970, the year Heaney went to Berkeley to teach, Queen's lecturers Michael Allen and Arthur Terry took over the workshops, but soon let them expire. According to one participant, Norman Dugdale, "The Group helped to put a generation of Ulster writers, poets in particular, on the literary map."[19] Once on the map, the writers would chart their own courses.

### TRUSTING THE GIFT

The Group, Arts Festival, and Club Rado enlivened the cultural scene in Belfast during the 1960s. Club Rado, which was built in a former Royal Irish Constabulary building, became an emblem of Belfast's Sixties Generation. Tired of conventional music and the repressive policies of the Ulster government, many young people went to the club to hear the latest rock 'n' roll bands. Homegrown musicians such as Van Morrison drew on American rhythm-and-blues legends, such as Muddy Waters and Ray Charles, to create what has been called "Celtic Soul." Morrison and his band gave electrifying performances at Club Rado, and so did other bands like Lovin' Kind, The Alleykatz, The Mad Lads, The Deltones, and Rory Gallagher and the Taste. Many of the musicians were rebels who despised the social injustices in Northern Ireland and endorsed the "Turn on, tune in, drop out" philosophy of the American anti-establishment guru Timothy Leary. Heaney liked the political idealism of these artists, but not their music. He felt the same way about the Beatles, the Rolling Stones, Bob Dylan, and other pop icons of the 1960s. "It was more like background music or fairground music," he said about rock 'n' roll. He was similarly indifferent to "whatever the Beats and the Liverpool Poets were doing," since they often worked in conjunction with the rock stars.[20]

By temperament reserved and contemplative, Heaney struggled to speak out on social issues with the vehemence of the musicians and Beats. As political activism gained momentum in the 1960s, though, he became more engaged. In 1964, he supported the formation of the Campaign for Social Justice (CSJ), whose founders, Dr. Conn McCluskey and his wife, Patricia, had befriended Heaney at one of his poetry readings. He also got involved with the Northern Ireland Civil Rights Association (NICRA).

On August 24, 1968, he joined a protest march led by CSJ and NICRA. The event that provoked the gathering was nothing out of the ordinary: a nationalist Member of Parliament, Austin Currie, had failed to secure a council house for a Catholic family in Dungannon (a town about twenty miles southwest of where Heaney grew up) because the local council chose to rent the house to a nineteen-year-old, unmarried Protestant woman who was a Unionist politician's secretary. Heaney knew Currie— they'd been classmates at Queen's—and supported his efforts on behalf of Catholics. In the end, about two thousand men, women, and children marched from Coalisland to Dungannon carrying signs that said END DIS-CRIMINATION and JUSTICE FOR ALL. A Protestant mob with the tacit support of the Royal Ulster Constabulary (RUC) prevented the protestors from entering parts of Dungannon. Eventually, the police had to separate the two groups. A violent clash was avoided, but the face-off was an omen of things to come.

The Dungannon protest, as many predicted, sparked other protests in Northern Ireland. A rally was organized in Londonderry/Derry for October 5, 1968. Heaney was drawn to the rally for both political and personal reasons: he'd spent much of the 1950s in the northern city, and school-mates from St. Columb's (John Hume, Eamonn McAnn) and Queen's stu-dents he knew (Michael Farrell, Bernadette Devlin) helped organize the rally. The number of participants was not as large as expected because the minister of home affairs, William Craig, issued a ban on protests and there was a football match in the Brandywell stadium. The assortment of politicians, housewives, students, and workers who skipped the match and defied Craig's ban sang "We Shall Overcome," just as they had done at the end of the march to Dungannon, out of a sense of solidarity with the nonviolent civil rights marches led by Martin Luther King in the United States. The protestors' hopes were dashed, though, when the RUC at-tacked them with batons. Police threw one man over a wall, fracturing his leg and arm. Another man's back was nearly broken. The RUC treated members of Parliament with the same belligerence. Blood ran down the faces of men, women, and children. For the first time in the city's history, police used water cannons to dispel a crowd.

Heaney observed the military-style battle from a distance, but in his detailed account of it in the *Listener* he argued that the four hundred protestors had every right to demand justice for Catholics. Three-quarters of the city's residents were Catholics, yet Protestant Unionists controlled the government and made it difficult for Catholics to vote, secure good jobs, and buy houses. Although 2,500 families had signed up for council housing, only about twenty new houses had been built for Catholics. Citizens had to be householders to vote in local elections, and most Protestants who owned houses had no intention of backing candidates who promised adequate housing for their opponents. Unionists knew that more Catholic voters would threaten their grip on power. Heaney made the obvious point that Catholics were simply "asking to be accepted as citizens of Derry."[21] The request seemed modest in a democratic country, but many Protestant politicians refused to grant it.

Some who watched the violence in Londonderry/Derry on TV compared it to the police assault on civil rights protestors in Birmingham, Alabama, in 1963 and in Selma, Alabama, in 1965. The night after the mayhem, Catholics vented their anger by pelting police cars with rocks and throwing petrol bombs in the streets. Conor Cruise O'Brien spoke to students and wrote an article for the *Listener* about using civil disobedience as a political weapon, framing his recommendations in terms of Antigone opposing tyrants such as King Creon in ancient Greece. (Heaney would later publish a translation, *The Burial at Thebes: A Version of Sophocles' Antigone*, that stressed the hero's repudiation of unjust laws.) Looking back at the period just before the march, Heaney told the writer Monie Begley, "There was an energy and excitement and righteousness in the air at that time, by people like myself who hadn't always been political."[22] Like his friend John Hume, who had helped form the Derry Citizens Action Committee to aid Catholics in the city, Heaney knew that the RUC's bloody response to the march would begin a new cycle of attacks and counterattacks. Hume, in fact, traced the resurgence of hostilities during the Troubles to the clashes on October 5, 1968.

To show their support for Catholic protestors and disapproval of the RUC's actions, a group of two thousand students marched from Queen's University toward Belfast's City Hall on October 9, 1968. Heaney commended the students, some of whom were in his classes, for their courage and tactics. He pointed out in his *Listener* article that the marchers came "from all kinds of political and religious backgrounds" and remained "quiet [and] orderly." By contrast, their opponents, who'd been organized by Ian Paisley, heckled the students and, with the help of police, stopped the march before it reached City Hall. Heaney was incensed that the police gave preferential treatment to the Protestant rabble-rousers. His *Listener* article made it clear that he backed a new political organization, called People's Democracy, that Farrell, Devlin, and McCann had started to advocate for "one man—one vote, houses on need, jobs on merit, free speech, fair electoral boundaries, and the repeal of the Special Powers Act which allows police to arrest and imprison citizens on suspicion."[23] In another article about the student protest movement, which he published in the Queen's journal *The Gown* on October 22, 1968, Heaney counseled members of People's Democracy to be "conciliatory" and to avoid "a fury of rhetoric."[24] Although he'd lost patience with the Ulster government's ability to control the volatile situation, he continued to call for civil, rather than uncivil, disobedience.

Heaney's political disappointments in the 1960s affected his poetry as well as his prose. Asked in October 1968 by the Northern Irish composer and conductor Seán Ó Riada to write a song about the Stormont government's handling of recent protests, Heaney came up with "Craig's Dragoons," which played variations on the Protestant song "Dolly's Brae" and the Percy French song "Clare's Dragoons." Heaney's lyrics castigate the minister for home affairs, who had banned the NICRA march in Londonderry/Derry. The song begins with a sardonic imperative: "Come all ye loyal Protestants and in full chorus join, / Think on the deeds of Craig's Dragoons who strike below the groin." Subsequent verses lampoon William Craig and his draconian police force: "They'll cordon and they'll baton-charge, they'll silence protest tunes, / They are the hounds of Ulster, boys, sweet William Craig's dragoons." Heaney was no doubt pleased when the English prime minister, Harold Wilson, demanded that the Ulster prime minister, O'Neill, institute reforms. He must have been pleased, too, when O'Neill sacked his minister for home affairs on December 11, 1968.

Heaney's protest poem was sung on Radio Éireann and printed in the English journal *The Review*, which had previously been dismissive of his work. Most of his poems, though, continued to shy away from overt political commentary. "In Memoriam Seán Ó Riada," which he published in *Field Work,* typifies the way he addressed the Troubles. The elegy compares the conductor's baton to "a black stiletto" and a "quill flourishing" before "the Ulster Orchestra." The baton resembles Heaney's gun-like pen in "Digging"; it's a weapon used for peaceful purposes. Heaney is thinking specifically of a concert Ó Riada conducted in Belfast's Whitla Hall as part of the 1968 Arts Festival (the program featured traditional Irish reels and jigs), and of a time when the conductor and the poet discussed the creative process. It is Ó Riada's ability to relax in a meditative state, "trusting the gift, / risking gift's undertow," that Heaney admires. Like Heaney, the conductor favors gift exchange with the muse as the "paradigm of good politics."[25] The bipolar inspirations and burdensome responsibilities that come with gift exchange can be an "undertow," but for both poet and musician they are worth the risk.

As Northern Ireland descended into chaos during the late 1960s, Heaney felt torn between devoting himself to his poetic gift in solitude and getting more involved in the political situation. He told Robert Druce roughly a decade later that "in a time of politics or violence, it wasn't the artist's function just to be liberal and deplore it, but if you believed in one set of values over the other, to maintain those values in some way."[26] As he suggested at the end of "Death of a Naturalist," he feared getting pulled down by the "undertow" into Ulster's sectarian quagmire. It was difficult, though, to stay aloof while his country spiraled into anarchy. After O'Neill pledged to work harder on reforming Northern Ireland, the prime minister did poorly in a general election on February 3, 1969, and resigned three months later. His replacement, James Chichester-Clark, tried to placate Catholics without much success. Protestant and Catholic paramilitary groups kept attacking each other and riots regularly broke out in cities. When the three-day "Battle of the Bogside" erupted between militant Catholics and the RUC on August 12, 1969, Chichester-Clark asked the British government to send soldiers to Northern Ireland to keep the peace. Harold Wilson pushed for policy changes that Protestants rejected. The Provisional IRA responded with bombings and shootings. More British soldiers arrived, and the cycle of killings continued.

As a Queen's lecturer, Heaney found himself in the middle of a combat zone. During one especially violent night, Protestants burned about 650 Catholic homes, driving the occupants into the streets. From July to

September, sectarian attacks forced about 1,500 Catholic families and 315 Protestant families from their homes. The diaspora in Northern Ireland over the next four years was one of the largest in Europe since 1945. Heaney had tried to tolerate bigoted Protestants for years; now he had to confront the real possibility of being injured or killed by them.

### MAKING ROOM TO RHYME

Unlike some of his students and friends, Heaney was too introverted to feel comfortable wielding a bullhorn on a political stage. Near the end of his life, he admitted, "I've never been actively involved in politics. Too much fervor and certitude and point-scoring, even in the right cause, wears me out. Something in me just wants to appeal to a higher court and get it over with."[27] He had an ingrained distrust of political rhetoric and political wrangling. Among politicians radiating certitude, he remained a poetic Incertus. Although he attended rallies at the Students' Union led by John McGuffin, Bernadette Devlin, and Michael Farrell, he distrusted McGuffin, a self-described anarchist and ally of the American radical Jerry Rubin, and he was wary of Devlin, a cofounder of the revolutionary Irish Republican Socialist Party who admired the American Black Panthers. (Her detractors called her "Fidel Castro in a mini-skirt.") "I'd go home to Ashley Avenue and the essays and the nappies," he said about this period of upheaval, "while they'd proceed to student flatland and get going on plans for shaking and shaping the future."[28]

Heaney's domestic duties increased in February 1968, when Marie gave birth to a son, Christopher, named for Heaney's brother who'd died fifteen years before in February. To accommodate his expanding family, Heaney moved from 37 Beechill Park South to a nineteenth-century house at 16 Ashley Avenue. Conveniently located near Queen's, the red-brick house with two towering, dome-shaped roofs became a salon for writers, teachers, filmmakers, broadcasters, clergymen, and painters who wanted to talk, drink, and sing late into the night. The Scottish writer George Mackay Brown visited in early 1968 and sang with David Hammond. Edna and Michael Longley were regular visitors. Marie liked to entertain the controversial Presbyterian clergyman Liam Barbour and the equally controversial Dominican Friar Herbert McCabe. McCabe, a scholar devoted to the writings of St. Thomas Aquinas and Ludwig Wittgenstein, was a socialist who opposed the Catholic Church's ban on contraception and ordination of women. The Belfast-born painter Colin Middleton, who once prided himself on being the only surrealist in Northern Ireland, joined the soirées with his wife, Kate. Heaney would hire him to illustrate his book *Sweeney Astray* and remember him in his poem "Loughanure" in *Human Chain*. The painter Terry Flanagan and his wife, Sheelagh, also visited, as did the English playwright Trevor Griffiths and the Ulster poet John Hewitt.

Heaney had met Hewitt with the Flanagans around 1965, when Hewitt moved back to Ulster from England. (In 1957, he'd taken a job at a museum in Coventry.) Heaney had read Hewitt's poetry at Queen's and his essays about regionalism at St. Joseph's. He was pleased that Hewitt had organized a reading for him at the Herbert Art Gallery in Coventry, but he was put off by the older man's mix of left-wing politics and puritanical elitism. Nevertheless, Heaney appreciated the generosity Hewitt showed toward younger poets like himself. To acknowledge the debt he and his generation owed Hewitt, he dedicated his poem "The Schoolbag" to the older poet.

In 1968, Ted Hughes made a memorable visit to 16 Ashley Avenue with his mistress, Assia Gutmann. Heaney had first met Hughes during the summer of 1967 at a teachers' conference in Hereford, England. Primed with whiskey, Marie sang Irish folk songs, Gutmann sang Israeli songs, and Hughes sang "The Brown and the Yellow Ale," a song about a man who lends his wife to another man only to die when she returns. Infidelity and the death of a spouse must have been on Hughes's mind at the time. About six years before, Hughes had started an affair with Gutmann while married to Sylvia Plath, and Plath had committed suicide. Not long after the Heaneys' party, on March 23, 1969, Gutmann would follow Plath's example by gassing herself and her daughter by Hughes, Shura, in London.

Heaney's admiration for Hughes and desire to promote Irish culture led to a proposal to create programs on BBC radio with one of Hughes's BBC collaborators, Moira Doolan. On May 24, 1967, Doolan discussed Heaney's ideas for a School Broadcasting program called "Listening and Writing" that would be designed for children between the ages of eleven and thirteen. Heaney later told Stuart Evans, a producer in the BBC's

School Broadcasting Department, that he wanted to write an "Exploration" script that focused on poems by Ted Hughes, Thom Gunn, Philip Larkin, and T. S. Eliot. Evans liked the idea and promised to visit Belfast at the end of November 1967 to record the program. A year later, Evans urged Heaney, Hammond, Longley, and Mahon to collaborate on three BBC school programs emphasizing their Northern Irish roots. Over the next few years, Heaney would work on numerous radio projects that tried to appeal to both Ulster's Catholic and Protestant communities.

As Heaney's reputation as a performer spread, more invitations came his way. During 1967 and 1968, he gave scholarly talks on Robert Frost at the University of Liverpool, on Michael McLaverty at the New University of Ulster, and on Thomas Hardy at a festival in Dorchester, England. He read his poems at Sheffield University Institute and the Belfast Arts Festival. He joined renowned Irish poets Austin Clarke and Thomas Kinsella at a reading in Dublin. (Often Heaney earned a pittance for these appearances—£10 or less.) He got together with another well-known poet, the Scotsman Hugh MacDiarmid, in Dublin on December 10, 1967. Ostensibly there to observe United Nations Human Rights Day, MacDiarmid made a scene by chasing Marie around a table, telling her how good she looked even though she was pregnant, and boasting to a group of nuns that he was a card-carrying Communist.

On an earlier trip to Dublin in June 1967, Heaney had met one of his literary idols, Patrick Kavanagh. Worried that the older writer might be jealous of the publicity generated by *Death of a Naturalist,* Heaney at first had shied away from him. Kavanagh's *Collected Poems* had just been published, and in the introduction he complained that critics had neglected his work. Heaney finally approached Kavanagh in the Bailey Bar on Duke Street and asked if he'd like a drink. "No" was Kavanagh's terse reply. Acting as a mediator, the young poet and future Irish diplomat Richard Ryan said, "Paddy, this man's come down here from Belfast, and he's just published a book of poems. His name's Seamus Heaney." Kavanagh looked surprised. "Are you Heaney?" he asked, deliberately mispronouncing Heaney's name as "Hainey." An awkward conversation ensued. Finally, Kavanagh agreed to let Heaney buy him a Scotch. A few days later, after a reading by the Irish poet Brendan Kennelly in a Dublin bookstore, Heaney offered Kavanagh a ride home. Once again, there was an awkward conversation. This time it began when the older poet's wife, Katherine, made a remark about Heaney owning a Volkswagen: "There you are now, Paddy, you can be a poet and have a car after all."[29] Kavanagh was in poor health and unamused. Before the end of the year, on November 30, 1967, he died. He was only sixty-three. On a cold December day, Heaney, Longley, and Mahon went to Kavanagh's funeral in his birthplace, Inniskeen, County Monaghan, to pay tribute to the influential poet.

Around this time, Heaney, Longley, and Hammond applied for an Arts Council grant to go on what they were calling a "Room to Rhyme" tour around Northern Ireland. They took the title from a mummers' play, *St. George and the Dragon,* that was performed in Heaney's community before Christmas when he was a boy. In a University of Dundee commencement address in 2003, he recalled viewing the itinerant Christmas Rhymers, who were generally young and dressed in old clothes when they came to Mossbawn. They carried an assortment of props—a hurricane lamp, a frying pan, a big stick, a doctor's bag, a tin can for donations—and scared Heaney when they showed up at night with faces blackened with burnt cork. He reminded his Dundee audience that "in the pre-electrified Ulster countryside, the blacked-out wartime Ulster of the early 1940s when the dark was truly dark . . . , strangers in the night always had a slightly problematical aura about them."[30] Nevertheless, he enjoyed their in-house performances.

"Room to Rhyme" was an allusion to the Fool in *St. George and the Dragon* who asks for the audience's attention: "So room, brave gallants all, / Pray give us room to rhyme. / We've come to show activity this merry Christmas time." In many versions of the play, a dragon and a Turkish knight named "Slasher" attack the iconic British hero and Christian soldier St. George. In retaliation, George wounds Slasher. Revived by a swig of whiskey, George ultimately defeats the dragon. Some scholars have speculated that the mummer plays grew out of sacrificial gift-exchange rituals and fertility narratives, since villagers in early iterations of the plays gave sacrificial gifts (trinkets, livestock, even humans) to the dragon with the hope that the dragon would reciprocate with gifts of prosperity and seasonal continuity. When a princess was selected as a sacrificial gift, though, the chivalric St. George came to her rescue and killed the dragon. The dragon's death was supposed to assure the birth of a new year after the traditional gift-giving season of Christmas. The mythic aspects of the mummers' plays made an indelible impression on Heaney. And the fact that the mummers staged their plays in houses and pubs gave him the idea of presenting poems and songs in similar settings with his friends.

The Arts Council funded a ten-day "Room to Rhyme" tour in May 1968. The three poets appeared mainly in parish halls, primary schools, pubs, museums, and city auditoriums. Later in the year, they performed at the Belfast Festival. To prod audiences into thinking outside their sectarian comfort zones, Hammond sang traditional Irish folk songs such as "The Boys of Mullaghbawn," which tells the story of an enlightened Protestant squire who takes care of his Catholic tenants. Longley read a poem he'd workshopped at a Group meeting, "Remembrance Day," which honored British soldiers who'd died in World War I. Heaney read "Requiem for the Croppies," even though he knew Protestants might regard it as inflammatory. Generally, they preferred the drinking song "Croppies Lie Down," which casts the anti-British rebels of 1798 as traitors and cowards. The Protestant song proclaims, with reference to the Irish fighters who died at the Battle of Vinegar Hill in southeastern Ireland, "Oh, croppies ye'd better be quiet and still / Ye shan't have your liberty, do what ye will / As long as salt water is formed in the deep / A foot on the necks of the croppy we'll keep." Heaney's countersong envisions a sacrificial gift exchange in which the rebels give the gift of life to their beloved land and the land reciprocates by giving them the gift of a second life in the form of crops and the promise of independence.

Not long after his "Room to Rhyme" tour, Heaney reviewed *The Year of Liberty*, Thomas Pakenham's historical account of the influence of the American and French Revolutions on the United Irishmen and their war against the British. For Heaney, the eighteenth-century rebels were martyrs who "believe[d] that violence was a necessary prelude to the planting of the tree of liberty," but they never "envisaged the sectarian massacres that left pigs rutting among the piled corpses on village streets all over south-east Ireland."[31] It was at the Battle of Vinegar Hill that some of the worst war crimes were committed. On June 21, 1798, thirteen thousand British troops attacked an Irish encampment, slaughtered the men, gang-raped the women, burned a makeshift hospital, and tortured prisoners by "picketing" (making them stand barefoot on sharp stakes), "pitch-capping" (pouring hot pitch or tar on their heads before ripping off their scalps), and "half-hanging" (hanging them until they were half-dead). Historians estimate that up to 1,200 United Irishmen were killed at Vinegar Hill. Heaney's "Requiem" for the croppies concludes with the image of barley seeds, which were carried for food in the rebels' pockets, sprouting from their graves. The seeds will produce edible crops in the future, just as the fallen rebels, who had "cropped" their hair short in solidarity with French revolutionaries with similar haircuts, will produce a new crop of fighters to avenge their deaths.

"Requiem for the Croppies" aroused controversy on Heaney's "Room to Rhyme" tour and elsewhere because some people took it to be an endorsement of nationalist violence by groups like the IRA. The 1960s band Flying Column, which had formed in Belfast, understood the revolutionary implications of the poem and included it with rebel songs on their popular 1971 album *Four Green Fields*. (The title song referred to Ireland's four provinces, one of which was still ruled by the British. The band's name proudly invoked the "flying columns"—small IRA cells that fought the British in the 1916–21 war.) Although Heaney knew his "Requiem" expressed nationalist sentiments, he resisted attempts to use it for overtly political purposes, and he bristled at any suggestion that it condoned or encouraged violence. "The poem may have been appropriated but it hadn't been written as a recruiting song for the IRA," he insisted. "In the Northern Ireland context, its purpose was to exercise the rights of nationalists to have freedom of cultural speech . . . , to make space in the official Ulster lexicon for Vinegar Hill as well as the Boyne and the Somme."[32] The Irish uprising in 1916, according to Heaney, "was the harvest of seeds sown in 1798, when revolutionary republican ideals and national feeling coalesced in the doctrines of Irish republicanism and in the rebellion of 1798 itself [that was] unsuccessful and savagely put down."[33] Heaney was heartened by the way Protestant Unionists at the "Room to Rhyme" performances listened attentively to his elegy for the eighteenth-century nationalists, even though he suspected they disapproved of its message. The signs of a new tolerance, unfortunately, would not last long, and Heaney would soon refuse to read the poem in public.

Heaney decided to use his £500 Somerset Maugham Award, which he'd received for *Death of a Naturalist,* to visit the European continent with his family during the summer of 1969. In July, he drove to Landes, a region in France that bordered the Atlantic Ocean near the Pyrenees. Once known for its sheep farms and shepherds who walked on stilts across boggy pastures, in the nineteenth century the sheep pastures had turned into pine forests, and the local economy had shifted to the production of timber and resin. Heaney was attracted to the bucolic setting and rented a house on a farm. He was soon writing friends about the delicious local wines, fruits, vegetables, and breads. In a letter to Longley on July 30, he said Marie was getting a good tan, Michael and Christopher were happily chasing ducks in the yard, and he was writing poems beneath swallow nests in a garage that reminded him of a shed near Mossbawn. With cows, pigs, hens, ducks, geese, cats, and a dog on the premises, it was almost as if he'd returned to his first home. The nearby village of Peyrehorade, with a population of six hundred, reminded him of small villages around Mossbawn. To make friends, Heaney bought a rod and joined residents in their favorite pastime on the banks of a nearby river: fishing.

A poem in *Field Work,* "High Summer," reveals that the Heaneys' French sojourn wasn't all idyllic bliss. Influenced by Robert Lowell's dyspeptic family portraits in *Life Studies,* Heaney's poem begins with an account of Christopher keeping his parents awake until 5:00 a.m. with his crying and the landlord's tractor waking Heaney shortly after his son falls asleep. The river where Heaney fishes with a bamboo pole is muddy and smells of festering silage. The maggots he uses for bait turn to flies, and the flies—like those in "Death of a Naturalist"—remind him of the rot and death in Ulster.

For a change of scene, Heaney planned to move from the area near Peyrehorade to a country house in Spain east of Madrid, and then visit Portugal before heading back to Belfast in mid-September. He wrote Longley that he was learning Spanish to prepare for a stay with his sister-in-law Anne, who lived in Spain. As for his writing, he was reviewing a book about the Orkney Islands by his friend George Mackay Brown and an *Introduction to Ireland* by Conor Cruise O'Brien. His big project, though, was a verse play for BBC radio titled *Munro.* His script would eventually contain three hundred heroic couplets about General George Nugent and General Henry Munro, who had clashed during the Rebellion of 1798.

Heaney's review of *The Year of Liberty* had included an eyewitness account of Munro approaching the gallows with his shop books to settle up with his clients after he was captured and sentenced to death by the British. Heaney had praised Munro's noble attempt to fulfill his ethical obligations: "Such behavior on the gallows constitutes a retreat into solitude, at least a retreat from partisan politics, a last frail attempt at healing the community."[34] While the Protestant Munro is a militantly democratic idealist in Heaney's radio play, the British General Nugent is a paternalistic, law-and-order simpleton who speaks in platitudes. As the two adversaries converse in a jail cell, Nugent reminds Munro, who has had little formal military training (he was a linen draper by profession), "Rebellion is not for the amateur. . . . Your trade's the pen."[35] Heaney had said the same thing about his literary "trade" in "Digging" when he decided to fight his battles with a pen rather than a gun.

*Munro* begins and ends with the gallows scene in which the draper-turned-rebel honors his responsibilities to clients by giving them linens or money he owes them. Munro becomes Heaney's alter ego here—a conscientious man who uses a pen to honor his debts. Shortly before he dies, he tells Nugent, "You will excuse me if I blot this solemn occasion / With a few strokes from my chosen weapon. / You did remind me, General, after all, of counter and pen."[36] As an Irish nationalist and devout Christian, Munro believes he owes something to his customers, country, and God. In the end, he gives the gift of life to Ireland and Christ with the hope that others will benefit from his sacrifice. *Munro*, however, is not overly optimistic about the future. Heaney reminds his audience in the last line of the play—just as he did in the last line of "Requiem for the Croppies"— that sacrificial gift-giving doesn't always repair bonds in the community. In fact, Munro's gifts do little besides sow the seeds of more uprisings and killings. The play concludes with Munro's sister vowing to use a sword rather than a pen to avenge her brother's death. Munro's other followers will resort to violence, as well. As some of Heaney's listeners knew, after British soldiers hanged and decapitated Munro, they sacked the town of Ballynahinch (the site of a revolutionary battle that began on June 12, 1798) and executed many rebels and civilians.

In France and Spain during the summer of 1969, events conspired to remind Heaney of Ulster. Even the bullfight he attended at a festival near Landes conjured up images of home. As an admirer of Hemingway, Heaney was curious about the blood sport that had so fascinated the American writer. After watching the bullfight, Heaney admitted to being "carried . . . away . . . in a kind of trance" by the ritualistic killing of the bull. It was as if he'd been "taken up to a high mountain and shown things," he said, alluding to the Gospel of Luke where Satan takes Jesus up to "an high mountain" and shows "him all the kingdoms of the world" (Luke 4:5) that He could rule if He only worships the devil.[37] Heaney's poem "Summer 1969," which he included in the *North* sequence "Singing School," implies that the bullfight as well as other unpleasant experiences on his European holiday (witnessing Spain's punitive Guardia Civil, looking at Goya's gruesome paintings in Madrid's Museo Nacional del Prado, smelling the stench of the fish market) correspond to satanic events in Ulster. Crouching before his sister-in-law's TV set like Robert Lowell watching televised civil rights protests in "For the Union Dead," Heaney chastises himself for "suffering / Only the bullying sun of Madrid" while Protestants are bullying Catholics at home. He feels especially guilty for escaping to a cool museum to look at Goya's *Shootings of the Third of May,* which depicts a man in a white shirt with arms raised before a firing squad. The image is a synecdoche for Spanish citizens who were executed for rebelling against the occupation of Napoleon's army in the early nineteenth century. For Heaney, the Spanish rebels recall Irish rebels, and Goya's complex political views recall his own. If Goya was "stained" by his work as a court painter for Napoleon's brother, Joseph, who became king of Spain in 1808, the painter redeemed himself in his art. For Heaney, Goya was a kind of noble bullfighter who "flourished / The stained cape of his heart as history charged." Heaney, it seemed, wanted to be the same sort of artistic bullfighter, even though he deplored the violence of bullfighting just as he deplored his father's cockfighting.

When Heaney returned to Northern Ireland at the end of the summer, history in the form of British soldiers "charged" into the cities to put an end to Protestants "bullying" Catholics. He told one reporter, "I remember coming back kind of exhilarated because the Army had come in and was protecting the Catholics."[38] Heaney was also excited by the

publication of his second book, *Door into the Dark,* on "Bloomsday"—
June 16, the day Leopold Bloom took his mock-epic journey around Dublin in Joyce's *Ulysses.* The reviews were generally positive. The Irish poet Eavan Boland wrote in the *Irish Times* that Heaney's new poems about women marked an advance over those in his first book; he now represented sex, pregnancy, and childbirth with a candor and empathy she admired. James Simmons praised the volume for its craftsmanship and range of subjects. Other critics, though, complained that the book was too similar in subject matter and style to *Death of a Naturalist.* Robin Skelton in the *Malahat Review* and Julian Symons in *Punch* criticized the poems for lacking vitality, while Anthony Thwaite lumped the poems together with those being written by "the Tribe of Ted [Hughes]."[39] Stung by the implication that his poems were derivative, Heaney addressed Thwaite's "Tribe of Ted" remark in an epistolary poem he sent to James Simmons. Heaney was also stung by A. Alvarez's negative review, "Homo Faber," that compared the book to "a flat-bottomed" boat that was "good only for shallow waters and calm days."[40]

What Thwaite, Alvarez, and like-minded critics failed to notice was the skillful way Heaney explored new territory in *Door into the Dark.* His poems contained traditional plots and characters, but, like Joyce's *Ulysses,* they deftly juxtaposed modern experiences against mythical paradigms. His realistic perspectives subverted traditional assumptions and romantic expectations. "No milk-limbed Venus ever rose / Miraculous on this western shore," he proclaims in "Girls Bathing, Galway 1965." Many of the other poems attempt to deconstruct and reenvision the mythical worldview that Heaney's classical and Judeo-Christian education had ingrained in him since childhood.

Heaney's personae in *Door into the Dark* continue to engage in gift-exchange rituals, but now for more secular than religious purposes. "The Peninsula," "The Forge," "In Gallarus Oratory," "Night Drive," "The Given Note," and "Bogland" all give empirical, as opposed to primarily mythical or Catholic, accounts of what Thomas Merton called the "vivid realization of the fact that life and being" are gifts that "proceed from an invisible, transcendent and infinitely abundant Source." God and the Holy Spirit recede into the background of many of the poems. "The Forge," for instance, offers an engaging account of a journey through a "dark night of the soul" toward a communion with an "invisible . . . abundant Source" that is grounded in an actual place: the forge at Hillhead on the Toome Road near Mossbawn that Heaney used to visit.[41] The spirited and in-spiriting God here is a Joycean artist-god but also a real person: Barney Devlin. "All I know is a door into the dark," Heaney says about the entrance to Devlin's forge. The horseshoes the blacksmith makes on an anvil that is "immovable [as] an altar" resemble the gifts of bread and wine that a priest consecrates on a church altar at Communion. Now, though, the symbolic objects are more like a poet's gifts than God's gifts. Heaney acknowledges that these artifacts—the horseshoes—are generally considered to be as archaic and useless as sonnets in the contemporary world. ("The Forge" is a sonnet.) After all, most people are driving cars, not riding horses or writing sonnets. Heaney's old artificer looks out at the road by his forge and "recalls a clatter / of hoofs where traffic is flashing in rows." He knows that if horses were still on the road, his occupation would be more profitable. Nevertheless, he doesn't despair. He insists that his labor has spiritual and aesthetic value, not just monetary value. He returns to his dark forge "to beat real iron out, to work the bellows."

Heaney's title *Door into the Dark* was undoubtedly suggested by Frost's poem "The Door in the Dark" and Joseph Conrad's phrases "door of darkness" and "door opening into a Darkness" in *Heart of Darkness*.[42] Heaney may have been echoing the Bible, too. Jesus declares in John's Gospel: "I am the door: by me if any man shall enter in, he shall be saved" (10:9). St. Teresa says something similar in *The Interior Castle*: "The door by which to enter this castle is prayer and meditation."[43] By the time Heaney wrote the poems for *Door into the Dark*, though, he was a lapsed Catholic intent on reenvisioning his former religious beliefs. As the scholar Benedict Kiely observed in his article "A Raid into Dark Corners," the forge recalls the "negative dark that presides in the Irish Christian consciousness . . . the gloom, the constriction, the sense of guilt, the self abasement," but Heaney was now examining that "Irish Christian consciousness" from a modern, secular perspective and charting a journey into "the dark centre, the blurred and irrational storehouse of insight and instincts, the hidden core of the self."[44] The door that opened into a mystical "dark night," despite its Christian associations, was essentially a door into the unconscious mind's storehouse of poetic gifts.

"In Gallarus Oratory" exemplifies the way Heaney reenvisioned his background in mystical contemplation and prayer to make his Catholic experiences correspond to his secular experiences as a poet. Based on a visit on August 19, 1966, to a small stone chapel on the Dingle Peninsula that Christian monks had constructed sometime between the ninth and twelfth centuries, his poem treats the monks as if they were precursors that he has respectfully moved beyond. "Inside, in the dark of the stone, it feels as if you are sustaining a great pressure, bowing under like the generations of monks who must have bowed down in meditation and reparation on that floor," he wrote after his trip to the holy site. "But coming out of the cold heart of the stone, into the sunlight and the dazzle of grass and sea, I felt a lift in my heart, a surge towards happiness that must have been experienced over and over again by those monks as they crossed the same threshold centuries ago."[45] If Heaney felt an urge to praise the natural world in specifically Catholic terms after emerging from the oratory, he resists. "No worshipper / Would leap up to his God off this floor," he declares. In fact, on the day Heaney visited the oratory, he was disappointed to find the site packed with American tourists. Yet after he left the Dingle Peninsula, he remembered the oratory's "core of old dark" that would have led the ancient monks in contemplation to "the heart of the globe" and to a "storehouse" of God's gifts. In Heaney's case, though, the gift he receives from the "old dark" is his poem "In Gallarus Oratory."

*Door into the Dark* begins with "Night-Piece" and retraces numerous forays into dark "storehouses" where literary gifts are preserved and revealed like bog artifacts. The concluding poem "Bogland" imagines this storehouse existing behind a mythical "eye." Irish "pioneers keep striking / Inwards and downwards" as if descending through this eye into Ireland's collective soul. What they excavate—an elk skeleton, fir trunks, butter that's "still salty and white"—are analogous to gifts in the poet's unconscious mind. The radio scripts Heaney wrote at the time for the BBC's *Today and Yesterday* series also recount journeys into the mind's and ground's dark spaces. One script broadcast on February 27, 1968, simply titled *The Dark,* documents another productive journey into a dark night. A subsequent radio script, *The Poet,* which was broadcast on March 15, 1968, lays out a plan for "a raid into the dark corners of memory" that will transport Heaney back to Mossbawn, where the nights were especially dark because there were no electric lights.

On May 1, 1968, Heaney was on the air again, this time reading Ted Hughes's poem "The Bull Moses" in the program *Exploration* to illustrate the way "a sudden shut-eyed look" can lead to a vision of an original "blaze of darkness." If he was thinking of the biblical account of God creating light from a dark void, once again he did so in secular terms. During his broadcast, he also read his own poem "Frogman," which compares poetic investigations of the private and collective unconscious to those of a diver who "pokes around in the rich darkness of the riverbed." After *Exploration*, Heaney wrote another script for the BBC, *Irish Writing I*, which his friend David Hammond produced for transmission on January 17, 1969. It begins with a story from John McGahern's *The Dark*, a novel about a Catholic farm boy struggling to break away from his abusive father. To emphasize the liberating nature of both writing and reading, which was the main subject of his BBC broadcasts, Heaney admonished his audience, "If you make yourself still and calm and quiet, like the water [in a pond], the words may sink and send ripples and echoes widening all through you."[46] This meditative state of mind, which he sometimes compared to the still water in a scullery bucket at Mossbawn, was his version of "the gifted state" during which words could enter the mind as if they were gifts of grace.

While he was in Spain in 1969, Heaney made a pilgrimage to Ávila, the city northwest of Madrid where the famous Catholic mystic St. Teresa had founded her reformed Carmelite convent in the sixteenth century. Here she had convinced her friend St. John of the Cross to work for the Carmelites and she had written her devotional works. Not far from Ávila, St. Ignatius of Loyola, after being wounded in the Battle of Pamplona, had composed his influential *Spiritual Exercises* and established the Society of Jesus. Heaney continued to gravitate toward St. John's concept of a mystical "dark night of the soul," but he also reflected on the way beliefs in a sublime God and His sublime creation could stir up violently intense emotions. St. Teresa, for example, conceived of her union with God as sado-erotic: "I saw in his hand a long spear of gold, and at the iron's point there seemed to be a little fire. He appeared to me to be thrusting it at times into my heart, and to pierce my very entrails; when he drew it out, he seemed to draw them out also, and to leave me all on fire with a great love of God. The pain was so great, that it made me moan."[47] It was as if God were a matador or picador, and St. Teresa was a bull being blissfully gored. The ongoing violence between Christians in Ulster contributed to Heaney's skepticism of all zealotry, no matter what ideological form it took.

While Heaney's *Door into the Dark* is full of violence, sex, and dark nights, the poems typically recount journeys to a contemplative realm where gifts of inspiration are quietly and gratefully received before being regifted by secular artist-gods. "The Given Note" is a good example of Heaney's penchant for following an artist with a spiritual bent through the stages of a "monomythical" journey that culminates with the reception and distribution of aesthetic gifts. Heaney's protagonist, an Irish fiddler, departs from familiar territory (the Irish mainland), is initiated into a mysterious otherworld (an island in the Atlantic Ocean where for years only Gaelic was spoken), and returns home with inspirational gifts. As in "The Peninsula" and "In Gallarus Oratory," Heaney's persona proceeds to a liminal place where land and ocean meet. The fiddler is on the most distant of the Blasket Islands off the southwestern tip of Ireland. (When Heaney wrote the poem, the Irish government had forced residents to evacuate the islands because of safety concerns; the last family had left in 1954.) Alone in a silent stone hut like a monk in the Gallarus oratory, Heaney's fiddler receives the gift of a tune "out of the night" that he calls "spirit music." Its source is mysterious; it comes "from nowhere," or nowhere he understands. Musician and musical instrument become mere conduits for the Muse's mystical gifts. When a gift arrives, "it comes off the bow" and "rephrases itself into the air" as if it has a will of its own.

Heaney admitted that he wrote "The Given Note" to communicate what he believed to be "at the heart of one of the big subjects of the species, really: the given-ness of art, the gift of music."[48] A companion poem in *Door into the Dark,* "Victorian Guitar," once again represents artistic creations and artistic instruments in terms of gifts. The inscription on the guitar, which Heaney incorporates in an epigraph, indicates that a Victorian woman, Louisa Catherine Coe, gave up her "gift of music" and gave her guitar as a gift to someone else after she married John Charles Smith in 1852. Heaney says at the beginning of the poem, "I expected the lettering [on the guitar] to carry / The date of the gift, a kind of christening." The implication is that Louisa's identity is so bound up with the guitar that she thinks of herself as a kind of musical instrument given as a gift to her husband on their wedding night. "More than a maiden name / Was cancelled by him on the first night," Heaney writes, revealing his disapproval of the husband who shows insufficient respect for his wife's gifts. From the husband's point of view, his wife's love for the guitar is incompatible with her love for him. He "did not hold with fingering," so he refuses to let her finger the guitar because he wants to spend more time "fingering" her. He forces her to abandon her "gift of music," her maiden name, and her maidenhead. Nevertheless, her artistic spirit lives on in her gift of a guitar, and the new owner appears to be vicariously enjoying Louisa as he plays it. He is "giving it the time of its life" and, in the process, passing on her "gift of music" to others. Like Heaney's talismanic pen in "Digging," the guitar is a gift that keeps giving, although in this case the original owner of the gift has had to sacrifice it to satisfy the desires of others.

# 8

# From Belfast to Berkeley and Back

## A CELT IN HIPPIELAND

Heaney had an almost erotic attachment to his muse and her gifts, but like the woman in "Victorian Guitar" and like most artists he found it hard to serve two masters. For Heaney, the tug-of-war was between his aesthetic and academic masters. As soon as he got a good job at Queen's, he felt constrained by classes and committees and wondered if he could find a job that would allow him more time for his poetry writing. During the 1960s, a number of his artistic friends tried to get teaching jobs in the United States, where salaries were usually higher and course loads lighter than in Britain, but Heaney was wary of American academia. He told the Irish poet Padraic Fiacc in 1968, "I wouldn't like to teach in a U.S. university; you'd always be studying the other poet's work; everything would finally channel into the other person's poetry, even your own perceptions."[1] It was as if he feared sacrificing his poetic gift to someone else the way Louisa Coe had sacrificed her musical gift to her husband when they married.

A Berkeley English professor, Tom Parkinson, helped change Heaney's mind about teaching in America. In the late 1960s, having heard about Heaney's work from the Irish poet John Montague, Parkinson went to a reading Heaney gave at the University of York in England, and was so impressed that he told Heaney to consider applying for a job at Berkeley. Heaney gradually warmed to the idea. He had relatives in the United States (maternal cousins had emigrated to Philadelphia in the 1920s), and he wanted to visit them; he also thought it would be interesting to meet some of the writers in the San Francisco Bay area. Teaching at a prestigious American university and going on reading tours would bolster his income and reputation in the United States. His lack of a doctorate concerned him, but he hoped Berkeley would consider his poetry books sufficient credentials for a visiting professorship.

The social unrest at Berkeley was another concern. Parkinson undoubtedly discussed this with Heaney when they met in York, since he bore scars of the unrest on his face. A political activist known for speaking out on behalf of trade unions, women, students, and persecuted authors (he testified in support of Allen Ginsberg's *Howl* at the famous San Francisco obscenity trial in 1957), Parkinson had been physically attacked for his views. In 1961, a conservative student who suspected him of Communist sympathies shot him in the face and fatally wounded his teaching assistant. Surgery had saved Parkinson's life, but his face was permanently disfigured.

Parkinson may have assured Heaney that Berkeley was more subdued than it had been in the recent past. Many of the notorious political battles of the 1960s had been fought in the university city and won by students and their allies. Local residents generally tolerated the students' libertarian values and freewheeling lifestyles. The campus demonstrations that had been a factor in turning public opinion in the United States against the Vietnam War had diminished in frequency and intensity. The chaotic "Summer of Love," during which one hundred thousand people flocked to the Haight-Ashbury section of San Francisco, had occurred in 1967. The legendary Monterey Pop Festival performances by Jimi Hendrix, Janis Joplin, the Grateful Dead, the Who, Jefferson Airplane, and other rock bands were also a thing of the past. Governor Reagan, who frequently railed against Berkeley's "communist sympathizers, protestors and sex deviants," had called in the police and National Guard to quell protests in 1969.[2]

After a good deal of deliberation, Heaney decided to apply for a job at Berkeley. The English Department chair, John Jordan, consulted Parkinson and another colleague, Tom Flanagan, and agreed that Heaney would add some luster to the department. On February 11, 1970, he wrote Heaney a letter offering him a salary of $13,100 (worth about $90,000 today) for one year of teaching. He said he'd pay for round-trip travel expenses and assured Heaney that he'd have more free time for his writing than at previous jobs. A graduate student would help grade his freshman papers, and he'd have no teaching duties on Mondays, Wednesdays, and Fridays. Heaney celebrated his good fortune with a big party in Belfast that he later mentioned in "September Song," a poem in *Field Work* that describes how the guests "lifted the roof" off the house until dawn. As he got organized to move his family to San Francisco at the end of the summer in 1970, he made sure to pack his new manuscript of poems, "Winter Seeds." The tentative title referred to seeds found inside the exhumed body of the Tollund Man. Heaney would be carrying his own seeds—the poetic seeds for his next book, *Wintering Out*—on his five-thousand-mile journey to California.

Tom Flanagan met the jet-lagged Heaneys after they landed at the San Francisco airport and took them out for a meal. Tom's wife, Jean, later drove them around Berkeley to look at rental properties, including an attractive first-floor apartment in a three-story house at 2444 Carleton Street, only an eight-minute walk from the English Department. Although the apartment was relatively small, renters had access to a pleasant lawn with an exotic-looking banana tree and an attractive peach tree. There was a House of Pancakes nearby that stayed open late into the night, where Heaney could go to buy the cigarettes he depended on for his nocturnal writing and reading. Marie liked the fact that the apartment was close to a supermarket and that it had an ample yard where her children could play and she could sunbathe. She also appreciated that it contained a furnished living room, dining room, kitchen, fireplace, and two bedrooms. The Heaneys promptly signed a lease.

The quickest route to the English Department was along Telegraph Avenue, a gathering place for those who had turned on, tuned in, and dropped out. In a letter to the Longleys written on September 22, 1970, Heaney said that, while walking down the avenue to work, he encountered "hippies, drop-outs, freak-outs, addicts, black panthers, [and] hare-krishna American kids with shaved heads, begging bowls and clothes made out of old lace curtains." He added sarcastically, "They're chanting Hare Krishna all the time but the most familiar chant is 'Got any spare change.' There's an overpowering reek of joss sticks and incense floating out of the gear shops and book shops and herb shops (notice on sunblind of herb shop—'All hail to the one cosmic mind'). Everywhere there are posters inviting you to 'personal exploration groups.' 'Lose your mind and come to your senses.' . . . It's lotus land for the moment."[3] To Paul Muldoon, he wrote with similar bemusement, "Imagine coming into Queen's and finding it like some curious dream vision with people in the most unconventional of garbs."[4] Having lived the life of a straightlaced Catholic during his formative decades, he felt as out of place in the psychedelic dreamworld of Berkeley as the Tollund Man in modern-day Denmark.

Heaney tried to be open-minded about Berkeley's counterculture, even though it made him self-conscious about his conservative roots. On their first Saturday, he took his family to hear renowned folk singer and political activist Pete Seeger. Heaney also learned about local eating trends and tried to convert to a healthier diet. On October 17, 1970, he reported to Ulster friends that his new eating habits were showing good results; he'd lost thirteen pounds. To get back to his writing, he set up a desk beneath a large wall map of the moon. (He alluded to this map at the beginning of "Westering" in *Wintering Out*.) As well as drafting new poems, he began writing short stories inspired by his fiction-writing colleague Leonard Michaels, who'd recently published the highly acclaimed book of short stories *Going Places*. To sample the local poetry scene, Heaney went to a reading by Robert Bly, who was living about ten miles north of San Francisco. The anti–Vietnam War activist and future men's movement guru was writing prose poems that became catalysts for Heaney's experiments with the form. In the introduction to the prose poems he collected in the pamphlet *Stations* (1975), Heaney said the poems derived from memories that "had lain for years in the unconscious as active lodes or nodes," and he was a pilgrim "on a psychic turas" (*"turas"* is an Old Irish word for pilgrimage or journey) intent on bringing the buried material to light.[5]

Writing late at night and early in the morning turned out to be a productive routine for Heaney in Berkeley. American journals began accepting his poems. He was especially pleased when the poetry editor of the *New Yorker,* Howard Moss, took his poem "Home" on October 6, 1970. (The magazine published "Home" on May 1, 1971, and it became section II of "Summer Home" in *Wintering Out*.) Heaney had placed poems in many of the best English and Irish journals by 1970, but the *New Yorker* acceptance signaled that he had "arrived" in America, and it marked the beginning of a long, rewarding relationship with the prestigious magazine. "Summer Home" dwells on personal and political wounds, but it differs from previous poems in the way it assigns blame to himself. Like Robert Lowell in "To Speak of Woe That Is in Marriage," Heaney focuses on a distraught wife. In this case, though, the narrator tries to console his wife with a gift. In Lowell's poem, the wife simply rails against her brutish husband. Heaney's narrator gives his wife "wild cherry and rhododendron / . . . for a May altar of sorts," and hopes the flowers will provide "sweet chrism" (sacramental oil) to "anoint the wound" he has inflicted.

"Summer Home" shows how Heaney was trying out the styles of American Confessional poets to see which ones suited his purposes. When the husband-narrator wonders who is at fault in the marital dispute, he sounds like Sylvia Plath vowing to "scald, scald, scald" the wound. When he laments that his "children weep out the hot foreign night," that his "foul mouth takes it out" on his wife, and that he and his wife "lie stiff till dawn" after their argument, he sounds like Robert Lowell. When Heaney says about his weeping wife: "[Her voice] hoarsens / on my name, my name. // O love, here is the blame," he sounds like Anne Sexton. When he tries to cure the "wound . . . / under the homely sheet" by having sex, and when he describes his lovemaking as "a final / unmusical drive" that forces "long grains . . . / to open and split," he sounds like Theodore Roethke in his greenhouse poems. Around the time he composed "Summer Home," Heaney told Longley in a letter that he wanted to appear vulnerable and self-revealing in his new poems. To underscore the importance of "Summer Home" in his stylistic development, he later sent sections II and IV to a young publisher, Peter Fallon, who had St. Sepulcher's Press print them as broadsides. Shortly before Christmas in 1971, Fallon gave Heaney fifty copies of "Chaplet" for him to sign. Over the next four decades, Fallon would publish broadsheets, limited editions, Christmas cards, lectures, and translations by Heaney at the Gallery Press, which he began at the age of eighteen at his family home in Dublin.

The marital squabble in "Summer Home" was not typical of Heaney's home life in Berkeley, which for the most part was happy. Marie liked the sunny weather, and Christopher and Michael were intrigued by their first encounters with American culture. Heaney wrote the Longleys on September 22 that Marie was getting a good tan and the boys were playing with their model airplanes in the yard. On October 17, he told Hammond that his son Michael was showing off his familiarity with American customs by saying "Hi" rather than "Hello" to friends, and that Christopher, pretending to be a rich American, had just promised to buy his father a new car. Despite his reservations about the motley denizens of Telegraph Avenue, Heaney appreciated the people in Berkeley who welcomed him and his family into their homes.

Not long after they settled on Carleton Street, a professor who taught English and Celtic literature, Bob Tracy, began to socialize with Heaney. Bob's wife, Rebecca, a Radcliffe graduate working in child-care services, befriended Marie. Michael and Christopher played with the Tracys' children at their home two blocks down the street. On one outing, the Heaney boys taught their American friends how to play "Black and Tans"—the Irish version of "Cowboys and Indians"—which dated back to the 1920–21 Irish War of Independence.

Of all the professors Heaney got to know in California, Tom Flanagan was one of the most significant for his writing career. Heaney credited the Hibernocentric Flanagan with expanding his vision of himself as a "Northern poet" and refocusing his mind on "the wound and the work of Ireland as a whole."[6] During long conversations about Joyce, Yeats, and other Irish writers, Flanagan convinced Heaney to shed his New Critical habit of concentrating on texts as aesthetic objects and to develop a greater understanding of their biographical and historical contexts. Deeply impressed by Heaney's imagination and intellect, Flanagan based a character—Owen McCarthy—on Heaney in his novel *The Year of the French*. Heaney repaid the debt by ending his poem "Traditions" with quotes from Shakespeare and Joyce that Flanagan had used in an epigraph to his book *The Irish Novelists*.

During his year at Berkeley, Heaney taught a class on contemporary poetry, a creative-writing workshop, a freshman composition course, and several courses on modern literature. His students were enthusiastic about his teaching style. One class wrote him a collective thank-you note: "We enjoyed the course very much, and found your lectures—and the wit and charm that went with them—most rewarding."[7] The future English professor David Wyatt, who served as a grader in Heaney's large course on modern poetry during the winter quarter in 1971, admired Heaney's erudition and friendliness. "Seamus would walk in [to the classroom], unclasp his briefcase, and begin talking," Wyatt recalled. "He just began reading poems and commenting on them. . . . The syllabus was nifty, with titles like 'Snow and Moonlight in America,' for the day on James Wright. He gave us no direction on grading and let us just run. It was my first experience grading papers." Wyatt and the other grader, Frank Cebulski, sometimes met their boss at Cebulski's apartment, where Heaney liked to drink beer, talk about poets he revered such as Robert Frost, and reminisce about Ireland. To show his approval of the graders' work, he gave them gifts. On June 1, 1971, which was Wyatt's wedding anniversary, he presented Wyatt with signed copies of *Death of a Naturalist* and *Door into the Dark*, and Marie treated Wyatt and his wife to a delicious dinner of boeuf bourguignon. On another occasion, noticing that Wyatt liked his leather briefcase, Heaney said, "Here, it's yours. It was a gift to me from an old girlfriend."[8] Wyatt never forgot Heaney's generosity.

### TURMOIL AT HOME AND ABROAD

Berkeley's "elysian airs and incensed avenues," as Heaney called them in a letter to Muldoon, could be intoxicating, but never so intoxicating that he forgot his Celtic roots.[9] He regularly exchanged poems and articles with friends in Northern Ireland. Perhaps worried that he would defect to America, some of his correspondents criticized what he wrote in the United States and what seemed to be his extended California holiday. Longley, who was stuck in an unsatisfying job at the Belfast Arts Council, was especially rancorous. In a letter written on January 8, 1971, he said he objected to the tone of a recent article Heaney had published in the *Listener*. Longley also disparaged some of the poets Heaney championed at the time, such as Robert Lowell and Ted Hughes. (He repudiated Hughes's "psychopathically narrow" sensibility and "the texture of grunts and groans" in his poems, and he found Lowell's sonnets in *Notebook* equally off-putting.)[10] Heaney responded to his friend's remarks with his usual equanimity and later tried to line up readings for Longley in the United States. He tried to find gigs for Hammond and Deane, too, and was similarly generous toward Muldoon. Aware that Muldoon was interested in Native Americans, Heaney sent him a copy of Dee Brown's *Bury My Heart at Wounded Knee* as a gift.

Some of Heaney's dispatches to friends and family were motivated by homesickness and concern about the political situation as much as by altruism. Remembering the simple pleasures of his childhood at Mossbawn, he sometimes bristled against the narcissistic attitudes of Berkeley students and self-destructive excesses of the local counterculture. The university city, he told Muldoon, was "an amazing and exciting place to be," but it had been overrun by "freaks, drop-outs, drug-addicts, [and] revolutionaries." The island of Alcatraz, which Heaney could see from his house on clear days, epitomized the revolutionary zeitgeist that could turn violent. Although its famous prison had been shut down in 1963, Native Americans had occupied the island since November 1969, and skirmishes with authorities were common. In a poster proclaiming, "ALCATRAZ IS NOT AN ISLAND . . . DIG IT . . . ALL POWER TO THE PEOPLE," which Heaney sent to Muldoon, militant students expressed solidarity with the Indians who wanted to turn the island into a cultural and ecological sanctuary.[11]

To a certain extent, Heaney shared the ideals of the Native Americans and their advocates, and so did Muldoon, who in April 1970 published "The Indians on Alcatraz," a poem highlighting similarities between persecuted minorities in America and Northern Ireland. In his *Listener* article, "Views," which Longley had criticized, Heaney expressed sympathy for the students' protests against American commercialism. He was especially repelled by the way local businesses during the Christmas season turned everything—no matter how sacred—into commodities. He preferred the noncommercial gift-giving of his boyhood Christmases at Mossbawn and scoffed at the cardboard Santas around hamburger joints and gas stations, overpriced Christmas trees on used-car lots, and television programs full of commercials for expensive children's toys.

Heaney was especially startled by the way money and religion went hand in hand in the United States, even for young people who'd supposedly disavowed capitalism. He had little patience for those who begged on the street and stole from shops while professing "blissful, eternal spiritual life is available to anyone who sincerely chants the name of God." The local "commune mores," he confessed, were "an irritation to the

Celt." The hate speech of radicals also bothered him. Citing a statement from the *Black Panther* newspaper that advocated a "shoot to kill" policy against all white "fascist" oppressors, he wrote, "The violence of the Panthers' rhetoric is shocking. . . . In contrast to the revolutionary language of America, the revolutionary voice of Ireland still keeps a civil tongue in its head." The grim irony, however, was that, "While Berkeley shouts, Belfast burns. Very little property has been destroyed here, even at the height of the campus violence, during the People's Park episode or the Cambodian aftermath. Nobody, to my knowledge, has lost a home and far fewer lives have been taken in the upheavals. It has been the police versus 'the people'; establishment versus emergence. But in Belfast the unproductive blood continues to be spilled and the heraldic oppositions hold."[12] Heaney should have known that plenty of blood had been spilled during the 1960s in the United States, and plenty more would be spilled in the years to come. In 1970 alone, there were sixteen thousand murders and 738,000 violent crimes. By contrast, there were only twenty-six deaths in Northern Ireland caused by the Troubles that year.

Around New Year's Day, an incident in Berkeley made Heaney reconsider his comments about agitators only shouting in Berkeley. He learned firsthand how violence could erupt in the city's haze of drugs and strident political rhetoric. One evening, while Marie was walking to the Tracys' house to pick up her children, a mugger hit her so hard on the head that she blacked out. When she came to on the sidewalk, she realized that her assailant was dragging her to a van and telling her that if she said anything he'd kill her. Rather than comply, she screamed, kicked, and bit the man. The commotion got the attention of some tennis players on a nearby court, and the mugger let go of Marie and took off in his van. Marie staggered to the Tracys' house with bloody cuts on her legs and a swollen black eye. In pain and tearful, she stayed away from the front door so her children wouldn't panic when they saw her. Bob Tracy accompanied her to the police station and the emergency room at Herrick Hospital, where doctors treated her wounds. Rebecca Tracy, who also visited the hospital, remembered how her "strong and determined spirit . . . carried her through this nasty episode," but added, "she was very lucky she was not abducted."[13]

Several days after Heaney returned to Berkeley from a Las Vegas wedding where he'd been best man, the police brought a suspect to the family's apartment for identification. Marie was unable to say for sure whether the person in custody was the one who'd attacked her, so he was set free. The Heaneys now feared the suspected mugger would seek revenge because he knew their address. Marie was even more frightened when she spotted him on the street several weeks later. To protect them, the Heaneys' elderly landlord, whose son was a warden at San Quentin prison, gave them a file that an inmate had sharpened into a razor-sharp blade. "It was a huge trauma and gave us a glimpse of the darker side of hippy-land," Heaney remarked years later.[14] Heaney got another glimpse of the "darker side" of Berkeley when a renter and her friends from Telegraph Avenue gutted the Tracys' house while the family was in Dublin. Bob wrote Heaney, "We have lost everything we have ever owned, barring the clothes and things we had with us in Ireland."[15] Heaney did his best to console his friends.

At times, it must have seemed that Berkeley was as bad as Belfast. Ulster friends wrote Heaney about the worsening conditions at home. On November 3, 1970, the Queen's English Department chair, Mark Roberts, told him that revenge killings had spiked and students were now demanding a complete overhaul of the university's organization and operation. On November 29, John Cronin reported that a bomb had exploded at the Finaghy branch of the Northern Bank, waking him in the middle of the night. Cronin also mentioned that a bomb blast in the city had thrown a teacher out of an armchair in her house. On January 12, 1971, an *Irish Times* journalist explained that the Provisional IRA had started sending guns to local Catholics, and that the IRA had carried out executions and tar-and-feather punishments against Catholics they considered to be traitors. Heaney would soon incorporate details of these brutal incidents in poems like "Punishment."

Meanwhile, Heaney thrived as a poet in North America. He gave readings at Beaver College on November 20, 1970, Trenton State College on November 23, Canada's University of Victoria on December 3, the University of Calgary on December 11, the University of Washington on March 3, 1971, and New York's YM-YWHA's Poetry Center in late March. He appeared at a dozen venues in and around the University of Michigan during the spring of 1971. He also spoke at the University of British Columbia in Vancouver while visiting his old Queen's friend George McWhirter. Touring improved his book sales, but not enough to please Oxford University Press or to entice another American publisher to give him a new book contract. Oxford was especially disappointing because it made Heaney pay for publicity copies of *Death of a Naturalist* and *Door into the Dark,* and it refused to send copies of the books to Berkeley's bookstores so they could be sold locally. On September 26, 1970, he wrote Matthew Evans at Faber about his frustration. Two weeks later, Evans replied that he'd contacted all the main American poetry publishers, but to no avail.

The mugging in January and the grim situation in Northern Ireland contributed to Heaney's low spirits at the start of Berkeley's spring quarter on April Fool's Day in 1971. He confided to Michael Longley on April 26 that his attitude toward teaching had changed. His large creative writing class (forty-three students) had become "an exhausting assignment" with a lot of "stupid, illiterate, long-haired, hippie, Blake-ridden, Ginsberg-gullible" students "wanting to hear they're the greatest thing since, say, Charles Olson."[16] His large "Introduction to Modern British and American Literature" class was full of needy, narcissistic students as well. He looked forward to the end of term in June, but then he had to teach two summer-school courses (from June 22 to August 4) before returning to Ireland.

The prospect of going home didn't offer much comfort, either, primarily because there was no foreseeable solution to the Troubles. He told Longley, "I've given up politics. . . . I'm beginning to think of our ever-loving community as a good starting point for personal redemption, but damned little else." In his disillusioned state, he wanted to write private, confessional poems that "risk the open self . . . rather than public poems."[17] His new poems, he explained, would be "drills and augers" burrowing into repressed memories. His focus on the "open self" was Janus-faced, though, since he vowed to make "wider connections, public connections."[18] Some of his paradoxical statements were influenced by Robert Bly, who had recently argued in an influential essay, "Leaping up into Political Poetry": "The writing of political poetry is like the writing of personal poetry. [It requires] a sudden drive by the poet inward. . . . Once inside the psyche, he can speak of inward and political things with the same assurance. . . . The political activists in the literary world are wrong—they try to force political poetry out of poets by pushing them more deeply into events, making them feel guilt if they don't abandon privacy. But the truth is that the political poem comes out of the deepest privacy."[19] Heaney agreed with these assertions.

Heaney's dialectical way of delving into private and public matters garnered mixed reviews. Even the political poems about Northern Ireland's recent IRA bombings and Loyalist reprisals, which he added to his new manuscript after submitting it to Faber on October 14, 1971, did little to appease some readers. Faber published the book, whose title Heaney had changed to *Wintering Out,* on November 20, 1972. The Scottish poet Douglas Dunn, in an anonymous *Times Literary Supplement* review, scolded Heaney for being evasive about the Troubles, and called *Wintering Out* a transitional book. Stephen Spender in the *New York Review of Books* also criticized Heaney for not confronting the Troubles more directly. The English writer Gavin Ewart, in the *London Magazine,* added his voice to the chorus of critics, advising Heaney to face the current realities of Ulster and stop writing about his rural roots, which he found uninteresting. Seamus Deane took a similar position: "The poems express no politics and indeed they flee conceptual formulations with an almost indecent success. Instead they interrogate the quality of the relationship between the poet and his mixed political and literary traditions. The answer is always the same. Relationship is unavoidable, but commitment, relationship gone vulgar, is a limiting risk." Deane wanted Heaney to jump on the political bandwagon. "Commitment is demanded during a crisis," he said.[20]

Heaney made it clear in interviews following the publication of *Wintering Out* that he had neither the desire nor the gift "to start plying the pros and cons of the Ulster situation in an editorializing kind of way." In *Ploughshares,* he told James Randall that he resented the presence of Unionist politicians and paramilitary forces in Ulster, but he also resented those in his nationalist community who demanded he act as their spokesman: "Apart from the politics of the thing, I was incapable, artistically, of breaking with my first ground and my first images. So *Wintering Out* tries to insinuate itself into the roots of the political myths by feeling along the lines of language itself. It draws inspiration from etymology, vocabulary, even intonations—and these are all active signals of loyalties, Irish or British, Catholic or Protestant, in the north of Ireland." Fearing that he'd lose himself in partisanship and propaganda, Heaney told Randall: "[I heeded] an early warning system telling me to get back inside my own head."[21]

Some reviewers applauded the way Heaney approached past and present conflicts in his country. Reviewing the book in a July 1973 issue of *Phoenix,* Edna Longley concluded that Heaney had produced a book that was both powerful and aesthetically pleasing. She knew Heaney well, and knew that his most vivid poems depended on gifts he found in the hidden areas of his psyche and country. The poet and editor Jonathan Galassi chimed in by calling Heaney "undoubtedly the most talented younger poet writing in the British Isles."[22] Before long, Galassi would publish Heaney's books at Farrar, Straus and Giroux.

*Wintering Out* benefited from Heaney's immersion in American poetry during his year in the Bay Area. One of the California poets he admired the most was Gary Snyder. He especially liked the way Snyder combined a scholarly understanding of myth and religion with a down-to-earth knowledge of manual labor and the natural environment. Heaney may not have shared Snyder's "Beat" propensities for wife-sharing and bow-and-arrow hunting on his Native American–style commune in the Sierra Nevada Mountains (Heaney once signed his name facetiously in correspondence: "Gary Snyder, West Gulch, Ballyscullion, Big Sur"),[23] but he emulated Snyder's concise, imagistic poems in *Wintering Out* and *North.* With regard to how California culture affected Heaney's view of Ulster, he said, "I could see a close connection between the political and cultural assertions being made at that time by the minority in the north of Ireland and the protests and consciousness-raising that were going on in the Bay Area." American poets protesting the Vietnam War resembled Ulster poets protesting the latest iteration of the British-Irish War. "Probably the most important influence I came under in Berkeley," he claimed, "[was] that awareness that poetry was a force, almost a mode of power, certainly a mode of resistance."[24] Most of the poets he got to know during his year in Berkeley were determined to move away from the formalist style that the New Criticism had made de rigueur in universities during the middle of the twentieth century. Heaney, at least for a while, moved in step with the rebellious Californians.

Although his point of view and style shifted in the United States, Heaney in *Wintering Out* continued to examine his British-Irish heritage. He told one interviewer that his new poems "harked back to the Irish language underlay" that existed in "the hidden Ulster" beneath the British "Plantation and the Siege."[25] Perhaps thinking of the way bog bodies represented gifts to and from the underworld, he said his place-name poetry "felt like [a] pure gift." Like most gifts, this new one was intended to establish civil bonds between donors and recipients. He didn't want his poems to be taken as divisive "mouthpieces for a party line" but, instead, as unifying agents "devoted to melting down the old categories of difference."[26] Having spent a year among democratic idealists in the Bay Area, he hoped Northern Ireland would become more like the American "melting pot."

Heaney's poems about places familiar to him as a child, such as Anahorish, Toome, and Broagh, bear witness to ethnic differences and fatal clashes in the past with the hope of resolving them in the future. "Anahorish," like "Gifts of Rain" that follows it in *Wintering Out,* recalls an Edenic Gaelic source of gifts that has turned dark and destructive. "Toome," the name of a town on Lough Derg not far from Heaney's first home, is similarly divided between fertile sources of life ("alluvial mud") and weapons used to destroy life ("flints, musket-balls"). The name "Toome" may have derived from the Scottish word "toom," which means "waste ground" or "rubbish heap." Following Eliot's example in *The Waste Land,* Heaney traces journeys through past and present debacles toward hopeful signs of regeneration.

Heaney wanted to believe that a common language in a unified Ireland would someday create peaceful, productive bonds between different ethnic groups. Perhaps thinking of the biblical story of the one language that existed before builders of the Tower of Babel were scattered around the world, Heaney looks back to Gaelic as Ireland's common language that was ruined by the British Empire. He also compares Gaelic to Eden after the fall. In "Traditions," Gaelic Ireland's "guttural muse" is a latter-day Eve who was "bulled"—that is, bullied and sexually assaulted—"by the alliterative tradition" of Anglo-Saxon England. To redress this violation and fall from grace, Heaney in "A New Song" calls for a return to a utopian "gift of tongues" spoken by a Gaelic Mother Ireland. His song looks forward to an apocalypse in which the Gaelic language initiates a new union after flooding all signs of the colonial past. He sounds like an angry prophet when he says, "Our river tongues must rise / From licking deep in native haunts, / To flood, with vowelling embrace, / Demesne staked out in consonants." The vowels on Gaelic tongues, in other words, must overpower the consonantal Anglo-Saxon words that were imposed on Ireland like boundary markers by British imperialists. When not speaking like an Old Testament prophet, Heaney adopts the voice of a military recruiter preparing for linguistic battle: "And Castledawson we'll enlist / and Upperlands, each planted bawn— / Like bleaching-greens resumed by grass— / A vocable, as rath and bullaun." Elucidating the linguistic and political aims of *Wintering Out,* Heaney said, "My hope is that the poems will be vocables adequate to my whole experience."[27] His "vocables" in "A New Song" combine different vowels and consonants, but the two words at the end of the poem have distinctly Gaelic referents. *Rath* is a Gaelic hill-fort, and *bullaun* is a ritual Gaelic basin stone. In his combative mood, he wants the sites of old British plantations (Castledawson, Upperlands) and the enclosed British estates or "bawns" with "bleaching-greens" for the planters' linen industry to undergo an Irish greening.

"Westering," which appears at the end of *Wintering Out,* gives more direct evidence of the way Heaney's year in the Bay Area affected his poetry. At the beginning of the poem, the expatriate poet sits in his Berkeley apartment beneath a Rand McNally map of the moon. His perspectives alternate between America, the moon, Northern Ireland, and the Republic of Ireland. Recalling a trip from Belfast to Donegal on a Good Friday during a more peaceful time, Heaney implies that Ulster and Ireland are as alien to him now as the moon. "The moon's stigmata" on the map reminds him of a wounded Christ and a wounded Ulster "six thousand miles away." Will his native land ever return to the stability he experienced during his Catholic boyhood at Mossbawn? "I imagine untroubled dust, / A loosening gravity, / Christ weighing by his hands," he says. Heaney seems to be indulging in "California Dreamin'" when he imagines Christ on the moon with American astronauts. (Neil Armstrong and Buzz Aldrin had landed on the lunar "Sea of Tranquility" in the summer of 1969.) Like Simone Weil in *Gravity and Grace,* a book he would allude to in future poems and essays, Heaney searches for a gift of grace that will offset the gravity in places like Ulster where everything seems to be falling into ruins. His poem and book end sadly with the implication that this sort of grace can only be found in an unearthly place like the moon.

As the end of summer in California approached and Heaney had to face another fall and winter in the "troubled dust" of Belfast, he tried to adopt the stoical attitude of his persona in "Servant Boy" who resolves to "outwinter" bad weather. "Outwintering" is a farming term applied to cows who persevere without shelter from the wintry elements. According to philologists, it may have derived from the word "wunthering" in the poem "Sarah Ann" by W. F. Marshall, a twentieth-century Presbyterian minister and professor from Omagh who wrote in the Ulster Scots dialect. In Marshall's poem, a woman who works for a cruel businessman named Robert says, "I wuthered in wee Robert's, I can summer anywhere." Heaney's servant boy who is capable of "wintering out / the back-end of a bad year," though, was modeled on a family friend, Ned Thomson, who lived in a primitive cottage near Mossbawn and worked diligently for different masters despite being poorly treated. The "servant" in the poem, Heaney said, was "also meant as a portrait of a minority consciousness, a minority artist's consciousness even," and "an emblem of the human call to be more than just 'resentful and impenitent,' even while injustices are being endured."[28] Heaney identified with this allegorical figure's dedication to service. Although social hierarchies and inadequate compensation frustrate him, he maintains his self-respect and honors his obligations by patiently "carrying the warm eggs" to his masters as if they were nourishing gifts.

Students who won State Exhibitions to attend St. Columb's College in 1957: *left to right*, Robert McLaughlin, Seamus Heaney, James McGrotty, Patrick Deery. Box 90, folder 45.tif, Emory University Special Collections.

Seamus Heaney, graduation portrait, Queen's University, 1961.
Emory University Special Collections.

Seamus, Catherine, Chris, Mick, and Marie Heaney. Copyright © The Bobbie Hanvey Photographic Archives, John J. Burns Library, Boston College. Found online in *Irish Times* article by Deirdre Falvey, June 30, 2018.

Seamus Heaney with his wife and children after receiving the Nobel Prize in 1995.
Photo by Eric Roxfelt; courtesy AP.

*Left to right:* Faber editor and poet Craig Raine with Ted Hughes
and Seamus Heaney.

Three Nobel laureates: *left to right,* Seamus Heaney, Derek Walcott, Joseph Brodsky. Box 91, folder 68, Emory University Special Collections.

Marie and Seamus Heaney with President Bill Clinton at a St. Patrick's Day party in the White House, 2000. Photo by David Scull. 0960-033.tif, Emory University Special Collections.

Seamus Heaney greets Queen Elizabeth with Ireland's
President Mary McAleese during the queen's visit to Dublin Castle in 2012.
Photo courtesy PA Images/Alamy Stock.

Seamus Heaney and Michael Longley.
Box 91, folder 91, Emory University Special Collections.

Seamus Heaney in his father's hat and coat among turf stacks in Bellaghy bog, near Mossbawn, his first home. Copyright © The Bobbie Hanvey Photographic Archives, John J. Burns Library, Boston College.

Seamus Heaney's grave, Bellaghy, Northern Ireland.
Photo courtesy Paul McErlane/Alamy Stock.

# 9

# Uprooting and Rerooting

The issue of service was often a vexing one for Heaney. Should he try to be like his noble "servant boy" or should he be more like Stephen Dedalus, who proclaims *non serviam* to various masters in *A Portrait of the Artist*? Should he try to "outwinter" the Troubles at home or go into exile? Thinking about obligations to his community, Heaney wrote to James Simmons in 1971 that he was tired of serving what he called "the Ulster team." In his unpublished poem "Ulster Poetry Circus," which he sent to Simmons with his letter, he declared: "I just don't want to be parading out / With the team. I want a solo run."[1] "Parading" was a loaded term in Ulster, since it was usually Unionists who went "parading out" to show their antipathy for Irish Catholics and support for British Protestants. After returning from California, Heaney wanted to avoid all parades, no matter what their sectarian affiliation.

In his article "Belfast's Black Christmas," which the *Listener* published on December 23, 1971, Heaney blamed his country's sociopolitical ills on fear, ignorance, and arrogance. He had satirized the excesses of American culture in a *Listener* article a year before; now he denounced Ulster's culture: "We survive explosions and funerals and live on among the families of the victims, those blown apart and those in cells apart."[2] He blamed the British army, which had entered Northern Ireland during the summer of 1969, for aggravating the situation. He told a story about the Ulster police apprehending him with his three-year-old son because his car tax was out-of-date as an example of the way Catholics were still being harassed.

Heaney feared for his family's safety when the Provisional IRA, which had split off from the official IRA on December 28, 1969, became more combative. He knew that the British army, Ulster constabulary, and Protestant paramilitary groups would respond in kind. In "Belfast's Black Christmas," he asked, "Who's to know the next target on the Provisional list? Who's to know the reprisals won't strike where you are?" The good cheer that normally accompanied the season of gift-giving was hard to find. Ordinary routines—like going to a pub or a grocery store—were getting more dangerous. A security guard stopped Marie in a department store, suspecting the clock she carried in her shopping bag was a bomb. A few days before she was interrogated, a bomb had exploded close to where Marie was walking on University Road. In California, Heaney had a vision of "a wounded man falling" toward him "with his bloodied hands lifted."[3] He now realized that his daydream might become a reality at any time.

The Stormont government's policy of internment, which had commenced on August 9, 1971, made the situation worse when it was discovered that no Protestant troublemakers were arrested; only those suspected of having ties to the IRA were arrested, and many of these suspects had little or nothing to do with the IRA. A march in Londonderry/Derry on January 30, 1972, which was organized by NICRA to protest the government's anti-Catholic policies, ended with British soldiers firing at protestors who approached barricades near the city square. Thirteen protestors were killed (some were shot in the back), and a fourteenth died later. Numerous others were wounded. "Bloody Sunday," as the day in Northern Ireland came to be known, was the worst assault on civilians by the British military in the United Kingdom since the Peterloo massacre in 1819.

Shortly before Bloody Sunday, when Heaney's Queen's colleague Robert Greacen had asked him to sign a letter to a newspaper protesting the way the government was handling the sectarian conflict, Heaney had replied, "I have never written a letter to the papers in my life and am waiting, I suppose, for an apocalyptic moment."[4] To many in Northern Ireland, Bloody Sunday was "an apocalyptic moment." Heaney was deeply upset by the Bloody Sunday massacre, but he refused to sign Greacen's letter. He did, however, join a protest march on February 6 in Newry, a city about twenty miles south of Lough Neagh. He planned to link up with his friends Brian Friel, Michael Longley, and Seamus Deane. Unfortunately, he never found them. Deane wrote Heaney on February 22, 1972, to apologize for the confusion, and asked if Heaney had made up his mind to leave Belfast for the Republic of Ireland. (Deane had moved south to teach at University College, Dublin.) "Take care of yourself in bombsville," he said at the end of his letter.[5]

Reluctant to speak out about the Troubles, Heaney nevertheless wrote about Bloody Sunday and the protest march in "The Road to Derry." He used the Irish ballad "The Boys of Mullaghbawn" as a model for describing his trip north on Wednesday, February 2, 1972, to attend funerals for the slain marchers. As in traditional elegies, Heaney imagines nature—rivers, wind, frost, clouds—mourning the dead. The poem also follows elegiac convention by offering a consoling afterlife, in this case a future "Derry" where justice can grow like an oak tree from the buried bodies. The poem ends with the resonant lines: "And in the dirt lay justice like an acorn in the winter / Till its oak would sprout in Derry where the thirteen men lay dead." As in "Requiem for the Croppies," lives sacrificed in the pursuit of justice are conceived of as gifts given to the land with the hope of return gifts.

Heaney wrote another political elegy when he heard that an old eel-fishing friend, Louis O'Neil, had been blown up by a bomb shortly after the Bloody Sunday funerals. The two men had spent many pleasant hours drinking in the Ardboe pub run by Marie's father. On the night O'Neil died, the police had imposed a curfew to prevent further violence. Heaney's father-in-law had closed the pub, so O'Neil went to another pub that opened its back door to customers. For Heaney, among O'Neil's virtues were his reticence and free-spirited resistance to authority. In the poem "Casualty," O'Neil shares Heaney's propensity for silence. He communicates without raising his voice and sometimes orders drinks "by a lifting of the eyes / And a discreet dumb-show / Of pulling off the top." O'Neil plays the role of a doppelgänger and father figure who returns from the dead to question Heaney's quietistic approach to the Troubles. Heaney's reference to his "tentative art" in "Casualty" may have arisen from guilt over how tentative he'd been with his protest elegy "The Road to Derry." Fearing readers would interpret the poem as nationalist propaganda, he withheld it from publication until allowing the *Derry Journal* to print it in 1997, on the twenty-fifth anniversary of Bloody Sunday.

What made Bloody Sunday especially galling for Ulster Catholics was the biased investigation conducted by John Widgery, Lord Chief Justice of England and Wales. Its conclusions, which were made public in April 1972, exonerated the British paratroopers who'd killed and wounded the marchers. It was not until Lord Saville issued a more comprehensive report decades later that the British government officially acknowledged that the paratroopers had committed a crime and lied about it. In 2010, Prime Minister David Cameron responded to the new report in a televised address: "There is no doubt, there is nothing equivocal, there are no ambiguities. What happened on Bloody Sunday was both unjustified and unjustifiable."[6] It had taken the British government almost forty years to reach this simple conclusion.

The English prime minister in office during Bloody Sunday, Ted Heath, realized that he had to do something about the crisis. In a bold gesture, he suspended the Stormont government in March 1972. He also appointed William Whitelaw as secretary of state and put the English government in charge of Ulster. Whitelaw tried to be a peacemaker, but the violence continued. Bloody Friday—July 21, 1972—followed Bloody Sunday. On that day, the IRA detonated twenty-two bombs around Belfast during an eighty-minute period, killing nine and wounding 130. The bombings were among 1,300 carried out by the IRA in 1972. During the IRA's bombing campaigns, Catholics were often the victims. (The IRA would kill more Catholics than the Protestant paramilitary groups, security services, and the British army combined.)

When Dennis O'Driscoll asked Heaney whether "fear or intimidation" had convinced him to leave Belfast, Heaney said: "No . . . , even though Belfast in the early seventies was a pretty unpleasant place to be."[7] The poems and articles he wrote at the time, however, indicate that he felt his home city was more than just "unpleasant." His poetic sequence "A Northern Hoard" depicts the city as a nightmare "of gunshot, siren and clucking gas" in which local citizens have only two options: "petrify or uproot." He told the Yeats scholar Mary Fitzgerald that he'd received a death threat on the phone for expressing his nationalist sympathies. He later confirmed in *Stepping Stones* that he'd gotten a threatening phone call after reading a poem that criticized the B-Special Constabulary on a 1970 TV program, "Heaney in Limboland."

Heaney's year in California had given him a new perspective on Ulster and also a sense of what it was like to make "a solo run" in a new place. As the situation in Belfast deteriorated, he applied for a fellowship to work in England and thought about going back to Berkeley (he had an open-ended offer to return). In addition, he visited a renovated barn near Marie's childhood home in Ardboe with the idea of living there with his family. He and Marie also talked about buying a house in County Antrim, County Londonderry/Derry, or County Tyrone. On trips to see the painter Barrie Cooke and his wife, Sonja Landjweer, who resided about sixty miles southwest of Dublin, Heaney considered moving close to them. Cooke was all for Heaney putting dysfunctional Ulster behind him. According to Heaney, Cooke's political ideals derived "from the Buddhist-oriented, environmentally conscious culture of Californian poets such as Gary Snyder." Born in England and educated at Harvard, Cooke had spent the early part of his career in the Irish countryside with no electricity or running water. Like Snyder on his commune in the Sierras, he hunted for food and pursued his career as an artist. He was, Heaney said, a "gifted painter" who "kept alive the gift for praise without ever averting his eyes from the worst that the age has to offer."[8] He counseled Heaney to focus on his artistic gifts and let the politicians sort out the mess in Northern Ireland.

Cooke's close friend Ted Hughes also played a crucial role in encouraging Heaney to leave Belfast. On March 19, 1972, Heaney told Hughes that his advice about resigning from Queen's "was one of the first things to bring the decision out of daydream into possibility." (Hughes had originally suggested that Heaney support his family by becoming a professional eel fisherman on Lough Neagh.) As luck would have it, Heaney heard about an opportunity to rent a stone cottage in the Wicklow Hills, about twenty-five miles south of Dublin. He worried that his Ulster friends would regard his departure as an abdication of his political responsibilities, but, in the end, he decided he would be sinning against his gift if he remained at Queen's. On the same day he wrote Hughes that part of him was "sorry to leave Belfast at the moment of truth,"[9] he told his Faber editor Charles Monteith that he planned to go to Wicklow for a year, and maybe longer, if he could make a decent living as a freelance writer.

There were numerous reasons for Heaney's departure from Belfast. In his *Ploughshares* interview with James Randall, he explained that he resented "being interviewed as, more or less, a spokesman for the Catholic minority during this early stage of the Troubles." He also felt that his social and academic responsibilities distracted him from his writing. "I didn't feel that my work was sufficiently the center of my life, so I decided I would resign; and I now realize that my age was the age that is probably crucial in everybody's life—around thirty-three [Christ's age when he was crucified]. I was going through a sort of rite of passage. . . . I wanted to leave Belfast because I wanted to step out of the rhythms I had established; I wanted to be alone with myself."[10]

The person most instrumental in enabling Heaney's move to County Wicklow was Ann Saddlemyer, a University of Toronto professor of Irish literature who had just finished editing a collection of John Millington Synge's letters. During one of her research trips to Ireland, she had heard that Heaney was looking for a place to live outside Belfast. On January 29, 1972, she wrote him a long letter explaining that she would be happy to rent her cottage to him until June 1973, and perhaps until her sabbatical year in 1976 or 1977, as long as the cottage was free for part of each summer so she could rent it to tourists or stay there herself. The cost would be minimal—about £25 per month. She promised to tidy up the grounds and make sure the roofers and electricians had finished renovations. If the Heaneys wanted a telephone, an extra storage heater, and other accessories, they could install them. She was sure Heaney would enjoy the rustic area around the cottage; there were outdoor tables for picnics, walking paths in Devil's Glen, and views of the Irish Sea from the hills. As for transportation, it was easy to travel to Dublin; buses left for the city from the nearby town of Ashford six or seven times a day.

Shortly before Easter 1972, Heaney visited Glanmore Cottage, which had once been the gate lodge on the Glanmore Estate owned by the Synge family. ("Glanmore" came from Gaelic words meaning "the big glen," and may have originally referred to the whole valley in Wicklow near Glanmore Castle, the home of John Synge's ancestors.) The cottage had a slate roof, iron gates, blue gingerbread trim, ornamental red brick around the windows, and rose gardens. On the first floor, there was a living room with a fireplace, and a bedroom Christopher and Michael could use. Heaney and his wife could sleep in the bedroom on the second floor. In another smaller bedroom, they planned to set up a cot if they had another child.

The sitting room had a fireplace, glass-topped walnut table, and pink armchairs. Heaney was thrilled to sign the lease.

In August 1972, after a raucous party with Ted Hughes and other literary friends in Belfast, Heaney drove his family to Saddlemyer's cottage. Once he'd settled into a routine in his new home, he told friends he felt as if he'd returned to his first farm near Bellaghy. "Everything in me felt connected up to an energy source," he said. "Maybe it was because of certain physical aspects of the house—cold cement floor in the living room, latches slapping up and down on the doors, a fire in the grate—things that connected back to the Mossbawn house."[11] He missed central heating, but found he could concentrate better on his writing without all the distractions of modern appliances and high-tech communications. He picked blackberries as he'd done on his way to Anahorish and took walks through the lush fields and rolling hills around the cottage. He felt even more at home when a dozen cows charged him on the road from Ashford. Noticing a local farmer's wife, Mrs. Johnson, hustling to catch up to the errant herd, he spread his arms wide and shouted a command he'd learned as a boy to make the cows halt. Mrs. Johnson was impressed by Heaney's cattle-herding skills, and soon she and her husband accepted Heaney's family into their small group of friends. Another farming family, the Chapmans, also befriended the Heaneys. Like their father as a youth, the children visited local farms, took baths in a tub in front of a fire, gazed at stars on the dark country nights, and got a Catholic education at a local convent school.

Heaney's friends reacted to his move to the Republic in different ways. On August 23, 1972, Douglas Dunn wrote, "It seems a good idea to be there rather than Belfast, and I hope you get the peace you deserve and write more splendid poems."[12] Michael Longley, who was now assistant director of literature and education for the Arts Council of Northern Ireland, envied Heaney's idyllic retreat from the madding crowd. David Hammond was sorry his good friend was no longer in Belfast, but continued to collaborate with him on BBC projects. On October 20, Harry Chambers, the editor of the journal *Phoenix*, wrote, "I take it you were virtually driven out of Belfast."[13] Many shared Chambers's opinion and concluded that Heaney would never return. To set the record straight, Heaney told the *Daily Telegraph* reporter Alan Riddel, "I *will* go back, but not for a long time."[14] In fact, Heaney regularly visited Northern Ireland to see family and friends or to give lectures and readings.

Some in the north were pleased that Heaney had gone south. On September 9, 1972, a writer calling himself the "Observer" wrote a sarcastic column about Heaney for Ian Paisley's newspaper, the *Protestant Telegraph*: "This man is described as being one of the foremost 'Irish' poets and intellectuals of modern times, but personally speaking, I cannot discern any aspect of his writings which would engender incredulous amazement at his talents. . . . Some months ago a programme for schools was broadcast which included a piece by Heaney, and I was filled with astonishment and resentment that such an item was considered suitable for dessimination [*sic*] by radio. It struck me as being as blatant a piece of papist propaganda as I ever listened to. . . . If reports be true, Heaney has removed himself to the Pope's colony and it is to be hoped he will remain domiciled in that land flowing with milk and honey."[15] Heaney didn't find out about this poorly written editorial, titled "Cheerio," until later in the fall of 1972, when he returned to Belfast, but he wasn't surprised by it. On November 8, he wrote Karl Miller that Paisley's newspaper had given him "a boot in the back." He also told Miller that he'd been "literally afraid to drive in the streets" and was glad "to be out of Belfast."[16]

Neighbors around Glanmore Cottage helped take the sting out of the "boot in the back" from Paisley's allies in the north. Not long after he arrived, Heaney went to a luxurious, eighteenth-century mansion in Luggala, a short distance away, where the music-promoter Garech Browne welcomed him. Browne, who'd married a princess from India, was related to the Guinness family and used his fortune to support traditional Irish music and Irish artists. He'd established Claddagh Records in 1959 with his friend, the Irish psychiatrist Ivor Browne. Together they recorded Irish music as well as poets such as Heaney. They were especially fond of the Uillean pipes. (Heaney would eventually have a Uillean piper, Liam O'Flynn, accompany him at poetry readings.) Browne's friend Paddy Moloney—a master of the pipes who performed with the Chieftains—was at the mansion with his friends Mick and Bianca Jagger when Heaney visited. Heaney took this serendipitous encounter with the Rolling Stones's lead singer and his glamorous wife as a sign of better times ahead.

Browne seemed to know all the celebrities in the British-Irish cultural scene and wanted to make sure Heaney didn't become a hermit in his stone cottage. He invited the Heaneys to an eightieth birthday party for Robert Graves on July 24, 1975. An admirer of Graves's work, Heaney asked the elderly English writer to write out his poem "Sick Love" and give it to Marie, who also liked Graves's poetry. Graves obliged, but then the crusty, competitive English poet got angry when Marie said she was fond of Theodore Roethke's poetry. The Heaneys had a more congenial time with another one of Browne's friends, the film director John Boorman, who lived in nearby Anamoe. In July, Boorman had released the film version of James Dickey's novel *Deliverance* and no doubt talked to Heaney about working on the blockbuster film with the talented but temperamental American poet-turned-novelist-and-screenwriter.

Various poets helped fortify Heaney during his self-imposed exile in Wicklow. At London's Poetry International festival in the early fall of 1972, he met Joseph Brodsky, who'd been imprisoned and later expelled from the Soviet Union after authorities accused him of being a paranoid schizophrenic and subversive poet. (He would win a Nobel Prize for Literature in 1987.) In London, Brodsky seemed nervous and wary among all the other poets, but he perked up when he learned that Heaney was from Belfast. The fact that Heaney had lived in a dangerous city and gone into exile for political and literary reasons made him more sympathetic to Brodsky. Heaney met Brodsky again in February 1973 in Amherst at a University of Massachusetts poetry festival and talked to him at length about poetry and politics. By that time, Brodsky was a professor at nearby Mount Holyoke College. They crossed paths again at the University of Michigan in 1974. For Heaney, Brodsky's subversive intellect and passion for well-crafted poetry reminded him of his Ulster friends.

Around this time, Heaney also got to know Robert Lowell, who, like Brodsky, combined a devotion to the Western canon with a rebellious attitude toward tradition and authority. Heaney corresponded with Lowell after broadcasting a complimentary review of his three books of free-form sonnets: *History, For Lizzie and Harriet,* and *The Dolphin* on RTÉ in July 1973. Lowell had praised some of Heaney's poems about the Bog People, which spurred him to write more of them and to visit the Tollund Man in Silkeborg and the Grauballe Man at Aarhus in October 1973, during a lecture trip on behalf of the Danish Association of English Teachers in Denmark. Lowell's ambivalence toward sacrificial gift-giving, which he expressed in poems like "For the Union Dead" (he called it "man's lovely, / peculiar power to choose life and die"), jibed with Heaney's mixed feelings about the sacrifices of the Bog People and Irish political martyrs. Recognizing a kindred spirit and equally skilled craftsman, Lowell soon wrote a book-jacket blurb for *North* extolling Heaney as "the most important Irish poet since Yeats."

In the 1970s, as he worked on his bog poems, Heaney paid close attention to reports of archaeological excavations in Ireland as well as in Denmark. In 1972, he went to the heather bog in Belderg, County Mayo, where the archaeologist Seamus Caulfield guided him around the dig. (The poem "Belderg" recalls the unearthed Norse settlement there.) Heaney was also interested in the excavations at Dublin's Wood Quay and got to know Brendán O'Ríordán and Tom Delaney, the archaeologists responsible for unearthing Viking relics that were exhibited at the National Museum of Ireland. During the summer of 1972, while driving around southwest England with Marie, he saw the chalk figures carved in the hills during the Bronze Age. The Heaneys stopped and rambled around the Dorchester earthworks, which were about 2,500 years old. They also visited an earthen fort called Maiden Castle erected in Dorset around 600 BC. While staying at a Tudor manor in Gloucestershire where a sister-in-law lived, he composed the poem "Bone Dreams" about his affinity for prehistoric craftsmen. The poem would appear in *North*.

On December 5, 1973, about two weeks after "Bog Queen" came out in the *Listener,* Philip Hobsbaum wrote Heaney a letter predicting that his interest in Iron Age rituals would result in major poetry. Ted Hughes agreed and, like Lowell, wanted to see more of "the bogman's offspring."[17] Stories about exhumed humans and animals had always appealed to Hughes. The first time he experienced "poetic frisson from literature," he told Heaney in a letter, was when he'd read a story about the preserved corpse of a saber-toothed tiger that was dug from a swamp. The day after receiving Hughes's letter, Heaney thanked his friend again for his poetic "confirmation" and indicated that he would be willing to send Hughes's sister, Olwyn, a series of bog poems that she could publish in a limited edition at her Rainbow Press.[18] Over the next two years, Heaney and Olwyn would correspond about the project and convince their mutual friend Barrie Cooke to illustrate the book. Olwyn asked Faber to delay the publication of *North* so it would not hurt sales of the special edition. In the end, Rainbow Press published 150 copies of *Bog Poems* in May 1975, and *North* came out a month later from Faber. Many critics thought the bog poems were Heaney's most distinctive work.

### MAKING THE GIFT PAY

Yeats in his poem "The Choice" contended that "The intellect of man is forced to choose / perfection of the life, or the work," and that if "the work" was chosen "an empty purse" could be expected. To avoid an empty purse, Heaney rented his Ashley Avenue house to students and lined up as many lectures, readings, and writing assignments as possible. In September 1972, he traveled to St. Anne's College, Oxford, to discuss Ted Hughes's poetry, and during the same month he gave a series of poetry readings in Leicestershire schools. On October 25, he read at Mary Immaculate College of Education in Limerick. On November 22, he returned to England to read at the University of Manchester. At the end of the year, he lectured at other venues in Ireland. During the first half of 1973 he gave numerous readings and lectures in the United States, Scotland, Wales, and England.

Heaney also bolstered his income by taking on editing and publishing jobs. He informed James Simmons on February 3, 1972, that he intended to start an international magazine called *Soundings*. He compiled annual anthologies for Blackstaff Press in Belfast, which he also called *Soundings*. Hoping to dismantle barriers between Ireland's northern and southern poets, he published Ciaran Carson and Frank Ormsby from the north and Peter Fallon, Harry Clifton, and Dermot Healy from the south. In the "Editor's Note" to *Soundings '72*, he applauded the way new Irish poets were exploring ancestral and cultural traditions, and the way these "soundings" might promote peaceful change in Ulster.

For additional revenue, Heaney stepped up his submissions of prose and poetry to journals such as the *Listener*, *Irish Times*, *Times Literary Supplement*, and *Hibernia*. Acceptances, however, were never guaranteed, and payments for poems were minimal. On October 6, 1972, the editor of *Evergreen* magazine in Northern Ireland asked Heaney for some political poems but then rejected the "Bog Queen" and some other bog poems Heaney submitted, arguing they weren't political enough. On October 30, Heaney's financial anxieties increased when Belfast's L'Estrange & Brett Solicitors told him he had to pay off the mortgage on his Belfast house. (He sold the house in 1976.) The welfare of his family now depended on his artistic productivity and marketability, but he found it difficult to write under pressure.

One of his moneymaking schemes was to translate *Buile Suibhne*, the poem about the Ulster king whose journey from northern to southern Ireland paralleled Heaney's. After offending a Christian saint and killing a cleric, the legendary Suibhne had been punished with a curse that turned him into a nomadic bird. "He was a very useful mask—or a very useful objective correlative . . . in so far as I began to think of him as being like myself," Heaney told an interviewer.[19] Above all, Suibhne—or "Sweeney," as Heaney translated his Gaelic name—embodied Heaney's conviction that he was an "inner émigré" in his own country. Hoping his move to the Irish-Catholic south would make him feel more at home, Heaney, like Sweeney, realized to his chagrin that he no longer felt at home anywhere. "When I came down here [to the Republic of Ireland]," he said, "I realized that I was probably more part of the [Northern] British literary thing, certainly, than I had realized. And I have a . . . very ambivalent feeling about some of the more vehemently 'Irish' writers [in the Republic]."[20] Like many immigrants, he inhabited a liminal space between homes rather than an actual, permanent home.

Faber offered a contract for Heaney's translation *Sweeney Astray* at the end of 1972. The jobs that assured him the steadiest income, though, were for BBC radio in Belfast and Radio Telefís Éireann (RTÉ) in Dublin. Heaney often traveled to Belfast to read poems and discuss Ulster's political situation on the radio. On December 15, 1972, he went to the BBC headquarters in London to record a conversation with Philip Oakes about *Wintering Out*. Three and a half weeks later, he participated in a conversation about Yeats's *Memoirs* on the BBC's *Now Read On* program. He continued to supply David Hammond with scripts for Belfast's BBC schools programs and began a weekly program for RTÉ that paid him for reviewing books.

In one his radio scripts titled *The Long Garden,* Heaney read passages from different works in which older people "look back to their first home . . . as a happy innocent place" and as a "kind of Garden of Eden." He alluded to Wordsworth's "Intimations of Immortality," Joyce's *A Portrait of the Artist,* Kavanagh's "The Long Garden," MacNeice's "Autobiography," Thomas's "Fern Hill," the Bible's book of Genesis, and other narratives that illustrate the romantic idea of a golden age of peace and joy in the past. As he contemplated his own past from the vantage point of Glanmore Cottage, he represented himself once again as an exiled Adam desperately trying to renew bonds with his Edenic home on the farm in Northern Ireland. He also identified with St. Colum Cille, who'd left his home in Donegal to build a monastery in Iona. Heaney was especially moved by the way the saint had put Irish soil in his shoes so he wouldn't forget his old home. As Heaney pointed out, the saint was "literally walking on his home ground, even though he was living miles away from it."[21] One reason Heaney translated *Buile Suibhne* (he completed a draft by April 1973) was because it gave him another opportunity to return to his home ground.

## MYTHICAL GIFT EXCHANGES IN *NORTH*

Dissatisfied with his first draft of *Sweeney Astray,* Heaney set it aside around the time his daughter Catherine Ann was born. Her due date had been his birthday, April 13, but she was late and had to be induced on April 25, 1973. (Heaney would write about her birth in his poem "A Pillowed Head.") Over the next year, his children kept him busy, and so did "the bogman's offspring." By the fall of 1974, he had assembled enough bog poems and other poems for his next collection, which he planned to supplement with the prose poems he'd written in Berkeley. On October 30, 1974, Monteith wrote Heaney that the prose poems would "upset the general feel and texture of the book," but added: "[they'd] fit beautifully into that autobiography which we've talked about."[22] A year later, the prose poems appeared in *Stations,* a pamphlet issued by Ulsterman Publications in Belfast. Heaney never produced an autobiography, although he and Dennis O'Driscoll published the 522-page, autobiographical *Stepping Stones* in 2008.

Heaney worried that many readers would find his new poems about ancient corpses in bogs and current atrocities in Ulster gruesome and inaccessible. The overall response to *North*, though, was enthusiastic. After its release on June 9, 1975, the first edition of 6,750 copies sold out quickly, and a second printing was ordered. Most of the negative criticism came from Heaney's peers in Ulster. His former student Ciaran Carson wrote one of the most scathing reviews for the *Honest Ulsterman*. Carson's "Escaped from the Massacre?" borrowed a phrase from the last poem in *North*, "Exposure," to cast Heaney as a befuddled, pusillanimous escapist. In Carson's eyes, Heaney had misrepresented Ulster "by falsifying issues" and "by applying wrong notions of history" to the Troubles. The journalistic poems near the end of the book were misguided, too, and even the portrait of Heaney on the back cover, which Edward McGuire had painted in 1973, was a failure. What especially irked Carson was the way his former professor had explained the sectarian violence in terms of fertility rituals and vegetation myths. Heaney had squandered his "gift of precision" by representing Ulster's battles in terms of sacrificial gift-exchange rituals. In the process, he'd become a "laureate of violence—a mythmaker, an anthropologist of ritual killing, an apologist for 'the situation,' in the last resort, a mystifier," and his poems had "degenerated into a messy historical and religious surmise—a kind of Golden Bough activity."[23] The "mythical method," which Eliot had championed in his famous review of Joyce's *Ulysses* as a way of "giving a shape and a significance to the immense panorama of futility and anarchy which is contemporary history," in Heaney's hands was a travesty.[24] Carson claimed that Heaney had fabricated a "Madame Tussaud's Gallery" of corpses for voyeurs. Changing metaphors to make sure readers understood his distaste for *North*, Carson said the book amounted to little more than a box of "verbal Cornflakes."[25]

Edna Longley's review, which also appeared in the *Honest Ulsterman*, was almost as contemptuous. She contended that *North* was a compendium of clichés, pretentious archaeological and philological allusions, and tedious discourses on history. Another Northern Irish writer, Eiléan Ní Chuilleanáin, echoed some of these damning remarks. To her, Heaney's sexual metaphors in "Ocean's Love to Ireland" and "Act of Union" pandered to a sexist audience. The only poem that the three reviewers approved of was the last one in the book, "Exposure," no doubt because in it Heaney also questioned the value of his poems. Set on a damp, cold, December day in Wicklow, "Exposure" suggests that his new work might be ill-conceived and futile. Obviously depressed, he asks himself why he keeps writing: "[Is it] for the ear? For the people? / For what is said behind-backs?" He thinks of himself as a beleaguered soldier, "a wood-kerne" who has fled an embattled country and is now homeless and disoriented. He would like to be a political David confronting a British Goliath, "a hero / On some muddy compound, / His gift like a slingstone / Whirled for the desperate." As in "Digging," he wants his pen—the material symbol of his gift—to be an effective weapon in the fight for justice. But he worries that his "responsible *tristia*" might be pointless. In the end, he might be what his detractors think he is—just another self-involved poet mulling over his frustrations on a rainy day.

Heaney's response to the history of ethnic strife in his country was not, as his critics argued, simplistic or smug or apologetic or entirely futile. It was agonizingly complex, and so was his view of the proper role of poets during political crises. If he'd failed to articulate an ethical or pragmatic response to the Troubles, so had his critics, which explains why he told an interviewer he was "very angry with a couple of snotty remarks [about *North*] by people who don't know what they are talking about and speak as if the bog images were picked up for convenience."[26] Rather than apologize for the killings in a mystifying way, as Carson asserted, Heaney critiqued the mythical assumptions that motivated the killings. He was not so much a "laureate of violence" as a judge of violence. *North* is predominantly an elegiac book that bears witness to gruesome deaths, whether ancient or modern, and that denies the mythical consolation that elegies traditionally offer as the ultimate gift. Heaney deplores the historical cycle of "thick-witted couplings and revenges," as he puts it in the title poem of *North*, in which "memory [keeps] incubating the spilled blood."

The two poems that bracket the first section of *North*, "Antaeus" and "Hercules and Antaeus," evoke Greek myths to mourn the multitudes in Ireland who have died fighting British imperialists. He feels akin to Antaeus, the son of the Greek Earth goddess Gaea and sea god Poseidon, and he suggests that the close connection between son and mother (like the one between Heaney and his mother) is inappropriately Oedipal. Even as an adult, Antaeus admits he "cannot be weaned" from his mother. Is he just a grown-up baby? Will he always have to be "cradled in the dark [earth] that wombed" him? The Antaeus poems underscore the paradox of Heaney's creativity: that his powerful gift came from an umbilical connection to an *omphalos* like Mossbawn and Glanmore Cottage. He told John Haffenden in *Viewpoints*, "I found in Glanmore . . . a period of confirmation, some kind of coming into home. . . . Glanmore was like the original place."[27] This "confirmation," like others in his life, referred to a rite of initiation that brought with it in-spiriting literary gifts like the original gifts of the Holy Spirit he'd received as a boy during Confirmation in that other "original place"—the Catholic Church. His retreat to Glanmore Cottage may have signified a regression to a womb-like origin, a substitute Mossbawn or church, but it was also a productive return to a "gifted state."

The title poem, "North," highlights the self-reflexive way Heaney circles back to his ethical and aesthetic obsessions. The narrator juxtaposes idealized assumptions about the Vikings and Norsemen with "the secular / powers of the Atlantic," "the unmagical / invitations of Iceland," "the pathetic colonies / of Greenland," and the bloodthirsty, land-grabbing conquerors buried "in the solid / belly of stone ships." The narrator communes with the ghosts of mythical raiders so he can denounce the myths that glorify them as heroes. In Heaney's judgmental imaginings, the dead confess that their conquests were spurred by a lust for illicit "gifts" of sex, property, and treasure. He counsels himself to examine the history of geographical and commercial exploits with an "eye clear / as the bleb of the icicle." Rather than "mythmaker" and "apologist," he is a clear-eyed demystifier who scrutinizes past and present evidence of violence.

What Heaney trains his eye on most frequently in *North* is history's graveyard. At one point, he conceives of himself as another Hamlet, a "skull handler . . . / coming to consciousness / by jumping in graves." In these memento mori scenes, he meditates on the causes and consequences of sacrifices, and weighs the losses against the gains. In "Bog Queen," a British aristocrat, Lady Moira, represents the capitalist forces in Ulster that interfere with the natural process of gift exchange in which dead bodies are given to the ground so that the ground can reciprocate with gifts of new life. In "Punishment," a community near Windeby, Germany, kills a young woman for her alleged adultery. Heaney compares the ancient woman's punishment to the rough justice meted out to contemporary Catholic women in Northern Ireland who have sexual relationships with British soldiers or Protestant police. (The IRA sometimes stripped, tarred, feathered, and shackled these "traitorous" women to lampposts or railings to publicly shame them.) Heaney suggests that violence against women who flout taboos hasn't changed much in two thousand years. Although he punishes himself for not protesting loudly enough (he admits to casting "stones of silence"), he bears silent witness to the way communities refuse to respect women as gifts and the gifts of life they create. (It should be noted that a Canadian professor's DNA analysis of Glob's "Windeby Girl," who was supposedly strangled for adultery, indicated that the body was actually that of a sixteen-year-old man who probably died from malnutrition.)

Most of the poems in *North* recount gift exchanges that have gone bad. One poem, "Ocean's Love to Ireland," compares the sexual violation of a young Irish woman by the Elizabethan poet-adventurer Sir Walter Raleigh with the widespread violation of Mother Ireland by the British Empire. "Act of Union" documents a similar assault by England against Ireland. In this case, a violently Oedipal son—an Irish rebel who will attack Father England and martyr himself to Mother Ireland—is produced by the fateful union. In "Hercules and Antaeus," a more archaic "act of union" produces Gaea's son, Antaeus, whose name in Greek means "antagonist." (Famous for killing his wrestling opponents, he built a temple of skulls until Hercules lifted him off the ground, thereby separating him from his mother, and strangled him.) To Heaney's revisionary point of view, Antaeus is a precursor of Irish martyrs and exiles who died after being uprooted from their Irish home ground, but who ultimately returned to the soil of Mother Ireland.

In *North*'s gendered allegories, the paternal, maternal, and filial actors normally come to tragic ends. Like *The Waste Land*, *North* is a kind of echo chamber in which the poet's personae speak in different voices about the breakdown of civility in a war-ravaged culture. Tragic events can be traced back to gifts being mistreated or given for the wrong reasons. Despite its dystopian vision of Northern Ireland and history in general, the book expresses hope that gift exchanges in the future will restore peaceful, productive bonds between antagonists. For Heaney, Wordsworth's epic poem *The Prelude,* with its emphasis on the growth of the poet's gift and awareness of the Earth as a divine gift, was one "working model for that evolution of a higher consciousness in response to an apparently intolerable conflict" that might, in the end, resolve the "intolerable conflict."[28]

Heaney placed "Mossbawn" at the beginning of his book to introduce readers to the sort of tranquil, enlightened consciousness he associated with his first home and, by extension, with Glanmore Cottage. Dedicated to his beloved Aunt Mary, the poem captures a scene of domestic peace and gift-making. She sits as if meditating in the "sunlit absence" of the Mossbawn kitchen after making scones. The tin scoop "sunk past its gleam" in a flour bin recalls the "visionary gleam" of Wordsworth's poetic gift in "Intimations of Immortality." When Heaney exclaims "here is a space / again," he implies that in Wicklow he has recaptured the original "space" and "gleam" of his gifted boyhood state.

### A FRIEND'S DISRUPTIVE GIFTS

Heaney hoped to see his friends Ted Hughes and Robert Lowell at the Kilkenny Arts Festival during the last week of August 1975. As one of the organizers, Heaney had invited Lowell and several other writers, including George Mackay Brown, Stephen Spender, and Seamus Deane, to the summer festival. Heaney had first met Lowell in 1972 at a London party hosted by Sonia Orwell to celebrate Lowell's marriage to his third wife, Caroline Blackwood. During a half-hour conversation, the American poet had dazzled Heaney with his knowledge of poetry and history. He had also disconcerted Heaney with a favorite pastime—ranking other poets. (Usually, Lowell reserved the top rank for himself.) Heaney had heard about Lowell's manic-depressive episodes that had earned him the nickname "Cal," an allusion to the mad Roman emperor Caligula, and realized that Lowell was one of those artists, like the composer Seán Ó Riada, who believed in "trusting the gift" and "risking gift's undertow."

It was at the Kilkenny festival that Heaney got a better understanding of Lowell's complex genius. Lowell stayed for the entire week, even though he'd agreed to give only one reading. Deane reported that Lowell indulged in the festival's "magnificent debauch." When Deane saw him, he was downing shots of whiskey and glasses of milk, even though he wasn't supposed to drink alcohol while taking medication for his manic-depression. One night after a cocktail party, according to Deane:

> [Lowell] summoned me over to talk to him, since I seemed to be the only person still conscious. A long monologue ensued, in which Lowell wondered about poetry and power, the relative status in world history of Shakespeare, Virgil, and Dante, on the one hand, and of Napoleon, Stalin, and Hitler, on the other. He was talking very fast, his eyes darting like fish, and he grabbed my arm every so often and then apologized for having done so. "Should we take poetry—all of that—seriously at all? Tell me yes, give me reasons." But he wouldn't have listened if I had replied.

As for Heaney's reaction to Lowell, Deane wrote:

> Heaney revered Lowell's patrician authority, his Daedalus-Icarus combination of the classical and the Romantic, repeatedly driving itself to the point of breakdown. I guess Heaney showed too much respect for people who took risks, because he disliked in himself a characteristic that he felt was a failure. He was, indeed, as cautious as a cat, and instinctively played safe, was nice to everyone, entertained . . . multitudes of people at his home, among whom the percentage of hangers-on must have been considerable. But, as usual, Heaney was also fomenting a little rebellion in his more recondite provinces of feeling. Heaney, the man who writes poems, can sometimes rail at Heaney the Poet, the public persona. The authority of reputation is not identical with the authority of the writer's voice; it may undermine it. What Heaney observed and admired in Lowell was his way of dealing with this conflict.[29]

As it turned out, Lowell regretted the way he acted at the festival. According to Lowell's biographer Paul Mariani: "As Cal feared, the Kilkenny event turned out to be a week of drunken and contentious readings" that continued at the estate of his wife's relative Garech Browne in Luggala.[30] Feeling contrite and exhausted after the long "debauch," Lowell returned to his wife Caroline Blackwood in London to rest.

During the festival, Heaney had other things to worry about besides Lowell's manic behavior. He heard from his family in Northern Ireland that his second cousin, Colum McCartney, had been killed by Protestants on his way home from a Dublin football match. Members of a Loyalist paramilitary group, who were disguised in Ulster Defense Regiment uniforms, stopped his car and shot him. In section VIII of "Station Island," McCartney returns from the dead to accuse Heaney of living it up with poets in Kilkenny while his "own flesh and blood / was carted to Bellaghy." McCartney's ghost also reprimands Heaney for the overly literary way he wrote about the murder in "The Strand at Lough Beg" in *Field Work*. In the earlier elegy, Heaney identifies with McCartney to the point of merging with him. Only at the end does a narrative "I" emerge as a distinct identity to remember how McCartney's assassins left his bloody, mud-smeared corpse by the road. The description of gathering up reeds to "plait / Green scapulars" for his cousin's shroud draws on imagery in *The Divine Comedy* and *The Bog People*. The "scapulars" (sacred garments) also resemble the "gift" of straw that Heaney's father "plaited" in the "The Harvest Bow." It is the ornamental beauty of this gift-giving ceremony that Heaney decries in section VIII of "Station Island."

Lowell's question in his poem "Epilogue"—"Why not say what happened?"—may have motivated Heaney to be more realistic about McCartney's murder and burial in "Station Island." In the latter elegy, Heaney recalls a plaster cast made from an ancient abbess's face that his archaeologist friend Tom Delaney gave him. "Your gift will be a candle in our house," he says. This illuminating plaster "gift" compels Heaney to depict McCartney as a "bleeding, pale-faced boy, plastered in mud." In the psychodrama of "Station Island," McCartney plays the role of an accusatory ghost who tells Heaney, "You confused evasion and artistic tact." As with his poems about bog people encased in mud and peat, Heaney resurrects his cousin so he can criticize gift-giving rituals. In this case, McCartney's ghost implies that Heaney indulged his gift for religious symbolism and decorative rhetoric in "The Strand at Lough Beg," and "whitewashed" and "saccharined" the facts of his cousin's gruesome death.

Heaney had a propensity for drawing "lovely blinds," as he put it, over those like McCartney and Lowell because of his inveterate desire to be congenial. He knew the unpleasant facts, but often preferred "artistic tact" over tactless candor. In a letter to Lowell after the Kilkenny festival, for example, he never mentioned the American poet's maniacal behavior. Instead, he tactfully thanked Lowell: "After that special and memorable time, I feel it not only proper but necessary to direct salutations towards you again. . . . And while it is probably needless to say my gratitude for all the talk and the confirmation through and in the talk, I'm saying it anyhow."[31] Alluding to the religious connotations of "confirmation" again, Heaney bestowed "scapulars" on Lowell, implying that Lowell had been priestly and generous at the festival.

Lowell, as Heaney knew very well, was often anything but a priestly gift-giver. After Heaney sent him "Glanmore Sonnets," which were partly inspired by the sonnet sequences in *Notebook, History,* and *The Dolphin,* Lowell wrote Heaney a derogatory letter on September 11, 1975, in which he faulted "the somewhat too full-dress" of Heaney's sonnets. Lowell conceded that "The Train" and "A Drink of Water" (the second poem would appear in *Field Work*) were well-written sonnets, but he still found it difficult to admire them: "Your Nature pours out images with a full hand; the cup (to work this figure to death) is so often dry for me, a town man in the end."[32] Lowell was referring to Heaney's drinking cup with the inscription "Remember the Giver"—a symbol for the nourishing gifts of nature and art.

Several years after Lowell died, Heaney reflected again on his difficult friend: "The tutorship that Lowell gave me was: not to be afraid of the mess that I had got into, with being almost a public poet, and to trust in the amphibious quality of being public and private at the same time."[33] Despite learning valuable lessons from Lowell, Heaney recognized their differences. Lowell was a Boston Brahmin who'd married an Anglo-Irish aristocrat in the Guinness family. Heaney had married a down-to-earth woman who'd grown up in a small town in rural Ulster. Heaney was descended from Irish-Catholic farmers and factory workers; Lowell was descended from New England's Protestant elite, who had helped found Massachusetts and America. Among Lowell's ancestors were Harvard presidents, political leaders, federal judges, influential theologians, army generals, and eminent poets. Aware of Lowell's unstable behavior—

drinking binges, physical and verbal abuse, extramarital affairs, obsessions with tyrants such as Hitler and Caligula—Heaney tried to shrug off the American poet's peccadilloes with humor, but it wasn't easy.

Heaney's "Elegy" in *Field Work* remembers Lowell's visit to Glanmore Cottage after the Kilkenny Festival. His portrait of Lowell here tries to be balanced, but it's hardly flattering. It represents Lowell as a "*retiarius*"—a Roman gladiator who holds down his victims before torturing or killing them. Heaney also compares Lowell to a "night ferry" plunging through an "ungovernable" ocean. (Journeys on night ferries between Wales and Ireland at the time were notoriously riotous affairs because of all the drinking.) Heaney may have identified with "the timorous or bold" way Lowell had lived his life, but "Elegy" accentuates the traits that made people think of Lowell as another Caligula.

Lowell's volatile personality was on full display at another occasion that involved Heaney—an awards ceremony in London for *North* after it won England's Duff Cooper Award in 1976. Heaney wanted P. V. Glob to officiate at the event, but Glob was receiving an honor of his own in Denmark at the time. Heaney's Faber editor suggested they invite the Prince of Wales, but in the end Heaney chose Lowell to give him the award, even though Lowell was recuperating from a series of manic episodes and refusing to take his lithium medication. Ever the devoted friend, Heaney promised to accompany Lowell in a taxi from his Redcliff Square apartment to an office on Harley Street where Lowell was scheduled to get acupuncture treatments. Before going, though, Lowell asked Heaney if he would like some Benedictine liqueur. Heaney said he would, only to discover that Lowell had filled the bottle with Imperial After Shave. The prank was an omen for things to come.

Lowell was in a London hospital right before the Duff Cooper Award ceremony began at London University, but he managed to escape from his room so he could join the festivities. "It was a sad, mad event," Heaney recalled: "Lowell going about with a jacket over his pyjama tops; Diana Cooper with a Chihuahua on her arm, telling him at some point that the prize was to be presented by some mad American; Lowell wild-eyed and nodding, 'I know, I know.'"[34] Lowell never gave a proper speech. At the lectern, he simply read a poem from *North* influenced by his poetry

("Summer 1969"), and then, like a deranged professor, asked Heaney questions about it.

Over the remaining two years that Lowell had to live, Heaney would sometimes meet him at one of Ireland's grandest Palladian mansions, Castletown House, located about twenty miles west of Dublin on a 120-acre estate owned by Caroline Blackwood's cousin, the Honorable Desmond Guinness. Having sold Milgate, her expensive country house in Maidstone, England, Blackwood now rented an apartment in Castletown House. (She didn't consult Lowell about the sale of their English home and relocation to Ireland; she took matters into her own hands after he announced his plan to rejoin his former wife Elizabeth Hardwick in New York.) The bipolar, paranoid Lowell felt imprisoned and depressed in the luxurious mansion. Hoping for some relief, he convinced Blackwood to meet the Heaneys for drinks on the evening of September 6, 1977. While Marie and Caroline were getting their coats after socializing, Heaney asked Lowell if he thought they could meet again, and Lowell said he didn't think so. On the drive to Lowell's new residence, the two poets stopped to urinate near the gates of the Guinness estate. Heaney later wrote in an uncollected poem "Pit Stop near Castletown" that before getting back in the car Lowell said he intended to separate from Blackwood. On September 12, Lowell flew to the United States to reunite with Hardwick. He was carrying a portrait of Caroline Blackwood painted by her first husband, Lucian Freud, when the taxi driver, pulling up in front of Hardwick's New York apartment, realized Lowell was dead in the back seat.

The fact that Lowell had given Heaney a gift—the American edition of his last book, *Day by Day*—during their last meeting in Dublin, and the fact that Lowell was bearing a gift—Freud's portrait of Blackwood—on his trip to New York, contributed to Heaney's view of Lowell as a problematic gift-giver. In "Elegy," Lowell appears, among other things, as a wandering dolphin like the dolphin featured in Lowell's "Fishnet," the sonnet that begins *The Dolphin*. Lowell's "dorsal nib," in Heaney's poem, is "gifted at last // to inveigle and to plash." Like Heaney's assessments of his own gift of a fountain pen, Lowell's nibbed pen-gift is liberating and entrapping, a boon and a bane, a useful tool and dangerous weapon. It steers him like a fin through chaotic waters, but in the end it "inveigles"; it deceives and leads him, as well as others, astray. With a nod to the pen-gun-spade analogy in "Digging," Heaney compares Lowell's pen to a trident or dagger wielded by a Roman "retiarius." (In Latin, *retiarius* means "net man" but can also refer to a fisherman's gear.) Lowell ends his sonnet "Fishnet" with a grim prediction: "The net will hang on the wall when the fish are eaten, / nailed like illegible bronze on the futureless future." Lowell says his gift, embodied here in the "net" of poetic lines, has "gladdened a lifetime," but it is also a sign of entrapment and death.

Heaney got another chance to address the complicated nature of Lowell's gifts on October 5, 1977, when he delivered a eulogy at Lowell's funeral in St. Luke's Church in London. As with Ted Hughes, he lauded Lowell's "confirming and enlivening presence" and the "nimbus of authority that ringed his writings and his actions." Despite evidence to the contrary, Lowell appears again in priestly garb delivering confirmation gifts from the Holy Spirit. He is a poet of conscience who ratified "the order and coherence of things," "established the practice of art as a moral function," and submitted himself to the same rigorous ethical judgments he applied to others. Now it was time, according to Heaney, to assume the "life values which he admired" and "conserve his unique energy" by honoring his gifts.[35] For the sake of propriety, Heaney glossed over (in what Mary McCarthy called "the biggest cover-up since Watergate") the darker aspects of Lowell's "nimbus of authority."[36]

# 10

# Professing Poetry Again

After spending three years as an "inner émigré" in the countryside, Heaney approached another critical juncture. He confided to Ted Hughes on July 22, 1976, that he was reluctant to leave his idyllic refuge, but he needed to earn more money and find better schools for his children. When a group of academic recruiters came to Glanmore Cottage from Our Lady of Mercy College, Carysfort, it was hard to resist their job offer, especially when they assured him that his teaching load would be light and that the Catholic college in Dublin was in the process of transforming itself into a more modern, secular university. In a way, he'd achieved what he'd set out to do in Wicklow. He said he'd "wanted the kids to have that sort of wild animal life" he'd experienced at Mossbawn and he "didn't want to lose that" in himself.[1] He'd also wanted to put poetry writing at the center of his life. The result of his bucolic retreat was *North,* arguably his most ambitious and engaging book. With a sense of completion, he agreed to take the job at Carysfort.

In 1975, Heaney began searching for a place to live in Dublin. He was distressed that he couldn't afford the £29,000 price tag on one of the first houses he liked, but soon found a handsome, semi-detached Edwardian house not far from Yeats's birthplace in the Sandymount section of the city. The house had an attic that he could convert into a study with a panoramic view of Dublin Bay. The house also had the sort of "winding stair" that Yeats had made famous in poems about his Thoor Ballylee tower. The city center was a short bus ride to the north, and Carysfort College was about a five-minute car ride to the south. The recent sale of his Belfast house made the Sandymount house affordable.

To blunt the shock of another move, the Heaneys installed furniture in their new house that comported with their humble origins. Heaney constructed a primitive desk from boards salvaged from old classroom benches at Carysfort College. He set up a large, secondhand refectory table downstairs that he obtained from the college dining hall. As if to recapitulate their Catholic schooling, Heaney and his wife sent their two sons to St. Conleth's College in Dublin. Catherine attended a local kindergarten before enrolling in a primary school in Booterstown, a short distance from Carysfort College. Marie resigned from her teaching job and focused on caring for the children.

Carysfort College had been established in 1877 to train young Catholic women to be primary-school teachers. At first, Heaney felt comfortable there. He respected the principal, Sister Regina Durkan, for her learning and open-minded approach to education, and he got along well with the nuns who taught. His stint at St. Joseph's College in Belfast had prepared him for training students how to teach. Beginning in October 1975, he had two full days and two half days of classes each week. Like most teachers, he learned from course preparations and student discussions. He attributed his new understanding of Yeats's poetry to a class in which he paid particular attention to midcareer poems such as "The Fisherman," "Easter 1916," and "Men Improve with the Years." He also developed a greater appreciation for Thomas Wyatt's sixteenth-century sonnets, and after writing "Glanmore Sonnets" and "A Dream of Jealousy," which echo Wyatt, he considered following Lowell's example by writing an entire book of sonnets. Andrew Marvell's "An Horation Ode upon Cromwell's Return from Ireland" and "The Nymph Complaining for the Death of her Fawn" won his respect, as well. From Lowell, Yeats, Wyatt, and Marvell, he got valuable lessons about articulating complex and even contradictory personal and political attitudes in well-crafted verse.

The poems Heaney wrote in the late 1970s document his ongoing debate about how to use his poetic gift to respond to the Troubles in Northern Ireland. He told one interviewer, "I didn't want to be writing political poetry that I didn't quite have the gift for."[2] In 1979, the year *Field Work* was published, he explained his conundrum in greater detail to Seamus Deane: "I . . . still do feel a tension within myself between the given part of whatever talent I have and the work it might be put to do. I don't think my intelligence is naturally analytic or political. But I felt that the gift for surrender—which I liked in my own work—of listening and of rejoicing in language was rebuked and challenged by another part of myself that recognized the world around me was demanding something more." Deane brought up Auden's elegy "In Memory of W. B. Yeats" and asked Heaney if "mad Ireland" still "hurt" him "into poetry." Heaney replied that the hurt he felt in Northern Ireland was not the same as the hurt he felt in the Republic, where an "absence of passion" and "a bland consumerism" were the rule. "Whatever scar there is on me, it is a Northern scar," he said.[3] Heaney had different names for this "scar." Sometimes he called it his "soul-mark," at other times his "spirit-mark" or "identity trace." In his article "Soul-Mark," he argued that poets should strive for a balance between "what is . . . given in you from the start, and what you make yourself into."[4] In his new poems, he wanted to submit to his lyrical gift as before, yet shape that gift in a more rational, conscientious, sociopolitical way.

"Oysters," the first poem in *Field Work*, introduces his gift problem in terms of savoring a feast with friends when there are ethical reasons for abjuring it. On the one hand, he wants to enjoy the oysters in an uncomplicated way, just the way he wants to enjoy the gifts of sex or poetry. During a time of social unrest and widespread deprivation, though, he finds it hard to take pleasure in such simple things because he knows many others have been denied them. In the poem that recalls dining at Moran's Oyster Cottage south of Galway, his mind fixates on a time when the Romans hauled oysters—their "glut of privilege"—over the Alps to the capital of their empire. He admits that his conscience won't let him indulge unselfconsciously in his oyster feast, even though he'd like to "repose / In the clear light" of the occasion. Like Lowell in "Beyond the Alps," he wants to free himself from the guilt and other burdens he inherited from Roman Catholicism, but he can't quite manage to.

Although Heaney claimed that in *Field Work* he tried to open doors into the light and write poems that would sound like conversations "in friendly, intimate situations," he kept opening doors into dark Catholic spaces, exploring the darkness of the unconscious mind, and writing with the sort of baroque diction he'd always relished.[5] The oyster feast, for example, is counterbalanced at the end of the book with a grotesque scene of a phantom feasting on the severed head of another phantom in the darkness of hell. This concluding poem, "Ugolino," translates passages from canto 32 and canto 33 of Dante's *Inferno* about cannibalism. (Hunger compels Count Ugolino to eat his hands, his children, and finally an archbishop.) Heaney may long to "repose / In the clear light, like poetry or freedom," but whatever repose he achieves is short-lived.

Heaney associated his year in California with "the clear light" of freedom and poetry writing, and he hoped to return someday. So when the chair of the English Department, John Jordan, asked if he'd like to teach during the summer and fall semesters in 1973, he wanted to say "yes," but he wasn't quite ready to abandon Glanmore Cottage. A few years later, though, he was happy to accept the position of Beckman Professor during the spring quarter of 1976. With approval from his family and the Carysfort administration, he flew to San Francisco shortly after Easter in 1976. At first, he stayed with his friends the Dillons and Flanagans; then he moved into Mark Schorer's spacious house at 68 Tamalpais Road in the Berkeley hills. Schorer, an emeritus English professor, had asked Heaney to housesit while he and his wife decamped to New York for several months.

Heaney's house-sitting produced one of his best-known poems, "The Skunk," about an animal most people consider repellent, but that appears to Heaney as another gift-giving muse on a dark night. On May 13, 1975, Heaney wrote David Hammond about the thrill of seeing the skunk walk across the Schorer's terrace. In the poem, the skunk goes through a series of metamorphoses that are religious and comical until it assumes the identity of Heaney's wife. The skunk's black fur reminds Heaney of a chasuble—a dark ecclesiastical vestment—at a funeral mass. Robert Lowell's "Skunk Hour," which tracks a solitary, tormented man on a night drive to a Golgotha-like graveyard in a small Maine town where couples have sex in cars, no doubt was one model for Heaney's poem. Lowell's mother skunk with her column of kittens is the only sign of fertility in the New England wasteland. Heaney's California landscape is a wasteland only in the sense that his wife is absent. (Schorer's property, with its lemon trees, orange trees, artichoke plants, squirrels, blue jays, and other wildlife struck Heaney as a paradise.) Unlike Lowell, who portrays himself unflatteringly as a Satanic, mentally ill lover ("My mind's not right / . . . I myself am hell"), Heaney casts himself as a bereft husband who yearns for his soulmate and welcomes the skunk as a substitute. His poem ends, not with a skunk searching through waste and finding a holy grail in a cup of sour cream, as in Lowell's poem, but with a sexy reunion with his wife after he returns to Ireland. It's as if Heaney has finally found his holy grail and gift-giving muse. It is her "head-down, tail-up hunt in a bottom drawer / For the black plunge-line nightdress" that reminds him of the California skunk, just as it is the skunk in California that reminds him of his Irish wife.

Not all of Heaney's time at Berkeley was spent gazing at skunks and pining for Marie. He was especially happy to socialize with Tom and Jean Flanagan, who on one occasion took him to Carmel to visit F. W. Dupee, a New York intellectual and former Columbia professor who had befriended Lowell and other writers while editing the *Partisan Review*. At other social gatherings, he met the Palestinian activist and writer Edward Said, who compared the Arab-Israeli conflict to the British-Irish conflict in Ulster. Heaney also met the English poet and critic Donald Davie, who taught at Stanford. Davie's graduate student, the poet Alan Shapiro, picked Heaney up in Berkeley and drove him to a party at Davie's house. The English expatriate poet Thom Gunn hitchhiked from San Francisco to join them.

As Beckham Professor, Heaney had to give one public lecture and teach two courses. (His lecture on the poetry of Geoffrey Hill, Philip Larkin, and Ted Hughes became the basis for his essay "Englands of the Mind.") Mona Simpson, the sister of Apple founder Steve Jobs and the model for Mona Simpson in the popular TV series *The Simpsons*, took one of Heaney's writing courses and remembered him fondly: "Seamus created an atmosphere of reverence and play, of praise more than criticism. He never seemed eager for us to go; we all secretly suspected he was lonely. We did see him after class at an Irish Bar . . . called the Plough and the Stars. He talked a great deal about Ireland; he seemed homesick, yet enchanted with California."[6] Heaney's enchantment, though, was undercut by reservations. On April 12, he wrote Muldoon, who was working at the BBC Broadcasting House in Belfast: "Berkeley is as Elysian as ever, and there are now roughly 3,000 poets in the Bay Area. Bewildering. The bookshops are crammed with small press publications, there are readings everywhere and I can't bring myself to believe in any of it."[7]

Heaney regularly corresponded with his Irish friends and tried to get together with them if they visited the United States. He made plans to reunite with Hammond in New York around April 30, 1976, during a reading trip to Stony Brook University. On May 13, he told Hammond that he'd recently spent a boisterous, bourbon-soaked day with the Chieftains in San Francisco. Heaney's Irish friends thought he might be tempted to get a permanent teaching job in the United States, especially after receiving offers from Princeton, Columbia, and the University of Michigan, but he told Hammond it was "out of the question" because he was committed to "settling quietly [in Dublin] for the next three or four years and tilling the garden of my verses."[8] His pastoral dream, though, would remain elusive.

Heaney returned to Dublin in the middle of the summer 1976, not to till his verses but to teach classes at Carysfort College. He told Michael Longley that he regretted leaving the sunny warmth and conviviality of California. Much of his ire was directed at an upcoming lecture he'd promised to deliver at the Ulster Museum in Belfast. "It seemed like a good idea at the time, but it's only a time waster and a scrabble for stuff to fill 60 minutes," he groused.[9] His frustrating "scrabble," however, produced "A Sense of Place," an insightful overview of how he and other Irish poets—from Yeats to Kavanagh, Montague, Muldoon, Longley, and Mahon—received "personal poetic gifts . . . from knowing and belonging to a certain place and a certain mode of life."[10] His essay also traces Dante's poetic gift back to his home in Florence, Italy, which, like Heaney's original home, was ravaged by religious disputes. (During Dante's lifetime, Black Guelphs supporting the pope fought against White Guelphs demanding more independence from the pope, and Dante was forced into exile when the Black Guelphs took power.)

Dante's example of artfully working through personal and political hardships informs much of *Field Work*. Heaney had read Dorothy Sayers's translation of *The Divine Comedy* studiously in the early 1970s, and he alludes to Dante's epic in "The Strand at Lough Beg," "September Song," "An Afterwards," "Leavings," and "Ugolino." A year after *Field Work* was published, Heaney wrote a review of C. H. Sisson's new translation of *The Divine Comedy* that touched on why the medieval poem had such a grip on his imagination. "Allegorical, theological, political, personal, en-cyclopaedic, all these it is," Heaney wrote. But what most attracted him was its "monomythical" story of "faring forth into the ordeal," receiving redemptive gifts during periods of struggle, and "returning to a world that is renewed by the boon."[11]

Heaney's habit of addressing Ulster's Troubles in terms of the "mon-omyth" was on display in *Field Work*, just as it was in *North*, and once again his mythopoesis irked those who believed he should write more realistically about current events. In his *Paris Review* interview, he talked about an encounter with an especially caustic critic. This occurred on a train when the former Sinn Féin publicity director Danny Morrison de-manded that he write "something on behalf of the republican prison-ers who were then on what was called 'the dirty protest' in the Maze Prison."[12] As Heaney was composing *Field Work*, IRA members and their sympathizers in the prison asked the authorities to give them the status of political prisoners, which the British government had recently revoked. When their request was turned down, they protested by dressing only in blankets or going naked. They also stopped taking showers and removing excrement from their cells. Prime Minister Margaret Thatcher insisted on referring to the prisoners as ordinary criminals, and conservative British politicians called members of the IRA murderers and terrorists. Some prisoners went on hunger strikes, and ten eventually died of starvation. The IRA responded by killing about nineteen prison officials during the Maze protests in the late 1970s and early 1980s.

Heaney's poem "The Flight Path" recalls the acrimonious conversa-tion he had with Morrison on a "bright May morning" in 1979, the year *Field Work* was published. After Heaney's all-night flight from New York to Ireland, Morrison approaches "as if he were some *film noir* border guard" on the train. He asks Heaney, "When, for fuck's sake, are you going to write / Something for us?" Heaney contended in *Stepping Stones* that the poem's "account of what went on in the train is as it happened. . . . I simply rebelled at being commanded. . . . This was . . . during 'the dirty protest' by Republican prisoners in the H-blocks. The whole business was weighing on me greatly already and I had toyed with the idea of ded-icating the Ugolino translation to the prisoners."[13] In a blog written in 2009, Morrison repudiated Heaney's account of their meeting. Morrison said he'd simply asked Heaney to make a statement about the H-Block prison, and a civilized conversation had ensued: "[Heaney] told me the story from Dante's *Inferno* of Count Ugolino who was imprisoned with his children and grandchildren underground and left to starve. . . . Seamus said he imagined this could be some sort of metaphor for hunger striking though I was lost as to what he meant." Morrison denied that he had "commanded" Heaney to take a political stand: "I find that explanation hard to reconcile with the fact that after our conversation we parted with a handshake, he gave me his address and telephone number and agreed to read the poetry of Bobby Sands."[14] In this version of events, Heaney was as polite and generous as usual.

Heaney originally planned to call his new book *Umber,* perhaps because its Italian cognate *ombra* (usually translated as "shade") frequently appears in *The Divine Comedy.* The muse figures who draw Dante through the umbrous shades toward paradise are the Queen of Heaven—the Virgin Mary—and Dante's beloved Beatrice, who had died young and ascended to heaven. The ultimate goal of Dante's journey is union with the Prime Mover of the universe, the Creator whom Dante personifies as Divine Love. The final cantos of the *Paradiso* are replete with images of transcendent circles of light, the most memorable being the mystical white rose that symbolizes Beatrice's love and God's love. Dante's quest culminates with a mystical communion that transports him beyond human understanding and language. "High phantasy lost power and here broke off," he writes in his last lines, "Yet, as a wheel moves smoothly . . . , / My will and my desire were turned by love // The love that moves the sun and the other stars."[15] Connecting with this gift-making and gift-giving life-force is the goal of Heaney's quests as well.

Heaney's unions and reunions in *Field Work* are more down-to-earth and erotic than Dante's in *The Divine Comedy.* Usually, they involve getting back together with his wife, Marie, rather than pursuing God or a divine woman. The title poem, "Field Work," deploys images of circles (bird's eye, vaccination mark, O, chestnut, moon, coin, sunflower) as obsessively as Dante does in the final cantos of the *Paradiso,* but Heaney's archetypal circle is a womb image associated with the fertility of Mother Earth, wife, and muse. Reflecting on his separation from Marie in Berkeley, he portrays himself as a "sunflower, dreaming umber" as he bends toward the sun and toward the ground in a desperate search for his wife, who is umber from sunbathing. He concludes his poem with an idiosyncratic ritual in which he "anoints" his wife's hand with the sticky juices of a leaf and his own spit, proclaiming: "My umber one, / you are stained, stained / to perfection." Here Heaney alters his Catholic predecessor Dante by celebrating physical love rather than divine love.

Heaney dedicated *Field Work* to Karl Miller, telling him, "Your trust in what I have done from the beginning has been vital and vitalizing, and your encouragement . . . was restorative and confirming."[16] It was as if Miller had been another priest giving him confirmation gifts and Heaney, out of gratitude, was reciprocating with the gift of his book. Not all responses to the book, however, "confirmed" it as a success. Jack Kroll's *Newsweek* review, "Bard of the Irish Soul," acknowledged Heaney's talent but attributed his "superstar" status to "his classic Irish gift of revelatory gab."[17] Heaney's old adversary A. Alvarez seconded this view by alleging Heaney's popularity was due to the way he channeled the stock Irishman's "boozy gift of the gab."[18] Others took potshots at Heaney, as well. Perhaps noticing the many echoes of Robert Lowell in *Field Work*, Ciaran Carson faulted Heaney for becoming too American. Marjorie Perloff, who had written her first books about Yeats and Lowell before devoting herself to avant-garde writers, scoffed at those who "enshrined [Heaney] as a Modern Classic." His poetry was marred, she said, by a reliance on "well-worn Romantic cliché[s]," "bland . . . classroom pieties," "easy solutions," and an "inclination to speechify rather than to engage his subject directly." Like Alvarez, she chastised Heaney for not being sufficiently modernist or postmodernist, and suggested that he'd never evolved beyond his early Incertus self: "The problem is that, as the prose pieces suggest, Heaney doesn't really trust his emotions or his intellect, that he doubts repeatedly whether his own particular response to things is significant."[19] Edna Longley agreed. To her, Heaney was "increasingly perplexed between feminine and masculine, instinctive and conscious, oblique and direct . . . , negative capability and the egotistical sublime," and he was "strangely sexist."[20] She hoped he'd grow out of his old-fashioned, binary way of conceptualizing aesthetic and ideological issues.

Other reviews were more complimentary. Christopher Ricks ranked *Field Work* above *North* in a *London Review of Books* article that focused on Heaney's preoccupation with trust. "The resilient strength of these poems," he declared, "is in the equanimity even of their surprise at some blessed moment of everyday trust."[21] According to Ricks, Heaney's new poems expressed trust in his wife, his readers, his mentors, and his gift. Denis O'Donoghue in the *New York Times Book Review* lauded *Field Work* in a comparable way, deeming it "the most eloquent and far-reaching book he has written."[22] Harold Bloom was equally enthusiastic in the *Times Literary Supplement,* hailing Heaney as a poetic Titan who "compels the same attention as his strongest American contemporaries, and indeed as only the very strongest among them."[23] Helen Vendler joined the chorus of praise, asserting in the *New Yorker* that *Field Work* gave further evidence that Heaney was "the greatest natural talent since Keats."

As in the past, jealousy motivated much of the harsh criticism aimed at Heaney. Seamus Deane wrote his friend at length about this, blaming it on the "the politics of the literary suburbia which have grown up around the city of Irish Lit." Deane understood the envy behind the rebukes. "I sometimes envy you the praise," he admitted, but "I do not envy you the backwash that comes with it."[24] Heaney knew that his increasing stature in the literary world made him more vulnerable to attack, and he may have suspected that some of the envy was due to rumors that he was a candidate for a Nobel Prize. During the spring of 1978, when Anthony Thwaite asked him to send poems for the twenty-fifth anniversary issue of *Encounter,* a journal he coedited, Heaney responded that he would be glad to submit his work and told a joke that revealed he knew about the Nobel speculation: "Did you hear about the Irishman who won the Nobel Prize?—He was out standing in his field!"[25] The Nobel Prize winner, at least in the joke, had been an Irish farmer like Heaney whose "field work" had shown the world he was "out standing in his field."

### OUTSTANDING IN HIS FIELD AT HARVARD

On the strength of his burgeoning reputation, Heaney received an offer to be a lecturer at Harvard University. He'd turned down other offers from American universities, but it was hard to say "no" to Harvard, especially since he was being asked to replace two poets he esteemed: Robert Lowell, who'd died in 1977, and Elizabeth Bishop, who'd been forced to retire in 1977 due to her age (she was sixty-six). Early in 1979, Heaney flew with his family to Boston to visit the university where he planned to teach for part of the year while Marie and the children stayed in Dublin. The Harvard alumnus and writer Alfred Alcorn met them at the airport. As the editor of the *Harvard Gazette,* Alcorn knew the university and city well and had found an apartment for Heaney several blocks north of Harvard Yard at 20 Crescent Street. Driving across the Charles River and through the campus toward the apartment, Heaney gazed at dormitories named after distinguished Boston families: Eliot House, Lowell House, Winthrop House, Adams House. Having started his education in a renovated World War II Nissen hut among fields where farmers still plowed with horses, he couldn't help but be astonished by the way his career had developed.

After his family flew back to Dublin, Heaney had no trouble making friends in the city that had welcomed so many Irish immigrants and that continued to cater to Irish Americans. A local newspaper stand that sold most of the major Irish papers made him feel at home. A day after he arrived, the writer Monroe Engel, who taught fiction in Harvard's creative-writing program, treated him to lunch at Mr. Bartley's Burger Cottage. Engel, who knew many American poets and novelists, told Heaney about the literary scene in Boston and Cambridge. Before long, Heaney would meet the local writers as well as Harvard's distinguished scholars, such as Walter Jackson Bate (a biographer of Keats and Samuel Johnson); Harry Levin (a specialist in American and European modernism); and Robert Fitzgerald (a translator of Homer, Virgil, and other classical writers). Heaney grew particularly close to Fitzgerald, who was a published poet and a Catholic as well as a classicist, and would soon share a study with him in Pusey Library.

Helen Vendler became one of Heaney's close friends, too, even though she hadn't left Boston University for Harvard yet. Vendler and Heaney had met at a 1975 Yeats Summer School session in Sligo, Ireland. "At the school's annual poetry reading a young man in his thirties named Seamus Heaney, wholly unknown to me, stood at the lectern and read some of the most extraordinary poems I had ever heard," she recalled. "I approached him afterwards, and asked whether these poems were to appear soon in a book as I wanted to write about them. Heaney replied that in fact he had galleys with him, and lent them to me. They were the galleys of *North,* which I thought then—and still think now—one of the crucial poetic interventions of the twentieth century."[26] Other friendships developed quickly, as well. Heaney enjoyed listening to music and drinking beer with Bernard McCabe, a professor who established the Irish Studies program at Tufts University and who had a house near Harvard Square. (When McCabe retired to Ludlow in southwest England, Heaney continued to visit him, and later eulogized him in "The Birch Grove," a poem collected in *District and Circle.*) Heaney also got to know the talented young poets Frank Bidart, Robert Pinsky, and Alan Williamson. Bidart, a close friend of Robert Lowell and Caroline Blackwood, had first visited Heaney in Dublin on a trip to see Blackwood after Lowell's death. Heaney had met Elizabeth Bishop in 1977, when Helen Vendler invited Bidart, Bishop, and the Heaneys to a dinner party that also included Bishop's lover Alice Methfessel, the poet-editor Barry Goldensohn, and the poet-scholar Lorrie Goldensohn, who had recently written an essay about Bishop's last book, *Geography III.* After the meal, the poet Jane Shore took Heaney and the Goldensohns to a party at the Plough and Stars, a popular pub in Cambridge owned by the O'Malley brothers. There was "a lot of high nationalistic talk going on and Seamus seemed in his element," Barry Goldensohn remembered.[27]

As with many of his friendships, Heaney established a bond with Bishop by exchanging gifts. He gave her a birthday present on February 8, 1979, and she reciprocated with a bottle of Rebel Yell bourbon from Texas. At the end of April, after his reading at the Ninety-Second Street YM-YWHA in New York, Bishop sang a song for him based on the Vassar College laundry list and "Yankee Doodle." To show his appreciation for Bishop's vocal talents, Heaney sent her a letter on July 12, 1979, with his poem "A Hank of Wool." Although he thought the poem wasn't up to her high standards, he hoped to include it with other gift-poems in a book with the working title *Giveaways.* After Bishop's death on October 6, 1979, Heaney revised "A Hank of Wool" and published it as an elegy in the *Times Literary Supplement.* The poem is another one of his encomiums about gifted makers. It points out correspondences between making a poetic text and making a woolen textile, and deftly knits together phrases from Bishop's poems with his own to convey their shared understanding of the "supple mysteries" of artistic gifts.[28]

Heaney once said that he formed a lifetime of friendships in the five months he spent at Harvard during the winter and spring of 1979. Some of these friendships were the result of his poetry readings that wowed audiences with his resonant voice and evocative accounts of life in rural Ireland. He came across as a natural-born performer, but only because he'd learned to disguise his anxieties about being an Irish poet on a foreign stage. He called himself "an insider of sorts" who was "at the same time situated at an angle to the place."[29] He admitted to the poet and literary critic Adam Kirsch, who'd been one of his students, that he felt "clenched and anxious" at Harvard.[30] His anxieties made it difficult to write, which convinced him that he was once again sinning against his gift. Despite his light course load (two poetry-writing seminars), he produced only a handful of poems during his decades of teaching at Harvard. Among these poems were "A Sofa in the Forties," the Harvard Phi Beta Kappa Poem "Alphabets," and the "Villanelle for an Anniversary" that commemorated Harvard's 350th birthday.

According to the Irish writer Belinda McKeon, Heaney had a lover's quarrel with Harvard related to his lover's quarrel with America. Like many professors in elite American universities, he disapproved of the way students were pampered. For an article in the *Irish Times,* he discussed with McKeon their "hunger to be comforted" and the "'bogus' language which rushed to offer that comfort." One of his dilemmas as a professor was "between giving and wrecking comfort." In his poetry workshops, he stressed the way Yeats and Lowell had toiled over their poems, and was dismayed that many of his students believed writing should be easy, spontaneous, and fun. One reason for their naïve aesthetic views, he speculated, was the critical success of John Ashbery's *Self-Portrait in a Convex Mirror,* which had won a Pulitzer Prize, National Book Award, and National Book Critics' Circle Award in 1976. Although Ashbery's abstract-expressionist poetry was notoriously difficult, Heaney told McKeon that it persuaded students that anything they wrote, no matter how slapdash, should be considered art. From his point of view, much of their poetry was solipsistic and "insulated within the 'centrally heated' American dream."[31] Heaney wanted his students to write more artfully about sociopolitical realities outside their "centrally heated" comfort zones.

A traditionalist devoted to classic texts, Heaney taught poems in the

Western canon from the fifteenth century to the present, and he emphasized that writing well was hard work. One of the poets he held up as a model was Robert Lowell. "Maybe Lowell," he said, "was the last American to be a dual citizen of the university and the world beyond it, at home in Harvard, but also at home among the metropolitan set, a figure to be photographed at cocktail parties and on marches to the Pentagon." By comparison, Heaney's students seemed to have bought into "the general, New-Agey, self-realization industries and the entrepreneurial turn in the university." Asked if a university like Harvard would recognize and nourish "a gifted new twenty-first-century poet," Heaney said he didn't think so.[32]

### PILGRIMAGE TO A "GIFTED STATE"

Struck by the differences between his experiences as a student and the experiences of his Harvard students, Heaney began to formulate plans for a mini-epic based on pilgrimages he took to St. Patrick's Purgatory as an undergraduate. By the end of the spring semester at Harvard, he had decided to turn his memories of the three-day pilgrimages into an archetypal quest for literary mentors and redemptive gifts that followed "the three-part Dantean journey" in *The Divine Comedy*.[33] He would commune with an assortment of writers, friends, and family members in "Station Island," and let them comment on the way he'd honored—or failed to honor—his gifts. He would let his "shades" comment on other matters that weighed on his conscience, too. The poem would be a contrarian's response to the "centrally heated American dream."

If the poetic sequence "Station Island" can be read as a counterpoint to American poetry in the 1970s, it can also be read as a counterpoint to the history and purpose of traditional Lough Derg pilgrimages. Records of the first pilgrimages date back to the twelfth century, when pilgrims from all over Europe walked through the Irish countryside to Lough Derg, and typically took a boat to Saints Island, where they fasted for fifteen days. Next, they took a boat to Station Island, where they confessed their sins, received communion, and descended into the purgatorial pit for twenty-four hours. After their confinement behind a locked door, they returned to Saints Island for an additional fifteen days of fasts and prayers. On several nineteenth-century maps, St. Patrick's Purgatory was not on Station Island, but on Saints Island. Some historians have argued that St. Patrick never went to the island and that the famous purgatorial pit God supposedly revealed to the saint may have been a small, underground sweathouse where medicinal plants were steamed or burned for their healing properties. (The Latin *purgatorium* refers to a place for therapeutic purifying or purging.) Archaeological evidence suggests that St. Dabheog or Dabheoc—rather than St. Patrick—was the one who established a monastery on Station Island during Patrick's lifetime, and that the stone circles on the island were the remains of beehive cells used by meditating monks.

Uncertainty about the origins of St. Patrick's Purgatory gave Heaney the incentive to create his own version of events. His long poem transforms his student pilgrimages with other Catholics into a journey whose main purpose is to converse with artist-gods rather than a Christian God. Dennis O'Driscoll hinted at this when he put the Lough Derg pilgrimage in the context of Heaney's other literary pilgrimages. "It strikes me," he said in *Stepping Stones,* "that 'Station Island' was only one of your pilgrimage places, since you must have visited more dead writers' houses than any poet alive."[34] After O'Driscoll cited trips to Yeats's tower and Hardy's birthplace, Heaney said he'd also visited sites associated with Carleton, Tennyson, Dylan Thomas, Alphonse Daudet, Hopkins, Joyce, Wilde, Emily Dickinson, Keats, Akhmatova, Brodsky, Shakespeare, Sir Walter Scott, Edmund Spenser, Oliver Goldsmith, and Hugh MacDiarmid. If *The Divine Comedy* was his primary model for the literary journey in "Station Island," accounts of journeys to St. Patrick's Purgatory by William Carleton, Patrick Kavanagh, and Denis Devlin were secondary models. From these diverse sources, Heaney fashioned a composite pilgrimage to pay tribute to a variety of literary gift-givers.

The giving and receiving of redemptive gifts on Station Island traditionally involved reenacting St. Patrick's reputed communions with God. According to legend, after pirates in fifth-century Roman Britain kidnapped Patrick, he prayed for deliverance, and God answered his prayers. He was freed and assured that when pagans came to the purgatorial pit on the island in Lough Derg they would convert to Christianity. Pilgrims visiting the island looked forward to obtaining gifts from God. To make themselves worthy, they walked barefoot around beds of sharp stones that surrounded crosses dedicated to St. Patrick and St. Brigid. In the purgatorial pit, they meditated on Christ's "Stations of the Cross" and prayed for God's grace. If they were lucky, God purged them of sins and granted indulgences that would alleviate punishments in Purgatory after death.

As in the early poem "Follower," Heaney in "Station Island" follows artistic father figures and is also followed by them. He places himself in the balance with other writers and wonders if he measures up to their standards. He describes his mental state most succinctly with a quote from Milosz in "Away from It All," a poem that precedes the title sequence in *Station Island*: "I was stretched between contemplation / of a motionless point / and the command to participate / actively in history." Heaney repeatedly implies that his quiet contemplative moments outweigh the moments he has participated actively in history. If he aims to confess and purge his sins in "Station Island," it's primarily because he feels guilty about not being a more vocal and effective activist in historical crises like the one consuming Ulster.

In his paper "Current Unstated Assumptions about Poetry," which he delivered at the Modern Language Association meeting in San Francisco at the end of 1979, Heaney laid out some of the religious concerns, including those related to gift exchange, that he took up in "Station Island." Sitting on a panel with Helen Vendler, Robert Pinsky, and Thomas Parkinson, he stated that poetry should "not be merely aesthetic"; rather, it should have "a binding force, a religious claim upon the poet," and it should create similar bonds with audiences. These binding "covenants," as he called them, were created when living poets accepted gifts from dead poets and regifted them in new poems. For Heaney, Robert Lowell was a good example of a contemporary poet who had forged a "covenant with the past and the future."[35] Another such poet was Lowell's friend Derek Walcott, as Heaney made clear in a review of Walcott's *The Star-Apple Kingdom* when he praised the Caribbean poet for creating a hybrid "language woven out of dialect and literature, neither folksy nor condescending, a singular idiom evolved out of one man's inherited divisions and obsessions that allows an older life to exult in itself yet at the same time keeps the cool of 'the new.'"[36] The biracial Walcott had forged covenants between contraries in his background and psyche, and between himself and his audience. In a 1979 interview, Heaney said Walcott was "tremendously gifted verbally with tremendous technique and richness; but he also has a theme that is very strong and very relevant to Ireland: how to discover a sure, confident voice, born out of a particular history and particular set of penalties arising from history, that will be able to walk out of its colonial circumstances and be a universal voice."[37] Like the mythopoetic Dante and Joyce, Walcott had used his literary gift to unite the local with the universal, the past with the present. As Heaney grappled with his problematic British-Irish heritage in "Station Island," Walcott served as another artistic guide.

Heaney fared forth with his pilgrimage poem in 1979 after a series of trips for work and pleasure. He flew from Boston to Dublin in June for two weeks of exam-grading at Carysfort College, then headed north to visit parents and friends. In July, he returned to the United States to vacation at Tom Flanagan's house in East Setauket, Long Island. By September, he was back in Dublin working on the section of "Station Island" that eulogized his friend, the archaeologist Tom Delaney, who'd been a Queen's professor and Keeper of Medieval Antiquities at the Ulster Museum. Heaney had known him for about a decade before his sudden death in 1979 from a heart ailment. Although Delaney died at the age of thirty-two, he'd established a reputation as a pioneer in the archaeological study of postmedieval Ireland. One of the sites he explored was at the twelfth-century Anglo-Norman settlement in Carrickfergus. Heaney visited him in hospital shortly before his death, and, as section VIII of "Station Island" attests, the final meeting left Heaney feeling guilty about having "somehow broken / covenants, and failed an obligation." This "covenant" was related to Delaney's gift of a plaster cast that reminded Heaney of his obligation to give him something in return.

It is significant that a failure to reciprocate lies at the heart of "Station Island." Guilt over this failure gets compounded when the shade of Delaney morphs into the shade of Heaney's murdered cousin McCartney in section VIII. The dead cousin forces Heaney to think again about being stretched between contemplative withdrawal and historical engagement. Around the time he composed his elegy for Delaney, sectarian fighting had surged in Ulster. Pope John Paul II had visited Ireland and begged the combatants "to turn away from the paths of violence and return to the paths of peace."[38] The IRA ignored the pope's pleas and stepped up their attacks. Protestant paramilitary groups retaliated. As for his Dantesque poem, Heaney said, "I needed to butt my way through . . . everything that had gathered up inside me because of the way I was both in and out of the Northern Ireland situation. . . . 'Station Island' was taken on . . . in order to have it out with myself, to clear the head."[39] Heaney expected to reenact the same sort of purge he'd experienced as a young man at St. Patrick's Purgatory. He also intended his poem to be a gift honoring those like Delaney who had given him gifts.

Heaney thought about ending his poetic sequence with a monologue delivered by Simon Sweeney, but instead he concluded with Joyce's advice about pursuing one's artistic gift with an independent, self-reliant, joyous spirit. Joyce's ghost promotes Stephen Dedalus's example of moving beyond the nets of religion and politics. He tells Heaney, "It's time to swim / out on your own." For Heaney, who was afraid of water and disinclined to swim, this was no easy task. At the beginning of "Station Island," the "old Sabbath-breaker" Sweeney gives Heaney similar advice: "Stay clear of all processions." Joyce has to repeat this message at the end because it's clear that Heaney still clings to his early Catholic concepts and practices.

For his entire career, Heaney had an unresolved quarrel with literary father figures who disapproved of his devotion to religious pilgrimages and gift exchanges with maternal figures such as muses and fertility goddesses. After Simon Sweeney voices his opposition to Heaney's pilgrimage in section I, William Carleton's ghost does the same. Heaney had reviewed Carleton's *Autobiography* in the 1960s and had read Carleton's essay "The Lough Derg Pilgrim," so he knew his predecessor had called the Station Island pilgrimage a "superstitious absurdity," a "mistaken devotion," and a "barbarous and inhuman" ritual full of illusory "religious terrors."[40] Not long after going to St. Patrick's Purgatory, Carleton renounced Catholicism and became a Protestant in Ulster's Established Church. Even priests like Terry Keenan, who knew Heaney in Bellaghy and who appears in section IV of "Station Island," are dismissive of Heaney's pilgrimage. Like the other masculine personae, Keenan accuses Heaney of foolishly returning to the Catholicism he should have outgrown. The women Heaney meets, by contrast, approve of his religious endeavors.

Heaney indicates to one of the male ghosts in the poem—his former football teammate William Straethern, who was murdered by Protestants during the Troubles—that he is revisiting St. Patrick's Purgatory to seek forgiveness for sins of omission. Heaney implores Straethern's ghost, "Forgive the way I have lived indifferent— / forgive my timid circumspect involvement." In section IX, with the sufferings of IRA prisoners in mind, he says, "I repent / My unweaned life that kept me competent / To sleepwalk with connivance and mistrust." At times he seems addicted to the "drugged path," as he calls it in section I, and the maternal religious figures and muses that lead him on that path. If he expects male figures to "wean" him from this drugged state or absolve him for his sleepwalking, he will be disappointed. As with Yeats's gyres, Eliot's spiral staircases, Joyce's circuitous plots, and Dante's circles of hell, Heaney seems destined to travel in a circle that never reaches a satisfying end. The ritual circling on Station Island's stone beds comes to represent the way he keeps brooding on his divided loyalties. Water imagery (rain, lakes, waves, flax ponds, springs, oceans, drain puddles, floods, fountains, barrel water, well water, morning dew, mist) contribute to the sense that he is drifting in the flux of his thoughts and can't "swim out" to a fixed resolution. His descriptions of rain in the last lines (a "shower broke in a cloudburst," a "downpour loosed its screens") recall his earlier poem "The Gifts of Rain," which began with a "cloudburst and steady downpour." But in this case, gifts of water seem incapable of absolving and renewing him.

### DEMANDS ON THE GIVER

During the fall of 1979, Heaney struggled to get back to work on "Station Island." One distraction involved a quandary about giving gifts. James Hart, the director of Berkeley's Bancroft Library, asked Heaney on May 13, 1980, if he would consider donating his papers. Heaney was flattered by the request but distressed by the thought of scholars reading his private letters. As a compromise, he sent the Bancroft a notebook with drafts of poems he'd written while teaching at the university in 1970 and 1971. Other librarians soon approached Heaney about his papers. Bothered by these and other requests, he wrote Paul Muldoon on September 9 about frittering away his summer and said he was "feeling a bit extinguished as the lights go up for another year's teaching."[41] At readings, such as the one he gave in December 1979 at the Tourist Centre in Cork, he looked bedraggled and nervous. The Cork-born writer Mary Leland was surprised that he sweated throughout the reading, even though the building was chilly, and that he was reluctant to discuss poems such as "Casualty." John Montague's introduction, which poked fun at Heaney's financial success, may have been one reason for his discomfort. Montague compared Heaney to the nineteenth-century Irish poet Thomas Moore and joked that Heaney's books sold more copies than Moore's wildly successful *Lalla Rookh* (1817)—a melodrama in verse and prose set in eighteenth-century India that had received the largest advance for a poetry book up to that time. Heaney resented the suggestion that he pandered to a mass audience in order to make a lot of money. He preferred thinking of poetry as a gift to be shared.

Along with classes and readings, Heaney's work on a number of book projects made it difficult to concentrate on his long poem "Station Island." In 1980, he started selecting poems with Ted Hughes for the *Faber Book of Verse for the Young.* He also worked with Faber editors on his *Selected Poems:1965–1975* and *Preoccupations: Selected Prose 1968–1978.* He told a friend that he'd settled on the title *Preoccupations* to highlight his tendency to meditate obsessively on certain subjects. He chose a quotation from Yeats's *Explorations* as the book's epigraph to stress the religious nature of these meditations: "If we understand our own minds, and the things that are striving to utter themselves through our minds, we move others . . . because all life has the same root. Coventry Patmore has said, 'The end of art is peace,' and the following of art is little different from the following of religion in the intense preoccupation it demands."[42] The essays on writers from Shakespeare and Wordsworth to Mandelstam and Lowell explored what Heaney considered to be exemplary or distinctive about their artistic gifts.

During this busy time, Heaney helped judge the 1980 Arvon Poetry Competition. At first, he was enthusiastic about joining Ted Hughes and the other judges, Philip Larkin and Charles Causley. Out of loyalty to the financially strapped Arvon Foundation, which organized writing workshops around Britain, Hughes had proposed holding a national poetry contest to raise money for the foundation. (Each poet who submitted work would have to pay a £1.50 entry fee.) In the end, the contest was more popular than expected. Approximately thirty-seven thousand poems flooded the office of Melvyn Bragg, who was promoting the event and its £5,000 first prize on his TV arts program *The South Bank Show.*

The competition seemed jinxed from the start. Larkin refused to read all the poems, even though Arvon had promised that the judges would do so. Larkin wanted a group of readers to make a short-list of poems for the judges. Heaney sympathized with Larkin's proposal, and on November 3, 1980, he complained in a letter to Derek Mahon that going through all the "bad verse, full of need and pain" was "physically and psychically exhausting."[43] Despite their gripes, the judges ended up plowing through all the poems and awarding the top prize to Andrew Motion for "The Letter," an elegy about a British woman reading a letter from a lover fighting in World War II while a German pilot falls to his death. Heaney agreed that the poem was moving and well-written, but he regretted having to single it out when other poems were just as deserving. He wrote Michael Longley that the judging process "was a great wound."[44] Hughes felt the same way and told his friend Keith Sagar, "That's the last judging I shall ever do. Ever. Ever. Ever. Ever. Ever."[45]

In an embattled mood at the beginning of 1981, Heaney sent off "The Loaning" to Karl Miller at the *London Review of Books* with an explanation that the poem was a response to A. Alvarez's sarcastic remarks about not being able to find the word "loaning" in a dictionary. The poem, whose title refers to a gift or loan as well as the space between cultivated fields on a farm, reveals how public service, like judging the Arvon competition, can be debilitating. When "tired or terrified," he confesses at the end of the poem, he regresses to a liminal space like a loaning: "Your voice slips back into its old first place / and makes the sounds your shades make there." On January 3, the day after he sent "The Loaning" to Miller, he mailed the poem and a letter to David Hammond, in which he referred to himself again with second-person pronouns. "Being busy," he said, "you get so keyed to attending outwards . . . rather than lining up towards what's at your own centre—you're so keyed that way that to relax and trust the relaxing is almost a hallucinatory experience."[46] Among other things, the poem conveys his desperate need to retreat to a place like Mossbawn— his "first place" and womb-like "centre"—where he once heard archaic words like "loaning."

One of the final images in "The Loaning" is of Dante snapping a twig in the *Inferno* and watching blood ooze from the wound, which is also a mouth. In Heaney's rendition of the speaking wound, "A voice sighed out of blood that bubbled up / like sap at the end of green sticks on a fire." As he indicated in his 1974 Chatterton Lecture, which he reprinted in *Preoccupations,* oozing sap was one of his favorite metaphors for a poem arriving as a gift. He quotes from a conversation in Shakespeare's *Timon of Athens* between a painter who carries a literal gift (a painting for Timon) and a poet who receives a literary gift in a "rapt" state. The poet tells the painter, "A thing slipp'd idly from me. / Our poesy is as a gum which oozes / From whence 'tis nourished."[47] As Heaney got busier in the 1980s, he often felt like one of Dante's broken branches, and could only hope that poems would ooze "idly" from the broken places.

Rather than withdraw inward to the place from whence his gift was nourished, though, Heaney advanced outward on multiple fronts. He negotiated a new contract with Carysfort College in 1981 that gave him permission to take time off for his visiting professorship at Harvard. David Perkins, Harvard's English Department chair, had asked Heaney to teach one semester per year for three to five years, and worked with Dean Henry Rosovsky to create a five-year appointment for Heaney as Senior Lecturer in Creative Writing. The salary for teaching two courses and a few tutorials would be $19,150 (about $65,000 today), with a travel allowance of $2,000. Derek Walcott was supposed to be at Harvard during the fall semesters, so Perkins proposed that Heaney come during the spring semesters. When Heaney eventually agreed to the terms in 1981, he was invited to live in Adams House. The rent would be $285 per month, a bargain considering the "Gold Coast" building had a swimming pool, a dining hall modeled on an eighteenth-century British spa, and palatial common rooms.

Heaney wrote Mahon on February 17 that his decision to resume teaching at Harvard might have been a mistake. To Michael Longley, he explained that he had wanted to escape the "clammy hold" of Carysfort College, where he felt "busy and useless" in his new role of English Department chair: "I have been here six years, and have more or less secured a life for the kids and for Marie. But I have an unease about the big hoods of domestic and professional routine settling too firmly or comfortably.

In one way, of course, I believe in them absolutely . . . but on the other hand, I have warning fears that what freedom the self might have had or tried to have is atrophying and the way to alert it to itself again is to be at risk. I want a bit of solitude, to try to settle under and down into the first levels again."[48] He must have known that it would be almost impossible to return to "the first levels"—presumably the "levels" of freedom and solitude he had enjoyed earlier in his life—if he was working at both Harvard and Carysfort.

The fact that his family had gone to Harvard and knew some of the people there made it easier for Heaney to leave his family behind for four months every year. He hoped Marie could cope with two teenaged boys and a nine-year-old daughter, and he was pleased that Marie's sister, who lived in Dublin, volunteered to assist with childcare every spring so Marie could visit him at Harvard. He promised Marie to fly back to Dublin as often as he could and reassured her that he'd stay at home during the summer and fall. To remind himself and others that his work at Harvard was only temporary, he never decorated his rooms in Adams House. He kept a few pieces of institutional furniture and propped a photo of his wife on the mantle. To those who were startled by the monastic décor, he said he wanted visitors to understand that he was "nesting on a ledge" like a nomadic Sweeney rather than inhabiting a second home.[49]

Heaney, though, could never nest in one place for long. Right around the time he told Longley he wanted to settle down and write without distraction, he organized an ambitious series of readings with Selma Warner's Program Services, a booking agency on Long Island. Beginning in late February 1981, he traveled to Minnesota, Arkansas, Illinois, Massachusetts, South Carolina, and New York. He also appeared in England, Ireland, and Mexico. Sometimes he justified his travels half-jokingly by saying he needed money to pay for a new Peugeot 305, which he'd bought after Christmas in 1980. In fact, like his restless father, he felt compelled to go out on the road. If he wasn't tending his gift on the "first levels" or "tilling the garden" of his verse in solitude, he was fulfilling his obligation to share his gifts with others around the world.

Some of the people Heaney met on the road, such as M. H. Abrams, contributed to his poetry in unexpected ways. At Cornell in the spring of

1981, the distinguished scholar of Romanticism and editor of the *Norton Anthology of English Literature* broached the idea of translating *Beowulf.* On June 26, Abrams followed up in a letter: "Have you found the opportunity . . . yet to try your hand at a few samples of *Beowulf?* I hope you have, or will soon; I'd like to turn out to have been midwife to something major, and permanent."[50] On September 28, 1981, Heaney wrote Abrams that he'd only translated five lines of *Beowulf* during the summer. Nevertheless, he was going back to the poem with renewed interest: "The strange thing is that the governing note for me is the big unlettered voice of a first cousin of my father's. He talks loudly and definitely and I have a feeling that the version I'd like to do is one that he could read out to a crowd; a word like *thole* would come naturally to him, and he would call a youngster a *cub.*"[51] Despite his excitement about personalizing the poem with a family voice, it would take Heaney two decades to complete his translation. In the end, though, he fulfilled Abrams's hope to be a "midwife to something major."

Two days before he wrote Abrams about his desultory progress with *Beowulf,* Heaney contacted Selma Warner about cutting back on his reading schedule. He told the agent that he only wanted to give three or four readings during his spring semesters at Harvard. He also insisted that Warner not raise his reading fee. "I do *not* wish to be a $1000 speaker," he said. "Apart from my moral scruples about whether any speaker or reader is worth anything like that, I do not wish to become a freak among my poet friends or to press the budgets of departments of literature at a time when the money for education is drying up in the United States." Heaney was adamant about this: "This is something I feel has to be definitely settled: it has been worrying me for some time, and involves not only money but principles and my reputation as an artist. Much as I enjoy the rewards of reading, the first basis of my enterprise is artistic and not financial. . . . It is often a cause of some unease to me that a more or less commercial enterprise has cut across a freedom to come and go in the name of old times and the cause of poetry."[52] His conviction was that a gift formed the "first basis" of his "enterprise," and this was at odds with the agency's view that poetry was a commodity that should make as much money as possible.

To relax after his busy spring and to make amends for being an absentee father, Heaney took his family to France and Spain in late June 1981. They first went to the Dordogne region, where they walked through the countryside, visited the caves near Lascaux, and sampled the exquisite cuisine. Memories of "the green // oak-alleys of Dordogne" and of a deer inscribed on a cave wall surfaced in *Station Island*'s "On the Road." In July, the Heaneys moved to Maubourguet, a small market town among the maize fields and vineyards of rural Gascony. They stayed in a spacious stone house by a pond with bulrushes and a tree-lined garden. On clear days, they could see the peaks of the Pyrenees. Maubourguet was close to Lourdes, the site of one of Heaney's early pilgrimages. It was also close to another pilgrimage site: Maubourguet's Church of Saint Martin, which was built in the eleventh century as part of a Benedictine monastery.

With "Station Island" gestating in his mind, Heaney decided to go on another pilgrimage—not to Lourdes or Maubourguet but to Rocamadour, where Catholics had built churches to honor St. Amadour, the husband of St. Veronica, the woman reputed to have wiped Jesus's face during His Stations of the Cross. Persecuted in Palestine, St. Amadour had traveled to the hilly area of southern France about one hundred miles north of Toulouse, built a chapel there to the Virgin Mary, and died shortly after as a hermit. The main attraction at Rocamadour was a statue of the Black Madonna in the Church of Notre Dame. Allegedly carved by St. Amadour, the Madonna was believed to bestow spiritual gifts that could enhance fertility and cure illnesses. On July 7, 1981, Heaney wrote David Hammond: "[I] made the pilgrimage . . . to Rocamadour, a penitential place full of steps up the cliff-face, which has been in business since the twelfth century."[53] The maternal aspect of this journey attracted Heaney and no doubt reminded him of his pilgrimages to Lourdes and Station Island.

On the last day of June 1982, Heaney wrote a letter from France to Carysfort's principal, Sister Regina Durkan, to announce his resignation. A few months later, he told his friend Henry Pearson that his nine-to-five job at Carysfort had threatened to destroy "something vital" in him.[54] As he explained in a 1979 interview, "You can sin against your own gift by not remembering always to keep it ready; and you can sin against it by . . . looking after a job."[55] Heaney felt an affinity for writers like Ted

Hughes who believed "a poet's first duty . . . is to his gift."[56] During his pilgrimage to the Black Madonna in the Church of Notre Dame, he may have concluded that he was neglecting that "first duty" by laboring at two academic jobs for the sake of financial security. By leaving Carysfort College, he hoped to have more time to settle down on the "first levels" that nourished his gift.

# Sweeney's Travels and Travails

Heaney often complained in the 1980s that his Dublin home resembled a travel agency or telephone exchange. He constantly made arrangements to give readings around the world, and Marie traveled to Ardboe to assist her ailing parents. (Her father had been disabled by a bad fall before Christmas in 1981, and her mother had also fallen, breaking her hip and wrist.) In addition to the family's comings and goings, the Heaneys were constantly hosting guests. Getting back to his "first levels" to finish work on several books, including *Station Island,* became increasingly difficult.

In a letter to Charles Monteith on January 4, 1982, Heaney promised to send final drafts of *Sweeney Astray* and the *Faber Book of Verse for the Young* (the anthology that would become *The Rattle Bag*) as soon as possible. Heaney had shelved his first draft of *Sweeney Astray* because he felt it was too autobiographical, too influenced by Robert Lowell, and too focused on Ulster's Troubles. Anxiety about sinning against gifts may have been one reason he returned to the manuscript. *Buile Suibhne* is a kind of cautionary tale about a powerful person who fails to respect gifts and barely manages to redeem himself at the end. As a book that Heaney would help edit, *The Field Day Anthology of Irish Writing,* notes, "[*Buile Suibhne* is] one of the great formulations of the plight of the artist who earns his gift at the cost of alienation and dispossession."[1] As he struggled to complete *Sweeney Astray,* Heaney shared his protagonist's concern for redeeming his gift.

Sweeney's ordeal can be traced back to a problematic gift exchange. King Congal Claon presents King Sweeney with a satin girdle and silk tunic decorated with gems and gold that he calls a "gift of fealty" and "reward of service."[2] In seventh-century Ireland, such gifts established bonds between leaders, so when Congal's servant asks Sweeney for support at the Battle of Moira in AD 637, Sweeney knows he must provide it. Dissatisfaction with the worth and number of the gifts he's just received, however, makes him hesitate. When he tells Congal he might switch allegiance to another leader, Congal ups the ante with more gifts: 150 horses, 150 swords, 50 servants, 50 servant girls, a gold tunic, and a silk girdle. Dazzled by such largesse, Sweeney writes a poem about the gifts and shows his gratitude by going to battle in his new clothes.

Sweeney's troubles begin when he assaults a missionary, Ronan Finn, who wants to build a church on the king's land. Sweeney grabs the pious man's psalter and tosses it into a lake. Later, he encounters Ronan and several fellow missionaries giving holy water and blessings to the two armies at the Battle of Moira. This gift-giving rite leads to a cease-fire, but Sweeney refuses to abide by it. He gets so angry at Ronan's peacekeeping efforts that he kills one of Ronan's colleagues and throws a spear that hits a bell hanging on Ronan's neck. Incensed, Ronan delivers a curse that strips Sweeney of his gifts and turns him into a bird. Sweeney ends up losing his home, his political power, his horses, his servants, and his sanity because, as Heaney says in his translation, "he killed his gift of friendship."[3]

Sweeney's penitential journey through the Irish wilderness follows the three-stage pattern of the "monomyth." He departs from the security of home, travels through a grueling otherworld, and returns to civilization when he arrives at St. Mullins's monastery in southeastern Ireland. In this Christian community, he embraces the principles of generosity and communion that he had abandoned. He tells one of the first monks he meets, "If you are Moling, / you are gifted with the Word," and he soon receives both material and spiritual gifts. Moling gives him clothes, the monk's female cook gives him milk, and God gives him the gift of grace.

Heaney wrote in the introduction to *Sweeney Astray,* which Field Day published on November 10, 1983, that his fundamental relation with Sweeney was geographical as well as artistic. The ancient king's domain in Ulster was close to where Heaney had spent the first thirty years of his life, and Sweeney's final destination was about fifty miles southwest of Glanmore Cottage. Heaney said that he took Sweeney to be "a figure of the artist, displaced, guilty, assuaging himself by his utterance," and carrying on a "quarrel between free creative imagination and the constraints of religious, political and domestic obligation."[4] Sweeney was another Irish "inner émigré" who was both constrained and liberated by the obligations of gift exchange.

The Irish poet Brendan Kennelly observed in a review of *Sweeney Astray* that Heaney was preoccupied with bonds "between the 'civilized' and the outcast, the accepted and the accursed, agonized aimlessness and calm resoluteness, the man of pain and the men of purpose." For Kennelly, "the balance" between these polarities in the text indicated "a long, imaginative bond between Mr. Heaney and Sweeney."[5] Heaney, in fact, wanted all citizens in Northern Ireland—whether Catholic or Protestant—to feel a bond with Sweeney. "Part of my intention of doing *Sweeney* was in the deepest (and least . . . offensive) sense political," he told an interviewer in 1985. "I wanted the Unionist population to feel that they could adhere to it, that something could be shared . . . I wanted the *Sweeney* to be a help; something that Ulstermen of both persuasions could have some identity with." Afraid that his translation would be "perceived as a . . . declaration of Sinn Fein culture," he Anglicized place-names that Protestants would recognize and downplayed the poem's Irish-Catholic roots. Ultimately, he wanted his *Sweeney Astray* to become "part of some united Ulstery mythology"—a kind of "monomyth" that brought disparate factions together.[6]

Despite his ecumenical intentions, Heaney was primarily interested in *Buile Suibhne* for what it revealed about his Catholic origins and the origins of Catholic culture in Ireland. His 1978 essay on early Irish nature poetry, "The God in the Tree," discusses the way the Gaelic poem highlights the tension between nature worship and Christian worship. Heaney alludes to the scholar Nora Chadwick, whose book *The Age of Saints in the Early Celtic Church* contends that some Christian officials around Suibhne's time disapproved of the "characteristic form of ascetic discipline known as *peregrinatio,* 'peregrination,' 'wandering,' literally 'pilgrimage.'"[7] Heaney, however, clearly approves of Sweeney's penitential journey and rhapsodic descriptions of nature, which for centuries inspired pilgrims to visit the holy well and stream at St. Mullins's monastery. Heaney's interpretation of Sweeney's *peregrinatio* as a poetic journey through nature was influenced by Robert Graves's commentary on *Buile Suibhne* in *The White Goddess*. For Graves, Suibhne was a prototype of the poet driven "astray"—both geographically and psychologically—by "service to the White Goddess, on the one hand, and respectable citizenship, on the other."[8] In Graves's view, Suibhne had received a gift of divine frenzy from the White Goddess, the mythical muse associated with the moon's power to drive poets to lunacy. *Suibhne* had strayed from his obligations as a citizen and king, but had atoned for his errant behavior through Christian *peregrinatio* and communion.

Like Kennelly, Heaney's friend Darcy O'Brien also noticed similarities between Heaney-the-lapsed-Catholic-poet and the half-pagan, half-Christian Sweeney. O'Brien joked in a letter, "Of course I see the strong identification between yourself and Sweeney except that you never go out of doors, probably would insist on taking your cress with a superior French olive oil, and I have never seen you throw a psalter; but these are incidental inconsistencies. Certainly you spent a great deal of time in the air and are often unhappy."[9] Heaney concurred with some of O'Brien's observations in a 1985 *Harvard Magazine* article that included a photo of Heaney perched like Sweeney in a tree. As an exiled bird-man on a modern-day *peregrinatio*, Heaney continued to insist that his Harvard apartment was like a bird's nest or monk's cell. "I am housed monastically . . . and eat meals in a student refectory," he told Michael Longley in 1982.[10] Like Sweeney, he was constantly on the go. Almost as soon as he unpacked his bags at Harvard in 1982, he began a series of readings and lectures that took him to Canisius College, Boston College, Georgetown University, SUNY Buffalo, Princeton, Fairleigh Dickinson, Vassar, and Sweet Briar. In March, he spoke at St. Lawrence University, Tufts, Williams, and Bryn Mawr. In early April, he attended a Joyce conference at the University of Leeds in England. Later that month, he read at Westfield State College, Swarthmore, and UCLA. In May, he went to Colby College and the University of Maine. At the end of the spring semester, he appeared at Fordham University and Queen's University in Belfast to receive more honorary degrees.

Heaney tended to think of the honorary degrees, speaking honoraria, and literary awards as gifts that confirmed his poetic gift. On November 16, 1982, when the *Hudson Review* presented its $12,500 Bennett Award to him in New York, he thanked the judges for "ratifying" his career and humbly noted that he was "only one of many . . . gifted poets now writing in Ireland." He reminded his audience, "The solitary encounter with more intractable and unpresentable aspects of ourselves and our world is the truly redemptive activity of the imaginative man or woman, and any writer will be superstitious about releasing himself too headily from those claims."[11] Public awards ceremonies, in other words, could lead one astray. Once again, he stressed the "binding force" of his commitment to writing and downplayed the financial value others placed on it.

One of Heaney's most dramatic peregrinations in 1982 was to a place that exemplified the sort of solitary, redemptive state he cherished—Orkney in the cold ocean north of mainland Scotland. The most famous poet who lived there, George Mackay Brown, had invited him to read at the St. Magnus Festival and to stay with the poet Elizabeth Gore-Langton. The isolation of the Orkney Islands reminded Heaney of Mossbawn, Glanmore Cottage, and the monastery where Sweeney ended his penitential journey. It was "a place of silence and solitude where a person would find it hard to avoid self-awareness and self-examination," Heaney said.[12] A poem about his stay there, "The Republic of Conscience," records how his "symptoms of creeping privilege disappeared" and how he returned, albeit momentarily, to a humble, contemplative "gifted state." In the end, he received a gift from his trip in the form of a poem, and he gave a gift to his Orkney host when she asked him to contribute to a small book intended to raise funds for the preservation of Orkney's St. Magnus Cathedral, which, after 850 years, had fallen into disrepair. Heaney donated a copy of "In Memoriam," his poem about intimate boyhood moments with his mother, which Gore-Langton printed along with poems by Ted Hughes, George Mackay Brown, and Christopher Fry in a limited edition of *Four Poets for St. Magnus.* By 2020, the book was worth $1,400.

Heaney had more reason to gravitate toward isolated places like Orkney after Faber published *The Rattle Bag* in 1982. The anthology, which included anonymous poets as well as canonical poets from Shakespeare to Yeats, was meant to create a stir. The "rattle bag" in the title referred to a penis-like musical instrument that scares off a young woman during a seduction scene in a bawdy poem by the fourteenth-century Welshman Dafydd Ap Gwilym. Heaney was proud of the anthology's robust sales and the Signal Poetry Award that it won, but Faber's publicity campaign on TV and elsewhere irritated him. During a visit to the University of Wisconsin in Oshkosh in October 1982, he told a newspaper reporter, "Poetry is a meditative way of thinking. One of the functions of the poet is to insist on the meditative instead of the calculative way of thinking of the world." During his early years, he admitted that he'd been "uncertain" about whether to "trust the gift or the hope [for the gift]."[13] Over the years, he'd learned to trust his gift, but also to distrust publishers who intended to monetize his gift with elaborate publicity campaigns, even though he realized that publishers had to be "calculative" to make money and survive. Much of Heaney's life was now a struggle to balance the meditative and the monetary aspects of his poetry.

Early in 1983, Heaney made a more concerted effort to assemble the poems for his book *Station Island.* While corresponding about the manuscript with his new editor at Faber, the English poet Craig Raine, he spelled out his complicated attitude toward English editors and English publishers in *An Open Letter,* and he sent his letter-poem to the Field Day Theater Company, which had been started in Londonderry/Derry in 1980 by playwright Brian Friel and actor Stephen Rea to advance art that dealt with the British-Irish conflicts in Northern Ireland. He composed his *Open Letter* after discovering that two of Raine's English peers, Andrew Motion and Blake Morrison, planned to reprint a selection of his poems in *The Penguin Book of Contemporary British Poetry.* The word in the title that bothered him was "British." He told *New York Times* reporter Francis Clines: "The Provos [the Provisional IRA] would see that as a kind of British imperialism. . . . They'd also see it as [a] betrayal of my Northern Irish Catholicism. I see it, on the contrary, as a kind of infiltration of the British, a takeover."[14] Heaney didn't want his Irish peers to think he'd submitted to a "takeover" by the British.

Like the etymological poems in *Wintering Out, An Open Letter* bears witness to the way empires have imposed their languages and other institutions on weaker countries like Ireland. The poem points out that the Roman Empire imposed the name "Britannia" on the region now known as Britain, and the British Empire did something similar when it Anglicized Irish names. "This 'British' word / Sticks deep . . . / Like Arthur's sword," Heaney complains, alluding to the British anthology being published by Penguin. Heaney knew Arthur's Excalibur had originally been a gift and that the British editors of the anthology had been generous in their selection of his poems. He also knew Motion and Morrison weren't out to conquer or marginalize or silence him with a sword. (They gave him more space than any other poet in the anthology.) Nevertheless, he regarded their use of the word "British" to be a sign of imperialistic infiltration and oppression. He even suggested that their inclusion of his poems under the moniker "British" was tantamount to rape. His Irish "identity [was] / rudely forced," he says, echoing Eliot's description of "Philomel, by the barbarous king / So rudely forced" in *The Waste Land*. According to Greek mythology, King Tereus cut out Philomela's tongue to prevent her from telling others that he had raped her. Heaney also places his anthology squabble in the context of Zeus's rape of Leda in Yeats's "Leda and the Swan."

*An Open Letter* tries to explain why Heaney's "anxious muse," which had agreed to being called British in the past, suddenly got so irate about British editors wanting to publish his work: "It is time to break / Old inclinations not to speak." When he speaks out in the poem, though, he tends to let other writers—Eliot, Yeats, Larkin, Livy, Horace, Daniel Corkery, Miroslav Holub, Donald Davie—speak for him. Letters to friends tend to be informal, but Heaney's letter to his British friends Motion and Morrison is full of scholarly allusions. In some of his other poems, he was trying to write in a more conversational style, but in *An Open Letter* he seemed hesitant to speak in a forthright way about the anxieties stirred up by the British editors.

Some of Heaney's critics accused him of being melodramatic and overstating his case. In an *Irish Times* review, Eavan Boland called Heaney's complaint "peculiar." She couldn't understand what had triggered his sudden display of pique and why he would take such offense at an anthology that aimed to be inclusive and diverse. "Seamus Heaney has been in and around anthologies of English poetry for nearly fifteen years," she wrote. "I cannot believe that the sudden appearance of the word 'British' on the title page came as a rude shock. He has either changed his mind or changed his friends. . . . Is this tentative piece to be taken as true commitment? . . . Personally, I think it would be a great pity if he thought he had to [renounce the British]. Poetry is defined by its energies and its eloquence, not by the passport of the poet or the editor."[15] Other critics also suspected Heaney was overplaying his Irish nationalist hand. When he announces in his poem that his "passport's green," he fails to mention that he had a British passport until he moved to the Republic of Ireland in 1972. (A decade before his move south, he'd even worked in a British Passport Office.) Heaney also proclaims, "No glass of ours was ever raised / To toast *The Queen*," which may have been true, but before long he was accepting invitations to do business with Queen Elizabeth.

Despite his angry gestures toward all things British in *An Open Letter*, Heaney was not about to boycott British anthologies, British journals, British universities, British friends, or British publishers. When his Polish translator, Piotr Sommer, wrote on September 14, 1982, about including some of Heaney's poems in an anthology of new "British" poets, Heaney did nothing to stop him. Sommer was well aware of the political significance of national passports and identities; Poland's Communist government had regularly refused to issue him a passport, and as a result it was hard for him to meet Heaney to discuss translation projects. As for the British editors of the Penguin anthology, Heaney continued to do business with Morrison, whose mother had grown up in Ireland, and with the *Observer*, the British journal that employed Morrison as an editor. In fact, while composing *An Open Letter*, Heaney agreed to review books for the *Observer* that Morrison sent him. In 1983, Heaney also let the *Observer* publish his poem "In a Basilica." And near the end of the summer of 1983, he sent *An Open Letter* to his British editor friend Karl Miller with the hope that he'd print it in the *London Review of Books*. Miller declined and alerted Heaney to Ian Hamilton's "Diary" column about the way Heaney handled the topic of nationality.

Heaney sought advice about the anthology imbroglio from his Field Day colleagues and other Irish friends. On June 15, after mailing an unfinished version of *An Open Letter* to Tom Paulin, he admitted that he wanted to maintain diplomatic relations with the British. He told Paulin, "I'm afraid the neurosis of trying to get something said on the well-known complex subject [of my British-Irish identity] made me insensitive to other decencies that were to be preserved."[16] The urge "to get something said" and the resulting outburst may have been fueled by Heaney's dispute with Morrison over a different matter. As *An Open Letter* indicates, Heaney was incensed by Morrison's proposal to use a phrase from "Glanmore Sonnets" in the title of the British anthology. Near the beginning of his epistolary poem, he exclaims, "To think the title *Opened Ground* / Was the first title in your mind! / To think of where the phrase was found / Makes it far worse!" Always touchy about others invading his private spaces, Heaney suggests that the phrase, which he'd used in the first line of "Glanmore Sonnets," had deep associations with his homes, and that the ghostly voices rising from "opened ground" in the sonnets were personal gifts from private property. *An Open Letter* comes close to accusing Morrison and Motion of trespassing and stealing his Irish gifts.

The pressure on Heaney to denounce the British came from numerous sources. An Irish woman named Nancy Tucker, having read Clines's article "Poet of the Bogs" in the *New York Times Magazine,* implored Heaney to break his silence about what the British were doing in Northern Ireland. "Isn't it possible for you to speak?" she asked. "Please do not keep silence in the long stream of traitors that have plagued our people for too long."[17] Tucker wanted Heaney to emulate the outspoken Sean MacBride, the son of Yeats's paramour Maud Gonne, who became an IRA chief of staff in the 1930s. Some of Heaney's friends also wanted him to speak out more forcefully against the British. Darcy O'Brien told him in a number of phone calls that he'd been too reticent for too long. In a letter written on December 15, 1982, he advised Heaney to be more openly confessional like Lowell and Berryman, and a few months later he pretended to be shocked by Heaney's new candor in *An Open Letter:* "What has happened to the famous Northern reticence? This time you have not merely bitten the hand that fed you, you have bitten it off, swallowed it, and farted it off. Jesus, I'm glad I'm not British."[18]

Heaney had previously been reticent or evasive about labels such as "British" and "Irish" partly because, as he intimated during a talk in Tulsa, Oklahoma, in April 1983, he was skeptical of labels. The best poems expressed a unique sensibility rather than some abstract idea of ethnic or national identity that was labeled. His goal as a poet, he told the audience in Tulsa, was to put his individual stamp—his "thumb print"—on his work. There was more to it than that, though, since a poem "can't be just personal. It has to have an otherness, a first person that is 'we' rather than 'I.'"[19] To engage an audience, poems couldn't be entirely private; they had to address common feelings and thoughts in a common language.

Heaney's conception of his "British" identity had always been complex. If he wanted to deconstruct the British heritage that had tried to stamp his identity with a label, like Joyce he was also "intent on deconstructing the prescriptive myth of Irishness."[20] After the brouhaha around *An Open Letter* faded, he concluded that he had overreacted. If he wanted to take a tough stand against the editors, he could have withheld his poems or only allowed two or three to be published. In the end, he let Motion and Morrison reprint twenty of his poems. When it came time for his British publisher to release *Sweeney Astray,* though, he took steps to prevent Faber from doing so in order for the Irish publisher Field Day to release the book first. (He also signed a contract that gave Farrar, Straus and Giroux the right to publish the book before Faber did.) Raine wasn't happy about this arrangement and said so in a letter to Heaney on July 21, 1983. Raine assumed that Field Day would publish an edition for the Irish market, and Faber publish a British edition before selling the rights to Farrar, Straus and Giroux. (Farrar, Straus and Giroux published *Sweeney Astray* on May 1, 1984; Faber published the book almost a half year later on October 15, 1984.)

### GOVERNING BRITISH AND AMERICAN GIFTS

Feeling pressure to do things against his will, Heaney informed Selma Warner on December 14, 1983, that she'd lined up too many readings for him during his upcoming winter-spring semester at Harvard. Traveling to all the different venues would force him to miss nine Thursdays and nine Fridays on campus, and this would amount to "a dereliction of duty" and a strain on his "nervous system." He told Warner he needed "to retreat" from "the distress and stress" of all his public appearances: "The fact is that my time aside from teaching should be employed more in contemplative and writing activity." He would not allow his agent to treat his gift as "just a parcel flying the airways," and insisted that she not book any readings during the fall of 1984 and all of 1985.[21] After settling his schedule for the near future, Heaney retreated to his study to complete the final arrangement of poems for his new book.

The last poem in *Station Island* is "On the Road," and the last word in the poem is "exhaustion." The narrator of "On the Road" is so tired that all his journeys seem to blend into one long road trip. "The trance of driving / made all roads one," he says. During his hallucination, he hears a Christ-like voice tell him, "Sell all you have / and give to the poor," and he imagines a cave with the carving of a deer bent over "a dried-up source." This "source" is reminiscent of the well in Heaney's "Personal Helicon," but the water, which Heaney associates with holy water in the Bible and Christian rituals, has evaporated. Heaney alludes to Psalm 42: "As the deer pants for water, so I long for you, O God." Like the deer, he, too, longs for sustenance from a sacred "source." He vows to "meditate / . . . until the long dumbfounded / spirit . . . raise[s] a dust / in the font of exhaustion." Heaney undoubtedly chose the title "On the Road" because it was the title of Jack Kerouac's famous Beat novel, and, like Kerouac and his fellow Beats, he felt beaten down by constant travel and in need of beatific restoration. Spiritual renewal, he implies, will only come when his source of gifts is replenished.

Near the end of June 1984, Heaney complained again about the ordeals of travel when the British Council—a charity independent of the British government—organized a tour of Spanish universities for him. On June 20, he demanded in a letter to a council representative that Ireland's Cultural Relations Committee (an organization set up after World War II to disseminate Irish culture) cosponsor his tour. "I have never travelled under the auspices of the British Council," he wrote, "and having just recently publicly expressed some demurral at the adjective 'British' as a description of my status, I am all the more reluctant to do so now."[22] Soon after this rebuke, Heaney wrote a testy, five-page letter to Matthew Evans about Faber's plan to promote *Station Island* on a helicopter tour of England and Scotland. The book signings might ultimately be profitable, he told Evans, but to him the trip would be profoundly demeaning. "Poetry, in spite of us is more than a saleable commodity," he declared. Convinced that his Northern Irish critics would grow even more disparaging if they heard he was selling books with the aid of a British helicopter (they undoubtedly associated helicopters with the British military occupation), he warned

Evans that "the attempt to induce the goose to lay more golden eggs" might end up "stopping the natural flow of the ordinary nutrient thing." He added, "More discretion in the approach to marketing poetry would not only be more dignified but, in the long run, better business."[23] Invoking Aesop's fable about the goose that laid golden eggs and Catholic principles of natural creation, he stressed that Faber's publicity scheme was *contra naturam*. Faber was acting like the owner of the goose who killed his profitable gift-giver by cutting it open in search of a treasure trove of golden eggs. Once again, Heaney accentuated the difference between the spiritual business of poetry writing and the capitalist business of bookselling. Nevertheless, he agreed to go on a book tour.

On August 2, shortly after chastising Evans about Faber's marketing strategies, Heaney made a pilgrimage with his wife and daughter to one of the hallowed sites of British poetry—Grasmere in the Lake Country—to deliver the Pete Laver Memorial Lecture. His topic was "Place and Displacement: Recent Poetry from Northern Ireland." Heaney's ongoing disputes with Faber and the British may have influenced his approach to Wordsworth. But rather than consider the British poet as an adversary, he showed how Wordsworth's dilemmas during a period of political strife—the French Revolution that the English government opposed—resembled his own dilemmas. Heaney contended that Wordsworth had resolved the "intolerable conflict" between his sympathy for the French revolutionaries and his loyalty to English traditions by reaching a "new level of consciousness" that put in perspective the contrary forces in his psyche and world.[24] (Heaney would develop these ideas further in the introduction to his selection of Wordsworth's poems that Faber published in 2016.)

Heaney aspired to a "new level of consciousness" partly in response to the ongoing bloodshed in Northern Ireland, but also to the ongoing ordeal of his writing life. The excitement of being "on the road" combined with his strong sense that he should share his gifts with fans was exhausting him. At times, he almost seemed addicted to the punishing routine of reading and lecturing around the world. In the early fall of 1984, despite telling Warner he wanted to cut back on readings, he continued to plan ambitious tours in Europe and the United States to promote *Station Island*. With the help of Margaret Hennessy, the counselor at the Department of Foreign Affairs in Dublin, he organized a trip to Spain for the second half of October. He also planned his British reading tour to promote *Station Island*. It would begin on October 14 at the Barbican, London's spacious arts center, and move on October 15 to the BBC for a TV interview. The same day, there would be readings and book signings at Reading's Bulmershe College and at either the Oxford Union or Oxford's Blackwell's bookstore that night. On October 16, after a champagne breakfast, he would go to the Leeds Playhouse and Manchester's Royal Northern College of Music. On October 17, he and Raine were scheduled to appear at Scotland's Edinburgh Bookshop and John Smith's Bookshop in Glasgow. On October 18, they would cross the Irish Sea for a presentation at Belfast's Whitla Hall and a book signing at the Queen's University bookshop. Heaney agreed to do multiple interviews with television stations and newspapers along the way. His mixed feelings about the tour were only partially tempered by Faber's promise to cancel the helicopter.

The day after fulfilling his marketing duties, Heaney flew from Dublin to Madrid and went with the Irish ambassador to Oriedo University in northern Spain for a reading. Two days later, on October 24, he read his poems and lectured on Yeats at the University of Malaga near Gibraltar. The trip had to be cut short when he heard that his mother had suffered a debilitating stroke on their family farm, The Wood. He rushed to Northern Ireland to join his father and siblings in Bellaghy. With family members around her bed, Margaret Heaney died on October 25, 1984. The next day, Heaney wrote Monteith that a "sense of completion now vies with the sense of loss."[25] He would score his anguish about his mother's passing into his sonnet sequence "Clearances" in his next book, *The Haw Lantern*.

Historically, the term "clearances" pertains to the removal of farmers from the Scottish Highlands and islands during the eighteenth and nineteenth centuries, when aristocratic landlords wanted to earn higher rent from farmers raising sheep or crops on larger, more profitable farms. Heaney turns this painful social uprooting into a metaphor for his mother's death, which he associates with the uprooting of a stately chestnut tree that grew for years near Mossbawn. He also takes comfort in thinking of her in the afterlife as "a soul ramifying and forever / Silent, beyond silence listened for." His mother is radically beyond him, but the memory of her—like the tree—continues to "ramify" (literally "grow branches") in Heaney's mind and poem. Her absence has left Heaney in a paradoxical state—"utterly empty," but close to the maternal source of his gifts. Many of the poems in *The Haw Lantern* would express guilt over leaving his mother and the farming community where she'd been rooted like the chestnut tree for so many years.

Heaney would never reconcile his desire for a rooted, meditative life with the nomadic life of a celebrity "on the road." At the end of the year, Harvard made his peregrinations more inevitable by officially appointing him to be the next Boylston Professor of Oratory and Rhetoric. A December 7, 1984, issue of the *Harvard Gazette* announced that he would succeed his friend, the translator Robert Fitzgerald, who had been ill. (Fitzgerald would die on January 16, 1985). With regard to Heaney's appointment, William Alfred spoke for many of his Harvard colleagues when he said, "[It is] the most wonderful thing I've heard in years. We couldn't have a better man. He has the widest range of human notice of any poet working today; and he is a master technician."[26] Heaney was flattered by his promotion but nervous about continuing to spend so much time away from his home and family, and away from his writing. At the end of his first semester as Boylston Professor, he told his Irish poet friend Desmond O'Grady, "I . . . feel like a parched and rib-split carrach, cast on the shore of my own imaginative life. The business, the busyness, of this place is . . . angering."[27] Once again, despite his efforts to spend more time composing poetry, he was sinning against his gift.

On April 30, at the Coolidge Auditorium in the Library of Congress, Heaney read "In Memoriam: Robert Fitzgerald," an elegiac sonnet like the sonnets he wrote for his mother in "Clearances." He alludes to the scene near the end of the *Odyssey* where Odysseus, after being away from home for twenty years, reveals his identity by shooting an arrow through a dozen axe heads. Heaney reimagines the event so that the holes in the axes resemble doorways in a megalithic tomb, and the arrow represents Fitzgerald's spirit traveling on a *via negativa* "out of all knowing / Perfectly aimed toward the vacant center." This complicated conceit treats his death in terms of a rite of passage in a Greek mystery cult, a Christian spiritual exercise, and a mythical homecoming. The arrow, like the body, leaves a breath or *spiritus* in the sockets to mark its path toward death, which Heaney regards as a source of new gifts. In his retelling of the Homeric scene, "There is no last door," no final "knowing," no ultimate union with a traditional goddess or god. There is only the ongoing passage to a "vacant centre" that is like the "utterly empty" source that remained after his mother died. This void recalls the sourceless source in his translation of St. John of the Cross's mystical poem in "Station Island." As Wallace Stevens's "Sunday Morning" declares, "Death is the mother of beauty, mystical, / Within whose burning bosom we devise / Our earthly mothers waiting, sleeplessly." For the mystically inclined Stevens, who would convert to Catholicism on his deathbed, and for Heaney, too, death creates the absence in which presences and presents are re-presented.

During the summer in 1985, the secretary of a Dublin branch of Amnesty International, Mary Lawlor, asked Heaney to write a poem for "Prisoner of Conscience Week," which gave him another opportunity to contemplate the paradoxical way deaths and absences create spaces for new gifts. Lawlor sent Heaney a dossier full of accounts of political regimes that had harassed, censored, banished, incarcerated, and tortured citizens. Although he approved of Amnesty International's work, he had no idea how to compress the painful subject matter of the dossier into a poem. He felt embarrassed and uninspired until he remembered asking his Harvard students to write an allegorical poem about a country that represented a mental or emotional state. Then he thought of his trip to Orkney, which in retrospect was like dying from the world into a "vacant center" for contemplation, and he thought of the death-in-life experiences of the prisoners in Lawlor's dossier. He quickly composed the "Republic of Conscience," and on August 18, 1985, he mailed the poem to Amnesty International as a gift.

Heaney got a chance to produce a different sort of gift when the Harvard administration asked him to write something for the university's 350th anniversary. According to the *Harvard Crimson*, "The festivities [in 1986], which drew 44,000 attendees, were part of one of the largest and most extravagant birthday parties the country has ever seen,"[28] The university celebrated with fireworks, a Boston Pops concert in Harvard Stadium, a posh ball, and symposia on subjects ranging from the Big Bang to the Protestant origins of Harvard. Before an audience of sixteen thousand on September 4, Prince Charles donned a gold-embroidered academic gown and gave a keynote speech that combined asides about the Greek ideal of a good education with jokes about standing where Americans had started a revolution against members of the British royal family. The following day, Heaney read his "Villanelle for an Anniversary," the first poem he'd written in that intricate form. As with his poem for Amnesty International, he'd struggled to find inspiration for the assignment. He got going only after discovering that John Harvard's father, like Heaney's father, had worked in the cattle trade and that Mossbawn-like cattle barns once stood near the college's first building. "There I was," he said, "travelling back to where I started."[29] The personal connection with the college's origins was the catalyst he needed to write.

Heaney's origin story in "Villanelle for an Anniversary" harks back to the account of America's origins in "The Gift Outright," a poem that Robert Frost (a former Harvard student and professor) recited at the inauguration of President Kennedy (Harvard class of 1940). Heaney's "Villanelle," though, returns to a time before America had been conceived or born, a time between prehistory and colonization when the "future was . . . in hibernation." For Heaney, this period was analogous to his childhood at Mossbawn, which he called a "doze of hibernation . . . between the archaic and the modern."[30] Heaney's directive to his Harvard audience—"Begin again where frosts and tests were hard. / Find yourself or founder"—echoes Frost's instruction in "Directive": "If you're lost enough to find yourself / . . . put a sign up CLOSED to all but me." Frost's guide directs the reader back to one of his early homes on a New Hampshire farm and to a "goblet like the Grail" hidden beside a spring whose water is cold because it's so "near its source." Heaney searches for a similar grail-gift at Harvard's source and finds it in John Harvard's "grace of works," which include the donation of his estate and library in 1638. These gifts ensured Harvard's survival during its difficult early years. As for John Harvard's compensation, Heaney imagines he received a "gift outright" of grace when his "soul . . . sped to its reward" in heaven.

Once he completed his duties at Harvard, Heaney worked on the four T. S. Eliot Memorial Lectures he gave at the University of Kent in Canterbury, England, in 1986. His lectures grapple with ethical and aesthetic matters that had preoccupied him from the start of his career, and he often returns to issues pertaining to the writer's gift. "To what extent should the tongue be in the control of the noble rider of socially responsible intellect, ethics or morals?" he asks in one lecture, alluding to Wallace Stevens's essay "The Noble Rider and the Sound of Words." His first lecture, "The Government of the Tongue," argues that the best poets bring their aesthetic and ethical principles to bear on their work, while still allowing their gifted tongues to express themselves. "The tongue (representing both a poet's personal gift of utterance and the common resources of language itself)" must be "granted the right to govern," he declares. He cites Hopkins as a poet who exemplifies the conscientious way a linguistic gift of tongues can be governed. Hopkins's Catholic principles "of monastic and ascetic strictness" govern—or at least try to govern—his gift for stylistic exuberance.[31]

### LOSS OF A PATERNAL GIFT-GIVER

The death of his father in early October 1986 made Heaney reexamine the problematic business of governing the tongue. Because Patrick was prone to stone-like silences, he often appears in *The Haw Lantern* as a tight-lipped, modern-day Hermes whose name, according to some scholars, derives from the Greek word *herma*—"stone pile." Heaney's poem "The Stone Verdict" portrays Patrick as "Hermes, / God of the stone heap." In death, he recapitulates his "old disdain of sweet talk and excuses," and becomes an enduring example of someone who governs his tongue so severely that he barely utters a word.

During his father's declining health in the 1980s, Heaney agonized over his fraught relationship with him. The first poem in *The Haw Lantern*, "Alphabets," introduces Patrick as a kind of home-schooler who teaches his son how to represent the world in a figurative way by using his hands to create silent shadow-plays on the walls. These primitive lessons prepare Heaney for his later education at St. Columb's, where Catholic priests advocate the sort of meditative silences that came naturally to Patrick. Heaney and his father ultimately coalesce in the image of "the scribe / Who drove a team of quills on his white field." As in the earlier poem "Follower," the father who doesn't speak as he plows (he guides his horse with a "clicking tongue" while his son is "yapping always") is the model the adult poet emulates when he silently "verses" and "reverses" with his plow-like pen on a "field" of white paper.

Other poems in *The Haw Lantern* draw connections between the father who represses speech in order to focus on his work and the son who expresses himself in silent writing. Hermes, the god of boundaries and crossroads who supposedly invented the alphabet, reemerges in "Terminus" as a guide for father and son as they try to navigate Ulster's divided culture. They both realize that silence is a coping mechanism in a country where speaking one's mind is dangerous, but Heaney in the end follows those who are "parleying" with Irish Catholics and British Protestants, rather than keeping quiet. The poem begins with a memory of digging up acorns at Mossbawn and moves on to the way Heaney's religious training teaches him to be charitable and communicative, and to treat words as gifts that should be shared. His origin as a writer is a liminal space between the archaic gift-exchange economy of his Catholic faith and the modern capitalist economy of his country. Caught in a dialectical force field between the two, he aims for a synthesis. Money, he concludes, should be distributed like symbols in the Eucharist for the benefit of others. "When they spoke of the prudent squirrel's hoard / It shone like gifts at a nativity," he says of his early Catholic instructors. "Terminus" recycles the biblical story of the Magi to emphasize Heaney's conviction that money and language should be exchanged like gifts rather than hoarded.

The Eliot lectures in the wake of his father's death left Heaney feeling depleted. As he rested at the beginning of 1987, he half-jokingly told Paul Muldoon that he'd developed an "immense gift for indolence."[32] Back at Harvard, though, he returned to his busy routine of traveling and socializing. He also tried to help his struggling friends. He reached out to Seamus Deane, who was suffering marital troubles, job setbacks, and physical ailments caused by a car accident. He did what he could for the Irish poet Nuala Ní Dhomhnaill, who visited Heaney during the spring and wrote him at length about her family problems and political grievances. Other women wrote him about their griefs and grievances, too. The Fordham professor Phyllis Zagano, whom Heaney had met on several occasions (including the university's 1981 Commencement, when he served as the main speaker), asked him to intervene in her antidiscrimination lawsuit against the university, which had denied her tenure. His Harvard assistant, Nancy Williston, who suffered severe bouts of depression, sought his counsel and consolation. He assisted his friend Joseph Brodsky, who suffered from heart disease, by commenting on the poems he wrote in

Russian and translated into English. On February 15, Brodsky sent him "Sextet," which had already been published in the *New Yorker,* and Heaney diligently suggested ways to improve it.

Most of the reviews of *The Haw Lantern,* which Faber published on June 22, 1987, corroborated a recent English poll that ranked Heaney as the most popular poet in the English-speaking world. In his *London Times* review "The Stain of Words," John Carey praised Heaney's allegorical style and attributed it to the death of his mother, even though many of the book's poems dealt with the legacy of his father. Carey's title echoed Samuel Beckett's provocative remark in a 1969 interview: "Every word is like an unnecessary stain on silence and nothingness."[33] Heaney, however, usually regarded words in poems as gifts from silence rather than stains on silence. If there were stains in his poems, they signified guilt caused by the absence or misuse of words. Always sensitive to the way critics elevated him above his contemporaries, he was annoyed by Carey's dismissive comments about Paul Muldoon's new book *Meeting the British.* On June 22, the day after the review appeared, Heaney sent Muldoon a postcard excoriating Carey for the way he judged their two books.

The title poem in *The Haw Lantern* cites Diogenes, the Greek Cynic who lived in the fourth century BC, as an example of someone who thinks of words as instruments to achieve truth and justice. Heaney conjures up the philosopher's ghost from an unlikely source: the diminutive fruit of a hawthorn tree. A bright berry hanging from a spiky branch reminds him of Diogenes's lantern, which the Greek philosopher supposedly carried through an Athens marketplace in search of one honest man. Heaney imagines the lantern trained on him. Much of *The Haw Lantern* delineates a place of "pure interrogation," as the poem "From the Frontier of Writing" calls it, where the poet is forced to reexamine his ethical and aesthetic concerns.

Fidelity to one's gift is one of these concerns. In "A Daylight Art," a poem about Socrates's last day alive, Heaney wonders if the famous philosopher should have remained faithful to his gift for intellectual debate or whether he should have explored other possible gifts. During his famous trial, he tried to convince the jury that he was God's gift to the Athenians and that it was natural for him to follow his natural gift, even though his accusers argued he was guilty of impiety. Well known for his conviction that philosophical dialogues were the best way to arrive at the truth, and that writing was a poor substitute for discovering and communicating the truth, Socrates surprised his friends by writing poetry shortly before he died. Was he abandoning his natural gift? Heaney's poem alludes to Plato's *Phaedo,* which opens with Cebes asking Socrates, "Why [are] you, who never before wrote a line of poetry . . . , turning Aesop's fables into verse, and also composing that hymn in honour of Apollo?"[34] Socrates says he often heard a voice in dreams exhorting him to write music. In Heaney's account, this dream voice repeats the command *"Practise the art."* But which art should Socrates practice: the art of philosophy, the art of poetry, or the art of music? "A Daylight Art" ends with a whimsical aphorism that echoes Dryden's translation of an ode by Horace: "Happy the man, therefore, with a natural gift // for practicing the right one from the start— / poetry, say, or fishing; whose nights are dreamless." Happiness, it seems, depends on remaining loyal to one's "natural gift" (which, for Socrates, was philosophy) and not having dreams about pursuing other gifts. But Heaney's cheerful ending is undercut by the fact that Socrates's peers judged his "natural gift" to be corrupting and a jury gave him the death penalty.

If Heaney quests for holy grails in *The Haw Lantern,* they continue to be natural gifts. At times, he puts the grail-gifts he finds in Lady Justice's scale for an unusual kind of judgment. A poem, he once said, should be "hung in the scale as a counterweight to the given actuality of the world."[35] Equilibrium between the poet's created gift and "the given actuality" is his idea of aesthetic justice. Simone Weil's *Gravity and Grace* helped him formulate this idea, although she was mainly interested in social and religious justice. "If we know the way society is unbalanced, we must do what we can to add weight to the lighter side of the scale," Weil writes. "Social order can be nothing but an equilibrium of forces." Balance, from her Christian point of view, is made possible by gifts of grace that offset the gravitational force of sin. God's grace is a gift, but also a loan. "Everything without exception which is of value in me comes from somewhere other than myself," she says. "[It is] a loan which must be ceaselessly renewed."[36] "Terminus" presents Heaney as a judicious weigher and balancer. In this case, he remembers weighing grain as a boy: "My left hand placed the standard iron weight. / My right tilted a last grain in the balance." The farmer's grain, after being weighed, is exchanged for money, but in Heaney's parable the monetary exchange is meant to suggest a spiritual gift exchange that establishes equilibrium.

Heaney constructs a similar parable about gravity and grace in "Hailstones," where the weight of ice hitting the narrator's face and covering the road where he drives is a testament to gravity, and "the light [that] opened in silence" during his journey signifies the "gifted state" of grace. As if recalling the grain image from "Terminus," he juxtaposes hailstones that create hazardous driving conditions with another image of grain. "Thomas Traherne had his orient wheat / for proof and wonder," he says, "but for us, it was the sting of hailstones." In *Centuries of Meditations,* the seventeenth-century mystical poet Thomas Traherne offers a litany of his "sublime and celestial" visions. "By the Gift of God they attended me into the world," he says about these wonderful visions, "and by His special favour I remember them till now. Verily they seem the greatest gifts His wisdom could bestow, for without them all other gifts had been dead and vain." Traherne received one of these early visionary gifts while gazing at an English field: "The corn was orient and immortal wheat, which never should be reaped, nor was ever sown. I thought it had stood from everlasting to everlasting."[37] In "Hailstones," Heaney wants to have the same sort of God-given visions that allowed Traherne to regard ordinary realities as extraordinary gifts. He indicates that he has achieved something akin to Traherne's "gifted state" when the hail stops falling, "the light opened in silence / and a car with wipers going still / laid perfect tracks in the slush." The tire's "perfect tracks" resemble the poet's "perfect" lines on white paper. In the end, the poet's mind, which was at first bombarded by hailstones, is granted a sudden reprieve: sunlight returns, the car keeps moving forward, the poem is written. A gift of grace has counteracted the weight of gravity.

*The Haw Lantern* garnered plenty of favorable notices and won England's prestigious Whitbread Award, but some critics regretted Heaney's turn toward allegory and metaphysical rumination. J. D. McClatchy predicted in a *New Republic* review that readers would "find *The Haw Lantern* something of a disappointment."[38] Ian Hamilton, Heaney's bête noir, contended that a "reluctance to reach for anything that might be thought of as poetic grandeur" and a preoccupation with "silence and emptiness" made his new poems insipid.[39] Helen Vendler, in one of the most complimentary reviews, worried that her friend was straying from his natural gift. "As the earth loses for him the mass and gravity of familiar presences," she wrote, "desiccation and weightlessness threaten the former fullness of the sensual life."[40] She hoped Heaney would go back to his Keatsean way of balancing the "mass and gravity" of sensual, down-to-earth experiences with his spiritual concerns with grace. The English poet Andrew Waterman, who had taught for three decades at the University of Ulster, called the book "a flawed, self-indulgent and unsuccessful collection of poetry, weakened precisely by its author's awareness of himself as a public figure, showing him over-eager to keep abreast with a gluttonous audience, and to explain himself to the fans."[41] He encouraged Heaney to return to his earlier preoccupations with the contested soil of his native land.

In early December 1987, while flying back to Boston after a reading at the University of Utah hosted by Mark Strand, Heaney suggested in a letter to David Hammond that he was painfully aware of the way the pressure of public activities was hurting his poetry. "It's strange, the way things have developed," he told his old friend. "What was once the domain of magnificent romance [has] become the humdrum of a slightly impatient, stressed, schedule-haunted, fat-bellied man. I rebuke myself for being in the land of Mormon, in the big sky of the west, and only being able to worry about the undone and overdue tasks of my life." He looked down from his plane window at the Rocky Mountains' snowy peaks and regretted that all he could think about was his obligations at Harvard: the letters to answer, recommendations to write, novels by friends to blurb, lectures to prepare, committee meetings to attend. "The chance to sit at a desk [and write poetry] has almost disappeared from my life," he groused. "It creates an enormous rage in me at times, a feeling I've allowed myself to be pushed to the edge of my own life."[42] But there was no let-up in sight. As soon as he got back to Harvard, he had to teach his classes, organize more readings, and prepare the Richard Ellmann Lectures, which he would deliver in April.

His complaints about all his obligations notwithstanding, Heaney began 1988 by trying hard to fulfill them. He teamed up with Ted Hughes to judge the Arvon Foundation's second poetry competition, even though he'd vowed not to. He contributed a poem, "New Worlds," to *In the Prison of His Days,* a collection of writings for the South African anti-apartheid activist Nelson Mandela on his seventieth birthday. (He was still in prison on Robben Island after being incarcerated there since 1964.) Heaney wrote another gift poem around this time for Richard Ellmann, the eminent scholar of Irish literature who'd spent his last years in a different kind of prison—a body wracked by Lou Gehrig's disease—and who'd died on May 13, 1987, while struggling to finish his Pulitzer Prize–winning biography of Oscar Wilde. Heaney's elegy for Ellmann, "The Sounds of Rain," speaks of the "feeling of immense debt" Heaney and others owed the scholar for his "masterwork"—his many esteemed books and essays—as if this work were a gift bequeathed to posterity. In a letter to a mutual friend at Emory University, Ron Schuchard, Heaney said, "I feel that the poem expresses both regret and replenishment, and in that way rehearses the double feeling one has about Dick's loss—that it was untimely and hard, yet that the riches of the work were a great recompense."[43] His comment frames Ellmann's life in terms of gain and loss, of gifts of grace that balance the gravitational forces of death and grief.

It had been Ellmann's dying wish for Heaney to inaugurate the lectures named in his honor at Emory. Heaney wrote in *The Place of Writing,* the book that assembled his three Ellmann lectures, which he delivered in 1988, that he was daunted by the prospect of being "measured against the unique standards of excellence" that Ellman exemplified. Once again, Heaney was thinking of writerly exchanges in terms of scales, judgments, and gifts. His first lecture praised Ellmann as an artful writer as well as a judicious critic: "I was always moved by a feeling that innate gifts of fortitude, tenderness and fairness had been consecrated to a discipline, one which placed immense intellectual and personal demands upon him but which rewarded him with a rock-bottom emotional verity."[44] Heaney's main intention in his lectures was to examine the sources of poetic gifts and the way poets represent and critique those sources. In his lecture, "W. B. Yeats and Thoor Ballylee," he noted that Yeats had transformed his Norman tower Thoor Ballylee, which he'd bought in 1916, into a "verifying force" and a "sacramental site" that signified the durability of his gift. It was not just Yeats's summer home; it was a symbol of his ability to preserve his gift during World War I, the Easter Uprising, and the Irish Civil War. Heaney believed that Yeats's "fortress of stone" helped make possible his "fortress of words," and he applauded Yeats for the way he wrote about his home as a "manifestation of the fortified mind, besieged yet ablaze, exalted and incontrovertible."[45] Heaney regarded his own "fortress of stone," Glanmore Cottage, and his former stone fortress, Mossbawn, in similar ways.

Heaney returned to the notion that a gift of grace could balance the gravity of the world in a discussion of the "justifying effect" of Yeats's "self-given music." When life is "menacing, the need for the steadying gift of finished art becomes all the more urgent," Heaney told his audience at Emory. That gift, according to Heaney, had the best chance of materializing when the poet shielded himself from the "constantly flickering horizon of violence and breakdown."[46] Yeats had hunkered down in his stone tower to create "one of [the] . . . great gifts to our century," which, for Heaney, embodied the resilience of his tower. "Another of his gifts was his own boldness to question the final value and trustworthiness of this powerfully composed tower."[47] Feeling as beset upon as Yeats, Heaney explored the themes of protection, distance, and criticism in his other lectures, too.

Around the time Heaney was analyzing the fortified safe zones of writers, Ann Saddlemyer gave him the opportunity to own Glanmore Cottage. It was during Heaney's visit to the University of Toronto in early 1988 that she offered to sell the cottage. "I nearly fainted at the table," he said. "She was prepared to give me access for a second time to the *locus amoenus* [lovely place]. Nothing that had happened since we left Wicklow was more important in my writing life."[48] It was as if Saddlemyer had given him a gift of grace that would permanently connect him to Mossbawn, his first *locus amoenus* and the *omphalos* of his gift.

## SEEING THINGS AND MARVELOUS GIFTS

Heaney complained to Medbh McGuckian on September 12, 1988, that he'd been a "mascot at every summer school and arts festival in the west, and host to every American friend and Co. Derry family relation that came near Dublin." He now wanted to isolate himself in his *locus amoenus*. "In a mood of screech and moan," he wrote, "I got out here [to Glanmore Cottage] twenty-four hours ago, into silence and self-recrimination, the

latter of which I can muster anywhere, of course. . . . It's in primitive order, but it's a godsend. . . . Even though it looks as if I have lots of time and
space, thanks to the Harvard deal, the world seems to eat it all. I intend to
make Glanmore a wee garrison against same world."[49] On September 12,
he wrote another friend, the scholar of Irish literature John Wilson Foster:
"Years ago at school at this time of the year, we did *Portrait of the Artist*–
type retreats. Self-abasement, silence, purposes of amendment. And it
seems I am beginning to revert. . . . I've come out to this gate-lodge on
my own, into an old stillness of stonewalls and stealthy fields, and on my
own for the first time in months."[50] He told others that Glanmore Cottage
was his "Colmcille beehive hut" where he could meditate in silence and
write behind stone walls.[51]

In 1988, Heaney wanted to retreat to a "garrison" in part because his
father's death, which had come two years after his mother's, represented
"the final 'unroofing' of the world."[52] His original "bawn" had been partially "unroofed" when his brother Christopher died and his family moved
to The Wood; the deaths of his parents had completed the "unroofing,"
and now he felt a profound sense of what Freud called "unheimlich"—an
"unhoming." His article "'Apt Admonishment': Wordsworth as an Example" deploys Freud's term, which is often translated as "uncanny," to
explain how "close encounter[s] between the poet and the muse" and
between the poet and significant precursors often occur during disori-
enting periods of loss:

> In the modern era, the sense of visitation and rededication will often
> derive from meetings and occasions which are . . . bathed in an un-
> canny light, occasions when the poet has been, as it were, unhomed,
> has experienced the unheimlich. Even in the modern period, however,
> the poet typically comes away from such encounters with a renewed
> sense of election, surer in his or her vocation. What is being enacted
> or recalled is usually an experience of confirmation, of the spirit com-
> ing into its own, a door being opened or a path being entered upon.
> Usually also the experience is unexpected and out of the ordinary, in
> spite of the fact that it occurs in the normal course of events, in the
> everyday world.[53]

After his parents died, his mind often drifted back to their early years together at Mossbawn, and Glanmore Cottage helped trigger his uncanny
sense of returning to his first home. His sonnet sequence "Glanmore Revisited," which he wrote shortly after buying Saddlemyer's cottage, emphasizes this. From his Freudian perspective, he had restored an umbilical
connection with his mother, his *omphalos,* his muse's gift-bearing womb,
and he had done so in a place of stone-like silence that he also associated
with his father. He even speculates that his chain-smoking in the cottage
recaptures the euphoria of his infantile "gifted state" at Mossbawn.

Emulating Yeats's propensity for self-criticism, Heaney in "Glanmore
Revisited" scolds himself for craving the "hibernated" and "chloroformed"
state of mind that is the by-product of smoking while sequestered in a
womb-like space. His quirky asides about the "thrill" and "scare" he gets
from "breaking and entering" into his own cottage are the results of his
suspicion that his new home is a taboo womb-substitute. Oedipal anxieties about regressing to a fetal state assail him in the last sonnet, "The
Skylight," where he berates his wife for wanting to open the roof with a
window. He doesn't want his first womb-like world "unroofed" again; he
wants to return to Mossbawn's familiar "low and closed" space with its
"claustrophobic, nest-up-in-the-roof / Effect."

Heaney told O'Driscoll in *Stepping Stones* that Glanmore Cottage was
his "completely silent place of writing" and that it stood "for what Wallace Stevens said poetry stands for, the imagination pressing back against
the pressures of reality."[54] Stevens in "The Noble Rider and the Sound of
Words" had called the imagination "a violence from within that protects
us from a violence without."[55] Heaney's fifty-page sequence "Squarings,"
which he began in September 1988 while annotating a selection of Yeats's
poems in Ireland's National Library, and which he placed at the end of
*Seeing Things,* plays variations on the idea that the imagination needs rock-
hard defenses against the "pressures of reality." It's as if Heaney wants
to build square poems (each is about the size of a "square" sonnet) to
replicate the sturdiness of Yeats's square stone tower or the sturdiness
of the stone-walled Glanmore Cottage and Mossbawn. In the first of his
forty-eight "squarings," he wonders if a door into the light or a door into
the dark is most conducive for entering a visionary "gifted state." He
has reconciled himself to "gazing out . . . alone" at the wintry light but

continues to pine for the hermetically sealed, dimly lit atmosphere of Mossbawn. "Roof it again," he commands. "Batten down. Dig in. / Drink out of tin. Know the scullery cold, / A latch, a door-bar, forged tongs and a grate." His directives are aimed at himself and point back to his original farmhouse and hearth culture.

Heaney said "Squarings" began mysteriously: "[It] felt given, strange and unexpected. I didn't quite know where it came from."[56] It was another poetic gift. The title of the first section, "Lightenings," refers to both a spirit moving toward a divine light before death and a fetus moving toward the world's light at birth. Heaney had stumbled across the word in *Romeo and Juliet*. Shortly before Romeo kills Paris in the tomb where Juliet lies dead, he says, "How oft when men are on the point of death / Have they been merry! which their keepers call / A lightning before death. Oh, how may I / Call this lightning?" (act 5, scene 3, lines 97–100). Heaney's "lightning" had come after his parents' deaths and after he'd felt reborn and reroofed at Glanmore. As he said in another poem, "Fosterling," it was "time to be dazzled and the heart to lighten"; it was time "to credit marvels." Although he argued with his wife about a skylight (Marie won the argument, and builders cut a hole in the roof), he eventually appreciated the way the "extravagant / Sky entered and held surprise wide open."

The most marvelous gift in "Squarings" arrives in the form of a visionary sailor who enters a church through a hole in the roof. According to a legend from the eighth century, a sailor who is crossing the sky above a monastery in Clonmacnoise, a town halfway between Dublin and Galway, shinnies down his ship's anchor-rope that has caught on the church's altar. Although the monks in the church may surmise God has delivered a supernatural gift, they fear the stranger will find their world painful, so they urge him to return to his medieval spaceship. Heaney read about this miraculous event in Kenneth Hurlstone Jackson's *A Celtic Miscellany*, but he altered it in his poem so the orphic voyager returns to his heaven with a vision of "the marvelous as he had known it." The irony is that he believes the mundane world is "marvelous," while the monks believe the high-flying sailor's world is "marvelous" and the actual world is unbearable.

Heaney said "Squarings" taught him "the difference between *les vers donnés* and *les verse calculés*." He also alleged that he "learned [from writing the sequence] what inspiration feels like but not how to summon it."[57] In fact, he had known the difference between verse that was donated as a gift (*donnés*) and verse that was crafted in a calculated way (*calculés*) for a long time, but in *Seeing Things* he reemphasized the process of waiting meditatively for poetic gifts. As he closed in on his fiftieth birthday, he confided to friends that his workaday life continued to undermine the conditions that made *les vers donnés* probable. Once again, he considered changing his life. He explained to Michael Longley that "the acquisitive brilliant young of Bush-ville" (the students at Harvard at the beginning of George H. W. Bush's presidency) sapped his creative energy. Did he "want to keep stepping on planes" and flying around the world? He conceded in his letter, "Eight months off work for four months on is a terrific arrangement, but it may have to go, for the sake of new life."[58] (His salary for four months of teaching at Harvard was equivalent to about $100,000 today.) He told Longley he yearned for a Dantesque *vita nuova*—a "new life"—of silence and contemplation so he could get back to the source of his gifts.

# 12

# Healing Wounds
# with Gifts

## IRISH DOG WINS ENGLISH RACE

Heaney's global stature made him an attractive candidate for the "Oxford Professor of Poetry" position that had been filled by a long line of distinguished poets since its founding in 1708. Charles Monteith had brought up the possibility of Heaney's candidacy in 1979, but Heaney demurred. On October 9, 1982, the English poet John Wain, who had held the post from 1973 to 1978, wrote Heaney a long letter prodding him to allow his name to be put on the ballot. Wain assured him that the Oxford Professor's duties were more honorary than onerous. If elected, he would serve for five years and deliver one lecture per term (Oxford had trimesters), judge the Newdigate poetry contest, give the Creweian Oration (a speech that honored university benefactors), and attend several academic ceremonies. The pay was minimal (Wain had earned about £1,100), and the residency requirement was also minimal (Wain said he spent about two weeks in Oxford during each of its three terms). Flattered by Wain's endorsement and promise to campaign for him, Heaney still worried about taking on more work and doing so on English ground. He had stressed in *An Open Letter* that his passport was Irish green, and the academic institution he'd be joining was steeped in British history and culture.

Seven years after Wain contacted Heaney, the Irish-born poet and Oxford don Bernard O'Donoghue encouraged him to reconsider the poetry professorship. On February 1, 1989, O'Donoghue sent Heaney an *Oxford University Gazette* announcement about the position. An *Oxford Times* article soon spread the rumor that Heaney was being recruited. Literary friends and well-wishers, including Iris Murdoch, Peter Levi, John Wain, John Jones, Tom Paulin, and John Carey, wrote in support of Heaney's candidacy. Anthony Smith, the president of Magdalen College at Oxford, promised Heaney a suite of rooms if he was elected. Moved by the groundswell of support, Heaney notified O'Donoghue in early April 1989 that he would accept the nomination.

On May 31, the day before voting commenced, Heaney reassured Dean Michael Spence at Harvard that, if elected Oxford Professor of Poetry, he would still fulfill his duties as Boylston Professor. As it turned out, he received an overwhelming majority of votes—361 out of a possible 485. (Sixty votes went to the scholar-poet C. H. Sisson, sixty to the Rastafarian reggae poet Benjamin Zephaniah, and nine to the relatively unknown poet Duncan McCann.) Fans around the world congratulated Heaney. On June 20, Ireland's consulate general asked him how he'd managed to overcome British prejudices. On August 2, Heaney's friend Tony Brophy joked about the unlikelihood of an Irish Catholic being crowned with laurels in such an ancient British institution and suggested that he write another nationalist poem reminding the English that his passport was green. Helen Vendler, Eamon Grennan, Jay Parini, and Toshi Furomoto sent less politicized compliments. Even those who disapproved of the Professor of Poetry position were pleased. On June 17, Marxist critic Terry Eagleton apologized for attacking the professorship in the past and said rather sheepishly, "I feel a bit like the atheist who doesn't reckon much to the papacy but would infinitely prefer John XXIII to Pius XII."[1] He said he was sorry to miss the upcoming reception that Magdalen College had organized to celebrate Heaney's victory. Although Gary Snyder shared Eagleton's disapproval of Oxford's encrusted traditions, he also congratulated Heaney. "We have many angles in common," he said, "and I'm grateful for the clarity and compassion & insight & calm wit that is so strong in your poetry." He hoped Heaney would visit his "corner of the [Sierra] mountains" the next time he was in California.[2]

One way Heaney dealt with all the hoopla surrounding the Oxford election was by retreating to Glanmore Cottage. "This is the bastion of silence, the ring-fort of reading, the guilt-granary," he told Padraic Fallon on August 2, 1989.[3] A few days earlier, he'd outlined his first Oxford lectures and asked the Oxford Clerk of the Schools if he could deliver them in late October, since he had to teach at Harvard in the spring. He thought of calling his lectures "Doing English: Poetry and Redressal" and "Throwing Shapes: The Freedom of Poetry." When the October dates were set, Anthony Smith informed him that rooms would be ready for him at Magdalen and that the college would welcome him as a Fellow in mid-October and hold a brunch in his honor on October 22, a few days before the lectures began. In late August, Heaney explained in a letter to Ted Hughes that he now planned to call his introductory lecture "The Redress of Poetry" and that he would elaborate on the word "redress more in metaphysical poetic terms than politically." He would "dodge the expectation of being a propagandist for the marginalized" and "go straight in and annex the centre." At the center of his discussion would be the canonical poetry of the Anglican priest George Herbert. Heaney was serious about his annexing strategy. At least to his Irish friends, he wanted to appear to be a rebellious colonist taking over an imperial capital. But he also joked about finding himself in the role of "Irish dog [who] wins English race."[4] In fact, his triumph in England was nothing new; he'd been winning English races ever since he began publishing in London during the 1960s.

Hughes responded to Heaney on October 8, 1989, dividing his letter between commentary on "Squarings" and advice about the Oxford Professor of Poetry. Heaney's new poems, Hughes pointed out insightfully, were ritualistic attempts to reconnect with his parents and original home. Hughes predicted that domestic deities, such as the Roman cluster of gods known as Lares and Penates, would act as Heaney's muses from now on. "I read ['Squarings']," he said, "as a reclaiming—of your own Lares & Penates. A quiet numbering & retaking possession of your house-gods—which with your father's death now come under your sole care. You handle them, salute them, & settle them into their new niches—in the new you, (the new head of the family)." According to Hughes, these muse-gods would enable Heaney to reclaim English poets like Herbert as well as his Irish home-ground, and they would dispense gifts to heal "the pituitary gland—of England."[5] Hughes was thinking of England as Eliot had in *The Waste Land,* as an ill person in need of sexual and cultural rejuvenation.

When Heaney went to Oxford, he may not have thought of himself as an Irish Percival questing for a Holy Grail that would heal the British wasteland, but at times he certainly felt like an alien wandering in a foreign land. Oxford customs puzzled him. Since he had to be affiliated with a college, there was a tug-of-war to determine which one would claim him. The president of St. John's College, the physicist William Hayes, convinced him to become a Supernumerary Fellow at St. John's. This grandsounding title allowed him drinking and reading privileges in the Senior Common Room, which was decorated with portraits and bronze heads of famous poets such as A. E. Housman and Robert Graves. The college governors, however, questioned the legitimacy of his Supernumerary Fellowship, so he had to have his title changed to Honorary Fellow.

Officers at Magdalen College also had to come up with an appropriate title for Heaney. On June 16, President Smith, after consulting the college constitution, dubbed him "a Supernumerary non-stipendiary Fellow" and placed him on the college's official list of members who didn't receive a salary. Heaney found it hard to take his new titles and privileges too seriously. Asked to speak at the college's Restoration Day dinner on October 25, 1989, he remarked in a letter to Karl Miller about the irony of commemorating the expulsion of Magdalen's Catholic administration and faculty on October 25, 1688, by King William, who'd caused so much misery for the Irish. (William replaced all the Catholics at Magdalen with Protestants.) Heaney soon discovered that the college treated Catholic Fellows much more hospitably than in 1688. Each morning, he woke to the dulcet voices of a choir practicing scales and singing hymns beneath his room. He attended Evensong services, strolled on the bucolic Addison's Walk near the Cherwell River, and gazed at the queen's deer in the park behind the college. Although John Wain had downplayed the amount of work he'd have to do, his schedule quickly filled up with activities. Wain invited him to meals at his home in Wolvercote and at his college in Oxford. Invitations to submit poems and do interviews came from the *Oxford Poetry* journal, the *Cherwell* newspaper, the *Isis* magazine, and the *Romulus* magazine. The Pegasus Theatre and Blackwell's Bookshop organized poetry readings for him. Bernard O'Donoghue, who was affiliated with Magdalen College, took him on literary pilgrimages to the homes of Matthew Arnold in Laleham and C. S. Lewis in Headington.

Heaney presented his lecture "The Redress of Poetry" to a large, attentive audience at Oxford's Examination School on October 24, 1989.

The British poet and literary critic Jon Stallworthy said he'd not "seen such a crowd, not sensed such excitement, at an Oxford lecture since [the late 1950s when] W. H. Auden was Professor [of Poetry]."[6] Following a preamble about poetry being an expression of "the imagination pressing back against the pressure of reality," Heaney applied Simone Weil's concepts of gravity and grace to Herbert's poetry. As a powerful figure in the Church of England, Herbert may have espoused the British Empire's cultural ideals, but he was no simple-minded imperialist. To Heaney, a typical Herbert poem examines the "contradictions of experience" and traces "the dialectic of thesis, antithesis, and synthesis" of philosophical reasoning in a way that was universal and therapeutic rather than merely political.[7] Herbert demonstrated how one could achieve a state of graceful equilibrium by pressing back against the world's gravitational pressures with a rational and imaginative mind.

Heaney's paean to Herbert's religious ideals of moderation and reconciliation may have disappointed some in the Oxford audience who expected a postcolonial critique of the seventeenth-century Anglican. Heaney told his Scottish friend Patrick Crotty that he'd originally considered calling his lecture "The Merit of Poetry" to highlight the way he wanted to approach aesthetic issues from a religious point of view: "I had this clear perception that underneath my understanding/search for the place of poetry in our lives there lay the structure of the doctrine of merit as we had it [at St. Columb's College] in Hart's *Christian Doctrine!*"[8] For Hart, God blesses a person with the gift of grace so he or she can do meritorious deeds. "Good works proceeding from grace are meritorious—i.e., are worthy of a reward in the sight of God," according to Hart.[9] (The Latin meaning of *meritum* is "a reward.") For Heaney, ideally, a poem should be an in-spirited gift of grace meriting rewards.

Heaney cited Herbert's poem "The Pulley" as an example of the way the Anglican poet conceived of meritorious gift exchanges. "When God at first made man," the poem begins, God gave him gifts of strength, beauty, wisdom, honor, and pleasure. God also made sure that humans had the power to revere Him as the original gift-giver. Herbert's anxious, jealous God worries that His original bond with humans might deteriorate if humans focus on the material gifts He had created rather than his sublime power as the Creator. In Herbert's poem, God is afraid humans will get too attached to the Creation. If that happens, God says, "[humans] would adore my gifts instead of me, / And rest in Nature, not the God of Nature." To avoid this, according to Herbert, God made humans restless in the material world and predicted that their dissatisfaction with the way things are would lead them back to His comforting "breast." The mystical reunion between God and humans, which Herbert conceives of as an erotic return to a mother's or father's "breast," had a powerful effect on Heaney. As he saw it, a productive bond with a creator, whether divine or artistic, male or female, was the goal of meritorious gift exchange.

Meritorious gifts were on Heaney's mind as the second millennium entered its last decade. Before returning to Harvard for the spring semester in 1990, he wrote a recommendation that argued his friend Helen Vendler merited the promotion to English Department chair because of her gifts: "I deeply admire and cherish her honesty, her forthrightness, her commitment to the University and her immense gift for hard work—to say nothing of her indispensable gifts as a literary critic and teacher."[10] He also corresponded with Ted Hughes about poets whose gifts merited inclusion in the anthology they planned to call *The Kit Bag* or *The School Bag*. Hughes wrote on January 20 that he wanted to select only those poets who were "spiritually great—voices of the whole tribe at a moment of crisis . . . and those who are obviously equally-gifted . . . but who are simply never picked up by the national gods." He looked forward to discussing the anthology at an Arvon dinner in England, but Heaney was too busy to attend. Hughes sent another letter to Heaney on February 7, proposing that they choose poems relevant to "the frightful battles of the next century (the famine battles, the Greenhouse flood-out battles, the refugee migration battles, the general devilry battles, the democratic mutual abuse battles, the roaming bands of hand-to-mouth warrior battles."[11] Their anthology, Hughes said, should resemble a "kit bag" of survival tools for the dystopian future. On April 1, Heaney told Hughes he didn't like "The Kit-Bag" as a title, since most readers would miss the reference to the English song, "Pack up Your Troubles in Your Old Kit Bag, and Smile, Smile, Smile," which had been written for soldiers during World War I. Instead, he suggested using an aeronautical term such as "The Black Box" or "The Flight Path" that would evoke a record of destruction or a journey beyond it.

Much of Heaney's letter to Hughes, which he wrote on a flight from Shannon Airport on April 1, 1990, was about his translation of Sophocles's play *Philoctetes*. In some ways, the play's main character resembled Hughes; he was a gifted, long-suffering man preoccupied with healing wounds. When Heaney decided to call his translation *The Cure at Troy*, he may have been thinking of Hughes's determination to find cures for personal and public afflictions. (Philoctetes's wounded foot had festered for ten years, and so had the siege of Troy.) Heaney also intended his version of the fifth-century play to be read as "a possible allegorical representation of the Ulster Unionist majority's 'refusal to join' and hence their deferral of any possibility of a United Ireland." He planned to make Philoctetes an allegorical Everyman—a composite of an Ulster Protestant and Ulster Catholic "bound to their wound-memory."[12] During the spring semester at Harvard in 1990, Heaney used a Loeb verse translation, a literal translation, and David Greene's modern translation as cribs for his work. By July 1990, he'd finished a first draft. Two months later, rehearsals began, and, in October 1990, *The Cure at Troy* was published.

The play's action revolves around a scheme hatched by Odysseus to steal the magical bow and arrows from Philoctetes, who has been abandoned by the Greek army on the island of Lemnos in the Mediterranean Sea. Heaney identifies Philoctetes as a "master" whose "old gifts as an archer / Stand him in good stead."[13] His weapons are actual gifts that Hercules gave him shortly before the mythical strongman died. Heaney's translation, however, dwells on the gift exchange between Philoctetes and Achilles's son, Neoptolemus, rather than on the gift from Hercules to Philoctetes. Odysseus instructs Neoptolemus to trick Philoctetes into handing over Hercules's powerful bow and arrows so that the Greek warriors can use them in their battle against the Trojans. The plan works, up to a point. Neoptolemus offers to take Philoctetes back to Greece from the island where he suffers in solitude, and Philoctetes thanks him by giving up his weapon. "You gave to me . . . / A way home to my father and my friends," Philoctetes says, so "I give [the bow] to you." This gift exchange illustrates what Neoptolemus refers to as their "economy of kindness."[14] The economic relationship falters, however, when Philoctetes discovers that it's based on a lie. To redeem himself and appease Philoctetes, Neoptolemus returns the bow. "The scales will even out when the bow's restored," he says. Negotiations with Philoctetes continue until he finally agrees to sail with his fellow Greeks to Troy. On the way, Asclepius and his sons cure the wound in Philoctetes's foot. With his body made whole and healthy, and with his gifted weapon in his possession again, Philoctetes can now "heal the wound of the Trojan war" and become a savior of his people.[15]

Heaney told Mary McCollum in an *Irish News* interview that he'd read about the Greek hero "as an undergraduate in the 60s in 'The Wound and the Bow' by the American critic Edmund Wilson," and that he'd been intrigued by Wilson's interpretation of the myth "as an allegory of the artist whose wound provides the basis for something miraculous which is the work of art."[16] For Wilson, Philoctetes is a type of aesthetic and sociopolitical healer who can cure himself and others when he is "able to forget his grievance and to devote his divine gifts to the service of his own people." According to Wilson, the Philoctetes-artist is "the victim of a malodorous disease which renders him abhorrent to society and periodically degrades him and makes him helpless," but he "is also the master of a superhuman art which everybody has to respect and which the normal man finds he needs."[17] In Northern Ireland, where the Protestant majority had systematically "degraded" the Catholic minority, Heaney found the myth of Philoctetes especially germane. As he told Karl Miller: "The wound the individual bears . . . can mark the soul for life."[18] To Heaney, Philoctetes stood for wounded Catholics as well as wounded Protestants who obsessively dwelled on their victim status.

Heaney's absorption in the Greek world of gifted heroes confronting illness and death influenced his second Oxford lecture, "Last Things in the Poetry of W. B. Yeats and Philip Larkin." On April 30, 1990, he told his Oxford audience that he sympathized with Larkin's view of death, but he found it difficult to accept the English poet's rejection of religion, which for Heaney was centered on gift-exchange rituals. He criticized Larkin's poem "Aubade" for being post-Christian and stated his preference for the way Yeats faced death with heroic defiance and creative energy. Yeats drew on principles espoused by classical heroes such as Philoctetes and Achilles, whereas the more modern Larkin posed as an atheist or nihilist.

Heaney's own gifts continued to be honored in 1990. On June 2, he flew in the supersonic airliner, the Concorde, from Paris to New York so he could receive an honorary doctorate and deliver a commencement address at Wesleyan University in Connecticut. That he flew in one of the world's fastest and most expensive jets (it cruised at around 1,330 miles per hour and crossed the Atlantic in three and a half hours) was partly a sign of his frenetic schedule. He had to get places fast. On June 28, traveling once again, he picked up another degree from the University of Stirling in Scotland and gave another commencement address. Immediately after that, he flew to Boston so he could receive the New England Poetry Club's Golden Rose Award at the Longfellow House. His next big trip, on July 6, was to Japan, where he was whisked from place to place to give readings and talks to ambassadors and academics.

The poem "Casting and Gathering" in *Seeing Things* reiterates his doubts about whether he deserved all this global acclaim and whether it was good for him. Why was he the chosen one? Weren't there others who were equally gifted and deserving? One persona in his fishing poem represents his inner Incertus. "You are not worth tuppence," he says. His more confident doppelgänger contradicts him. Heaney's ongoing debate between Incertus and Certus was prompted in part by his friendship with Ted Hughes. On August 12, five days before Hughes's sixtieth birthday, Heaney sent him a copy of "Casting and Gathering" to once again honor "the verifying and releasing power *Lupercal* [had for me in 1962]." Heaney intended his poem to be a birthday gift; he inscribed it, "For Ted, with love and gratitude for helping me to hear myself. Happy Birthday."[19] "Casting and Gathering" extols the give-and-take of an ongoing exchange in which gifts are given "entirely free" by both parties. A fisherman on one side of the river casts line as if giving a gift, and a fisherman on the other side pulls in line as if receiving a gift. The lines are like lines of poetry that create a lasting bond between the two men as they pass back and forth between them.

Heaney's preference for gift exchange as opposed to commercial exchange arose in part from his nostalgia for his Catholic hearth culture. "The Sharping Stone," an elegy for his father-in-law, once again reflects on the sort of agricultural work he did as a youth in terms of gift exchange. The poem opens with a description of "the sharping stone that was to be

/ Our gift" to Marie's father. Heaney finds the stone, which had once been used to sharpen farming tools, still encased in its wrapping paper, and he's ashamed he "failed to pass" it on before his father-in-law's death on September 28, 1990. To make amends, he launches the drawer with the gift on a river as if it were an Anglo-Saxon ship containing gifts for the hallowed dead. The makeshift craft drifts toward an old-fashioned farm "where scythes once hung all night in alder trees" and "mowers played dawn scherzos on the blades." The stone creates heavenly music when farmers use it to sharpen their harp-like scythes, and it becomes another emblem for the artist's gift that transports both giver and recipient to a better—in this case a more pastoral and peaceful—place.

A day after his father-in-law died, Heaney sent a thank-you note to the Lannan Foundation, which had just given him a $35,000 poetry prize. "The boost to the coffers is mighty," he said. "The confirmation to one's sense of purpose and one's trust in the meaning of the enterprise of poetry is deeply gratifying also."[20] On October 1, two days after writing his note, he wondered if *The Cure of Troy* would receive another "confirmation" when it premiered at the Guildhall in Londonderry/Derry. A reunion with Derek Walcott and his partner, Sigrid Nama, helped assuage Heaney's opening-night jitters. As he watched and listened to his lines come to life onstage, he was pleased by the audience's reactions. By the end of the play, he was convinced it was a success. Doubts about his talents as a verse-dramatist surfaced, though, when he read the reviews. As the play moved around the world (it soon appeared at Dublin's Abbey Theatre, London's Tricycle Theatre, Edinburgh's fringe theater, and other British and American venues), many reviewers complained that he'd failed to resuscitate the ancient play.

These negative reviews may have helped determine the subject matter for his Oxford lecture in late October, "Above the Brim: On Robert Frost," in which he portrayed Frost as a latter-day Philoctetes whose great gift had been maligned and misunderstood by many critics. "Among major poets of the English language in this century," Heaney told his audience, "Robert Frost is the one who takes the most punishment." Heaney identified with the "contrariness at the centre of his nature" and with the stubborn way Frost declared independence from stylistic and political trends. Heaney observed that Frost had a "Sophoclean gift for making the neuter outback of experience scrutable in a way that privileges neither the desolate unknown or the human desire to shelter from it." What especially intrigued Heaney was Frost's need for traditional order that was at variance with his enchantment with extravagance and freedom. Heaney concluded that Frost's best work was done when he let his imagination go "beyond skill and ego into a run of energy that brimmed up outside [his] . . . conscious intention and control." It was the exuberant, transcendental side of Frost that most impressed Heaney: "When Frost comes down hard upon the facts of hurt, he still manages to end up gaining poetic altitude. As his intelligence thrusts down, it creates a reactive force capable of raising and carrying the whole burden of our knowledge and experience."[21] That reactive force compelled his poetic gift to surge beyond the "brim" of his conscious mind. As Frost's "Directive" showed, that gift, like Philoctetes's gift, had the power to heal—to make whole—those suffering from various troubles.

On January 28, 1991, facing another semester at Harvard, Heaney wrote Medbh McGuckian, "More and more I hate the disruption of the travel" and "the busyness of teaching, appointments, committees, references."[22] The reviews of *The Cure at Troy* made him even more eager to follow Philoctetes's example and retreat into solitude. One article by the Belfast-born scholar Desmond Fennell, which appeared in the *Irish Times* several months after *The Cure of Troy* premiered, was especially upsetting. Fennell maintained in "The Heaney Phenomenon: 'A Disparity between the Work and the Reputation'" that Heaney's success had been engineered by Faber's public-relations machine and by powerful academic critics such as Helen Vendler. His main beef with Heaney was political: "His poetry says nothing, plainly or figuratively, about the war [in Northern Ireland], about any of the three main parties to it, or about the issues at stake." Fennell attacked Heaney on aesthetic grounds, too, arguing—despite much evidence to the contrary—that he'd failed to engage "most people who find sustenance and delight in poetry." Educated like Heaney by devout Catholics, Fennell used Simone Weil as a stick to beat Heaney. Weil had been a politically astute "mystic whose mysticism was intellectually disciplined by Christian doctrine," Fennell wrote, while

Heaney was nothing more than "a free-lance mystic."[23] While Fennell was mean-spirited and wrongheaded, he echoed others who belittled Heaney in the wake of *The Cure at Troy*.

In mid-November 1991, Heaney returned to Oxford to expound on two literary figures who'd also been subject to their fair share of negative criticism—Christopher Marlowe and Dylan Thomas. On November 19, he discussed the way some scholars had connected Marlowe's reputation as a playwright to his persona as an enfant terrible, and the way postcolonial critics tended to construe Marlowe's dramatic verse "simply and solely as a function of an oppressive discourse, or as a reprehensible masking [of British imperialism]."[24] To Heaney, the Renaissance poet, who'd died in 1593 at the age of twenty-nine after a fight over a bill at an English tavern, was a genius like Frost who had married orderly craftsmanship with disorderly extravagance. Marlowe possessed a "gift for outstripping the reader's expectation" with "an inventiveness that cannot settle for the conventional notion that enough is enough, but always wants to extend the alphabet of emotional and technical expression." His powerful gift came from a "mysterious . . . source" like the healing spring at the end of Frost's "Directive."[25] Heaney later pointed out that Dylan Thomas had tapped a similar linguistic source and had tried to shape his lyrical gift with similar craftsmanship. In the lecture "Dylan the Durable" on November 21, he saluted Thomas's "spellbinding power" to transport readers to an Eden of "prelapsarian wholeness," even though he was well aware of Thomas's peccadilloes and death at the age of thirty-nine from alcoholism.[26]

Heaney's interest in the power of poetic gifts to heal and make "whole beyond confusion" became more personal in November when he began to suffer from heart fibrillations. He wrote Ted Hughes about his health concerns, and on November 28, 1991, Hughes, who had experienced similar health problems during his tempestuous marriage to Sylvia Plath, wrote a letter full of sympathy and advice. Hughes said doctors had diagnosed his heart condition as tachycardia and prescribed tranquilizers, which were ineffective. Taking matters into his own hands, he had hypnotized himself and, like the shamans he so admired, implored his guardian spirits to guide him toward a healthier life. The spirits had warned him to avoid social situations that harmed his true self and that cut him off from his "bodily being as a mobile mother's womb substitute." Hughes prescribed a variety of cures for Heaney's fibrillations: smoking (since a cigarette is a "substitute mother's breast"); Buddhist renunciation of all "social duties & domestic obligations"; kelp tablets, since the Incas had eaten dried kelp to strengthen their hearts at high altitudes; exorcism of "the contradictory imperatives from the . . . forebrain"; and vitamin E. Hughes also passed along an Arab proverb: "Wherever you go—go with your whole heart. If you can't go with your whole heart—don't go." Hughes admitted that his advice was "freakish," but he hoped it would help his friend.[27]

### THE FIELD DAY ANTHOLOGY CONTROVERSY

Heaney had more reasons to burrow into "womb substitutes" when he read critical responses to *Seeing Things* in late 1991 and early 1992. Tom Clyde in the journal *Fortnight* rated the translations of Virgil and Dante, which framed the collection, as superior to Heaney's own poems, which he considered to be lackluster. James Wood in the *Guardian* objected to the prosaic diction in the book. Hilary Corke in a *Spectator* review, "A Slight Case of Zenophilia?," echoed Fennell's charges that Heaney had become overly academic and obscure. While the Scottish writer Lachlan MacKinnon praised *Seeing Things* in the *Times Literary Supplement* for its range of styles and subjects, he speculated that Heaney had been "lamed by the extra-poetic authority of civic and largely externally imposed responsibility."[28] Heaney's compulsion to be an ambassador of poetry, according to MacKinnon, had turned him into another "lamed" Philoctetes.

These reviews were tame compared to those that began appearing in November 1991 in response to the *Field Day Anthology of Irish Writing*, which Heaney and his editorial cohorts had assembled under the direction of Seamus Deane. To much fanfare, Heaney, Deane, Brian Friel, and former Irish president Charles Haughey launched the four-thousand-page anthology on October 31, 1991, at Dublin's elegant Newman House, part of a former university where Gerald Manley Hopkins once taught and James Joyce once studied. Haughey hailed Field Day's publication as "one of the most important events of our present era." Eight days later, during an interview with Deane on RTÉ's *Booklines,* the Irish feminist writer Nuala O'Faolain began what would become a multipronged offensive against the all-male editorial board. While seeking to make amends for the centuries-old suppression of Irish-Catholic culture by British Protestants, the editors, according to O'Faolain, had neglected to pay sufficient attention to the Catholic Church's suppression of women in both Northern Ireland and the Republic of Ireland. Without realizing it, Field Day had colluded in this disenfranchisement of women by failing to include them in the anthology. To his credit, Deane admitted his oversight: "To my astonishment and dismay, I have found that I myself have been subject to the same kind of critique to which I have subjected colonialism. . . . I find that I exemplify some of the faults and erasures which I analyze and characterize in the earlier period."[29] He promised to rectify matters by including more women in the paperback edition of the anthology.

O'Faolain and other feminists were not so easily mollified. On November 11, O'Faolain restated her objections in an *Irish Times* review, "The Voice That Field Day Didn't Record." She singled out volume 3, the one to which Heaney had contributed, as being especially egregious. "I want it revised at the earliest opportunity," she said. "As it stands . . . it is immensely wounding. And I hope that other people will protest with me, so that the next time an anthologist bends to his task, he won't be able to forget that there are watchful women out there." She supported Deane's original plan to expose "the way in which canons are established and the degree to which they operate as systems of ratification and authority," but she complained that the editors had been so busy "demolishing the patriarchy of Britain on a grand front" that they'd ignored the way Ireland's "native patriarchy" remained intact, dictatorial, damaging, and "smug as ever."[30]

Heaney reacted to these and other feminist charges in a long letter to John Wilson Foster on January 8, 1992. He first congratulated Foster on his new book, *Colonial Consequences: Essays in Irish Literature and Culture,* citing the essay "Who Are the Irish?" for particular praise. Then he mentioned "the (entirely justifiable) ire of feminist Ireland gathering round one's Field Day head, and . . . an enforced sense of one's 'old fashioned-ism' for being unable to go with the swish revisionist (entirely justifiable, or maybe *not entirely*) tide." Heaney attributed his short-sightedness as an editor to the "petrified rings" in his Irish-Catholic sensibility and hoped that Ulster Protestants such as Foster and Irish feminists such as

O'Faolain would "not feel 'erased' or excluded" or "unfairly assailed" by his work in the future.[31]

Despite the editors' apologies, feminists attacked the *Field Day Anthology* for the next decade. The controversy grew so heated that on February 21, 1992, the Irish Writers' Union convened a public debate in the Dublin Writers' Museum to try to resolve matters. Eavan Boland, who'd been included in the anthology, was among those who decried the editors' exclusions. At a Trinity College conference later in 1992, Boland stated that the ratio of thirty-four male poets to three women poets in the contemporary Irish section, as well as the "other absences," were "ethically indefensible." Even when Deane in August 1992 commissioned a new volume that would include more women, the criticism didn't subside. Edna Longley at the Yeats Summer School in August complained that Deane's "damage-limitation exercise" was too little, too late.[32] Not until September 23, 2002, when former president Mary Robinson launched the 3,100-page *Field Day Anthology of Irish Writing, Volumes IV–V,* did the furor die down.

One of the projects Heaney was proud to finish during the Field Day imbroglio was an introduction to Robert Fitzgerald's translation of the *Odyssey.* As if to appease his feminist critics, he made sure to emphasize the importance of women in the *Odyssey.* He even went so far as to suggest that the author had been a woman, or at least a woman in the form of a muse who had given the author multiple gifts. One of these was "her gift" for knowing "the good of life"; another was her narrative "gift for collapsing the distance" between readers in different places and different times.[33] Heaney had celebrated this sort of transformative feminine vision in *Seeing Things,* and especially in "Field of Vision," where his muse takes the form of a down-to-earth woman in a wheelchair (probably his Aunt Mary) staring out a window at ordinary things—sycamores, hawthorns, calves, a mountain—and observing how the world "grew more distinctly strange."

Fitzgerald's *Odyssey* appealed to Heaney partly because it was a deft translation of a timeless war story that dramatized the pros and cons of gift exchanges. As the classicist Moses Finley wrote in *The World of Odysseus,* "There were times and conditions when even the fiercest of the heroes preferred peace. An exchange mechanism was then the only alternative, and the basic one was gift-exchange." As in other ancient cultures (the *Odyssey* is set in the Bronze Age around the eleventh and twelfth centuries BC), the ethical obligation to give and receive gifts was paramount. The Greeks had a special word for friendships based on gift exchanges: *xenia*. In their culture, a host was expected to provide gifts to a guest, and a guest was expected to reciprocate. The failure to abide by the ideal of *xenia* could have dire consequences, while successful gift-giving could help pacify even the most die-hard foes. Agamemnon, for example, offers Achilles an abundance of gifts—horses, money, women, cities—in an attempt to resolve their feud, which had started when Achilles was forced to give a gift he'd received after the battle at Lyrnessus—the woman Briseis—to Agamemnon. According to Finley: "No single detail in the life of the heroes receives so much attention in the *Iliad* and the *Odyssey* as gift-giving. . . . There was scarcely a limit to the situations in which gift-giving was operative. More precisely, the word 'gift' was a cover-all for a great variety of actions and transactions which later became differentiated and acquired their own appellations. There were payments for services rendered, desired, or anticipated; what we would call fees, rewards, prizes, and sometimes bribes. . . . The whole of what we call foreign relations and diplomacy, in their peaceful manifestations, was conducted by gift-exchange."[34] Heaney also thought of the word "gift" as a term with many referents.

During the 1990s, Heaney practiced his own kind of *xenia* by giving gifts to organizations that were trying to resolve conflicts in Ulster and other countries around the world. He became a patron of Initiative '92, which established a commission in Ulster to reconcile sectarian groups. He made donations to Arts Care, which organized artistic performances and workshops for patients in Ulster's health-care system. He contributed to the Youth Campaign Against Racism, Xenophobia, Anti-Semitism, and Intolerance; the National Library for the Blind; the Russian Poets Fund; and the Action Group for Irish Youth. He wrote letters on behalf of prisoners he believed were wrongly accused, such as George Long, a mentally ill man serving a life sentence at a maximum-security prison in Worcestershire, England. (Heaney and others persuaded solicitors to reexamine the case, which led to Long's acquittal on July 13, 1995, and his release after sixteen years behind bars.) Heaney sent financial gifts to Peter Fallon's Gallery Press; the Monastery of St. Catherine of Siena in Drogheda,

Ireland; the Irish Peatland Conservation Council; and the Grolier Poetry Book Shop in Cambridge, Massachusetts.

Heaney's charitable impulse made it almost impossible for him to alter the pace of his life. By July 1992, he was so exhausted by all his "community service" activities that he worried his Oxford lectures in the fall would further damage his heart. He wrote Desmond O'Grady, "My mistake—at least one of them obvious to me—was to let myself in for the Oxford job. It will be over in two years, but the clamp tightens over the breast just when the breathing should be getting easy."[35] Sometimes he had to cancel readings and lectures when he'd promised to be in two places at once. On September 11, 1992, the editor of Berkeley's *Threepenny Review*, to which he'd contributed funds, wrote a letter that quoted Thom Gunn on Heaney's largesse: "He's a very generous person and he obviously just says yes to too many things, to be nice, and then finds himself occasionally in this sort of bind."[36] Heaney had promised to give a reading at Berkeley and somewhere else, too, and in the end he had to cancel his trip to Berkeley.

Heaney repeatedly made halfhearted attempts to sever the bonds that got him into "binds." At the end of 1992, he considered cutting ties with the Field Day company. One of the directors, the novelist and playwright Thomas Kilroy, had recently resigned from the board because he felt the other directors didn't support his political agenda. On September 22, Heaney wrote Tom Paulin: "The Field Day is shaken and sorry. The acknowledgement at meeting level of the theatrical 'split' and the wobbly nature of our approach . . . to volume A [of the *Field Day Anthology*]; not to mention Seamus [Deane]'s fall-back in the face of the hostile reception—it has all been dispiriting."[37] Two years later, Heaney was still bemoaning the fate of the anthology: "The odd thing is that the anthology was very much a postcolonial reading of the Irish situation and therefore should have been sensitive to the silencings that women and women's writing had undergone, but I think that for everybody involved the pressure at the horizon was from Northern Ireland politics rather than gender politics." Despite its faults, the *Field Day Anthology* remained for Heaney "a monument to the genius of Seamus Deane."[38]

Two days after writing Paulin, Heaney sent Ted Hughes a more candid assessment of the Field Day controversy. Referring to Hughes's demands that feminist critics respect the privacy of his marriage to Sylvia Plath, Heaney wrote, "It's shocking that you had to be as explicit as that about the rules of the game; obtuseness and hostility and galvanized vindictiveness combined helplessly at first and then proceeded willfully against you. I had a faint taste of it this year myself through association with the *Field Day Anthology*." He acknowledged the editors' mistakes but deplored "the immense rage which man-speak, or even men speaking, now produces." He told Hughes, "The historical tide is running against almost every anchor I can throw towards what I took to be the holding places."[39]

On September 29, 1992, after an evening of wine and singing at his Dublin house with his Japanese friend Kazuo Kawamura, Heaney got entangled in another controversy. This one began when the Irish journalist Michael O'Toole in Dublin's *Evening Press* accused him of demeaning Larkin in "The Journey Back," a poem in *Seeing Things*. Angered by O'Toole's obtuseness, Heaney wrote a rebuttal that attempted to clarify his opinion of Larkin, which had always been respectful, even though Larkin's letters, which Faber had published on January 1, 1992, contained insulting remarks about him. Heaney's Oxford lecture "Joy or Night" had lamented Larkin's post-Christian attitudes, but "The Journey Back" had compared him to one of the Magi: "a wise king setting out" with his poetic gifts "under the Christmas lights." On another occasion, Heaney observed that one of Larkin's great "gifts was the ability to win the respect of two kinds of reader: the non-specialist . . . [and] the scrupulous literary invigilator."[40] His avowals of atheism notwithstanding, Larkin's gift—at least in Heaney's view—was Magi-like or Christ-like in the way it unified worldly and otherworldly perspectives.

On October 20, Heaney reflected on another gifted but irascible poet in his Oxford lecture "John Clare's Prog." Rather than dwell on Clare's troubled and troubling life, however, he again drew attention to the poet's gifts. Clare's "persistent theme," Heaney declared, was "the gift for keeping going and the lovely wonder that it can be maintained—the gift which is tutored by the instinctive cheer and courage of living creatures, and heartened by every fresh turn and return of things in the natural world." In early November, he brought up this animal-like "gift" again in his Oxford lecture on Elizabeth Bishop. Bishop was well-known for her poems about animals and what Heaney called her joy in the "mysterious otherness of the [natural] world."[41] She possessed a "famous gift for observation," he said, but her "supreme gift" was her ability "to ingest loss and to transmute it" into well-crafted, consolatory verse.[42] She had a "gift for raising the actual to a new linguistic power" so readers could "enjoy life" and "endure it."[43] Like Clare, she redeemed the "givens of experience," which she cherished and inevitably lost, and turned her losses into gains. (One definition of "prog" is "gain.")

Despite a persistent concern for his ailing heart, Heaney tried to channel Clare's "gift for keeping going." He installed a fax machine in his house to make it easier to communicate with his innumerable correspondents, and he did his best to fulfill his obligations around the world. He helped open the Ireland House for Irish Studies at New York University in early May 1993 and accepted a Presidential Medal there. He traveled to Dickinson College in Pennsylvania on May 23 and Dartmouth College on June 13 to receive two more honorary degrees. He met friends at the Poetry International Rotterdam Festival in Holland and gave the Creweian Oration in Oxford. The stress of constantly being in the limelight took its toll. Upon returning to Dublin, he complained of a pinched nerve in his shoulder, a rheumatic back, and extreme fatigue. Friends such as Medbh McGuckian begged him to slow down. Having recently lost her father, she was afraid she might now lose Heaney. In his response to her on July 30, 1993, he said he hoped the "whole dread and cruelty of the politico-military thing" in Belfast, where she lived, was "not too intolerable," and he admitted that he felt "the wound of the news items far more in the last year or so than ever before."[44] As usual, he showed more solicitude for a friend's and a community's hardships than for his own.

# 13

# The Bounty
# of Sweden

## ORPHIC GIFTS

The feminist response to the *Field Day Anthology* may have been one reason Heaney translated Brian Merriman's eighteenth-century Gaelic poem "Cúirt An Mheán Oíche" and published his version as *The Midnight Verdict* in 1993. Merriman had constructed his story of women punishing men as a dream-vision that parodies the traditional Irish genre of *aisling*. In his nightmarish fantasy, a "dangerwoman" summons a man to a court presided over by a female judge who, Heaney writes, is "full of fight, with a glinting eye, / Hot on the boil, ill-set and angry." Women in this court question Irish men about their failures to respect, love, marry, and impregnate Irish women. In the case Merriman dramatizes, the judge concludes that young Irish women "deserve redress," and she approves of them hunting down young bachelors, stripping off their clothes, and whipping them until "their backs and asses [are] scourged."[1]

Heaney contextualizes this sadistic tale by interspersing it with accounts of Orpheus's punishment at the hands of the fanatical women known in Greek myth as the Maenads or Bacchantes. Heaney's translations from Ovid's *Metamorphoses* tell how the Greek women "commit atrocities against [the] . . . sacred poet," tearing his body apart with their "blood-filled nails" and scattering his "mangled flesh and bones" over the earth.[2] This gruesome "redress" is the consequence of another masculine failure to give gifts at a crucial time. Orpheus fails to deliver the gift of new life to his wife, Eurydice, which was promised to her by the gods after she died. "There was one term set: / Until he left Avernus, he was not / To look back, or the gift would be in vain," Heaney writes. When Orpheus ignores the divine decree and looks back, the gods renege on their promise. Instead of being given a second life, Eurydice is forced to return to the underworld. Orpheus, on the other hand, returns to the world with his lyrical gifts intact until the Maenads accuse him of being a "misogynist" and "his magic note / that should have stalled their weapons was drowned out / By blaring horns and drums, beatings and yells."[3] The frenzied women dismember him, but his musical gift lives on, and his soul descends to the underworld to join his beloved wife. He gets another kind of "redress," too, when Bacchus punishes his assailants by turning them into trees.

If Heaney intended *The Midnight Verdict* to be a parable of the rough justice meted out to him and his Field Day colleagues by feminists, he also intended it to reflect similar attacks against his Orphic friend Ted Hughes. In his Oxford lecture delivered on October 21, 1993, "Orpheus in Ireland," he was undoubtedly thinking of Hughes when he argued that poets who had "Merriman's vital gift for 'the stylistic arrangements of experience' . . . should be immune to the common feminist castigation."[4] As soon as the Gallery Press published *The Midnight Verdict* in December 1993, Heaney mailed a copy to Hughes, and his friend sent an enthusiastic reply that recalled how Merriman's poem had been "a cult object" for him and his undergraduate friends at Cambridge University in the 1950s. He complimented Heaney for bringing the poem "alive into the present," predicted the "lovely little book" would attract lots of readers, and welcomed Heaney as a fellow antifeminist insurgent who had "smashed through the perimeter [of] electrified barbed wire and scampered clear of the Academy tower machine-gunners."[5]

In his letters to the overwrought Hughes, Heaney invariably played the role of loyal ally. On March 25, 1994, while in Missoula, Montana, he wrote a letter lavishing praise on Hughes's recently published collection of prose, *Winter Pollen*. He especially liked the chapter on Sylvia Plath. Hughes had written that "her poetic gift" was the "most intriguing mystery" and added, "Few poets have disclosed in any way the birth circumstances of their poetic gift, or the necessary purpose these serve in their psychic economy."[6] Invoking Jungian psychoanalysis, the Ouija board, and mystical theology, Hughes proposed that Plath had used "the extreme peculiarity" of her gift to redress the traumatic wound caused by her father's death. Heaney must have known that many scholars had made similar observations about the painful loss of her father when she was a child and the therapeutic way her poetry tried to redress that loss. Nevertheless, he said he was "in awe" of "the intentness and focus and big strength" displayed in "Sylvia Plath and Her Journals" and Hughes's other essays in *Winter Pollen.*[7]

Ever the diplomat, Heaney hardly touched on Hughes's role in Plath's death. Instead, he complimented his friend's stoical perseverance in the aftermath of her death when he was pilloried by Plath's advocates. Heaney apologized for being "inadequate to the job of saying anything commensurate with your own great 'durance,' as GMH [Gerard Manley Hopkins] might call it." Fearing that the recent death of Plath's mother might trigger painful memories of Hughes's marriage, Heaney said, "I wish I could have absorbed some of the shock that you are applying to yourself a bit better. And I hope your self-flagellation has eased. . . . More and more when I think of you, I think of the immense complexity of your sorrows and constraints, of the stove-hot labyrinth you've been caught in, what one took for granted—the abundance and ecology of your whole work."[8] For the empathetic Heaney, Hughes was another Daedalus trapped in a labyrinth or another Orpheus assailed by irate women.

When Hughes's poems about his marriage to Plath began to appear in print (they would be collected in *Birthday Letters* in 1998), Heaney's defense of Hughes remained steadfast. On March 14, 1995, he wrote Hughes, "When I saw 'Chaucer' in the New Yorker a few weeks ago [on January 16] I reeled for joy." He summed up his reactions to the elegiac "letters" by saying, "The total engagement of those poems is exhausting and beautiful because of the total candour and the unleashed, justified anger." Heaney's claim that his friend's new poems were "as lightning packed" as his "early poems in the 1960s" was a fulsome exaggeration. And so was Heaney's claim that *Birthday Letters* provided more evidence that Hughes was an "example of good behavior."[9] The verse "letters," as many readers and critics have pointed out, were often prosaic and self-serving. Few were as well-crafted and engaging as his early poems.

Heaney's determination to cheer up the embattled Hughes may have had something to do with *The School Bag* anthology, which the two men were editing. The manuscript was due by November 1, 1995, and, like the original *Field Day* anthology, it contained a preponderance of male poets. Would *The School Bag* elicit the same sort of feminist backlash as the *Field Day* anthology? Heaney's jitters intensified in March 1994 when Matthew Evans at Faber said he hoped the new anthology would outdo the success of *The Rattle Bag*, which had sold 160,000 paperback copies and 5,000 hardback copies. Faber was concerned about making a profit on *The School Bag* after paying the editors a substantial advance of £35,000, worth about $95,000 today. When the anthology finally appeared in 1997, Heaney told Joanna Mackle at Faber that she should be careful about promoting it as a schoolbook since he and Hughes had paid little attention to the socio-political ramifications of the poems and had included no footnotes or headnotes. He predicted reviewers would wonder "why . . . 'silenced' or 'marginalized' groups are not being given special emphasis."[10] He also asked Mackle not to line up any interviews with journalists who might be unsympathetic to the editors' choices.

During the 1990s, as Heaney wrote poems for *The Spirit Level* (1996), he kept striving for levelheadedness—as the book title implies—in the aesthetic and ideological controversies erupting around him. The poem that opens his new book extols a specific Orphic gift that continues to flourish despite the forces arrayed against it. The gift, in this case, is a rain stick that Heaney's friends Rand and Beth Brandes gave him during a get-together in North Carolina. The instrument, made from a dried-out saguaro cactus stalk, possessed the same magical power over nature as Orpheus's lyre and voice. At least it was believed to have that sort of power by Native Americans, who used such sticks in ceremonies to bring rain to the desert. For Heaney, the rain stick is another material symbol of the poet's "undiminished" gift for writing. He adapts the biblical parable of the rich man's difficulty entering heaven to illustrate his conviction that such gifts are more valuable to him than monetary gifts. Drawing on Jesus's parable, which states "it is easier for a camel to go through the eye of a needle, than for a rich man to enter into the kingdom of God" (Matthew 20:24), Heaney proposes that a literary gift can transport anyone to a heavenly place for free.

Like his other books, *The Spirit Level* emphasizes the spiritual as opposed to the financial benefits of the poet's gift. "A Brigid's Girdle" compares the poem that Heaney wrote as a gift for a friend, Adele Dalsimer, to the sort of healing gifts the Irish make from straw on St. Brigid's Day. According to Heaney, Dalsimer "had a gift for lifting spirits into vision and cooperation" when she worked in the Irish Studies program at Boston College.[11] Because she'd invited Heaney to read there, helped establish a Heaney archive, and endorsed the plan to give Heaney an honorary degree in 1991, he reciprocated with his poem. Heaney hoped his "Brigid's Girdle," woven from "straw that's lifted in a circle / To handsel and to heal," would help his friend. Dalsimer, sadly, died in 2000 at the age of sixty.

For Heaney, even something as mundane as a cheap piece of farmhouse furniture could have the liberating power of a gift. "A Sofa in the Forties" takes another look at a site of transformative gift-giving in Heaney's first home, where "insufficient toys appeared . . . // On Christmas mornings." The Heaney children would make up for the lack of material gifts by turning the family sofa into a fantasy train that transported them into a heaven of spiritual gifts. "St Kevin and the Blackbird" is another poem that dramatizes the compensatory power of the imagination. According to the legend that Heaney retells, St. Kevin, while living in a hermitage close to Glanmore Cottage, prayed for so long with his arms stuck outside a window that a mother blackbird built a nest in his hands and laid eggs. The good saint felt obligated to wait until the nestlings had hatched and flown before he withdrew his hands. Heaney uses St. Kevin's story to reflect on the pros and cons of gift exchange. He wonders if St. Kevin's sacrifice on behalf of the birds has "linked [him] / Into the network of eternal life," or just exhausted him. Has the pain of holding up the birds made it impossible for him to enjoy the fruits of his labor? Is it possible to "labour and not . . . seek reward"? Should he expect a return gift to compensate for his arduous gift-giving? Heaney doesn't answer these questions in a straightforward way, although he implies that it's hard to appreciate the gifts of life when the work that has gone into making them possible is so excruciating. In the end, St. Kevin seems to have "forgotten self, forgotten bird," and forgotten the reasons for enabling the mother bird to produce her gifts.

As Heaney got older, his saintly personae examine gift-giving with minds tempered by experience. Caedmon in "Whitby-Sur-Moyola" is one such saintly person who is aware of both the joy of discovering a gift and the hard labor required to turn it into exemplary art. Heaney identifies with the Anglo-Saxon poet who herded cows and attended church before becoming a lay brother at Whitby Abbey on the north Yorkshire coast. Like Heaney, Caedmon went through an Incertus phase as a young man; he'd doubted his vocal talents and refrained from singing hymns with the other monks until one night he dreamed of a divine voice commanding him to sing about the Creator and His Creation. Heaney called this dream "a free gift from God" in his "Room to Rhyme" lecture at the University of Dundee in 2003 and suggested that he'd received a similar command as an undergraduate: "I heard the equivalent of the voice telling me to make room to rhyme and to sing." At this time, he also realized "that poetry was a vocation" (a *vocatio* or "spiritual calling") and that he had a gift as well as an obligation to realize that gift, which he considered to be his "truest self."[12] Caedmon's famous thanksgiving "Hymn" about "the Creator's might and His mind-plans, / the work of the Glory-Father," reminds Heaney of the work of numerous creators, both divine and human. The "Hymn" also reminds him of his cattle-raising father and Scullion relatives. When Heaney says Caedmon's "real gift was the big ignorant roar / He could still let out of him, just bogging in / As if the sacred subjects were a herd / That had broken out and needed rounding up," he's equating Caedmon's vocal gift with the rough speech of the "big-voiced Scullions."[13] Heaney's point, though, is similar to the point he made in "St Kevin and the Blackbird" and other poems in *Spirit Level*: fulfilling one's gift is hard but necessary work.

### BEOWULF AND GIFT EXCHANGE

To Anglo-Saxon monks like Caedmon or Anglo-Saxon warriors like Beowulf, the world appeared to be divided between walled-in communities made stable by gift exchanges and regions beyond the walls where violent conflicts took place. This binary worldview was one aspect of *Beowulf* that appealed to Heaney and that made the poem relevant to divisions in his native country. As early as March 17, 1984, Norton editor John Benedict had asked him for translated sections of the poem. On April 30, referring to Heaney's earlier communications with M. H. Abrams, Benedict quipped, "As Mike [Abrams] mentioned to you, it'd be marvelous to have Heaney both at the beginning of Volume 1 and, as he already is, at the end of Volume 2 [of the *Norton Anthology of English Literature*]."[14] For many years, Heaney had made little progress with the translation. On August 3, 1992, another Norton editor, Mary Cunnane, offered him an advance of twenty-five thousand dollars to entice him back to the translation work. Still, he procrastinated. She sent him a follow-up letter on May 11, 1993: "At the risk of doing my best imitation of editor as Chinese water tor-turer (the drip-drip-drip of inquiries), can I ask whether you've thought about our BEOWULF proposition?" The drip-drip-drip of inquiries per-sisted, as did Heaney's apologies for stalling. Cunnane reminded Heaney on January 10, 1994: "An editorial candle still burns in the window here for BEOWULF if you ever change your mind."[15]

Heaney formulated a concrete plan for translating *Beowulf* during the summer of 1995. He asked the American scholar Marijane Osborn, who had published a translation of *Beowulf* in 1983 and a study guide in 1986, to assist him. Osborn was eager to collaborate. Heaney also sought scholarly advice from Professor Alfred David, a medievalist at Indiana University. In 1997, the New Historicist and Renaissance scholar Stephen Greenblatt, who had taken a job at Norton, urged Heaney to submit something by Feb-ruary 1998. Heaney, though, still found it difficult to apply himself to the task. On December 1, 1997, he sent Greenblatt his work-in-progress and apologized for his meager output. Over the next couple of years, he worked on *Beowulf* in five-day or ten-day bursts, usually composing about twenty lines per day. (He compared his translating efforts to breaking rocks with a sledgehammer.) By the end of the millennium, he'd nearly finished.

Heaney had always relished the sonic and imagistic qualities of *Beo-wulf*. He also felt a sense of kinship with the fortified halls in *Beowulf*, which reminded him of Mossbawn. His introduction reveals that he'd sometimes use "the word 'bawn' to refer to Hrothgar's hall" since in "Elizabethan English, bawn . . . referred specifically to the fortified dwell-ings which the English planters built in Ireland." The halls in *Beowulf* are places of "actual and a symbolic refuge," he says, where leaders give gifts in accordance with the "value system upon which the poem's action turns."[16] Gift exchange is at the center of this "value system." The poem lavishes attention on gifts of neck rings, arm rings, helmets, swords, goblets, and even women, and pays little attention to commercial exchanges of money and commodities. According to the scholar Roy Naismith, the Anglo-Saxon bard who committed the poem to paper near the end of the first millennium, "invested [gifts] with a value that runs deeper than their considerable material worth. In themselves, they are frequently tools of war and feasting—central activities of elite life, at least as portrayed in the poem—but also serve as physical embodiments of memory and honour. . . . Making a gift of treasure was more than simply a reward for good service; it built personal bonds and shared memories which were supposed to hold society together." The refusal by a king, lord, or dragon to abide by the ethics of gift exchange, Naismith avers, "could bring disorder and violence."[17] Hoarding gifts in treasure troves is a sign of evil; it is what dragons do. Heroes like Beowulf, by contrast, dispense gifts to preserve the all-important "comitatus" bond between leader and warriors.

Beowulf dutifully gives gifts, but he is also the recipient of gifts. According to the Christian scribe who wrote down the oral poem, it is the "wondrous gifts God had showered on [Beowulf]" that enables his heroic deeds.[18] When he dies, his followers treat his body as a divine gift and offer it, along with valuable possessions—helmets, shields—as a return gift to God. They pray that the "Lord of All" will accept it on a burning pyre and reciprocate with gifts of grace and peace. The poem concludes, however, with ominous signs that the community's sacrificial gifts might not prevent future conflicts.

Norton had commissioned Heaney's translation, but Faber and Farrar, Straus and Giroux published it first in 1999. To the amazement of many, including Heaney, the text often considered to be the bane of high school and college students climbed the bestseller lists in both Britain and the United States. By the end of April 2000, Farrar, Straus and Giroux had sold close to 120,000 copies. Faber's sales figures in England were similar and soared to new heights after the book won the prestigious Whitbread Book of the Year Award, somehow beating out *Harry Potter and the Prisoner of Azkaban*. "Marie thought I was going to faint, I got so white," Heaney said after hearing the news of the Whitbread Award. He gratefully accepted his £22,000 check (worth about $55,000 today) and tried to ignore all the hoopla in the press. "Maybe it can be survived, but I'm not sure," he told Dennis O'Driscoll in a letter. "The lookalike who goes to the platform and the camera-calls has been robbed of much of himself these past few weeks, and I just hope the scullion/scullery man can nurse himself to secret strength again."[19] Once again, he wanted to retreat to one of his "secret nests" and reconnect with the source of his gifts in Mossbawn-like solitude and silence.

The controversy around the award was especially galling. Rumors circulated that one of the Whitbread judges, Mick Jagger's former wife Jerry Hall, had argued that Heaney's book didn't deserve the award. Many thought that Hall, an avid Harry Potter fan, would prevail during discussions on the awards committee, and J. K. Rowling would be the winner. To quiet these rumors, the chairman of the Whitbread committee issued a public statement in January 2000: "Beowulf was the clear winner. There was no real disagreement. This was a master poet breathing life into a great work of art which has only been known to a small number of academics."[20] At the Whitbread ceremony in January 2000, Heaney deflected attention from the controversy by saying he would receive the award "on behalf of the anonymous master who conceived the Beowulf 1,000 years ago." With a shrug of his shoulders, he added, "Fate goes ever as fate must."[21] He also told Alfred Hickling, a reporter for the Yorkshire Post, "No writer can measure themselves in terms of awards. . . . Being ignored is a test. Being somewhat over-attended to is a different kind of test. . . . I simply hope I pass."[22] As usual, Heaney tried to downplay the significance of a monetary award.

Heaney had intended his translation of Beowulf to show how gift-giving in a war-torn culture, whether in ancient Scandinavia or modern Ulster, could achieve the sort of peace he'd known as a boy at Mossbawn. In 1994, shortly before taking up his translation again, he wrote several poems that expressed optimism about a resolution of the Troubles. One of these, "Tollund," was inspired by a trip he took in September to the Jutland peat bogs where turf-cutters had unearthed the Tollund Man. Could some contemporary, gift-giving Beowulf or Tollund Man reestablish peace and prosperity in Ulster? A few days before Heaney composed "Tollund," the Provisional IRA had announced a suspension of its military operations. On September 4, Ireland's Sunday Tribune printed Heaney's editorial "Light Finally Enters the Black Hole" (retitled "Cessation" in Finders Keepers) about the possibility of peace. He compared his hope for change to what he'd felt during the political protests in the late 1960s: "There was now an opportunity for everybody to get involved again. The excitement being expressed about the new developments was more than hype."[23] As Heaney knew, there were still plenty of obstacles to overcome. As it turned out, it would take the rest of the decade to work out a viable truce, even though the Combined Loyalist Military Command called for a cease-fire on October 13, 1994.

Another poem Heaney wrote near the end of 1994 that dealt with the role of gift exchange in peace-building was "Mycenae Lookout." This poem examines current events through the lens of Aeschylus's tragic play *Agamemnon* in the *Oresteian Trilogy*. Heaney identifies most closely with Aeschylus's watchman, who spends years patiently looking for a "victory beacon" to signal the end of the Trojan War, but Heaney also identifies with Cassandra, whose gift of prophecy allows her to predict that the war will last a long time. "Mycenae Lookout" supports Cassandra's realistic vision of gifts resolving historical conflicts, and it supports her recognition of the abuses of gift exchange by those in power. In the *Oresteia,* the Greek army denigrates Cassandra's gift of prophecy, which she receives from Apollo, by forcing her to be a sex slave. Agamemnon brags, "she / Came to me by the army's gift, of all Troy's wealth / The chosen jewel."[24] To the ancient warrior-king of Mycenae, the prophetic woman is primarily an erotic commodity—a "jewel" to decorate his ego and satisfy his lust.

Aeschylus obsessively recounts the effects of perverse acts of gift-giving. To his pessimistic point of view, gifts often disable or simply fail to enable productive bonds between donors and recipients. The Trojans offer sacrificial gifts to the gods to win victory, but "No gift, no sacrificial flame / Can soothe or turn / The wrath of Heaven from its relentless aim." The gods punish the Trojans for Paris's abduction of King Menelaus's wife, Helen, which was set in motion by a series of bungled gift exchanges involving the golden apples of the Hesperides. Perhaps the most barbaric act of gift-giving is when Atreus, Agamemnon's father, gives parts of a nephew's cooked body to Thyestes, Atreus's brother, as a "host's gift" at a dinner.[25] Thyestes's act of cannibalism as well as other crimes lead to the murders of Agamemnon, his ex-wife Clytemnestra, and her lover Aegisthus. In multiple ways, *Agamemnon* is a cautionary tale about the way a society's appetite for "feud and vengeance" can undermine the salutary effects of *xenia,* the Greek tradition of gift-giving. For Heaney, that appetite was as powerful in ancient Greece as it was in modern Ulster.

In between finishing *The Spirit Level* and correcting proofs for *The Redress of Poetry* during the summer of 1995, Heaney gave a keynote address, "Further Language," on June 26 at a Queen's University Irish Studies conference and used the occasion to tell his audience that making peace in Northern Ireland was like making a difficult poem. "Just as the work of poetry depends for successful completion upon turning that original excitement into a process of sustained and resourceful composition," he said, "so in the work of peacebuilding, the outcome will depend upon the ongoing alertness and thoroughgoing technique of the workers at every stage of the process."[26] During the 1990s, Heaney promoted "the work of peacebuilding" in poems and in editorials he sent to the Irish and British press. Under no illusions about his power to effect change, he nevertheless hoped that a new spirit of goodwill would prevail. On August 30, 1995, he sent a fax about peace negotiations to London's *Independent* newspaper: "The [IRA's] ceasefire created new conditions. There was the sheer surprise that people experienced when they allowed themselves to believe that change for the better was possible; this minimal hope represented an immense psychic (if not political) shift and put new spirit into all that happened since. It is to be hoped that the British government, in spite of its perilous sluggishness, can still find ways to match these expectations."[27] There was still a chance, he believed, that hope and history could rhyme in Northern Ireland.

### THE GIFT FROM STOCKHOLM

As a political solution to the Troubles looked more promising, Heaney at times despaired that he hadn't done enough to promote it. He even wondered if his poetry had done any good at all. In a mood of self-incrimination, he told Peter Fallon, "[I have an] increasingly infirm sense of what [my writing] . . . (or I) add up to." He wished he had "more certitude" about his "ongoing vitality" as a poet and citizen.[28] To revitalize himself, he proposed going to Greece with his wife and their two friends Cynthia and Dimitri Hadzi. The Hadzis, who spoke Greek and worked at Harvard's Carpenter Center for the Arts, promised to give the Heaneys a tour of Corinth, Mycenae, Epidauros, Arcadia, Delphi, Sparta, and other well-known historical sites. The two couples took off for Greece near the beginning of the fall in 1995.

After the sightseers reached Pylos, a small coastal town in southwestern Greece, Heaney spent a morning on his hotel balcony catching up on correspondence. He posted a thank-you letter to a former student who had dedicated a book to him, then ate lunch at a restaurant by the harbor. Back in his hotel room, he called his son Christopher, who was teaching in Dublin. "Dad," his son said excitedly, "have you heard the news? You've won the Nobel Prize!"[29] Caught off guard, Heaney replied that his son had better speak to his mother. Once he'd regained his composure, he called his siblings and friends in Northern Ireland. To celebrate his latest triumph, according to the final poem in *Electric Light*'s "Sonnets from Hellas," he got "boozed, borean / . . . and manic" at a dinner with Marie and the Hadzis in Pylos that night.

Heaney later said about this momentous day—October 6, 1995—that he felt like Odysseus's son Telemachus, who'd once visited Pylos in an attempt to find out his father's fate during and after the Trojan War. There was a difference, though: "Telemachus was about to get some guidance from wise old Nestor whereas there's no instructor to tell you how to handle the bounty of Sweden."[30] What's surprising about Heaney's reference to the *Odyssey* is that he feels akin to a bereft and bewildered son rather than a crafty, victorious father. Clues for why Heaney identifies with Telemachus can be found in his "Sonnets from Hellas," which repeatedly describe scenes in which Heaney acts like a restless, confused, intemperate, boyish Incertus. On his tour of cultural landmarks with the Hadzis, he plays the role of a "borean" alien from the north who disregards local laws and customs. During one of his fits of pique, he ignores "keep out" signs at the Castalian spring, thinks "to hell with all who'd stop me," and trespasses to get a drink. At other places, he seems determined to affirm his humble origins and the sort of declarations of independence he made as a son against the expectations of his father.

Did Heaney feel guilty about receiving "the bounty of Sweden"? Was he acting in a boorish or "borean" way to show others he didn't deserve the prize? "Consider . . . all the writers who did not get the Nobel Prize," he said in *Stepping Stones*. "You would have to be pretty self-satisfied to list yourself in that company, never mind the company of ones who *did* get it."[31] He informed his family he didn't want them to make a big deal of the prize. Pretty soon they jokingly referred to the Nobel as the "N-word" that they weren't supposed to say at home. Out of humility and consternation about his big award, he insisted on acting the role of the befuddled Telemachus rather than the self-confident Odysseus.

Heaney acted more appropriately when he viewed a votive relief of Orpheus and icons devoted to Artemis at a museum in Sparta. He made a sketch of Orpheus and later mentioned the museum artifacts in his Nobel Prize lecture. He was especially entranced by the iconic gifts offered to Artemis. One of his most cherished memories of the Greek trip, he said in an article about Dimitri Hadzi, was the "cache of votive items that had been retrieved over the years from the nearby sanctuary of Artemis, especially the many sickle-shapes, some in metal, some in terra cotta, some large, some small, which had been dedicated once upon a time by the victors at the festival of Artemis Orthia. I felt completely at home because, among other things, the sickle-blade in its ancient Spartan shape was something which I myself had plied when facing hedges at home on our farm."[32] In ancient Greece, the festival for Artemis honored the fertility goddess of the moon and hunt with a variety of gifts.

Heaney tried to cope with the media frenzy that resulted from the Nobel Prize announcement by refusing to grant interviews with any reporters other than those from Ireland's RTÉ. Nevertheless, Greek reporters descended on Pylos, and journalists from around the world kept phoning Heaney at his hotel. RTÉ's Tommy Gorman eventually arrived in a helicopter for an interview. During their conversation, he asked Heaney if winning the Nobel Prize had made him think of a particular poem. Heaney answered by reciting his sonnet in "Clearances" about peeling potatoes with his mother. He was following his advice in "A Drink of Water"—"*Remember the Giver.*" After his meeting with Gorman, Heaney took off with Marie in the reporter's helicopter. They circled the theater at Epidauros where ancient pilgrims had exchanged gifts with the god of medicine, Asclepius, eventually landed at the Athens airport, and boarded a plane for Ireland.

Heaney got a hero's welcome when his Olympic Airlines plane landed at the Dublin airport. Ireland's President Robinson arranged for a limousine to whisk the Heaneys away from the crowds of well-wishers to a reception in her posh residence in Phoenix Park. Soon, congratulations poured in from around the world. The distinguished American poet Anthony Hecht wrote on the day Heaney won the Nobel Prize, "How splendid! How just! How absolutely right. Things have gone as they ought, for once. Jubilant congratulations."[33] Darcy O'Brien quipped, "You ennoble the Nobel."[34] The southern poet Dave Smith chimed in, "There is proper justice in the world! . . . You must be cheered, too, by how happy this makes everyone of us who are your partisans."[35] Derek Walcott, Michael Longley, Paul Muldoon, Donald Hall, and many other poets joined the chorus. Heaney's loyal opposition spoke up, too. On October 8, 1995, the Irish journalist Eaman Dunphy declared in Dublin's popular *Sunday Independent* newspaper that Heaney was a "sham national poet."[36] Others agreed. As usual, Heaney took the negative comments in stride. In "the land of taunt and banter," he observed, "the beginning of praise is the beginning of execration."[37] Never a fan of excessive publicity, he decided it was time once again to return to his "attic life of stillness and concentrated solitude" so he could write.[38]

Heaney tended to think of the Nobel Prize as a miraculous gift that rewarded him for the way he'd developed and shared the miraculous gift of his poetry. When his old friend John Hume, who'd been schooled in the same Catholic doctrines as Heaney, won the Nobel Peace Prize in 1998, Heaney told him, "The prize is like a grace streaming in. . . . Try to enjoy it utterly, try to let the sheer celebration enter you." Heaney sent Hume an admonitory poem inspired by a bridge he'd seen in Strasbourg, France, hoping his letter and poem would help Hume deal with the stress that accompanied the prize. To emphasize the sort of strength one needed, the poem repeats the lines, "Steady under strain and strong through tension . . . , / Bridges stand their ground without contention."[39] Heaney here is no doubt thinking of Weil's concepts of grace offsetting the pressure of gravity, and using the bridge as a metaphor for a person who can maintain equilibrium and grace under pressure.

A few weeks after returning from Greece, Heaney withdrew to the "concentrated solitude" of Glanmore Cottage to write his Nobel acceptance speech. By the end of November, he'd finished "Crediting Poetry," which he wanted his friend Peter Fallon to publish as a small book featuring a photograph of the votive relief of Orpheus on the cover. The carving, which he'd seen at Sparta, portrays Orpheus with a lyre beside someone who could be a fellow poet giving him a piece of papyrus. Animals enchanted by Orpheus's music surround them. Orpheus seems to be accepting a gift—perhaps an award?—that acknowledges his lyrical gift.

If Heaney imagined himself to be an Orpheus or Telemachus in Stockholm, it was mainly because he felt so alien there. According to Seamus Deane, who attended the Nobel festivities with a group that included Anne Friel, David Hammond, Matthew Evans, Carolina Michel, Peter Fallon, and Helen Vendler, Heaney slipped back into his shy, Incertus personality. He admitted in an interview that a combination of excitement, nervousness, and a bad cold left him "dry mouthed and hot browed."[40] The hectic schedule nearly exhausted him. On December 6, 1995, he met other Nobel Prize recipients; the following evening he gave a talk and went to a dinner hosted by the Swedish Academy; on December 8, the Irish ambassador in Sweden, Martin Burke, held an honorary lunch at his residence; the next day, there was a lunch with the Swedish Academy. During the main ceremony on Sunday, December 10, sitting on a stage in a concert hall with the king, queen, and princess of Sweden, Heaney listened to introductions for the various prizewinners and tried to relax during the intermissions when an orchestra played baroque music. Finally, a member of the Swedish Academy read a brief account of his achievements and presented him with the Nobel Prize for Literature.

Heaney later told Deane he found it hard to believe he'd won the illustrious prize. Deane also felt a "sense of unreality" in Stockholm, especially during the dinner when a group of singers in Nordic folk costumes descended the stairs while their leader slid down the balustrade backward, yodeling over his shoulder. Because the Nobel Prize had such mythic status around the world, Deane worried that Heaney would "recede into an abstraction" and become "a writer reified into a prize."[41] Heaney was about to become a wealthy man, since the check that came with the prize exceeded $1 million, and also a man sought out by heads of state around the world. President Clinton was one such leader eager to befriend Heaney. While visiting Northern Ireland in 1995, Clinton delivered a speech about the peace process in which he quoted the passage in *The Cure at Troy* about hope and history rhyming. In Dublin on December 1, the U.S. president quoted *The Cure at Troy* again, this time to a jubilant crowd of about one hundred thousand. Later in the day, the American ambassador, Jean Kennedy Smith, arranged a get-together for the Heaneys and Clintons at her residence. To show his gratitude, Heaney gave the Clintons gifts: a handwritten copy of the stanza in *The Cure at Troy* that Bill Clinton had quoted in his speech, and a copy of the play for Hillary, inscribed with lines from the final chorus about love prevailing after immense hardship. At home that night, the Heaneys watched President Clinton give a televised speech in Dublin. Once again, he quoted Heaney's lines about hope and history rhyming.

When Clinton returned from Ireland to Washington, he had Heaney's handwritten excerpt from *The Cure at Troy* displayed on a wall in the Yellow Oval Room of the White House, right next to a photograph of President Kennedy addressing the Irish Parliament. The excerpt included the inscription, "To President Bill Clinton with highest regard. It was a fortunate wind that blew you here. Seamus Heaney, Dublin, 1 December 1995."[42] The line about "a fortunate wind" came from the end of *The Cure at Troy* where the Chorus speaks for the Greek warriors who'd gone to Lemnos to recruit the man with the magic gift of bow and arrows who would end hostilities at Troy. Heaney's inscription implied that Clinton would do something similar with his political gifts in war-torn Ulster. It was someone appointed by Clinton, though—Senator George Mitchell— who brokered the Good Friday Agreement in 1998 that led to peace.

Heaney always found it difficult to rebuff his admirers, but after becoming a Nobel laureate he had to turn down their invitations at an ever-increasing rate. His reply on December 20, 1995, to the World Centre of Poetry's request that he join its governing board in Italy was typical: "I have had to make a rule forbidding myself to join any more boards or committees or councils or academies—already I am involved in more bodies of this kind than I can adequately serve."[43] Three weeks later, he wrote the Italian poet and poetry scholar Marco Fazzini, who taught at Venezia University, "Since the Nobel Prize, there are about three or four invitations arriving every day asking me to attach myself to very good causes. Unless I proceed with extreme caution, I am going to sign my life away and lose any time or peace in which to do my own writing. I am, of course, deeply aware of the honour implicit in these invitations."[44] He told the writer Connie Brothers that he was in "crisis-country, end-of-the-tether time, straw-that-breaks-the-camel's-back time" because of all the demands.[45]

One of the reasons he was in "crisis-country" was his stepped-up work with political figures around the globe. On December 21, 1995, on behalf of the peace process in Ulster, he attended a political ceremony organized by the British government at Hillsborough Castle, an official residence of the British secretary of state for Northern Ireland. Heaney graciously accepted a commemorative spade as a gift from the secretary of state, Sir Patrick Mayhew. A few months later, Prince Charles invited him to stay with him at Sandringham House, a historic mansion his family owned on a twenty-thousand-acre estate in Norfolk, England. Prince Charles gave him gifts of drinking glasses etched with his initials, which helped solidify their friendship. Hobnobbing with celebrities was exciting, but he confided to Darcy O'Brien that all he really wanted to do after receiving the Nobel Prize was chat quietly in a pub over a pint of beer with old friends. He complained about all the mail he got from strangers and admitted that he needed to hire a secretary. Even the much-hyped Nobel Prize ceremony had disappointed him because he hadn't been able to include some of his close friends and family:

> The actual presentation ceremony and banquet in Stockholm on Sunday 10 December were utterly beyond expectation. I had anticipated some higher commencement, but in the event was daunted by the sheer force of the pomp and the scale of the feasting. Trumpets and royalty, decorations and costumes, cleavage and glitter, staircase and escort, torch flames and flirtings. It was like a coronation. An ordination. A canonization. It was a moment which I could not have anticipated and I was deeply sorry that all my friends were not there at that particular juncture. In fact, I was so tense over the nomination of my ten allowed guests that I almost lost pleasure in my own attendance—through the consciousness of all those not in attendance.[46]

Concerned about honoring commitments to others, he almost forgot to enjoy the event designed to honor him.

It was impossible for Heaney to fulfill the expectations of all his fans. Not long after he returned home from Sweden, Michael Schmidt asked him to participate in a memorial ceremony for the poet-critic Donald Davie, who had died in September 1995. Jackie and Caroline Kennedy implored him to read at the John F. Kennedy Presidential Library in Boston on May 28, 1996. Hillary Clinton proposed having a party for him at the White House in the same month. Tufts University and the University of Genoa asked him to attend their commencement exercises so he could receive more honorary degrees. Michael Horovitz invited him to read at London's Royal Albert Hall on July 7. Michael Longley pleaded with him to join the campaign to reinstate his wife as academic director of the John Hewitt Summer School, after she was forced to resign. Various research libraries sent queries about his papers. A German travel agency contacted him about a "Seamus Heaney Information Tour" to Bellaghy, Castledawson, and Glanmore. He wrote the organizer, Aideen Shannon, a stern letter on February 26, 1996, stipulating that no tourists should approach anyone in his family. To help manage his accumulating correspondence, he finally hired a secretary, Susie Tyrrell, and instructed her to decline most of the requests that arrived every day in the mail.

The news of Joseph Brodsky's death on January 28, 1996, at the age of fifty-five, made Heaney even more determined to alleviate some of the debilitating stress in his life. He had last seen Brodsky in early January 1996 for the New York opening of Brian Friel's play *Molly Sweeney*. A blizzard had made driving in the city perilous, so Brodsky walked through the snow from Brooklyn to Union Square Café to have lunch with Heaney, Jonathan Galassi, and Roger Straus. Even after several operations on his heart, Brodsky refused to moderate his smoking, drinking, and traveling. Heaney had strained his body in similar ways and also had heart problems. Shocked by the death of his friend and fellow Nobel laureate, he immediately began composing "Audenesque," an elegy that urges readers to commune with Brodsky's Eucharistic gifts: "Do again what Auden said / Good poets do: bite, break their bread." (Auden's elegy for Yeats proclaims, "The words of a dead man / Are modified in the guts of the living.") Heaney may have been thinking of Brodsky's goal as U.S. poet laureate to make poems as available to the masses as Gideon Bibles in hotel rooms. From Heaney's post-Catholic point of view, breaking bread with dead and living poets allows readers to commune with their redemptive gifts. Heaney reiterated this message at Brodsky's memorial service at the Cathedral of St. John the Divine in New York on March 8, 1996.

On Mother's Day in 1996, Heaney made a similar point when he received an honorary degree from the University of North Carolina. On this occasion, he told the graduating students a story about his mother giving him and his siblings simple gifts—a tin milk can, a couple of wooden spoons—so they could play in the sand on a trip to the beach. He admitted that, at first, he was ashamed of the gifts, and when he wrote a paper for school about the beach trip he claimed that his mother had given them a shovel and pail. Still feeling guilty about his fibs, he said, "The true and durable path into and through experience involves being true to the actual givens of your lives." He told the students to embrace the "givens" of their lives, affirm "the gift of keeping going upon your own terms," and pursue "the further and more fulfilling gift of getting . . . renewed and revived by some further transformation."[47]

After returning to Dublin, Heaney hoped to get back to his poetry, but his social calendar interfered. On June 5, he joined Ted Hughes at a Buckingham Palace lunch to discuss candidates for the Queen's Gold Medal for Poetry. (They recommended Peter Redgrove for the honor.) The next day he flew to Edmonton, Canada, for a brother's birthday party. On the plane, he wrote a letter to David Hammond in which he groused about an all-too-familiar scenario: "I'm a function of timetables, not an agent of my own being. And it's going to be like this for weeks and months still."[48] His upcoming timetable included visits to Rotterdam, Paris, Cork, and Oxford. Vacationing with Marie in Spain during the first weeks of July, he again tried to make time for writing. Asked by the organizers of the European Poetry Festival why he couldn't participate in the spring of 1997, he responded, "Unless I take drastic measures, I am going to become a mere blip in airlines' computers. Instead of being a farmer on Helicon, I'll be a jet-trail fading beyond Delphi."[49] On July 26, 1996, he wrote sardonically to Piotr Sommer about his travails as a "parcel on a conveyor belt."[50] He vowed in 1997 to spend more time in his monastic writer's cell.

At the Frankfurt Book Fair in late September, Heaney gave a lecture titled "Ireland and Its Diaspora" in which he commiserated with the many Irish people who'd been uprooted from their native land. St. Colum Cille, who'd been banished from Ireland for fighting in the battle of Cooldrenva and for refusing to give up a manuscript belonging to Finnian of Moville, was Heaney's "archetypal figure" in the diaspora. The saint had physically left Ireland, but remained spiritually bound to it. "Behind and beyond the historical facts of a people's dispersal from their country," Heaney said, "a mystical ethnic body persists and stays united."[51] This was as true, he felt, for early Celtic saints launching boats into the Atlantic Ocean as modern Irish immigrants seeking opportunities in the United States. Heaney soon signed his faxes "Colmcille the Scribe" to underscore his kinship with those who left Ireland and remained united with their "mystical" home.

Now that the Nobel Prize had made Heaney's name even more marketable, businesses increased their demands on him. Dillons Bookstore in London, for instance, wanted him to sign nine hundred copies of *The School Bag* anthology after it was published in 1997. Scholars contacted him about making himself accessible for possible biographies. So did publishers and literary agents. Several years after Michael Parker published his literary biography *Seamus Heaney: The Making of the Poet,* the Yeats specialist Alexander Norman Jeffares proposed writing another biography. Heaney's reaction was similar to his reaction to the German travel agent who wanted to bring tourists to the area where he'd grown up: stay away. On February 5, 1997, he told Jeffares: "[I will not] be in any mood to collaborate with anybody at this stage. I feel leached of all privacy. Imperiled by publicity."[52] Before long, he told the editor of the *Dictionary of Hiberno-English,* Terence Dolan, that, like the basketball superstar Michael Jordan, he was afraid of becoming "more logo than human being."[53] Seamus Deane's prediction that Heaney would be "reified into a prize" and marketed like a brand-name commodity seemed to be coming true.

Heaney's generous nature continued to entangle him in the commercial publicity machine that he longed to escape. When Queen's University wanted to publicize his work at the new Seamus Heaney Centre for Irish Poetry, he sent some of his private papers. He took steps to sell a much larger cache of letters and manuscripts to libraries at Harvard and Emory. The National Library of Ireland also expressed interest in establishing an archive. On February 13, 1997, he wrote his Emory friend Ron Schuchard that he would examine the collections of Irish writers at Emory before deciding what to do. Later, he told Michael Longley that he was "both impressed and daunted" by what he found at Emory: "They do a wonderful job on the manuscripts, but, Christ, it's odd to see the whole thing turning into an 'archive.' Before we've been archived ourselves. But Mahon . . . is probably right—there's no such thing as privacy no more."[54] On June 25, 1998, he apologized to Schuchard for discussing Harvard as a potential repository for his papers before consulting him, and said he was sick of the deliberations. On June 28, 1999, Emory's president, Bill Chace, said he understood Heaney's quandary and asked about a check for a half million dollars that Emory had sent as a kind of down payment. Heaney knew, of course, that as soon as his papers were available to scholars, his privacy would be further compromised.

As he seemed to lose more control of his life, Heaney at times lashed out at those who threatened his privacy. Asked by the photographer Eamonn O'Doherty about taking pictures of Glanmore Cottage, he responded angrily, "The only place in my life that has not been photographed, featured, interviewed, nationalized, 'shared' is the Wicklow place—I want to keep the site as unseen as possible."[55] Heaney's refusals to get involved in public events were often terse. In a note to Fordham University's president, who had asked him to help inaugurate a new campus library, Heaney wrote, "No travel in 1997."[56] Wary of his poems being used for political causes, he told Stephanie Ault at *Frontline* that she couldn't include audio recordings of four poems on a website linked to a PBS history of the Troubles. On November 6, 1997, he responded similarly to Michael Healey's query about recording a selection of Yeats's poems: "Over the years, for a variety of reasons, I have declined many invitations to get involved with Yeats projects of different sorts and I am going to stay consistent in the recording you propose."[57] But he wasn't always consistent. He soon published a selection of Yeats's poems at Faber and a long, favorable review in the *Atlantic* of *The Apprentice Mage*, volume 1 of Roy Foster's biography *W. B. Yeats: A Life*.

Heaney was also inconsistent in his responses to the many institutions that offered him awards. In 1997, he refused an honorary degree from Northeastern University, where he'd read his poetry before, but agreed to accept a degree from Oxford, a Foreign Honorary Membership to the American Academy of Arts and Letters, and the honorary title of "Saoi" (Gaelic for "wise one") from the Irish association of artists known as the Aosdána. In a special gathering of the Aosdána in Dublin on May 1, 1998, Ireland's President McAleese gave him a gold torc, a symbol of the office of Saoi. Heaney began his acceptance speech:

> In old Irish times, it is said that the poet was rewarded by the lord of the tuath with a gift of cattle. In Anglo-Saxon society, the gift-giving element was present also, but there the lord handed out "coiled gold," as it was called in the Old English texts. And so it came to pass that one of the old poetic titles for the lord of the land was "ring-giver," a term which I myself have occasionally translated as "giver of torcs." It is, therefore, particularly apt and I am particularly honoured to receive this torc of twisted gold from the hand of our own "ring-giver," President Mary McAleese.[58]

Once again, Heaney's gift had been honored with a gift.

In another effort to secure more time for his writing, Heaney in June 1997 contacted an associate dean at Harvard, Laura Fisher, about resigning as the Boylston Professor. The administration agreed to his request but convinced him to accept the Ralph Waldo Emerson Poet in Residence position, which required that he be at Harvard for only six to eight weeks each fall. As he scaled back his teaching, he also cut down on the number of interviews he granted. He told the editor Patricia Harty, who wanted to reprint an interview that had already appeared in the *Irish America Magazine*, that there were "far too many interviews" and that he'd like to put a "full stop to the whole business."[59] In a few years, though, he began work with Dennis O'Driscoll on a book-length series of interviews, *Stepping Stones*.

Heaney had more reason to be concerned about the effects of stress and fatigue on his health after an accident near the end of 1997. On the morning of November 14, right after he flew home from a conference in Japan, he rushed to the Dublin airport to meet his American accountant. Still jet-lagged from his flight, he slipped on the floor and damaged his knee so badly that an ambulance had to take him to St. Vincent's hospital for surgery. For the next six weeks, he wore a leg cast, and for the first months of 1998 he regularly went to a physical therapist to strengthen his leg. He also had to contend with gout in his foot and a pinched nerve in his neck, which made walking painful. Some of his friends took his fall as another sign that he needed to slow down. To put them at ease, he joked about his physical ailments. With regard to his trips away from home, he said he had the Oisin Syndrome: "It means that after an enchanted journey you fall to earth and grow to be 300 years old in a second."[60] The mythical Irish bard Oisin had returned to Ireland after a long journey but only showed his age after his feet touched Irish soil.

## LAST GIFTS BETWEEN HEANEY AND HUGHES

On December 14, 1997, having just read through an advance copy of *Birthday Letters,* Heaney wrote Hughes an eight-page letter to thank him for the gift. He asked rhetorically: "How [can] I . . . salute you after the immensity I've come through these last few days, reading—and re-reading . . . Birthday Letters?" Heaney saluted Hughes with a flurry of compliments. He compared Hughes's sequence of poems to *The Divine Comedy,* Hopkins's best poetry, heroic Irish legends, and Shakespeare's plays. Hughes's epistolary verse, Heaney enthused, was capable of "doing the Cuchulain warp-splash, the salmon-feat, showing a wild Shakespearean back above their element." Hughes was a great admirer of Shakespeare, enjoyed fishing for salmon, and no doubt appreciated the praise, but he may have been taken aback by the allusion to Cuchulain, since the Irish hero was deformed (he'd been given seven fingers on each hand, seven toes on each foot, and seven pupils in each eye), and sometimes became so deranged by bloodlust that he failed to distinguish friend from foe. In the end, Cuchulain killed his son and was beheaded. Heaney returned several times in his letter to the image of Hughes as a Cuchulain-like warrior. Like Yeats in his poem "Cuchulain's Fight with the Sea," Heaney imagined Hughes fighting an "invulnerable tide" of enemies. He advised Hughes not to "dread the vulgarity and vehemence" of feminists who held him responsible for Plath's plight. "Publication may unleash" a backlash, he warned, but he hoped *Birthday Letters* would remind readers of Hughes's unassailable talent.[61]

Hughes's book, which Faber published on January 29, 1998, was a popular success. Readers on both sides of the Atlantic were eager to find out what Hughes had to say about his fateful marriage to Plath. There were plenty of critics who pointed out that the poems had neither the colloquial energy of letters, nor the compressed vigor of prose poems, nor the vitality of his early free verse. In an interview, Dennis O'Driscoll confronted Heaney about the negative reviews: "Might it not be said that the writing is banal in places and that the attempts at self-exculpation through mythologization are less than convincing?" Heaney conceded this was a plausible assessment, but he still defended the book. The verse had rhetorical power, he insisted, and Hughes had done a noble job of breaking his silence and releasing the "emotional pressure" that had built up around his difficult marriage to Plath.[62] Once again, Heaney extolled his friend as a Cuchulain-like hero trying to heal his wounds so he could keep fighting the good fight.

On December 29, 1997, Heaney wrote Darcy O'Brien about healing his own wounds after his fall in the airport and his worry that physical therapy would further disable him. He told his friend Bert Hornback in January 1998: "My mummy case has been unlidded and the limb trans-ferred to a bolted and strapped caliper/brace thing, bolted in two sides of the knee with those washers that you last saw . . . on the Frankenstein monster."[63] By February, Heaney was mobile enough to travel to London and Norwich, England, to give readings. On March 3, he flew to San Fran-cisco to be honored at an American Ireland Fund dinner. It was at the air-port arrival gate that he learned that Darcy O'Brien had died in Tulsa the previous day. Shortly afterward, he paid tribute to his talented friend by donating two thousand dollars to the University of Tulsa, where O'Brien had taught, so the university could establish a prize for the best honors thesis on an Irish subject. His complaints about a packed schedule and a bad leg notwithstanding, Heaney showed up at literary events around the world with remarkable alacrity for the rest of the year.

During 1998, some of Heaney's "purposeful work," as he called it in a letter to Michael Longley,[64] was done on behalf of the Good Friday Agree-ment, which political leaders in Northern Ireland, Ireland, and England approved on April 10, 1998, after long and acrimonious negotiations. Heaney had supported human rights organizations for years, but he paid special attention to the peace process in his native country. He wrote editorials, gave talks, and stressed the importance of the Good Friday Agreement in his communications with President Clinton and President

McAleese. In his public appearances in Ireland, Clinton continued to make use of Heaney's poetry as a goad for peace. On September 6, 1998, he ended a speech in Limerick, Ireland, with a quotation from Heaney's short poem "Song" about "the music of what happens"—a phrase originally attributed to the legendary Irish hero Finn McCool. Clinton hoped that the new "music of what happens" in Northern Ireland would be harmonious and no longer include the cacophony of bullets, bombs, and sirens.

Heaney knew how quickly Ulster's "music" could become discordant again. On August 22, 1998, he wrote an editorial for the *Irish Times*, "The Reciprocity of Tears," bemoaning the IRA's attempts to destroy the prospects of peace. The Real Irish Republican Army, a splinter group of the former Provisional IRA, had just packed a stolen Vauxhall Cavalier with five hundred pounds of fertilizer-based explosives and parked it outside a clothing shop in Omagh's Lower Market Street. The courthouse had been the intended target, but no parking space was available, so a different site was chosen. The IRA had warned local citizens of the impending explosion. In the confusion, the police had moved people from the courthouse to the shopping area where the IRA detonated the bomb. Glass shards and car parts flew three hundred yards, ripping apart bodies and scattering debris from buildings. The bomb killed 29 people and injured 220 others. Tony Blair and Queen Elizabeth denounced the atrocity. Bill and Hillary Clinton visited Omagh to offer condolences. Irish Labour Party president John Hume called the bombers fascists. Sinn Féin leaders Martin McGuinness and Gerry Adams also deplored the incident. It was Northern Ireland's worst single terrorist attack. Among the casualties were Protestants, Catholics, Mormons, women, and children.

Heaney began his editorial by stating that silent sorrow and anger were his natural responses to such carnage. As for the responses of Ulster citizens, he said, "I think what most people now curse is not primarily the political motivation of those who planted the bomb but their callousness. What is shared by both communities in the North is awe at the enormity of the killers' indifference to human life, their imperviousness to simple affection." Heaney alluded to Wilfred Owen's poem "Insensibility," which chastised "the armchair patriots on the home front, hardliners shooting their mouths off with impunity." The rhetoric of politicians and patriots seemed irrelevant when people were being slaughtered. As a soldier in the trenches of World War I, Owen had felt more empathy for his German enemies than his countrymen at home because his enemies had a better understanding of warfare and shared with him "the eternal reciprocity of tears."[65] Heaney implied that this reciprocal giving—even though the gifts were tears—was a sign that antagonistic groups could form sympathetic bonds.

In June, Heaney experienced the same "reciprocity of tears" in his friendship with Hughes, who was now fighting a losing battle with colon cancer. When Hughes arrived in Dublin, Heaney was at first encouraged by his friend's high spirits and the fact that his hair had grown back after chemotherapy. Nevertheless, Heaney sensed Hughes was visiting old friends to say goodbye and, over the next few months, tried to be as solicitous as he could. On September 19, after Hughes received the Order of Merit from Queen Elizabeth, Heaney wrote, "The honour not only ratifies you in the order of the present time and our present lives, but it magnifies itself by being continuously present." For Heaney, Hughes exemplified "what they used to call in our Christian apologetics 'Continuous creation.'"[66] Theologically, "continuous creation" referred to God's creation of the universe as a sacred gift that was continuously preserved, re-created, and regifted. Once again, Heaney conceived of Hughes as an artist-god producing gifts. Although Heaney looked forward to meeting his friend in November after returning from Harvard, Hughes's cancer metastasized to his liver, and he died on October 28, 1998, from a heart attack. He was only sixty-eight.

Heaney wrote a number of friends about how devastated he was by Hughes's death. He had hoped that Hughes, like the hero of the Joycean "monomyth" who journeys to a menacing otherworld and returns triumphant with life-enhancing boons, would somehow overcome his latest ordeal. Heaney wrote Hughes's friend Roy Davids about this, and Davids responded, "As you say, he took to his forest to hide, conserve, recoup and return."[67] But Hughes never recouped or returned. Reflecting on his friendship with Hughes in *Stepping Stones,* Heaney said, "He was the one who fortified me the most, the most intuitive about what I worked from and how I worked. . . . Right up until the end I still experienced a sense of privilege in his company. There was something foundational about my relationship with him. I felt secured by his work and his way of being in the world, and that gave the friendship a dimension that was in some sense supra-personal."[68] After his death, Hughes's spirit and poems continued to fortify Heaney in a "supra-personal" way.

In November 1998, Heaney met with Queen Elizabeth to discuss the search for a new poet laureate to replace Hughes, and, on December 1, he officially recommended Geoffrey Hill in a letter to John Parson, the queen's deputy treasurer. Heaney noted that "Hill has set himself up in Boston University and has been writing jeremiads about the state of England, so he might want to redeem the country by his own efforts."[69] Heaney's other suggestions were Derek Walcott, Michael Longley, James Fenton, Andrew Motion, Wendy Cope, and Carol Ann Duffy. The recommendation of Hill typified Heaney's largesse. As Heaney's fame had grown, so had Hill's jealousy of his perceived rival. Three days after Hughes died, Heaney sent a curt note to Hill about his most recent insults, which had appeared in his long poem *The Triumph of Love*. Heaney wrote, "Even though I realize you may intend the accent to be wrong, you may still like to know that the effect at page 58, line 19 was picked up by at least one reader."[70] Heaney didn't sign his note, although he may have been tempted to sign it "Sean O'Shem," since that was the clownish Irish nickname Hill had given him in *The Triumph of Love*. "It's self-evident he can't / keep up a fiction, even for twenty lines," Hill had said about O'Shem. Hill also scoffed at a phrase from Joyce's *Ulysses* that Heaney had used in his essay "Now and in England" to praise Hill's linguistic gift: "*Morosa / delectatio* was his expression, that Irish /professor of rhetoric—forget his name." Heaney, the Boylston Professor of Oratory and Rhetoric until 1995, was the obvious target of Hill's heavy-handed sarcasm. Hill ended with a vulgar slur: "*up / yours, O'Shem.*"[71] Despite Hill's remarks, Heaney still nominated him to be Britain's poet laureate.

On November 3, 1998, Heaney delivered a eulogy at Hughes's funeral in St. Peter's Church, not far from Hughes's Devonshire home. He began, "No death in my lifetime has hurt poetry or poets more than the death of Ted Hughes. No death outside my immediate family has left me feeling more bereft." He compared Hughes's poetic gift to Caedmon's and Shakespeare's and praised him as "a tower of kindness and strength, a great arch where the least of poetry's children could enter and feel safe."[72] Reverend Terence McCaughey, a professor at Trinity College, Dublin, who'd known Hughes since their undergraduate years at Cambridge, reiterated Heaney's sentiments. He lauded "the generous way" Hughes "made others part of new plans and projects," and quoted the apostle Paul's discourse on spiritual gifts in his First Letter to the Corinthians. Paul had written, "And though I have *the gift* of prophecy and all knowledge; and though I have all faith, so that I could remove mountains, and have not charity, I am nothing" (13:2). McCaughey explained, "Paul reckons that, unless it informs what we say and do—unless it informs our exercise of the other gifts we receive from that Other we have learned to name as 'God'—absolutely nothing we say or do is worth anything at all. . . . [Love] is a gift that comes unbidden which we receive from God through other people—and which then we can by God's grace nurture, cultivate, [and] share."[73] McCaughey cited Hughes's ability to endure personal trials and to be charitable toward others as examples of his noble spirit.

Heaney echoed this biblical account of gifts in a longer eulogy he gave at Hughes's memorial service in Westminster Cathedral on May 13, 1999. In this hallowed setting, he said Hughes had been a great man as well as a great poet whose life had resembled the "sacred drama" of a mythical hero who realized his "destiny was bound to involve a certain ordeal." His "healer's vision" had helped him recuperate from his wounds and uplift others in the process. "His ultimate gift," Heaney declared, "was for setting experience afloat upon that pure river of the water of life which was revealed to [St. John] the evangelist. And it was, as the scripture says, 'in the midst of the street of it' that he was carried away from us, down the aisle, into 'the starry dew.'"[74] For Heaney, Hughes's poetry was a nourishing gift that had issued like the "water of life" from a sacred source.

At the end of 1999, Ireland's President Mary McAleese invited Heaney to write a poem for a special candle-lighting ceremony at Dublin Castle to mark the end of the millennium and beginning of the new one. Heaney sent his regrets—occasional poems were always difficult for him to write—and suggested that someone read lines from Yeats's poem "To Ireland in the Coming Times." The president's Millennium Office pressed him to reconsider, so he sent a poem he'd already written, "Bann Valley Eclogue," which echoed Virgil's "Fourth Eclogue." Perhaps realizing that Heaney had originally intended his eclogue to be a gift for a newborn niece, the Millennium Committee chose to distribute an excerpt from

Yeats's poem along with candles that Irish citizens could light on the last day of December.

With regard to his own plans for "the coming times," Heaney decided to begin the new millennium with a well-deserved vacation, so he booked a flight to the island of St. Lucia in the Caribbean, where his friend Derek Walcott lived. On February 17, 2000, he informed Tom Flanagan that he was in a tropical paradise: "Already I have drunk coconut water from a trepanned coconut, shown my pale belly to the dismayed beach-[combers] . . . , wobbled in the turquoise waters of the sea, drunk the habit-forming rum punch and generally slackened. . . . I even smoked a cigar on our-separate-cottage verandah last night. . . . It's the first time I've relaxed in a couple of years. . . . This lotus-interlude is indeed a trip."[75] Heaney also socialized with the writer Peter Balakian, who had rented a cottage for his family in a nearby town. His relaxation on the sunny island left him feeling healthier and happier than he had in a long time. He told Ron Schuchard, "Since I was a lad at the seaside, I have never had such a time. . . . I relaxed totally, dumbed down, came home with a brown face and a changed pace, a determination not to get too hurried ever again."[76] Heaney's interlude among the Caribbean Lotus-eaters came to an abrupt end in March when he traveled to the United States for meetings with his publisher Roger Straus, interviews with the *New York Times* and PBS NewsHour, and a poetry reading at a White House St. Patrick's Day party organized by Bill and Hillary Clinton. His fate, it seemed, was to be an airborne Sweeney.

# 14

# Final Gifts

For Heaney, much of 2000 was spent rushing around the world to give poetry readings and lectures, conduct interviews (including one with Karl Miller that was published as a book), and receive honorary degrees (from the University of Wales, the University of Pennsylvania, the University of Birmingham). In 2001, his travel destinations included Aberdeen, Oxford, Leeds, London, Lisbon, Colorado Springs, Houston, Los Angeles, San Francisco, Tulsa, St. Lucia, Cambridge (England), St. Andrews, New York, and Princeton. At most of these places, he read at least a few poems from *Electric Light,* which Faber published in March 2001. Recognizing the demand for his work in the United States, Farrar, Straus and Giroux printed 17,000 copies of the book on April 8, 2001. (By that time, his American publisher had sold over 173,000 copies of *Beowulf;* eventually, sales of his translation would exceed 400,000.) *Publishers Weekly* reported at the time that "just about anything under the Heaney brand should sell solidly."[1] As his good fortune continued, so did his philanthropy. He supported the County Derry Society's efforts to renovate St. Mary's, the church he'd attended as a boy. In 2001, he gave a signed copy of "The Rain Stick" to Energy Action Ltd, an environmentally friendly power company in Australia, which sold the poem for £1,400. He donated one of his signed books to OutReach Moldova, a charity established by an Irish doctor to raise money for orphanages in Africa; the book was auctioned for £2,000. He supported other good causes, too.

Heaney had written many poems to honor other artists, but *Electric Light* was more crowded with homages than his previous books. Lines from "On His Work in the English Tongue"—"Poetry . . . is, as Milosz says, / 'A dividend from ourselves,' a tribute paid / By what we have been true to"—could have served as the book's epigraph. His numerous elegies offered tributes in acts of reciprocity to gift-givers. "Out of the Bag" pays tribute to Doctor Kerlin for delivering "gifts of life" at Mossbawn. "The Real Names" remembers gifted schoolmates at St. Columb's who performed with him in plays. "The Gaeltacht" acknowledges those who contributed to his "gift of tongues" by speaking Gaelic with him at Queen's University. Literary friends and acquaintances—Vladimir Chupeski, Rafael Alberti, Caj Westerburg, Hans Magnus Enzensberger—appear in "Known World," a poem about the Struga Poetry Festival in North Macedonia that bestowed a Golden Wreath on Heaney. Other poems pay poetic "dividends" to Virgil, Dante, Hardy, Kavanagh, Auden, Brodsky, Zbigniew Herbert, Norman MacCaig, Iain Crichton Smith, Sorley MacLean, David Thomson, Nadine Gordimer, Eamon Grennan, and Brian Friel. In "Montana," he even commemorates a farmer he knew at Mossbawn, John Dologhan.

*Electric Light* begins and ends near the *omphalos* from which Heaney drew so many of his gift-like "dividends." The book's first poem, "At Toomebridge," returns to the "continuous / Present" of the Bann River that flows out of Lough Neagh near Heaney's first home. Like the Muse's fertile waters in "Personal Helicon," the river represents the "continuous creation" of gifts: it is a "present" that is always present and giving. The "negative ions in the open air / Are poetry to me," Heaney says. The charged particles created by the flowing water (ions are atoms or molecules that have more electrons than protons) are reputed to relieve stress and depression by releasing serotonin in the brain. For Heaney, they possess the same power to energize and heal as poems, and aren't that different from the electric currents flowing through his grandparents' light bulbs in the book's title poem. Once again, he is genuflecting to what he earlier called "the most unexpected and miraculous thing in my life . . . —the arrival in it of poetry . . . as gift, surprise, bonus, grace."

Many reviewers of *Electric Light* admired the book's noble intentions but disapproved of the conventional language used to present them. Patrick McGuinness wrote in the *London Review of Books*, "Some of the poems are burdened by literary self-consciousness and a kind of ruminative fireside recollection that is neither electric nor electrifying."[2] Robert Potts remarked in the *Guardian,* "Heaney has always been a gift to the academic community, in that a 'career' has been discernible from volume to volume . . . , [but] Heaney's commentators are going to be hard-pressed to see this volume as a development in a career. It restates all Heaney's themes and approaches to date, and in doing so manages to make many of them look like mannerisms."[3] In *Electric Light,* he paid tribute to gifts and gift-givers again but without the rhetorical energy that made his earlier poems so enthralling.

During the last decade of his life, Heaney in poems, essays, and lectures repeatedly engaged in Eucharistic thanksgiving rituals to show gratitude for gifts from the dead. His introduction to Darcy O'Brien's autobiographical *A Way of Life, Like Any Other* was a testimonial to his friend's "gift for the immaculate" and, paradoxically, for "the uncensored and the incorrect."[4] O'Brien's stylistic "gift of tongues" had grown from an imagination energized by the friction between sacred and profane compulsions. On March 28, 2001, before an audience at Westminster Abbey, Heaney highlighted similar contraries in a eulogy for the Welsh poet and Anglican priest R. S. Thomas, who had died on September 25, 2000. Sympathizing with the devout Welshman's attempts to reconcile the soaring rhetoric of religious texts and the terse, down-to-earth speech of farmers in his congregation, Heaney said, "[It was] as if the poet bore a grudge against his own lyric gift—and I liked that a lot. I liked it especially because the lyric gift was genuine and was yearning to give itself over to its own delicious exercise."[5] Unlike his Welsh countryman Dylan Thomas, R. S. Thomas had avoided the perils of overindulging his "lyric gift."

Heaney found an outlet for his own "lyric gift" and for lyrical music in general when he teamed up with his friend Liam O'Flynn, a traditional Irish musician and master of the uilleann pipes. On May 29, 2001, poet and piper performed at New York's Lincoln Center. As he implied in "The Given Note," which he read, Heaney wanted to transmit a "note" to the audience that resembled the sonic gift delivered by the wind off the Atlantic Ocean to an Irish fiddler hunkered down in his stone hut on a Blasket Island. At the beginning of the new millennium, Heaney continued to long for that solitary fiddler's "gifted state." On June 30, 2001, he wrote Danny Weissbort, "At times I fear I am lost to myself, or have allowed myself to get lost—by not reneging on various 'duties,' good causes, 'decent' behavior—the festschrifts, the catalogue notes, the introductions to books, the launches of exhibitions." The "failure to say no" amounted to "an absconding from harder dedication to more inward tasks," he admitted.[6]

### SEPTEMBER 11, 2001: SUBLIME GIFTS

In late August 2001, Heaney published an article in the *New York Times*, "Poetry's Power Against Intolerance," which called on artists to bear witness to "the darker levels to which human beings can descend" and to aid the downtrodden by "raising spirits and creating hope."[7] Heaney's belief that poetic gifts could overcome intolerance and create peaceful bonds between people was sorely tested when Al-Qaeda terrorists crashed commercial jets into the World Trade Center, the Pentagon, and a Pennsylvania field on September 11, 2001. He responded to the cataclysm in an unusual way—by translating a Latin poem about pagan gods written by the Roman poet Horace in the first century BC.

In a short essay, "Reality and Justice: On Translating Horace, *Odes*, 1, 34," Heaney argued that classical art had the "power to keep itself whole and its viewers hale" when the world was collapsing.[8] His translation of Horace's "Book 1, Ode 34" follows precedents he'd established in his bog poems, although now he addresses sacrifices committed by Islamic militants in the United States rather than by Christian militants in Ulster or by worshippers of fertility goddesses in ancient Europe. As in his bog poems, though, victims and victimizers merge; the powers that be who demand sacrificial gifts are as problematic as the sacrificial gift-givers. From Heaney's point of view, President Bush's "Shock and Awe" campaign in the Middle East to punish the terrorists was as brutally indifferent to the loss of innocent lives as Osama bin Laden's campaign of terror in America.

Horace's ode attracted Heaney because of the way it set a catastrophe in a mythical context. (The poem alludes to the mythical figures Jupiter, Atlas, Fortune, Styx, and Tartarus.) Although Horace had been skeptical of myth and religion as a youthful follower of Epicurus and Lucretius, as he matured he came to accept Lucretius's view that religion and myth could represent occurrences in nature for which there was no plausible explanation. The beginning of his "Ode 34" contains a confession: "Now backward am I forced to turn my sails, and retrace the course I have forsaken." As he ponders his intellectual evolution, he decides he should no longer dismiss myths as silly fictions; he should accept them as expressions of surprising paradoxes, random changes in fortune, and unfathomable mysteries. "God has power," he asserts, to make "mean the man of high estate" and "change the highest for the lowest"; sometimes "the Father of the sky" drives "his thundering steeds and flying car" through "the undimmed firmament" when no storm clouds are there to produce thunder and lightning.[9] Like the mystical texts Heaney read as a young man, Horace's ode focuses on events that defy human reason and language.

A lecture titled "Bright Bolts," which Heaney gave at Harvard in 2000 as the Ralph Waldo Emerson Poet in Residence, sheds light on his idiosyncratic approach to the September 11 attacks. Heaney's lecture title comes from Robert Graves's poem "The White Goddess," which in some ways resembles Horace's ode. Both poems deploy images of lightning bolts to represent overwhelming power. Although "The White Goddess" features a matriarchal goddess who inspires poetry rather than a patriarchal god who destroys things, both divine beings evoke sublime feelings of terror and awe in those who witness them. For Graves, the archetypal muse-goddess compels a select few to go their "headstrong and heroic way / Seeking her out . . . / Careless of where the next bright bolt may fall."[10] The goddess's in-spiriting "bolt[s]" are as awe-inspiring as Jupiter's lightning, but her power is directed at a poet's mind, whereas Jupiter's power is directed at anything that gets in its way on Earth.

When Heaney mulled over how best to describe the hijacked planes flying through the "undimmed firmament" and exploding in thunderous "bright bolt[s]" on September 11, 2001, he recalled his Harvard lecture in which he pointed out that Graves and Horace had written about "the 'bright bolt' of terror." In his essay "Reality and Justice," he said for Graves the lightning bolt symbolized "a psychosomatic frisson, which he associated with the presence of the goddess," and for Horace it symbolized "the tremendous force of unexpected thunder and lightning which announced the power and presence of Jupiter." As for the connection between these poems and the attacks on September 11, Heaney explained,

"When the World Trade Center attacks happened, I suddenly found that the shock-and-awe factor in the Horace poem matched what I and everybody else was feeling."[11] In a number of interviews, Heaney suggested that the terrorist attacks, the U.S. "War on Terror" in Afghanistan, and the U.S. "Shock and Awe" bombing of Iraq in 2003 were not only examples of the sublime; they were also examples of misguided gift exchanges.

With respect to the perverse aspects of the gift-giving muse, Graves's "The White Goddess" illustrates the way her "nakedly worn magnificence" and "bright bolt" can drive poets insane and make them want to sacrifice themselves to receive more gifts. Graves argues in his encyclopedic study of myth, *The White Goddess:* "Every Muse-poet must, in a sense, die for the Goddess whom he adores" as he pursues "the gift of inspiration" or "the gift of prophecy."[12] The White Goddess's "habit has never been to coerce, but always to grant or withhold her favours according as her sons and lovers came to her with exactly the right gifts in their hands." This habit of sometimes granting and sometimes withholding gifts is one reason her zealous devotees oscillate between the sublime poles of "exaltation and horror."[13]

Heaney had other reasons besides the writings of Graves and Horace for framing the September 11 attacks in terms of gift exchange. He knew that radical Muslim clerics viewed the lives of devout militants as gifts that should be sacrificed to secure divine gifts (including nubile women) in the afterlife. Heaney must have seen the similarity between these heavenly gifts and those Graves envisioned in his poem. Graves was no apologist for jihad, but he supported the idea of male poets sacrificing themselves to a muse who was a beguiling sex goddess. Her "eyes were blue," he says of this femme fatale, and she had "rowan-berry lips" and "hair curled honey-coloured to white hips."[14] Heaney's poem counters the expectations of muse-addled poets and virgin-obsessed jihadists by reiterating his view that sacrificial gift-giving can provoke violence as well as peace. "Nothing resettles right," the narrator of "Anything Can Happen" says. Out of the "telluric ash" and generative "fire-spores," new terrorists will rise like phoenixes to hurl more bright bolts and kindle more fires.

Heaney told the poet-critic Adam Kirsch that he disapproved of the American government's "War on Terror" because he thought it would foment more war and more terror. When the Bush administration invaded Iraq in 2003, he denounced its "arrogance and stupidity" and its "blatant lies about Iraq's involvement in al Qaeda."[15] He told his friend George Watson, "I can't help thinking how little has changed, in spite of the great achievement of Owen and his comrade poets, between the first war of the 21 c and the first big one of the 20 c."[16] Combatants were once again engaging in Owen's "eternal reciprocity of tears." They were also acting like the sectarian factions during Northern Ireland's Troubles, and the long line of martyrs who had sacrificed themselves to their idealistic versions of Mother Ireland.

When Heaney gave a commencement address at Emory University on May 12, 2003, he was still thinking about the victims of the terrorist attacks and Bush's "War on Terror." He told the students, "Acts of coldly premeditated terror such as those of Sept. 11, carefully premeditated acts of war such as the campaign in Iraq—these things have had a quality of mirage about them. . . . We know these things are real, but it is hard to bring their terrible reality home."[17] One way to bring their reality home and to redress it, in Heaney's view, was by returning to the classical foundations of Western civilization. In a lecture he gave to Ireland's Royal College of Surgeons on November 5, 2001, "The Whole Thing: On the Good of Poetry," he restated his conviction that traditional concepts and traditional narratives help people heal during crises. He discussed how his poem "Anything Can Happen" made use of "Robert Graves's notion that all poems are the gift of a muse," and he explained how his fiddler in "The Given Note" stood for all artists who journeyed "alone into the island of themselves and their world," found "a whole and healing gift," and returned to share that gift with others.[18] Once again, he alluded to the pattern of departure-initiation-return in the "monomyth" to explain his conception of the creative process, and he emphasized the healing power of gift-givers rather than the destructive power of gods and goddesses wielding "bright bolts."

## GIFTS FROM THE ISLAND OF THE SELF

The lackluster reviews of *Electric Light* made Heaney even more convinced that he needed to retreat to a solitary inner island, commune with his healing muse, and return with new poetic gifts. He told the journalist

Geordie Greig, who asked to interview him for the *Tatler* after *Electric Light* was nominated for the T. S. Eliot Prize, "I am secluding myself for a couple of months."[19] On February 18, 2002, after dining with Prince Charles, he wrote Ron Schuchard about his social responsibilities: "[I just] saw off the Prince of Wales from Irish soil and my latest smiling public man stint ended." His civic duties, in fact, never ended. He made plans to attend his fiftieth reunion at St. Columb's College on May 10, receive an honorary degree from Charles University in Prague on May 15, and visit Milosz's home in Lithuania on May 19. "Even Kissinger would blench [at all my travelling]," he told Schuchard. "The truth is I am in panic at the way I've let things develop and it would be self-destructive madness to load on more, however right and true the occasion."[20] Schuchard had invited Heaney to Emory again, but this time he refused to go. He was tired of being an ambassador of poetry, shuttling from country to country the way Henry Kissinger did when he practiced his famous "shuttle diplomacy."

The strain of public appearances continued to affect Heaney's poetry. As he explained to a University of North Carolina graduate student, Elizabeth Lunday, frustration with the burdens of public speaking spurred him to translate the section from Aeschylus's *Agamemnon* where the "honour-bound" sentinel imagines losing his voice when his "tongue / Like the dropped gangplank of a cattle truck" is "trampled" and, as a result, he feels as if his mouth is "running piss and muck." Heaney wrote Lunday about getting interested in the *Oresteia* after returning from a Melbourne Writers Festival in 1994: "[I was in a] rage at myself for not having got enough writing done. So I sat down and gritted my teeth and very deliberately started . . . [translating the] Watchman's speech." He had played the honorable and honored public man to a fault at the festival and was tired of being "Mr. Niceguy."[21]

In an August 2002 lecture on Sorley MacLean at Edinburgh's International Book Festival, Heaney looked to the Scottish poet as a possible guide for navigating between social and personal obligations. MacLean had possessed a strong "puritan conscience" that drew him toward humanitarian service in the world as well as an equally strong artistic spirit that drew him toward the solitary study of a "Gaelic tradition of music and poetry." MacLean had felt conscience-bound to support the Republican cause during the Spanish Civil War, yet, unlike other members of his literary generation, he stayed at home on the Isle of Skye to write poetry, teach school, and care for his family. Heaney admired MacLean's poems about his conflicted allegiances to hearth culture and international culture, to self and others, and he considered MacLean's "Hallaig," which he translated from Gaelic, to be a testament to MacLean's "Orphic gift [that] had survived the test of awakening to the nightmare of history." Registering the shocks of a public crisis—the eviction of farmers from their lands during the Scottish "Clearances"—the poem was also a "dividend paid to MacLean by his lyric muse."[22] Like many of Heaney's best poems, it had arrived as a private gift, but it bore witness to crucial events in the public domain.

During his trip to South Africa in 2002, Heaney reflected again on the difficulty of navigating between conscience and muse. At Rhodes University on August 29, he gave a lecture, "The Guttural Muse," in which he elaborated on the Orphic "gift of tongues" that had inspired him to address the Troubles in his native country. At first ashamed of the dialect and accent he'd inherited from his farming ancestors, he'd hesitated to accept the private "givens" of his heritage. As for his conscience, one reason he was traveling to the southernmost tip of Africa to accept yet another honorary degree was because he wanted to pay tribute to the politically engaged scholar Malvern van Wyk Smith, who had tried to make "hope and history rhyme" in racially divided South Africa. Smith was another example of a principled intellectual who had united conscience with art.

Asked by the scholar Michael Roberts to participate in a commemoration of Samuel Beckett in 2003, Heaney felt he'd reached another limit. "From now on, I'm in retreat: 2003 a no-go area," he wrote Roberts. "Beckett-lessons to be learnt, even at this late stage. Hugh Kenner dubbed him an 'immobilist,' so leaf is being taken from that book."[23] Since many considered Heaney to be an extrovert with a passion for community service and Beckett to be a nihilistic introvert, Heaney's insistence that he shared more than a birthday (both were born on April 13) with Beckett usually made people laugh. Yet when overwhelmed by the world's demands, Heaney treated Beckett as a kindred spirit. His conscience, though, never allowed him to be immobile for long. After returning from South Africa, he traveled to New York for a public conversation about

Elizabeth Bishop, then headed to North Carolina for an exhibition of his work organized by Rand Brandes at Lenoir-Rhyne College. He returned to Harvard as the Ralph Waldo Emerson Poet in Residence and took an excursion to Lawrence, Massachusetts, to lecture on Robert Frost. Crossing the Atlantic again, he joined friends at Belfast's Lyric Theatre to honor his old mentor Philip Hobsbaum. And in mid-February he flew to St. Lucia to visit Derek Walcott. He also traveled to Atlanta for Emory's commencement on May 12, 2003, where he told the graduating students "to maintain that balance between the call to be true to your mysteriously essential inner self and the need equally to operate capably and self-respectingly in the outer world of affairs."[24] He was reminding his audience, but also himself, of the need to balance different commitments.

On a return trip to Emory in September 2003, Heaney celebrated President Bill Chace's retirement and spoke to Ron Schuchard about giving his papers to the university's special collections library. Although Harvard was also hoping to get the papers, Emory issued a formal announcement on September 23 that they had acquired them. Even though the university paid a substantial price, Heaney still considered them to be, at least in part, a gift and "a memorial to the work" President Chace had done "to extend the university's resources and strengthen its purpose."[25] He would later donate a smaller portion of his papers, which were valued at $2.2 million, to Ireland's National Library.

During his final years, Heaney continued to ponder the pros and cons of gift-giving, and he continued to send financial gifts to various causes. Among the numerous beneficiaries were the West of Ireland Cardiology Foundation, the Women's Peace Camp in Britain, the Irish-based group Concern Worldwide, the Inishbofin Community Arts Festival, the Ulster Cancer Foundation, and the Hope and History Campaign at Queen's University. On October 10, 2001, after being asked by the social activist Breda Keena to make a donation to Dublin's National Anti-Racism Awareness Programme, he wrote that "people in Ireland need only go back to the basics of their beliefs" to redress problems such as racism. Then he crossed out his message and wrote a new one: "Every time questions of racism and multi-culturalism come up, I realize that I was equipped to deal with them very early on." He sent Keena his poem "The Catechism," which consisted of two lines: "Who is my neighbor? / My neighbor is all mankind."[26] For

Heaney, "Catholicism"—at least according to its root meaning—was a "universal" doctrine that supported diversity, inclusiveness, and charitable gift-giving.

## MYSTERY CULTS AND GIFTS

In late 2003, Heaney hired builders to renovate Glanmore Cottage. To keep it like Mossbawn, though, he didn't want a lot of new appliances installed that would distract him and make it easy for people to contact him. In the end, there was no landline, no TV, a poor BBC radio signal, and spotty cell phone service. He carried an iBook now (he generally shunned computers), but he still preferred writing with a fountain pen. As he aged, he also grew more preoccupied with the past—and often with the distant past—than with the present. Unfazed by recent criticism that his aesthetic tastes were increasingly archaic, he began translating another Greek tragedy, Sophocles's *Antigone,* which had been written around 441 BC. Heaney planned to highlight parallels between the political turmoil surrounding a civil war in ancient Thebes, which was the subject of the play, and recent wars in Northern Ireland, Afghanistan, and Iraq.

In *Antigone,* a despotic king named Creon rises to power after Antigone's two brothers, Eteocles and Polyneices, die fighting each other in the war caused by Eteocles's refusal to follow through on his promise to rule Thebes with his brother. To punish Polyneices for attacking Thebes, King Creon refuses to grant him burial rites because, according to Theban law, traitors are not granted such rites. Heaney's "Note" in the American edition of his translation contends that President Bush was a latter-day Creon who had a similarly simplistic view of right and wrong: Bush believed American citizens were either "in favour of state security" by going to war against Iraq's leader, Saddam Hussein, or they were "on the wrong side in 'the war on terror.'"[27] Once again, Heaney was going back to the past to evaluate the present.

The most consequential dispute in Heaney's translation, *The Burial at Thebes,* is between Antigone and Creon. Antigone insists on her right to honor familial and cultural traditions by burying her brother; Creon denies her request because he regards Polyneices as a criminal. The prophet Tiresias warns Creon that his refusal to allow Antigone to bury her brother is a mistake. In the end, Antigone disobeys Creon's injunction. She recovers her dead brother from the battlefield and buries him. In response, Creon expels Antigone from Thebes, and multiple disasters ensue: Antigone hangs herself, her fiancé fatally wounds himself with his sword, and Creon's wife commits suicide. All these deaths occur shortly after Creon has decided to rescind his orders and accept the traditional view that "Religion dictates the burial of the dead."[28] It's too late; Tiresias's prophecy has come true.

Some critics were skeptical of Heaney's way of turning a play written in the fifth century BC into an allegory for President Bush's "War on Terror." Like so many poems Heaney wrote at the time, his translation amounts to a Eucharistic homage to the dead. Antigone honors the dead, just as Heaney honors the dead Sophocles, but it was no easy task to convince contemporary audiences that ancient political conflicts resembled wars in the twenty-first century. After *The Burial at Thebes* premiered at the Abbey Theatre on April 5, 2004, as part of its centennial celebrations, many reviewers were nonplussed. Michael Billington in the *Guardian* complained that the play lacked "political animus" and "cultural specificity."[29] Neil Corcoran in the same newspaper said he'd expected the play to "crackle with poetic, political and cultural static" like Heaney's earlier poems about the Troubles, but there was little of the old linguistic energy.[30] The critic Paul Taylor was also disappointed, claiming in the *Independent* that Heaney's allusions to current events were awkward and unconvincing. Heaney's text, in fact, often resorted to clichés and hackneyed expressions to make its points. Antigone's sister says, "I want to throw myself / Like a lifeline to you in your sea of troubles." Creon remarks about his son, "He has other fields to plough." When the king refers to rebelliousness in his family, he says, "That is a bitter pill to have to swallow"[31]

During the first years of the new millennium, Heaney returned to Greek, Roman, and Christian classics that dramatized losses and gains in gift-exchange relationships. When Milosz died on August 14, 2004, he published a eulogy in the *Guardian* that alluded to a mysterious gift exchange in Sophocles's *Oedipus at Colonus*. At the beginning of that play, Oedipus enters a grove sacred to the Eumenides in Colonus, a city in southeastern Greece, and the Chorus tells him that he has to leave. As a notorious sinner who has killed his father and married his mother, he has no right to be trespassing on sacred ground. Theseus, the king of Athens, is more lenient and gives Oedipus credit for his years of penitential wandering. "I am sorry for you," Theseus says. "And I should like to know what favor here / You hope for from the city and me." Oedipus asks for a simple gift—permission to be buried in the sacred wood—and he agrees to reciprocate with a countergift if his request is granted. He tells Theseus, "I come to give you something, and the gift / Is my own beaten self." That "self," he adds rather cryptically, "[contains] a more lasting grace than beauty." Theseus wants to know more about this "gift," but Oedipus says the king must "wait to be enlightened."[32]

Shortly before Oedipus dies, he promises that his mysterious gift will bring power and success to those, such as Theseus and the Athenians, who treated him with generosity during his nomadic life. Theseus, it turns out, is the only person who learns the precise nature of the gift and where it will be given. "I'll lead you to the place where I must die," Oedipus tells the Athenian king. "But you must never tell it to any man." Oedipus assures Theseus that the gifts he is about to give are greater "than many shields and many neighbors' spears," but they are also "mysteries, not to be explained."[33] Oedipus's essential gift seems to be the spirit or life force in his body. When he commits his body to the ground, his spirit will establish an enduring bond between the Earth, the Athenians, and their gods. As in Greek mystery cults, his sacrificial gift will ensure the land's and the community's productivity. Heaney was so enthralled by this story that he planned to translate Sophocles's entire play. He only abandoned the idea after he learned that his poet friend Eamon Grennan was about to publish a translation of *Oedipus at Colonus* with Oxford University Press.

The lines from the play that Heaney translated for Milosz's eulogy are spoken by a messenger who has failed to witness Oedipus's death and descent into the underworld. Nevertheless, the messenger observes, "That man surely went / In step with a guide he trusted down to where / Light has gone out but the door stands open." In the rest of the eulogy, titled "In Gratitude for All the Gifts," Heaney expounds on Milosz's attributes as a writer, political activist, and religious man. He invokes Milosz's assertion in *The Separate Notebooks* that "There are nothing but gifts on this poor, poor Earth,"[34] and quotes from Milosz's short poem "Thankfulness," which begins: "You gave me gifts, God-Enchanter. / I give you thanks for good and ill."[35] On August 14, 2004, the day Heaney got a telephone call about Milosz's death, he said the news made him think of the poem "Gift" and Milosz's remark: "One can believe in God out of gratitude for all the gifts."[36]

An enchantment with gifts characterizes "Out of This World," the elegy Heaney wrote after going to Milosz's funeral on August 27, 2004, in Krakow's Mariacki Church. In the poem, Heaney bows "during the consecration of the bread and wine," receives "the mystery" of God's presence on his tongue, and refuses to "disavow words like 'thanksgiving' or 'host' / or 'communion bread.'" The Polish mass brings back memories of a mass in the subterranean church Heaney visited during his early pilgrimage to Lourdes. At Milosz's funeral, he may not proclaim the Nicene Creed (the "*unam sanctum catholicam* acoustic") with the fervent faith of his youth, but he still acknowledges the "catholic" or universal significance of the Church's liturgy and rituals. To Heaney, the Eucharist remains an apt expression of gratitude for what Milosz called the "God-Enchanter's" gifts. From Heaney's "monomythical" point of view, Demeter and Persephone at Eleusis, Oedipus in the sacred grove at Colonus, Jesus at the Last Supper in Jerusalem, God at the moment of Creation, and Milosz in Krakow are all heroic gift-makers and gift-givers.

As the twenty-first century gained momentum, Heaney's life seemed to devolve into an endless series of gift-giving and gift-receiving rituals. On January 23, 2005, he joined friends bearing presents to Derek Walcott on St. Lucia at a party celebrating his seventy-fifth birthday. In May, it was his turn to receive presents after entertaining the empress and emperor of Japan at Glanmore Cottage. Empress Michiko sent him a photograph with a chrysanthemum emblem on it. This was special, since the chrysanthemum was a symbol for happiness, health, and longevity usually used in correspondence with heads of state. On June 2, at the opening of the Jenwood Centre in Grasmere, England, Heaney used the occasion to praise the archive of Wordsworth's letters, books, paintings, and other artifacts as a great gift. "The voluntary gifting from the Wordsworth family alone makes [this] . . . place worthy and proper as a centre of romantic and Wordsworth studies," he said.[37] This "voluntary gifting" may have prompted Heaney to "gift" his substantial collection of papers to Ireland's

National Library in 2012. It was another example of the way a generous gift could bring people together.

A month after his talk in Grasmere, Heaney discoursed on the social benefits of gifts again—this time at the museum in Silkeborg, Denmark, where the Tollund Man and numerous artifacts related to the apocalyptic End Times of Ragnarök had been displayed. Ever the allegorist, he pointed out typological correspondences between the disaster scenario in Norse mythology and the modern disasters of terrorism and climate change. But he was mainly interested in the Norse artifacts as gifts intended to create productive bonds between different people and between communities and their gods. Saluting the archaeologists who had discovered the artifacts, Heaney compared their digging to the sort of poetic digging he'd done throughout his career: "For the archaeologist, coming upon the buried shard can be as thrilling as coming upon the buried city, just as for the poet, the gift of a perfect three line lyric can be as gratifying and immortal as the achievement of a three part epic. Physical size, commercial value, importance in the eyes of the world, these considerations are not the primary ones."[38]

Heaney's visit to the Silkeborg Museum inspired a six-part sonnet sequence, "The Tollund Man in Springtime," which became the centerpiece for his 2006 book *District and Circle*. In *Wintering Out*, he had predicted that he would feel "lost, / Unhappy and at home" while visiting the Tollund Man in Denmark. In 2005, as a global celebrity who never felt completely "at home" anywhere, he had all the more reason to identify with the ancient man who had been uprooted from his bog and put on display for the multitudes in a city. Adopting the Tollund Man as his persona, Heaney said he was "neither god nor ghost, / Not at odds or at one, but simply lost." Like Heaney, he pines for his original home—his *omphalos* —in the bog. When Heaney says at the end of the sonnet sequence, "I straightened, spat on my hands, felt benefit, / And spirited myself into the street," he indicates his resolve to set things right.

Heaney's revenant Tollund Man is akin to the "familiar compound ghost" who accompanies a despondent T. S. Eliot in "Little Gidding" as he patrols London's wreckage during the Blitz. Eliot's Dantesque communion with the ghost discloses "the gifts reserved for age," which include an awareness of the body's decline, the "impotence of rage / At human folly," and guilt over "things ill done and done to others' harm."[39] The gifts disclosed during Heaney's communion with the Tollund Man's spirit are similarly distressing, but they motivate his search for redemption. With a "Newfound contrariness / In check-out lines, at cash-points, in those queues / Of wired, far-faced smilers," he affirms the gifts from his down-to-earth past and resists the seductive commodities that surround him at every turn in the city. To demonstrate his contempt for modern commercial culture, he carries what is valuable to him: not cash, but "Tollund rushes—roots and all— / Bagged in their own bog-damp." The vegetation is an emblem of the geographical and genealogical roots of his gift.

The title poem, "District and Circle," is another sonnet sequence that registers Heaney's attitudes toward gift exchange and monetary exchange. Here he assumes the role of Aeneas, who, like the Tollund Man, travels between the living and the dead with the help of a gift: the golden bough. Before Heaney descends into his modern-day Hades (London's District and Circle underground line), he contemplates exchanging gifts with an Orpheus-like or Charon-like tin-whistler who offers music to passing crowds at a tube station. Heaney "trigger[s] and untrigger[s] a hot coin" in his pocket, debating whether to give it or keep it. Perhaps he would have preferred donating something akin to the Tollund Man's "rushes— roots and all." In the end, he heads to a subway car without giving the musician anything. "Had I betrayed or not, myself or him?" he asks as the car rumbles along like his guilty conscience. Impersonating a shade in a circle of Dante's *Inferno,* he wonders if he has committed a sin of omission and wonders if he has inherited his father's parsimonious temperament. He also suggests that some art should be shared and accepted as a free gift.

*District and Circle* chronicles a variety of gift exchanges, some of which transport Heaney into a "precinct of vision" (as he calls it in "Out of the Bag") and others that plunge him into an inferno of consternation and guilt. "Helmet" refers to a "Boston fireman's gift" that Bobby Breen gave him at a Cambridge poetry reading. Though Heaney shows gratitude for the gift, the "scarlet letters on its spread / Fantailing brim" make him feel ashamed, since he never "served time" under any sort of helmet. He wishes he could think of himself as a Boston fireman like Breen or one of the Beowulf-like firemen who heroically saved people at the World Trade

Center after the September 11 explosions. Instead, he feels more like a guilty Hester Prynne in *The Scarlet Letter*.

Other poems in *District and Circle* confess to shame or guilt over failing to take strong stands in a world wracked by injustices. The book's introductory poem, "The Turnip-Snedder," describes a hand-operated machine at Mossbawn as if it were a monument to someone's formidable stance. The snedder, which "dug its heels in among wooden tubs / and troughs of slops" to chop up vegetables "in an age of bare hands / and cast iron," harks back to the Iron Age cultures of the Tollund Man and Beowulf. The snedder has "body armour" and brandishes "a barrel-chested breast-plate // standing guard / on four braced greaves." It seems ready to repel whatever hostilities come its way. The book's second poem, "A Shiver," recognizes another obdurate stance, this time taken by someone who "stand[s] to swing the sledge" with "knees locked" and "lower back shock-fast / As shields in a testudo." The trembling in the earth from the sledgehammer "that could make air of a wall" is a reminder of the earthquake felt by New Yorkers when the walls of the World Trade Center fell. Breastplates, greaves, shields, and testudoes are types of ancient armor used by those trying to stand up to or stand against whatever threatens to knock them down.

Like Robert Frost, who envisioned the world as a place divided between those who wanted to build walls and those who wanted to tear them down, Heaney in *District and Circle* obsessively imagines walls rising and falling. The poems accentuate the need for "walling in" treasured gifts and "walling out" the forces that threaten them. Early in his career, he'd lamented childhood walls breaking down, and as a newly married man he implored his wife to "arrange the world / Within our walls, within our golden ring." The wedding gift of a "golden ring" was supposed to provide the security of a walled ring-fort. Heaney's title *District and Circle* alludes to the same sort of protective rings and boundaries that he'd espoused in his early marriage poems. Now, whether imagining a "moulded verge" as a "stockade" and "bulwark" in "Polish Sleepers," or a "cast-iron pump" as an ancient Greek boundary "herm" in "Quitting Time," or "sentries . . . guarding every locked-up hurt and secret" in "Cavafy," he concludes that certain fences "make good neighbors" by creating the stability needed for productive gift exchanges.

The matter of taking a strong stand—or simply standing on one's feet—became more crucial when Heaney suffered a stroke in 2006 after another summer of hectic travels. In Donegal with David Hammond, John Hume, Peter Fallon, and other friends to celebrate Anne Friel's birthday, Heaney woke in the middle of the night unable to move his left leg and left arm. One of the guests, Desmond Kavanagh, called medical personnel while his wife, a physiotherapist, tried to keep Heaney and Marie calm. Paramedics soon arrived, and Fallon helped Heaney get to the ambulance, which drove him about thirty miles west of Londonderry/Derry to a hospital in Letterkenny. After Heaney regained movement in his left foot, another ambulance drove him to Dublin, where he began five weeks of physical therapy at the Royal Hospital, Donnybrook.

One unexpected hospital visitor was Bill Clinton, who had flown to Ireland for a meeting with the Irish president and a social gathering at the Ryder Cup golf tournament. In between official duties, the former American president spent a half hour talking to Heaney. With Clinton, Heaney tried to dismiss his health troubles with humor, just as he'd done on September 19, when he wrote Derek Mahon, "Theology professor Jim Mackey once averred that 'original sin was only a temporary setback.' Thus, happily, it is with my stroke."[40] To others, Heaney remarked sardonically that "the curse of Field Day" had laid him low.[41] In early October, he had to be transferred to St. Vincent's Private Hospital for more procedures. Concerned about his slow, erratic heartbeat, doctors soon installed a pacemaker.

### REMEMBERING THE GIFT-GIVERS

On March 18, 2009, Heaney got another opportunity to pay tribute to gift-givers and their gifts when he received the David Cohen Prize for lifetime achievement. At a ceremony in London, he thanked Andrew Motion and the other judges for giving him the prize and said he viewed it as a "corroboration" for "somebody whose first poems were published under the pseudonym Incertus—somebody not sure, uncertain." He considered reading his prose poem "The wanderer" about the gift of a half crown he'd received at Anahorish School when he was twelve, but opted for "The Underground" to express his "gratitude for all that London and the people I have known in London have given by way of literary inspiration and confirmation." He told his audience that the other poem he would read, "A Drink of Water," was "about receiving a gift and being enjoined to 'remember the giver.'"[42] The Cohen Prize brought with it a check for £40,000 (worth about $70,000 at the time) and another check for £12,500 (worth about $17,500) that he could give to a charity of his choice. (He donated the money to Ireland's Poetry Aloud, an annual poetry-speaking competition for post–primary school students.)

Heaney's last book, *Human Chain,* published on September 2, 2010, and his posthumously published translation *Aeneid Book VI* revisit themes of mythical journeys and ritual thanksgivings. As if realizing the end of his career was near, he returned to one of the mythical narratives that had captivated him from the start: Aeneas's descent to the underworld. Like Aeneas, he wanted to commune with precursors who'd made his remarkable career possible. The first poems in *Human Chain* recollect family relationships, his difficult departure from Mossbawn to St. Columb's, his parents' gift of a Conway Stewart fountain pen, and his early struggles as a scholar and writer. As an older man, anxious about his infirmities and mourning the loss of loved ones, he honored his enablers. "Chanson d'Aventure" adapts the medieval genre of poetic songs to recount the way friends came to his aid after his stroke at the Friel's party. The poem expresses his fear of being separated from his wife during the high-speed drive to the hospital. "Hooked-up [to a] drip-feed" in the ambulance, he can do nothing but lie back and ponder the *"aventure."* When he remarks that his and his wife's "postures all the journey [were] still the same," he points to the bond, which resembles the restorative "drip-feed" in the ambulance, that has sustained him whether he and his wife were together or apart.

Gifts of sustenance appear throughout *Human Chain.* The title poem juxtaposes sacks of grain distributed by aid workers in an impoverished country with sacks of grain Heaney once handled on his family farm. He plays on the phrase "to give purchase" in a description of heaving a sack of grain onto a trailer and getting something valuable (a "purchase") in return. His gain comes in the form of a "quick unburdening, backbreak's truest payback / A letting go which will not come again." Here and elsewhere, he intimates that his compulsion to "pay back" has been both uplifting and backbreaking, liberating and constraining. The conclusion of the poem implies that total freedom from this sort of give-and-take will only come in death—in the final "letting go" when one's body is unburdened "once. And for all."

Many of the most memorable poems in *Human Chain* are those in which Heaney adopts the familiar role of a pilgrim following the footsteps of Orpheus, Odysseus, Aeneas, Virgil, and Dante into the underworld. Gifts enable these journeys and the communions with shades along the way. The second poem in the book, "Album," retraces Aeneas's famous *katabasis*—his descent to the land of the dead made possible by the golden bough, which he plants by the Groves of the Fortunate Ones. The passage from the sixth book of the *Aeneid* that haunts *Human Chain* is the one where Aeneas turns his gaze from the shade of his dead father to the meadow by the river Lethe, where "spirits destined to live a second life / In the body" gather to drink. The water "heals their anxieties and obliterates / All trace of memory." This restoration allows Anchises to converse with his son about "the future glory of the Trojan race" that will make their names "illustrious." During their talk, he predicts the gods will take "the gift / Of . . . life" from some of their noble descendants, and he tells his son: "Load my arms with lilies, let me scatter / Purple flowers, let me lavish these gifts at least / On the soul of my inheritor and perform / My unavailing duty."[43]

Having felt duty-bound to perform gift-exchange rituals his whole life, Heaney translates parts of this section of the *Aeneid* in "The Riverbank Field," interspersing Virgil's descriptions of Elysium with images of the fields and rivers around his own Elysium—Mossbawn. He tells the story of a journey to his childhood home in "Route 110," the impressive twelve-part poem that starts with an exchange in which a Sybil-like woman at a Belfast market sells him a used copy of the *Aeneid VI*. He leaves with his "purchase / In . . . a deckle-edged brown paper bag" that harks back to the bag of grain he gains "purchase" on in "Human Chain." As in the previous poem, which contrasts "soldiers / Firing over the mob" with the good deeds of aid workers, "Route 110" showcases heroic peace-building efforts in a world of violence and death. The bus taking Heaney home reminds him of Charon's barge as it passes by dead neighbors and blown-up friends. On this dismal journey, gifts act as guiding beacons. One gift in

particular—"a votive jampot" with oat stalks wrapped in glittering foil—
serves as a makeshift golden bough.

After encountering an assortment of shades in "Route 110," Heaney
arrives at an Elysian "riverbank field" near Mossbawn. Here he slips
into the role of a gift-giving Anchises. He turns his gaze from "the age of
ghosts" to "the age of births," and appears to regift Mrs. Nick's "bunch of
stalks and silvered heads // Like tapers" to his granddaughter, Anna Rose,
who was born in 2006. The gift is meant to bind past, present, and future
generations in a human chain. At the end of "Route 110," he calls the
silver-headed stalks, which were originally given to him by a Mossbawn
neighbor, a Eucharistic "thank-offering for one / Whose long wait on the
shaded bank has ended." Through the looking glass of the *Aeneid,* Anna
Rose resembles one of the mysterious souls who has waited a thousand
years in Elysium to receive the gift of life.

The Irish writer Colm Tóibín wrote in the *Guardian* that *Human Chain*
was Heaney's "best single volume for many years."[44] Reviewing the volume for the *Independent,* Sean O'Brien referred to it as a "very rich and
substantial collection."[45] Robert Tracy in the *Irish University Review* said
Heaney's new book revealed him "at the height of his powers."[46] Eamon
Grennan agreed with this assessment in the *Irish Times,* praising Heaney's
"customary strength and subtlety."[47] These reviews written by Heaney's
friends, however, seemed more eager to applaud Heaney's career than to
grapple with the book's aesthetic merits. The poet-critic William Logan
offered a more discriminating assessment in the *New York Times* that
compared Heaney to Robert Frost and argued that the distractions of
fame had compromised the imaginations of both poets. "There's a state
of innocence poets need, a state hard to reach when they've been frog-
marched out of paradise to the memorial dinners and honorary degrees of
experience," Logan wrote. "Many of Heaney's new poems start with the
old flair and dash, but after a few lines they lose their way and sputter out.
The late work has been solid, composed to a high level of craftsmanship;
but the poems are like footnotes to poems already written, with all of his
mastery but little of his passion and less of his subdued outrage. They become that evil thing, poems written for the sake of writing poems."[48] As
the acknowledgments and dedications in *Human Chain* indicate, many of
his new poems were written out of a sense of obligation to others.

Heaney had once made comments similar to Logan's about William Wordsworth, a poet whose career in some ways resembled Heaney's. "As the years proceeded," Heaney wrote about the esteemed English poet, "Wordsworth became more an institution than an individual. It is an impression reinforced by the sonorous expatiation of his later poetry and the roll call of his offices and associations—friend of the aristocracy, Distributor of Stamps for Westmoreland, Poet Laureate. He had lost the path that should have kept leading more confidently and deeply inward; still vivid as an intelligence, nationally celebrated, domestically fortified, he ended up industriously but for the most part unrewardingly marking time as a poet."[49]

Like most of Heaney's books, *Human Chain* was both nationally and internationally celebrated. It garnered Britain's Forward Poetry Prize (£10,000) and the Irish Times Poetry Now Award (€5,000). It was shortlisted for Canada's lucrative Griffin Poetry Prize. In a couple of years, Heaney would win the Griffin Lifetime Recognition Award and the AWB Vincent Literary Award for lifetime achievement from the American Ireland Fund. During the Vincent Award ceremony in Cork, Ireland, on June 27, 2012, he told the audience, which included Bill Clinton and the Taoiseach Enda Kenny, that a woman from Mayo had told him many years before that he was "steeped in luck." He mentioned that his father had been "a silent man" who "regarded speech as an affectation," and said he was tempted to follow his father's example and remain silent about all his good luck. Then he made an eloquent speech placing prizes and gifts in the context of Aristotle's discussion of "magnificence" in the *Nicomachean Ethics*. A person demonstrated magnificence, according to Aristotle, by giving "gifts and counter-gifts . . . for the good of public things so that even the private gifts have some resemblance to votive offerings."[50] Gifts should contribute to public improvement, Aristotle said, and also be symbols of thanksgiving for the gift-giving gods. Heaney concluded his remarks by telling his benefactors, "I thank you very much for all the gifts."[51] Then he read "A Drink of Water" about remembering gift-givers.

On March 20, 2013, Heaney returned to the idea of "magnificence" in a speech introducing the exhibition *History of Ireland in 100 Objects* at the National Museum of Ireland. He was there, he said, to "pay tribute to . . . this magnificent venture." On display were artifacts such as Mesolithic fish traps and Neolithic axe-heads that reminded him of the premodern world he'd known as a farmboy. He again spoke up for a culture that valued making, preserving, and distributing well-made artifacts as gifts rather than a culture obsessed with marketing commodities and accumulating money. He hoped that the display would remind Irish citizens that they were "not simply a credit rating or a [capitalist] economy but a history and a culture, a human population rather than a statistical phenomenon." He continued:

> When we think of things preserved from the past we often use the expression "handed down"—"handed down" instead of the more abstract "inherited." "Inherited" is slightly legalistic whereas "handed down" presupposes the physical handover of a gift; it situates the exchange in a social context, implies a kind of handshake. And it is that sensation of human contact, of a covenant with the past, of an at-homeness experienced in silence and stillness, it is that combination of distance and familiarity which can give us some sense of belonging with those who have gone before. So it might be said that if we have inherited a debt, we have also been handed down a treasury.

For Heaney, the treasures on display "were no one person's property; they belonged to everybody."[52] Like Aristotle's "magnificent" votive offerings, these Irish gifts established covenants between givers and receivers that helped unify a community.

Heaney remained candid about the benefits and burdens of gift exchanges to the end of his life. In one of his last poems, "On the Gift of a Fountain Pen," which he read at Baylor University on March 4, 2013 (the poem was published as a broadside for the university's Beall Poetry Festival), he wondered if he'd betrayed his gift by devoting so much energy to "public things." The poem alludes to lines in Keats's sonnet "When I Have Fears That I May Cease to Be" that express Keats's fear that he might die before his pen has "gleaned . . . [his] teeming brain," and his "love and fame to nothingness do sink." Heaney's "Gift of a Fountain Pen" also cites Jesus's Golden Rule in the Bible. In Matthew's rendition of the Sermon on the Mount, Jesus warns that some people don't deserve or appreciate gifts: "Give not that which is holy unto the dogs, neither cast ye your pearls before swine, lest they trample them under their feet, and turn against and rend you" (Matthew 7:6). Jesus advocates pragmatic generosity and compares the smart gift-giver to a father who knows what to give his children. "If ye then . . . know how to give good gifts unto your children," Jesus says, "how much more shall your Father which is in heaven give good things to them that ask him. Therefore, all things whatsoever ye would that men should do to you, do ye even so to them: for this is the law" (7:11–12). Jesus commands his followers to emulate God's gift-giving, but Heaney questions "All that 'Do unto others / As you would have done unto you'" rhetoric in the Bible. He wonders if Jesus was "mistaken." Once again, he circles back to his Incertus self: "I dip and fill [my pen with ink] / And start again, doubts / Or no doubts. Heigh-ho."

Richard Rankin Russell, the English professor who organized Heaney's visit to Baylor, remembered, "He inflected that concluding 'Heigh-ho' with weariness, then instantly looked up and smiled."[53] Heaney had read to an audience of nine hundred at Emory University and given several other readings before ending his tour in Waco, Texas, so he was tired. At Baylor, one thousand people packed into a concert hall, despite the fact that one of the most talented female basketball players, Brittany Griner, was playing her final home game on campus. Heaney was gracious as ever. He read poems Russell requested, dutifully answered questions from the audience, and entertained his hosts at a three-hour dinner. If Heaney felt weighed down by all the "obligation[s] / Imposed and undertaken," he kept singing in his human chains like Dylan Thomas in "Fern Hill."

Heaney's health deteriorated during the months after his return to Dublin. In August 2013, he stumbled on some restaurant steps after a lunch with Peter Fallon, hit his head, and went to St. Vincent's hospital, where doctors discovered he had a split aorta and would need risky heart surgery. He was transferred to Blackrock Clinic a short distance from his home. He texted his wife "Noli timere"—Don't be afraid—on August 30, 2013, as orderlies wheeled him to the operating room. The Latin command had been given by a biblical angel to calm Joseph's fears after he discovered the Holy Spirit had delivered a miraculous gift to his wife—a divine son. Jesus had also used the phrase when his disciples were disturbed by a vision of the Holy Spirit walking over the water during a storm (Matthew 1:20, 14:27). Fifteen minutes after texting his wife, Heaney died.

During the subsequent days and weeks, there was a global outpouring of grief and gratitude. Marie expressed the sentiments of many when she said, "He was . . . an extraordinarily kind person who used to spend his life doing things for people."[54] The Irish people felt especially bereft. To show their appreciation for all Heaney had done for their country, eighty thousand fans at an All Ireland Gaelic Football match gave him a three-minute ovation. His funeral in Donnybrook's Sacred Heart Church in south Dublin attracted both ordinary citizens and global celebrities. Irish president Michael Higgins, Sinn Féin leader Gerry Adams, and U2 star Bono attended. In their eulogies, Heaney's family and friends praised his genius and generosity. Bill Clinton told the press, "Both his stunning work and his life were a gift to the world. His mind, heart, and his uniquely Irish gift for language made him our finest poet of the rhythms of ordinary lives and a powerful voice for peace. . . . His wonderful work . . . will be a lasting gift for all the world."[55] The scholar Roy Foster said something similar: "He possessed what he himself ascribed to Yeats, 'the gift of establishing authority within a culture.' . . . Generosity, amplitude and sympathy characterized his dealings with people at every level."[56]

A man from Armagh named Pat McParland told a *Guardian* journalist at the funeral a typical story about Heaney's charitable nature. He and his fiancée had met Heaney by chance at a Dublin restaurant on the night they got engaged. "We kept getting mobile phone calls as people rang in to congratulate us," McParland said. "Seamus must have overheard us and went over to wish us all the very best. Then he pulled out a poetry collection which contained his [marriage] poem 'Scaffolding.' He then wrote a couple of verses from that poem into the book by hand and then gave it to us as an engagement present. This gift from Seamus has become a very precious thing for Joanne and myself."[57] At an early age, Heaney knew he'd been blessed with extraordinary gifts, and throughout his life, "doubts / Or no doubts," he shared those gifts with others at home and around the world.

# Notes

ABBREVIATIONS

APPR    Seamus Heaney. "The Art of Poetry." Interview by Henri Cole. *Paris Review,* no. 75 (1997). www.theparisreview.org/interviews/1217/the-art-of-poetry-no-75-seamus-Heaney.

P    Seamus Heaney. *Preoccupations: Selected Prose 1968–1978.* London: Faber and Faber, 1980.

RP    Seamus Heaney. *The Redress of Poetry.* New York: Farrar, Straus and Giroux, 1995.

SHLP-NLI    Seamus Heaney Literary Papers. National Library of Ireland.

SHP-EU    Seamus Heaney Papers. Emory University. These papers are stored in the Stuart A. Rose Manuscript, Archives, and Rare Book Library at Emory University.

SS    Dennis O'Driscoll. *Stepping Stones: Interviews with Seamus Heaney.* New York: Farrar, Straus and Giroux, 2008.

In the endnotes, "Heaney" refers to Seamus Heaney. To avoid cluttering the book with superscript endnote numbers, I deliberately didn't give page numbers for quotations from Heaney's poems. Most of the poems are readily available online or can be found easily in his books.

INTRODUCTION

1. Heaney, *APPR.*

2. Michael Ross, "The Art of Rhyme and Reason," *Sunday Times of London,* October 24, 1999, "Eire Culture," 4.

3. Michael Huey, "Interview: Seamus Heaney," *Christian Science Monitor,* January 9, 1989, 16.

4. June Beisch, "An Interview with Seamus Heaney," *Literary Review* 29, no. 2 (Winter 1986): 165.

5. John Breslin, "Seeing Things: John Breslin Interviews Seamus Heaney," *Critic* 46, no. 2 (Winter 1991): 32.

6. Nicholas Wroe, "Son of the Soil," *Guardian,* October 9, 1999, "Books."

7. Michael Huey, "Interview: Seamus Heaney," *Christian Science Monitor,* January 9, 1989, 16.

8. Heaney, "A Poet's Blessing," *Listener,* April 19, 1984, 13.

9. Heaney, *The Government of the Tongue* (London: Faber and Faber, 1988), 163.

10. Heaney, "The Ugly Suckling," *New Republic,* August 11–18, 1986, 34; Heaney, "Anubis of Cwmdonkin Drive," *Irish Times,* September 2, 1989, "Weekend," 9.

11. Heaney, "Full Face," *Irish Times,* April 1, 1978, "Weekend," 3.

12. Heaney, "Bowstring, Harpstring," *Sunday Tribune,* June 23, 1985, 20.

13. Heaney, "An Authentic Poetic Voice," *Boston Globe,* February 9, 1986, 30.

14. Heaney, "A Poet Remembered," *Scotsman,* January 27, 1996, 16.

15. Heaney, "Unresting Death," *Observer,* October 9, 1988, 44.

16. Heaney, "Laureate in the Time of Catastrophe," *Irish Times,* December 17, 1988, 9.

17. Heaney, "What the Applause Was About," *New York Times Book Review,* November 8, 1987, 63.

18. Theo Dorgan, "Seamus Heaney," RTÉ NewsNow, August 30, 2013, www.youtube.com/watch.

19. Marcel Mauss, *The Gift: The Form and Reason for Exchange in Archaic Societies,* trans. W. D. Halls (London: Routledge, 1990), 13, 16.

20. Heaney, "Kavanagh of the Parish," *Listener,* April 26, 1979, 577.

21. O'Driscoll, *SS,* 318.

22. Heaney, "Kavanagh of the Parish," 578, 577.

23. Robert McCrum, "Seamus Heaney: A Life of Rhyme," July 18, 2009, www.theguardian.com/books/2009/jul/19/seamus-Heaney-interview.

24. Patrick Garland, "Poets on Poetry," *Listener,* November 8, 1973, 629.

25. Heaney, *Beowulf* (New York: Farrar, Straus and Giroux, 2000), xiv.

26. Leon Wieseltier, "Czeslaw Milosz, 1911–2004," *New York Times,* September 12, 2004, www.nytimes.com/2004/09/12/books/review/czeslaw-milosz-19112004.html.

27. Czeslaw Milosz, *The Collected Poems, 1931–1987* (New York: Ecco, 1988), 438.

28. Neil Corcoran, "Seamus Heaney Obituary," *Guardian,* August 30, 2013, www.theguardian.com/books/2013/aug/30/seamus-Heaney.

29. Heaney, "In Gratitude for All the Gifts," *Guardian,* September 11, 2004, 4.

30. Joseph Campbell, *The Hero with a Thousand Faces* (Princeton, NJ: Princeton University Press, 1949), 30, italics original.

31. Heaney, "'Apt Admonishment': Wordsworth as an Example," *Hudson Review* 61, no. 1 (Spring 2008): 21–28.

32. Lewis Hyde, *The Gift: Creativity and the Artist in the Modern World* (New York: Vintage, 2007), 195.

33. Heaney, *Opened Ground: Selected Poems, 1966–1996* (New York: Farrar, Straus and Giroux, 1998), 415.

34. Heaney, *APPR.*

35. Karl Miller, *Seamus Heaney in Conversation with Karl Miller* (London: Between the Lines, 2000), 53.

36. Bel Mooney, *London Times,* October 11, 1984, 8.

37. "Why I Write," *Inscape '95,* 1995, Pasadena City College, 8–11.

38. Padraic Fiacc, "Seamus Heaney," *Hibernia,* May 1968, 23.

39. Robert Druce, "A Raindrop on a Thorn," *Dutch Quarterly Review* 9, no. 1 (1979): 27.

40. Heaney, *An Open Letter* (Londonderry/Derry: Field Day Theatre Company, 1983), n.p.

41. Heaney, *APPR.*

42. Bill Lewis, "Seamus Heaney," *Arkansas Gazette,* May 20, 1984, 10C.

43. O'Driscoll, *SS,* 65.

44. Seamus Deane, "Unhappy and at Home," *Crane Bag* (Spring 1977): 62.

45. O'Driscoll, *SS,* 373.

46. Hyde, *The Gift,* 199.

47. Joseph Conrad, *The Nigger of the Narcissus* (New York: Doubleday, Page, 1926), xi–xii.

## 1. ANCESTRAL GIFTS

1. Robert Lowell, *History* (New York: Farrar, Straus and Giroux, 1973), 115.

2. Heaney, *APPR.*

3. Heaney, *APPR.*

4. Heaney to Peter Fallon, September 12, 2000, SHP-EU.

5. Tom Adair, "Calling the Tune," *Linen Hall Review* 6, no. 2 (1989): 6.

6. Marshall Sahlins, *Stone Age Economics* (Chicago: Aldine-Atherton, 1972), 205–6, 182.

7. O'Driscoll, *SS,* 222.

8. Heaney, fax to Suzanne O'Brien, March 16, 1998, SHP-EU.

9. Heaney, *Boy Driving His Father to Confession* (Farnham, UK: Sceptre, 1970), n.p.

10. Heaney to Wilhelm Brockhaus, June 3, 1996, SHP-EU.

11. "Belfast Group Poetry," SHP-EU.

12. Heaney, *Cuchulainn and Ferdiad,* March 23, 1973, p. 12, SHP-EU.

13. Heaney, *Opened Ground,* 415.

14. Heaney, *APPR.*

15. Heaney, *Among Schoolchildren* (Belfast: Queen's University, 1984), 6.

16. O'Driscoll, *SS,* 27.

17. John Haffenden, *Viewpoints: Poets in Conversation* (London: Faber and Faber, 1981), 60, italics original.

18. O'Driscoll, *SS,* 39–40.

19. Heaney, "Tribute to Tony Smith," July 22, 2005, SHLP-NLI.

20. Heaney, *APPR.*

21. O'Driscoll, *SS,* 134.

22. Heaney, *APPR.*

23. Heaney, *P,* 20.

24. Heaney, *P,* 17.

25. Heaney to Roger Haney, December, 2002, SHP-EU.

## 2. MOSSBAWN

1. Heaney to Paul Muldoon, April 13, 1999, SHP-EU.

2. Heaney, *P,* 17.

3. Alison Flood, "Seamus Heaney Chooses Two Poems to Sum up His Lifetime Achievement," *Guardian,* March 19, 2009, www.theguardian.com/books/2009/mar/19/david-cohen -seamus-Heaney.

4. Steve King, "Young Seamus Heaney," www.todayinliterature.com.

5. O'Driscoll, *SS,* 8.

6. Heaney, *P,* 17–18.

7. Heaney, *P,* 19.

8. Heaney, *P,* 19.

9. Heaney, letter published in *Northern Constitution* newspaper, ca. 1987, SHP-EU.

10. John McCann, *Passing Through: The 82nd Airborne Division in Ireland, 1943–1944* (Newtownards: Colourpoint, 2005), 5.

11. Heaney, "The Guttural Muse," Rhodes University Lecture, August 27, 2002, p. 20, SHP-EU.

## 3. ANAHORISH PRIMARY SCHOOL

1. Heaney, *SS,* 242.

2. Heaney, *SS,* 246.

3. Heaney, *SS,* 244.

4. Hopkins, *The Sermons and Devotional Writings of Gerard Manley Hopkins,* ed. Christopher Devlin (London: Oxford University Press, 1959), 122–23.

5. Walt Whitman, *Leaves of Grass and Selected Prose* (New York: Random House, 1950), 27–28.

6. Heaney, *P,* 25.

7. Heaney, *P,* 21–22.

8. Heaney, *P,* 23.

9. Heaney, *P,* 23.

10. Maurice Fitzpatrick, *The Boys of St Columb's* (Dublin: Liffey, 2010), 65.

## 4. ST. COLUMB'S COLLEGE

1. FJM Madden and Thomas Bradley, eds., *Seeking the Kingdom: St Columb's College, 1879–2004* (Derry: St. Columb's College, 2004), 72.

2. Fitzpatrick, *The Boys of St Columb's,* 60.

3. Madden and Bradley, *Seeking the Kingdom,* 73.

4. Madden and Bradley, *Seeking the Kingdom,* 6.

5. Madden and Bradley, *Seeking the Kingdom,* 73.

6. Seamus Deane, "The Famous Seamus," *New Yorker,* March 12, 2000, 54.

7. Robert Greacen, *The Sash My Father Wore* (Belfast: Mainstream, 1997), 10.

8. Greacen, *The Sash My Father Wore,* 22.

9. Greacen, *The Sash My Father Wore,* 34–35.

10. Fitzpatrick, *The Boys of St. Columb's,* 61.

11. Fitzpatrick, *The Boys of St. Columb's,* 53.

12. Fitzpatrick, *The Boys of St Columb's,* 59.

13. Fitzpatrick, *The Boys of St. Columb's,* 59–60.

14. Fitzpatrick, *The Boys of St Columb's,* 107, 176.

15. Deane, "The Famous Seamus," *New Yorker,* 63.

16. Fitzpatrick, *The Boys of St Columb's,* 106.

17. Heaney, *Aeneid Book VI* (New York: Farrar, Straus and Giroux, 2016), vii.

18. Seamus Deane, *Reading in the Dark* (London: Jonathan Cape, 1996), 155–56.

19. James Joyce, *A Portrait of the Artist as a Young Man,* ed. Chester Anderson (Harmondsworth: Penguin, 1964), 109, 127.

20. Charles Hart, *The Student's Catholic Doctrine* (London: Burns, Oates and Washbourne, 1931), 165, 277, italics original.

21. Seamus Heaney, "The Guttural Muse," p. 18, SHP-EU.

22. O'Driscoll, *SS,* 22.

23. Monie Begley, *Rambles in Ireland* (Old Greenwich: Devin-Adair, 1977), 161.

24. David Young, "Schoolboy Seamus Heaney Thumped Firebrand," *Belfast Telegraph,* October 23, 2015, www.belefasttelegraph.co.uk/archive.

25. Fitzpatrick, *The Boys of St Columb's,* 65, 118.

26. Madden and Bradley, *Seeking the Kingdom,* 274.

## 5. QUEEN'S UNIVERSITY

1. Heaney to Alfred McCreary, March 24, 1994, SHP-EU.

2. O'Driscoll, *SS,* 42.

3. Heaney to Alfred McCreary, March 24, 1994, SHP-EU.

4. Heaney to Alfred McCreary, March 24, 1994, SHP-EU.

5. Deane, "The Famous Seamus," *New Yorker,* 62.

6. George McWhirter to Henry Hart, October 26, 2010, author's private collection.

7. Deane, "The Famous Seamus," *New Yorker,* 63.

8. O'Driscoll, *SS,* 43.

9. Heaney, "The Poet as a Christian," *Furrow,* October 1978, 604.

10. Thomas à Kempis, *The Imitation of Christ* (Harmondsworth, UK: Penguin, 1952), 122–23.

11. Heaney to Henry Hart, June 4, 1987, author's private collection.

12. St. Ignatius, *The Spiritual Exercises of St. Ignatius* (Garden City, NY: Image Books–Doubleday, 1964), 43.

13. Evelyn Underhill, *Mysticism* (Oxford: Oneworld, 1993), 3–4, 129.

14. Campbell, *The Hero with a Thousand Faces,* 21, 30, italics original.

15. Heaney, "Treely and Rurally," *Quarto* 9 (August 1980): 14.

16. Dante Alighieri, *The Divine Comedy: Paradise,* trans. Dorothy Sayers and Barbara Reynolds (Harmondsworth, Penguin, 1962), 344–47.

17. Thomas Merton, *Seeds of Contemplation* (Wheathampstead: Anthony Clarke, 1961), 174, 178, 208.

18. Merton, *Seeds of Contemplation*, 1, 2.

19. Merton, *Seeds of Contemplation*, viii–ix.

20. Heaney, "Seamus Heaney at the Pierpont Morgan Library," *Envoy*, no. 47 (1985): 20.

21. Heaney, *Among Schoolchildren* (Belfast: Queen's University John Malone Memorial Committee, 1983), 9.

22. Heaney, *RP*, 20–21.

23. Frank Kermode and John Hollander, eds., *The Oxford Anthology of English Literature, Volume 1* (New York: Oxford University Press, 1973), 288, 294.

24. Kermode and Hollander, *Oxford Anthology*, 330, 331, 336, 346–47.

25. Thomas Malory, *King Arthur and His Knights* (New York: Oxford University Press, 1956), 18–19, 213.

26. Heaney to Dominique Orozco, November 15, 1994, SHP-EU.

27. Incertus, "October Thought," *Q*, Michaelmas Term, 1959, 27.

28. Incertus, "Song of My Man-Alive," *Gorgon*, Hilary Term, 1961, 19.

29. Deane, "The Famous Seamus," *New Yorker*, 63.

30. Heaney to Rachel Buxton, February 19, 2000, SHP-EU.

31. Haffenden, *Viewpoints*, 70.

32. Heaney, *The Government of the Tongue*, 92.

33. Heaney, *P*, 28.

34. Deane, "The Famous Seamus," *New Yorker*, 64.

35. Heaney, fax, June 24, 1997, p. 1, SHP-EU.

36. George McWhirter to Henry Hart, October 26, 2010, author's private collection.

37. Incertus, "There's Rosemary——," *Gorgon*, Hilary Term, 1961, 30.

38. Incertus, "There's Rosemary——," *Gorgon*, Hilary Term, 1961, 30.

39. Incertus, "The Seductive Muse," *Gorgon*, Hilary Term, 1961, 5–6.

40. Heaney, "Shall We Jive This Jig?," *Irish Digest*, April 1961, 12.

41. Michael Parker, *Seamus Heaney: The Making of the Poet* (London: Macmillan, 1993), 26–27.

42. Heaney to Sonja Landjweer, January 26, 2002, SHP-EU.

6. FROM INCERTUS TO MASTER

1. Alan Ryan, *The Reader's Companion to Ireland* (New York: Harvest, 1999), 226.

2. Heaney, "Old Derry Walls," *Listener*, October 24, 1968, 522.

3. Ian Paisley, *Protestant Telegraph*, January 4, 1967, n.p.

4. Heaney, "In Our Own Dour Way," *Trench*, St. Joseph's TTC, April 1964, 4.

5. Heaney, "In Our Own Dour Way," *Trench*, St. Joseph's TTC, April 1964, 3.

6. Tom Adair, "Calling the Tune," *Linen Hall Review* 6, no. 2 (1989): 6.

7. Heaney, "Michael McLaverty: Part of His Own Posterity," *Fortnight*, no. 306 (May 1992): 31.

8. Jack Holland, *Irish Echo*, October 18–24, 1995, 10.

9. Holland, *Irish Echo*, 10.

10. Parker, *Seamus Heaney: The Making of the Poet*, 46.

11. Heaney, *Interest*, November 1964, 16–17.

12. O'Driscoll, *SS*, 117.

13. Polly Devlin, *All of Us There* (London: Virago, 2003), 20.

14. Devlin, *All of Us There*, 34, 31, 49.

15. O'Driscoll, *SS*, 62–63.

16. Suzanne Lowry, *Belfast Telegraph*, November 21, 1968.

17. Devlin, *All of Us There*, 15.

18. O'Driscoll, *SS*, 98.

19. Heaney to Ted Hughes, May 24, 1979, SHP-EU.

20. "Walkthrough of the Confirmation Rite," http://rclbsacraments.com/confirmation /walkthrough-confirmation-rite.

21. Joyce, *A Portrait of the Artist*, 135.

22. Heaney, APPR.

23. Heather Clark, *The Ulster Renaissance: Poetry in Belfast 1962–1972* (Oxford: Oxford University Press, 2006), 41.

24. Heaney, "Poetry from a Co-operative Society," *Hibernia*, September 1963, 15.

25. Parker, *Seamus Heaney: The Making of the Poet*, 50.

26. "Philip Hobsbaum in Conversation," with Gerry Cambridge, *The Dark Horse*, no. 14 (Summer 2002): 39.

27. O'Driscoll, *SS*, 74–75.

28. "The Belfast Group," *Honest Ulsterman*, no. 97 (Spring 1994): 8.

29. Stephen Ennis, "Seamus Heaney and the London Origins of the Belfast Group," author's private collection, 6.

30. "The Belfast Group," *Honest Ulsterman*, 5–6.

31. Clark, *Ulster Renaissance*, 66, 67.

32. Heaney, *P*, 29.

33. "The Belfast Group," *Honest Ulsterman*, 12.

34. Clark, *Ulster Renaissance*, 61.

35. Heaney, *The Government of the Tongue*, xxi.

36. Clark, *Ulster Renaissance*, 16, 23.

37. O'Driscoll, *SS*, 74.

38. Parker, *Seamus Heaney: The Making of the Poet*, 52.

39. Norman Dugdale, "The Belfast Group: A Symposium," *Honest Ulsterman*, no. 53 (November/December 1976): 56–57.

40. Heaney, "Prospero in Agony," *Outposts* (Spring 1966): 21–22.

41. Heaney, "Prospero in Agony," 22.

42. Parker, *Seamus Heaney: The Making of the Poet*, 58.

43. O'Driscoll, *SS*, 81.

44. Anonymous, "Son of the Soil," *Guardian*, October 9, 1999, www.theguardian.com /books/1999/oct/09/books.guardianreview10.

45. Heaney, draft of an essay on Philip Larkin, folder 145, SHLP-NLI.

46. Philip Larkin, *Selected Letters of Philip Larkin: 1940–1985*, ed. Anthony Thwaite (London: Faber and Faber, 1993), 636.

47. Heaney, folder 145, SHLP-NLI.

48. O'Driscoll, *SS*, 67.

49. John Carey, "Eleven Poems," *New Statesman,* December 31, 1965, 1033.

50. Anonymous, *Observer,* November 21, 1966, 12.

51. Rae Rosenfield, "Belfast Fortnight of Culture and Gaiety," *Hibernia* (December 1966): 33.


7. MARRIAGE AND FIRST BOOKS

1. O'Driscoll, *SS,* 61.

2. Arthur Rimbaud, *Complete Works* (New York: Harper/Colophon, 1976), 100.

3. Padraic Fiacc, "Seamus Heaney," *Hibernia,* May 1968, 23.

4. O'Driscoll, *SS,* 62.

5. Parker, *Seamus Heaney: The Making of the Poet,* 52.

6. Peter Marsh, "Props for a Proposition," *Observer,* June 19, 1966, 26.

7. Giles Sadler, "Gummidge and Others," *Review, no. 16* (October 1966): 43–44.

8. O'Driscoll, *SS,* 84.

9. C. B. Cox, *Spectator,* May 20, 1966, 638.

10. Christoper Ricks, "Growing Up," *New Statesman,* May 27 1966, 778.

11. Ricks, "Growing Up," *New Statesman,* 778.

12. Heaney, *P,* 47.

13. William Wordsworth, *The Prelude,* http://triggs.djvu.org/djvu-editions.com/WORDS
WORTH/PRELUDE1850/Prelude1850.pdf.

14. O'Driscoll, *SS,* 15.

15. John Cronin to Henry Hart, February 7, 2009, author's private collection.

16. Heaney, fax, June 24, 1997, SHP-EU.

17. Heaney to Paul Muldoon, May 30, 1968, SHP-EU.

18. Heaney, "Letter to an Editor," *Honest Ulsterman,* no. 29 (1971): 39.

19. Norman Dugdale, "The Belfast Group," *Honest Ulsterman* 97 (Spring 1994): 6.

20. O'Driscoll, *SS,* 100–101.

21. Heaney, "Old Derry's Walls," *Listener,* October 24, 1968, 522.

22. Begley, *Rambles in Ireland,* 165.

23. Heaney, "Old Derry's Walls," *Listener,* 522.

24. Heaney, "Civil Rights, Not Civil Weeks," *The Gown,* October 22, 1968, 5.

25. O'Driscoll, *SS,* 383.

26. Robert Druce, "A Raindrop on a Thorn," *Dutch Quarterly Review* 9, no. 1 (1979): 27.

27. O'Driscoll, *SS,* 119.

28. O'Driscoll, *SS,* 120.

29. O'Driscoll, *SS,* 72–73.

30. Heaney, *"Room to Rhyme": The Greatest Minds Lecture* (Dundee: University of Dundee, 2004), 6.

31. Heaney, "Delirium of the Brave," *Listener,* November 27, 1969, 757.

32. O'Driscoll, *SS,* 118.

33. "Requiem for the Croppies, Responding to the Poem," https://resources.teachnet
.ie/ckelly/Heaney/Responses%20Requiem.htm.

34. "Delirium of the Brave," *Listener,* 759.

35. Heaney, *Munro, Everyman,* no. 3 (1970): 61–62.

36. Heaney, *Munro,* 64.

37. O'Driscoll, *SS,* 183–84.

38. Begley, *Rambles in Ireland,* 165–66.

39. Anthony Thwaite, "Country Matters," *New Statesman,* June 27, 1969, 914.

40. A. Alvarez, "Homo Faber," *Observer,* June 22, 1969, 27.

41. Merton, *Seeds of Contemplation,* 1.

42. Joseph Conrad, *Heart of Darkness* (New York: St. Martin's, 1989), 25, 36.

43. St. Teresa of Ávila, *The Interior Castle* (London: SCM, 1958), 19.

44. Benedict Kiely, "A Raid into Dark Corners," *Hollins Critic,* no. 4 (1970): 10.

45. Heaney, *P,* 189.

46. Heaney, BBC radio scripts, author's private collection.

47. St. Teresa of Ávila, *The Life of St. Teresa of Jesus,* www.gutenberg.org/files.

48. Cole Moreton, "A Wandering Voice in the Storm," *Independent,* April 3, 1999, www .independent.co.uk/arts-entertainment/books-a-wandering-voice-in-the-storm-1085106 .html.

8. FROM BELFAST TO BERKELEY AND BACK

1. Fiacc, "Seamus Heaney," *Hibernia,* May 1968, 23.

2. Seth Rosenfeld, "The Campus Files," *San Francisco Chronicle,* June 9, 2002.

3. Heaney to Michael and Edna Longley, September 22, 1970, SHP-EU.

4. Heaney to Paul Muldoon, September 30, 1970, SHP-EU.

5. Heaney, *Stations* (Belfast: Ulsterman, 1975), 3.

6. O'Driscoll, *SS,* 143.

7. Berkeley students to Heaney, ca. 1971, SHP-EU.

8. David Wyatt to Henry Hart, March 11, 2009, author's private collection.

9. Heaney to Paul Muldoon, September 30, 1970, SHP-EU.

10. Longley to Heaney, January 8, 1971, SHP-EU.

11. Heaney to Paul Muldoon, September 30, 1970, SHP-EU.

12. Heaney, "Views," *Listener,* December 31, 1970, 903.

13. Rebecca Tracy to Henry Hart, March 20, 2009, author's private collection.

14. O'Driscoll, *SS,* 139.

15. Bob Tracy to Seamus Heaney, November 4, 1972, SHP-EU.

16. Heaney to Michael Longley, April 26, 1971, SHP-EU.

17. Heaney to Michael Longley, April 26, 1971, SHP-EU.

18. James Randall, "An Interview with Seamus Heaney," *Ploughshares* 5, no. 3 (1979): 16.

19. Robert Bly, *American Poetry: Wildness and Domesticity* (New York: Harper Perennial, 1990), 246–47.

20. Seamus Deane, "The Appetites of Gravity," *Sewanee Review* (Winter 1976): 203.

21. Randall, "An Interview with Seamus Heaney," *Ploughshares,* 16–17.

22. Jonathan Galassi, "Dealing with Tradition," *Poetry,* November 1973, 118.

23. Heaney to Michael Longley, June 14, 1971, SHP-EU.

24. Randall, "An Interview with Seamus Heaney," *Ploughshares,* 19–20.

25. O'Driscoll, *SS*, 124.

26. Heaney, "Turning Points," *The Age* (Melbourne, Australia), October 15, 1994, 1.

27. Heaney, *P*, 37.

28. O'Driscoll, *SS*, 130.

### 9. UPROOTING AND REROOTING

1. Heaney to James Simmons, "Ulster Poetry Circus," ca. 1971, SHP-EU.

2. Heaney, *P*, 30.

3. Heaney, *P*, 33.

4. Heaney to Robert Greacen, January 24, 1972, SHP-EU.

5. Seamus Deane to Seamus Heaney, February 22, 1972, SHP-EU.

6. "Bloody Sunday Report," *Guardian*, June 15, 2010, www.theguardian.com/uk/2010/jun/15/bloody-sunday-report-saville-inquiry.

7. O'Driscoll, *SS*, 148.

8. Heaney, "Total Absorption," in *Barrie Cooke Profiles*, ed. John O'Regan (Oysterhaven: Gandon Editions, 1998), 5–7.

9. Heaney to Ted Hughes, March 19, 1972, SHP-EU.

10. Randall, "An Interview with Seamus Heaney," *Ploughshares*, 7–8.

11. O'Driscoll, *SS*, 198.

12. Douglas Dunn to Seamus Heaney, August 23, 1972, SHP-EU.

13. Harry Chambers to Seamus Heaney, October 20, 1972, SHP-EU.

14. Alan Riddel, "Poet of Divided Ireland," *Daily Telegraph*, February 14, 1976.

15. Anonymous, "The Passing Show," *Protestant Telegraph*, September 9, 1972, n.p.

16. Heaney to Karl Miller, November 8, 1972, SHP-EU.

17. Ted Hughes to Seamus Heaney, December 5, 1973, SHP-EU.

18. Heaney to Ted Hughes, December 6, 1973, SHP-EU.

19. Robert Druce, "A Raindrop on a Thorn," *Dutch Quarterly Review*, 34.

20. Helen O'Shea, "Interview with Seamus Heaney," *Quadrant*, September 1981, 15.

21. Heaney, *The Long Garden*, BBC Radio script, January 21, 1973, author's private collection.

22. Charles Monteith to Seamus Heaney, October 30, 1974, SHP-EU.

23. Ciaran Carson, "Escaped from the Massacre?," *Honest Ulsterman* (Winter 1975): 187, 183.

24. Eliot, *Selected Prose*, 177.

25. Carson, "Escaped from the Massacre?," *Honest Ulsterman*, 185.

26. Randall, "An Interview with Seamus Heaney," *Ploughshares*, 19.

27. Haffenden, *Viewpoints*, 59, 69.

28. Heaney, *Place and Displacement: Recent Poetry of Northern Ireland* (Cumbria: Trustees of Dove Cottage, 1985), 1.

29. Deane, "The Famous Seamus," *New Yorker*, 66.

30. Paul Mariani, *Lost Puritan: A Life of Robert Lowell* (New York: Norton, 1994), 434.

31. Heaney to Robert Lowell, September 5, 1975, SHP-EU.

32. Robert Lowell, *The Letters of Robert Lowell* (New York: Farrar, Straus and Giroux, 2005), 642.

33. Helen O'Shea, "Interview with Seamus Heaney," *Quadrant*, 13.

34. O'Driscoll, *SS*, 216.

35. Heaney, "Robert Lowell: A Memorial Address," *Agenda*, no. 3 (Autumn 1980): 23, 24, 26.

36. O'Driscoll, *SS*, 220.

## 10. PROFESSING POETRY AGAIN

1. Parker, *Seamus Heaney: The Making of the Poet*, 153.

2. Michael Glover, "Interview with Seamus Heaney," *Poetry Life*, 1996.

3. Seamus Deane, "Seamus Deane Talks with Seamus Heaney," *New York Times Book Review*, December 2, 1979, 12.

4. Heaney, "Soul-Mark," *The Reader: The Journal of the English Association North*, no. 8 (2001): 14.

5. Dennis O'Driscoll, "In the Mid-Course of his Life," *Hibernia*, October 11, 1979, 13.

6. Mona Simpson to Henry Hart, June, 1 2009, author's private collection.

7. Heaney to Paul Muldoon, April 12, 1976, SHP-EU.

8. Heaney to David Hammond, May 13, 1976, SHP-EU.

9. Heaney to Michael Longley, January 4, 1977, SHP-EU.

10. Heaney, *P*, 148, 136.

11. Heaney, "Treely and Rurally," *Quarto*, 14.

12. Heaney, *APPR*.

13. O'Driscoll, *SS*, 258.

14. Danny Morrison, "Seamus Heaney Disputed," January 31, 2009, www.dannymorrison.com.

15. Dante, *Paradise*, trans. Sayers and Reynolds, 485.

16. Heaney to Karl Miller, October 20, 1978, SHP-EU.

17. Jack Kroll, "Bard of the Irish Soul," *Newsweek*, February 2, 1981, 67.

18. A. Alvarez, "A Fine Way with Language," *New York Review of Books*, March 6, 1980, www.nybooks.com/articles/1980/03/06/a-fine-way-with-the-language.

19. Marjorie Perloff, "Seamus Heaney: Peat, Politics and Poetry," *Washington Post*, January 25, 1981, 5, 12, 11.

20. Edna Longley, "Heaney-Poet as Critic," *Fortnight*, December 1980, 16.

21. Christopher Ricks, "The Mouth, the Meal and the Book," *London Review*, November 8, 1979, 4.

22. Denis O'Donoghue, "Field Work," December 2, 1979, https://archive.nytimes.com/www.nytimes.com/books/98/12/20/specials/Heaney-field.html.

23. *Times Literary Supplement* review reprinted in *Seamus Heaney: Modern Critical Views*, ed. Harold Bloom (New Haven, CT: Chelsea House, 1986), 10.

24. Seamus Deane to Seamus Heaney, June 1, 1978, SHP-EU.

25. Heaney to Anthony Thwaite, May 16, 1978, SHP-EU.

26. Helen Vendler, *Seamus Heaney* (Cambridge, MA: Harvard University Press, 2000), 3.

27. Barry Goldensohn to Henry Hart, September 18, 2009, author's private collection.

28. Heaney, "A Hank of Wool," *Times Literary Supplement,* March 7, 1980, 261.

29. O'Driscoll, *SS,* 270, 272.

30. Adam Kirsch, "Poet's Perspective," *Harvard Magazine,* November–December 2006, 55.

31. Belinda McKeon, *Irish Times,* April 13, 2009.

32. O'Driscoll, *SS,* 274–75.

33. O'Driscoll, *SS,* 235.

34. O'Driscoll, *SS,* 251.

35. Heaney, "Current Unstated Assumptions about Poetry," *Critical Inquiry* (Summer 1981): 649.

36. Heaney, "The Language of Exile," *Parnassus* (Fall/Winter 1979): 5.

37. O'Driscoll, "In the Mid-Course of His Life," *Hibernia,* 13.

38. Michael Parker, *Seamus Heaney: The Making of the Poet,* 178.

39. O'Driscoll, *SS,* 235–36.

40. William Carleton, *Traits and Stories of the Irish Peasantry* (London: Ward, Lock, 1881), 69, 85.

41. Heaney to Paul Muldoon, September 9, 1979, SHP-EU.

42. Heaney, *P,* front matter.

43. Heaney to Derek Mahon, November 3, 1980, SHP-EU.

44. Heaney to Michael Longley, ca. February 4, 1981, SHP-EU.

45. Elaine Feinstein, *Ted Hughes: The Life of a Poet* (New York: Norton, 2001), 212.

46. Heaney to David Hammond, January 3, 1981, SHP-EU.

47. Heaney, *P,* 79.

48. Heaney to Michael Longley, ca. February 1981, SHP-EU.

49. Heaney, *APPR.*

50. M. H. Abrams to Seamus Heaney, June 26, 1981, SHP-EU.

51. Heaney to M. H. Abrams, September 28, 1981, SHP-EU.

52. Heaney to Selma Warner, September 26, 1981, SHP-EU.

53. Heaney to David Hammond, July 7, 1981, SHP-EU.

54. Heaney to Henry Pearson, September 24, 1981, SHP-EU.

55. Haffenden, *Viewpoints,* 58.

56. Heaney, "'Apt Admonishment': Wordsworth as an Example," *Hudson Review* 61, no. 1 (Spring 2008): 23.

## 11. SWEENEY'S TRAVELS AND TRAVAILS

1. Angela Bourke, ed., *The Field Day Anthology of Irish Writing, Vol. IV* (Cork: Cork University Press, 2002), 226–27.

2. Heaney, *Sweeney Astray* (Derry: Field Day, 1983), 16.

3. Heaney, *Sweeney Astray,* 47.

4. Heaney, *Sweeney Astray,* viii.

5. Brendan Kennelly, "Soaring from the Treetops," *New York Times Book Review*, May 27, 1984, 14.

6. Marilynn Richtarik, *Acting between the Lines* (Oxford: Clarendon, 1994) 150.

7. Nora Chadwick, *The Age of Saints in the Early Celtic Church* (Oxford: Oxford University Press, 1961), 76.

8. Robert Graves, *The White Goddess* (New York: Farrar, Straus and Giroux, 1948), 456.

9. Darcy O'Brien to Seamus Heaney, May 11, 1984, SHP-EU.

10. Heaney to Michael Longley, February 24, 1982, SHP-EU.

11. Heaney, "Bennett Award Acceptance Speech," *Hudson Review* (Winter 1982–83): 519.

12. O'Driscoll, *SS*, 292.

13. *Weekly Northwestern,* October 16–17, 1982, B3, SHP-EU.

14. Francis X. Clines, "Poet of the Bogs," *New York Times Magazine,* March 13, 1983, 42.

15. Eavan Boland, "Poets and Pamphlets," *Irish Times,* October 1, 1983, 12.

16. Heaney to Tom Paulin, June 15, 1983, SHP-EU.

17. Nancy Tucker to Seamus Heaney, March 13, 1983, SHP-EU.

18. Darcy O'Brien to Seamus Heaney, March 10, 1983, SHP-EU.

19. Anonymous, *Tulsa World,* April 17, 1983, B8, SHP-EU.

20. Heaney, *Among Schoolchildren,* 11.

21. Heaney to Selma Warner, December 14, 1983, SHP-EU.

22. Heaney to Ms. Hennessy, June 20, 1984, SHP-EU.

23. Heaney to Matthew Evans, July 27, 1984, SHP-EU.

24. Heaney, *Finders Keepers,* 122.

25. Heaney to Charles Monteith, October 26, 1984, SHP-EU.

26. Anonymous, *Harvard Gazette,* December 7, 1984.

27. Heaney to Desmond O'Grady, May 24, 1985, SHP-EU.

28. Mhamed and Sebenius, "Harvard Turns 350," *Harvard Crimson,* www.thecrimson .com/article/2012/5/23/350-Anniversary-Celebration.

29. O'Driscoll, *SS*, 283.

30. Heaney, *Opened Ground,* 415–16.

31. Heaney, *The Government of the Tongue,* 166, 92, 96.

32. Heaney to Paul Muldoon, January 9, 1987, SHP-EU.

33. John Gruen, "Samuel Beckett Talks about Beckett," *Vogue,* December 1969, 210.

34. M. J. Knight, ed., *Passages from Plato* (Oxford: Clarendon, 1895), 137.

35. Heaney, "Human Rights, Poetic Redress," March 15, 2008, www.irishtimes.com /news/human-rights-poetic-redress.

36. Simone Weil, *Gravity and Grace* (London: Routledge, 1952), 171, 31.

37. Thomas Traherne, *Centuries of Meditations,* www.ccel.org/ccel/traherne/centuries .iii.html.

38. J. D. McClatchy, "The Exile's Song," *New Republic,* December 21, 1987, 38.

39. Ian Hamilton, "Excusez Moi," *London Review of Books,* October 1, 1987, 11.

40. Helen Vendler, "Second Thoughts," *New York Review of Books,* April 28, 1988, 41.

41. Andrew Waterman, "Keep It in the Six Counties, Heaney!," *PN Review,* no. 6 (July–August 1989): 37.

42. Heaney to David Hammond, December 11, 1987, SHP-EU.

43. Heaney to Ron Schuchard, January 5, 1988, SHP-EU.

44. Heaney, *The Place of Writing* (Atlanta: Scholars Press, 1989), 17, 18–19.

45. Heaney, *The Place of Writing*, 23, 25, 27.

46. Heaney, *The Place of Writing*, 25.

47. Heaney, *The Place of Writing*, 32.

48. O'Driscoll, *SS*, 431.

49. Heaney to Medbh McGuckian, September 12, 1988, SHP-EU.

50. Heaney to John Wilson Foster, September 12, 1988, SHP-EU.

51. Heaney to Dennis O'Driscoll, January 4, 2000, SHP-EU.

52. O'Driscoll, *SS*, 322.

53. Heaney, "'Apt Admonishment': Wordsworth as an Example," *Hudson Review* 61, no. 1 (Spring 2008): 21.

54. O'Driscoll, *SS*, 325.

55. Wallace Stevens, *The Necessary Angel* (New York: Vintage, 1951), 36.

56. O'Driscoll, *SS*, 320–21.

57. O'Driscoll, *SS*, 320.

58. Heaney to Michael Longley, October 13, 1988, SHP-EU.

## 12. HEALING WOUNDS WITH GIFTS

1. Terry Eagleton to Seamus Heaney, June 17, 1989, SHP-EU.

2. Gary Snyder to Seamus Heaney, June 26, 1989, SHP-EU.

3. Heaney to Padraic Fallon, August 2, 1989, SHP-EU.

4. Heaney to Ted Hughes, August 31, 1989, SHP-EU.

5. Ted Hughes, *Letters of Ted Hughes,* ed. Christopher Reid (New York: Farrar, Straus and Giroux, 2007), 564–65.

6. Jon Stallworthy to Seamus Heaney, October 28, 1989, SHP-EU.

7. Heaney, *RP*, 1, 12–13.

8. Heaney to Patrick Crotty, July 23, 1991, SHP-EU.

9. Hart, *The Student's Catholic Doctrine*, 142.

10. Heaney to Michael Spence, January 9, 1990, SHP-EU.

11. Hughes, *Letters of Ted Hughes*, ed. Reid, 574, 576.

12. Heaney to Barbara (no last name), March 31, 1992, SHP-EU.

13. Heaney, *The Cure at Troy* (New York: Farrar, Straus and Giroux, 1991), 13.

14. Heaney, *The Cure at Troy*, 37.

15. Heaney, *The Cure at Troy*, 65, 73.

16. Mary McCollum, "All the World's a Stage," *Irish News*, September, 22, 1990, 7.

17. Edmund Wilson, *The Wound and the Bow* (Boston: Houghton Mifflin, 1941), 294, 263.

18. Karl Miller, *Seamus Heaney in Conversation with Karl Miller*, 52–53.

19. Heaney to Ted Hughes, August 12, 1990, SHP-EU.

20. Heaney to Lannan Foundation, September 29, 1990, SHP-EU.

21. Heaney, "Above the Brim: On Robert Frost," *Salmagundi* (Fall–Winter 1990–91): 275–76, 278, 285.

22. Heaney to Medbh McGuckian, January 28, 1991, SHP-EU.

23. Desmond Fennell, *Whatever You Say, Say Nothing: Why Seamus Heaney Is No. 1* (Dublin: ELO, 1991), 16, 23, 42. The article first appeared in the *Irish Times* on March 30, 1991.

24. Heaney, *RP,* 22, 24.

25. Heaney, *RP,* 36, 20.

26. Heaney, *RP,* 125, 133.

27. Hughes, *Letters of Ted Hughes,* ed. Reid, 600–602.

28. Lachlan MacKinnon, "A Responsibility to Self," *Times Literary Supplement,* June 7, 1991, 28.

29. Catriona Crowe, "Testimony to a Flowering," *Dublin Review,* no. 10 (Spring 2003): 2.

30. Nuala O'Faolain, "The Voice That Field Day Didn't Record," *Irish Times,* November 11, 1991, 14.

31. Heaney to John Wilson Foster, January 8, 1992, SHP-EU.

32. Crowe, "Testimony to a Flowering," *Dublin Review,* 8–9.

33. Robert Fitzgerald, trans., *The Odyssey* (New York: Penguin/Random House, 1992), xxiv–ix.

34. M. I. Finley, *The World of Odysseus* (New York: Viking, 1965), 61–65.

35. Heaney to Desmond O'Grady, July 15, 1992, SHP-EU.

36. Anonymous to editor of *Threepenny Review,* September 11, 1992, SHP-EU.

37. Heaney to Tom Paulin, September, 22, 1992, SHP-EU.

38. Heaney, *APPR.*

39. Heaney to Ted Hughes, September, 24, 1992, SHP-EU.

40. Heaney, folder 142, SHLP-NLI.

41. Heaney, *RP,* 78, 178.

42. Heaney, *RP,* 165, 172.

43. Heaney, *RP,* 168, 179, 185.

44. Heaney to Medbh McGuckian, July 30, 1993, SHP-EU.


13. THE BOUNTY OF SWEDEN

1. Heaney, *The Midnight Verdict* (Loughcrew: Gallery, 1993), 24, 28, 30.

2. Heaney, *The Midnight Verdict,* 30, 40–42.

3. Heaney, *The Midnight Verdict,* 17, 39.

4. Heaney, *RP,* 55, 52.

5. Hughes, *Letters of Ted Hughes,* ed. Reid, 660–61.

6. Ted Hughes, *Winter Pollen* (New York: Picador, 1994), 178.

7. Heaney to Ted Hughes, March 25, 1994, SHP-EU.

8. Heaney to Ted Hughes, March 25, 1994, SHP-EU.

9. Heaney to Ted Hughes, March 14, 1995, SHP-EU.

10. Heaney to Joanna Mackle, January 3, 1997, SHP-EU.

11. "A Brigid's Girdle," https://fawbie.info/the-spirit-level/a-brigids-girdle.

12. Heaney, "Room to Rhyme," University of Dundee, 2004, 23.

13. Heaney, *Beowulf,* xxvii.

14. John Benedict to Seamus Heaney, April 30, 1984, SHP-EU.

15. Mary Cunnane to Seamus Heaney, May 11, 1993, January 10, 1994, SHP-EU.

16. Heaney, *Beowulf,* xxx, xv–xvii.

17. Rory Naismith, "The Economy of Beowulf," https://core.ac.uk/download /pdf/45312042.pdf.

18. Heaney, *Beowulf,* 89.

19. Heaney to Dennis O'Driscoll, January 4, 2000, SHP-EU.

20. Fiachra Gibbons, "Beowulf Slays the Wizard," *Guardian,* January 25, 2000, www .theguardian.com/books/2000/jan/26/costabookaward.seamusHeaney.

21. Penelope Dening, "'Beowulf' Brings Heaney Second Whitbread Award," *Irish Times,* January 26, 2000, www.irishtimes.com/news/beowulf-brings-Heaney-second -whitbread-award.

22. Alfred Hickling, *Yorkshire Post,* January 29, 2000, SHP-EU.

23. Heaney, *Finders Keepers,* 49.

24. Aeschylus, *The Oresteian Trilogy* (Harmondsworth, Penguin, 1956), 75.

25. Aeschylus, *Oresteian Trilogy,* 44, 97–98.

26. Heaney, "Further Language," Queen's University lecture, June 26, 1996, SHP-EU.

27. Heaney to Mary Braid, August 30, 1995, SHP-EU.

28. Heaney to Peter Fallon, April 20, 1995, SHP-EU.

29. O'Driscoll, *SS,* 370.

30. O'Driscoll, *SS,* 369.

31. O'Driscoll, *SS,* 370.

32. Heaney, "On the Art of Dimitri Hadzi," *Harvard Review* 32, no. 12 (Spring 1997), www.jstor.org/stable/pdf/27560854.pdf.

33. Anthony Hecht to Seamus Heaney, October 6, 1995, SHP-EU.

34. Darcy O'Brien to Seamus Heaney, January 3, 1996, SHP-EU.

35. Dave Smith to Seamus Heaney, October 6, 1995, SHP-EU.

36. Eamon Dunphy, www.independent.ie/life/controversial-selection-dunphys-starting -eleven/26623210.html.

37. Dennis O'Driscoll, "Letter from Dublin," *Harvard Review* (Spring 1996), www.har vardreview.org/print-issue/harvard-review-10/.

38. O'Driscoll, *SS,* 373.

39. Heaney to John Hume, with "Pont de L'Europe" enclosed, November 30, 1998, SHP-EU.

40. O'Driscoll, *SS,* 368.

41. Deane, "The Famous Seamus," *New Yorker,* 68, 79.

42. Taylor Branch, *The Clinton Tapes,* books.google.com.

43. Heaney to World Centre of Poetry, December 20, 1995, SHP-EU.

44. Heaney to Marco Fazzini, January 12, 1996, SHP-EU.

45. Heaney to Connie Brothers, December 28, 1995, SHP-EU.

46. Heaney to Darcy O'Brien, December 31, 1995, SHP-EU.

47. Heaney, University of North Carolina Commencement Address, May 12, 1996, www .ibiblio.org/ipa/poems/Heaney/unc-commencement.php.

48. Heaney to David Hammond, June 6, 1996, SHP-EU.

49. Heaney to European Poetry Festival, July 10, 1996, SHP-EU.

50. Heaney to Piotr Sommer, July 26, 1996, SHP-EU.

51. Heaney, "Ireland and Its Diaspora," Frankfurt Book Fair, 1996, SHP-EU.

52. Heaney to Alexander Jeffares, February 5, 1997, SHP-EU.

53. Heaney to Terrence Dolan, June 29, 1998, SHP-EU.

54. Heaney to Michael Longley, November 13, 1997, SHP-EU.

55. Heaney to Eamonn O'Doherty, November 9, 1997, SHP-EU.

56. Heaney to Fordham University president, April 15, 1997, SHP-EU.

57. Heaney to Michael Healey, November 6, 1997, SHP-EU.

58. "AOSDÁNA," *Art Matters,* no. 29, June 1998.

59. Heaney to Patricia Harty, July 24, 1997, SHP-EU.

60. Heaney, written on letter from Department of Architecture and Town Planning, November 25, 1997, SHP-EU.

61. Heaney to Ted Hughes, December 14, 1998, SHP-EU.

62. O'Driscoll, *SS,* 391.

63. Heaney to Bert Hornback, ca. January 1998, SHP-EU.

64. Heaney to Michael Longley, April 13, 1998, SHP-EU.

65. Heaney, "The Reciprocity of Tears," *Irish Times,* August 22, 1998.

66. Heaney to Ted Hughes, September 19, 1998, SHP-EU.

67. Roy Davids to Seamus Heaney, ca. November 1998, SHP-EU.

68. O'Driscoll, *SS,* 395.

69. Heaney to John Parson, December 1, 1998, SHP-EU.

70. Heaney to Geoffrey Hill, October 31, 1998, SHP-EU.

71. Geoffrey Hill, *The Triumph of Love* (Boston: Houghton Mifflin, 1998), 39, 76, italics original.

72. Heaney, eulogy for Ted Hughes, November 3, 1998, author's private collection.

73. Terence McCaughey, eulogy for Ted Hughes, author's private collection, italics original.

74. Heaney, "A Great Man and a Great Poet," *Observer Review,* May 16, 1999, 4.

75. Heaney to Tom Flanagan, February 17, 2000, SHP-EU.

76. Heaney to Ron Schuchard, ca. mid-March 2000, SHP-EU.

### 14. FINAL GIFTS

1. Anonymous, *Publisher's Weekly,* April, 2001, www.publishersweekly.com/9780374 146832.

2. Patrick McGuinness, "Roaming the Stations of the World," *London Review of Books,* no. 1 (January 3, 2002), www.lrb.co.uk/the-paper/v24/no1/patrick-mcguinness/roaming -the-stations-of-the-world.

3. Robert Potts, "The View from Olympia," *Guardian,* April 7, 2001, www.theguardian .com/books/2001/apr/07/poetry.tseliotprizeforpoetry2001.

4. Heaney, introduction to *A Way of Life, Like Any Other,* by Darcy O'Brien (New York: New York Review Books, 2001), v.

5. "R. S. Thomas Memorial," *Poetry Ireland Review,* no 69 (summer 2001): 11–12.

6. Heaney to Danny Weissbort, June 30, 2001, SHP-EU.

7. Heaney, "Poetry's Power Against Intolerance," *New York Times,* August 26, 2001, www.nytimes.com/2001/08/26/opinion/poetrys-power-against-intolerance.html.

8. Heaney, "Reality and Justice: On Translating Horace," *Irish Pages,* no. 2 (Autumn/Winter 2002–3): 50.

9. Heaney, "Reality and Justice," 32.

10. Graves, *The White Goddess,* 5.

11. O'Driscoll, *SS,* 423–24.

12. Graves, *The White Goddess,* 5, 75, 45.

13. Graves, *The White Goddess,* 485, 14.

14. Graves, *The White Goddess,* 5.

15. Heaney, "The Poet's Perspective," *Harvard Magazine,* November–December 2006, 55.

16. Heaney to George Watson, September 17, 2001, SHP-EU.

17. Heaney, "Holding Reality and Justice," *Emory Report,* May 27, 2003, www.emory.edu/EMORY_REPORT/erarchive/2003/May/erMay27/5_27_03firstperson.html.

18. Heaney, "The Whole Thing," *The Recorder: A Journal of the American Irish Historical Society* (Spring 2002): 17, 20.

19. Heaney to Geordie Greig, January 25, 2002, SHP-EU.

20. Heaney to Ron Schuchard, February 18, 2002, SHP-EU.

21. Heaney to Elizabeth Lunday, SHP-EU, August 1, 2002.

22. Heaney, "The Trance and the Translation," *Guardian,* November 29, 2002, www.theguardian.com/books/2002/nov/30/featuresreviews.guardianreview20.

23. Heaney to Michael Roberts, November 5, 2002, SHP-EU.

24. Heaney, *Emory Report on Commencement,* online.

25. Heaney, *Emory Report on Commencement,* online.

26. Heaney to Breda Keena, October 10, 2001, SHP-EU.

27. Heaney, *The Burial at Thebes* (New York: Farrar, Straus and Giroux, 2004), 76.

28. Heaney, *The Burial at Thebes,* 33.

29. Michael Billington, "The Burial at Thebes," *Guardian,* April 6, 2004, www.theguardian.com/stage/2004/apr/07/theatre.

30. Neil Corcoran, "The State We're In," *Guardian,* April 30, 2004, www.theguardian.com/books/2004/may/01/poetry.seamusHeaney.

31. Heaney, *The Burial at Thebes,* 35, 37, 41.

32. Dudley Fitts and Robert Fitzgerald, trans., *Sophocles: The Oedipus Cycle* (New York: Harvest, 1939), 112–13.

33. Fitts and Fitzgerald, *The Oedipus Cycle,* 158.

34. Czeslaw Milosz, *The Separate Notebooks,* trans. Robert Hass and Robert Pinsky (New York: Ecco, 1984) 186.

35. Milosz, *Collected Poems,* 438.xx

36. Heaney, "In Gratitude for All the Gifts," *Guardian,* September 11, 2004, www.theguardian.com/books/2004/sep/11/featuresreviews.guardianreview25/.

37. David Ward, "Heaney Opens Lakeland Centre," *Guardian,* June 4, 2005, www.theguardian.com/uk/2005/jun/04/books.poetry.

38. Heaney, *Trowel* 10 (2005), ed. Brian Dolan and Nial Kenny, University College, Dublin, https://issuu.com/btdolan/docs/trowel_volume_x_2005.

39. T. S. Eliot, *Complete Poems and Plays* (New York: Harcourt, Brace & World, 1971), 194–95.

40. Heaney to Derek Mahon, September 19, 2006, SHP-EU.

41. O'Driscoll, *SS*, 461.

42. Alison Flood, "Heaney Chooses Two Poems" *Guardian*, March 19, 2009, www.theguardian.com/books/2009/mar/19/david-cohen-seamus-Heaney.

43. Heaney, *Aeneid Book VI*, 73, 79, 91.

44. Colm Tóibín, *Human Chain, Guardian*, August 20, 2010, www.theguardian.com/books/2010/aug/21/seamus-Heaney-human-chain-reviewonline.

45. Sean O'Brien, "*Human Chain,* by Seamus Heaney," *Independent*, September 3, 2010, www.independent.co.uk/arts-entertainment/books/reviews/human-chain-by-seamus-Heaney-2068708.html.

46. Robert Tracy, "*Human Chain,*" *Irish University Review* (Autumn/Winter 2011), https://www.jstor.org/stable/i24573367.

47. Eamon Grennan, "Seamus Heaney's Book of Resurrections," *Irish Times,* August 28, 2010, www.irishtimes.com/culture/books/seamus-Heaney-s-book-of-resurrections-1.644008.

48. William Logan, "Ply the Pen," *New York Times,* September 24, 2010, www.nytimes.com/2010/09/26/books/review/Logan-t.html.

49. William Wordsworth, *William Wordsworth: Poems Selected by Seamus Heaney,* ed. Heaney (London: Faber, 2011), xi.

50. Aristotle, *Nicomachean Ethics,* http://classics.mit.edu/Aristotle/nicomachaen.html.

51. Heaney, Award Ceremony, June 27, 2012, https://irelandfunds.org/news/seamus-Heaney-1939-2013/.

52. Heaney, *History of Ireland in 100 Objects* (exhibition), National Museum, March 20, 2013, author's private collection.

53. Richard Rankin Russell, "Remembering the Giver: Seamus Heaney," *Irish Studies South* 1, no. 1 (August 2014), https://digitalcommons.georgiasouthern.edu/iss/vol1/iss1/.

54. Kathy Sheridan, "Marie Heaney: 'I Had a Very Public Grief,'" *Irish Times,* September 10, 2016, www.irishtimes.com/culture/books/marie-Heaney-i-had-a-very-public-grief-1.2785781.

55. "Clinton Hails Poet Seamus Heaney," *Independent,* August 30, 2013, www.independent.ie/irish-news/clinton-hails-poet-seamus-Heaney/29540030.html.

56. Roy Foster, "Seamus Heaney Remembered," *Guardian,* August 31, 2013, www.theguardian.com/books/2013/sep/01/seamus-Heaney-roy-foster-appreciation.

57. Henry McDonald, "Seamus Heaney's Last Words," *Guardian,* September 2, 2013, www.theguardian.com/books/2013/sep/02/seamus-Heaney-last-words-funeral/.

# Index